CAMALDOLESE EXTRAORDINARY

B. Paulus Iustini
anus Patritius Venetus Eré
mita Camaldulensis et Congregationis Eremita
rum S. Romualdi Montis Coronæ Institutor.

Romæ Sup. perm. ann.   1725 Roccus Pozzi Fecit

CAMALDOLESE EXTRAORDINARY

*The Life, Doctrine, and Rule
of Blessed Paul Giustiniani*

By Dom Jean Leclercq and Blessed Paul Giustiniani
Edited by the Camaldolese Hermits of Montecorona

Ercam Editions
Bloomingdale, Ohio
www.Camaldolese.org

The English translation of *Alone with God* by Elizabeth McCabe, from the French *Seul avec Dieu: La Vie Érémitique*, and preface by Thomas Merton, copyright ©1961 and copyright renewed 1989 by Farrar, Straus and Giroux, Inc.

Saint Romuald's Brief Rule for Hermit Novices, by Raphael Brown, originally printed c.1973 by New Camaldoli Hermitage

Second edition, revised and reset, 2008

NIHIL OBSTAT and IMPRIMATUR: P. Lanfranco Longhi, er. cam., Superior Major

ISBN 978-0-9728132-6-6

Library of Congress Control Number: 2003104630

Typeset by M. Fontecchio
Printed in the United States of America

Front cover: Icon by Bengt Kälde
Back cover: *The Vision of Saint Romuald*, attributed to Brother Venantius (+1659), altarpiece at the Sacro Eremo Tuscolano

Contents

Section I
A HUMANIST HERMIT
Dom Jean Leclercq

hermit "proclaims God's kingdom" by renouncing the world for the sake of the kingdom of heaven. The meaning of religious profession in this context. Through the communion of saints, the hermit's personal sanctification helps his neighbor. The contemplative life is fruitful. Why Giustiniani seldom refers to the prayer of intercession.

Section III
RULE OF THE EREMITIC LIFE
Blessed Paul Giustiniani

SUPPLEMENT — **Saint Romuald's Brief Rule**

Abbreviations

Gn	Genesis	Mt	Matthew
Ex	Exodus	Mk	Mark
Nm	Numbers	Lk	Luke
Dt	Deuteronomy	Jn	John
Jos	Joshua	Acts	Acts
1 Sm	1 Samuel	Rom	Romans
1 Kgs	1 Kings	1 Cor	1 Corinthians
2 Chr	2 Chronicles	2 Cor	2 Corinthians
Jb	Job	Gal	Galatians
Ps(s)	Psalm(s)*	Eph	Ephesians
Prv	Proverbs	Phil	Philippians
Qo	Ecclesiastes	1 Thes	1 Thessalonians
Si	Sirach(Ecclesiasticus)	2 Thes	2 Thessalonians
Is	Isaiah	1 Tim	1 Timothy
Jer	Jeremiah	2 Tim	2 Timothy
Lam	Lamentations	Heb	Hebrews
Bar	Baruch	Jas	James
		1 Pt	1 Peter
*Hebrew numbering in parentheses		1 Jn	1 John

ACW	Ancient Christian Writers
CCC	*Catechism of the Catholic Church*
CCL	Code of Canon Law
CS	Cistercian Studies series
F	folio
FC	Fathers of the Church
HE	*Un humaniste ermite*, by Dom Jean Leclercq
NCE	New Catholic Encyclopedia, first edition
NPNF	Nicene and Post-Nicene Fathers
PG	Migne's *Patrologia Graeca*
PL	Migne's *Patrologia Latina*
Q	quarto
RB	*Rule of Saint Benedict*
RM	Roman Missal
RVE	*Rule of the Eremitic Life*, by Blessed Paul Giustiniani, revision of 1520
VFr	*Life of the Five Brothers*, by Saint Bruno of Querfurt
VR	*Life of Saint Romuald*, by Saint Peter Damian
Vulg.	Vulgate

Note: Editorial additions have been placed within square brackets.

General Introduction

DA PER MATREM ME VENIRE

O ne day Philip the Apostle brought Bartholomew or Nathanael, as he was sometimes called, to Our Blessed Lord. As soon as He gazed upon him, and read his soul, He described the future apostle and martyr as follows:

Here comes one who belongs to the true Israel;
There is no falsehood in him. [Jn 1: 47]

Mysterious words these — they harken back to the Old Testament times to Jacob whose name was changed to Israel. If there ever was a schemer, a plotter, one who used his brains to swindle other people out of birthrights and sheep and blessings, it was Jacob or Israel. After Jacob had wrestled with the Lord, and his name changed to Israel, he became a more worthy representative of the Most High.

A sudden transition from the singular to the plural happens when Our Lord says: "You will see heaven opening"; Jacob had seen the heavens opened and angels ascending and descending on the ladder, bringing the things of man to God and the things of God to men. Jesus was now telling Nathanael that he would see even greater things. The implication was that He Himself would henceforth be the Mediator between heaven and earth, God and man; in Him, all the traffic between time and eternity would meet as at a crossroad.

Life of Christ

Now this vision of the ladder on which angels ascended and descended, which was the symbol of the Incarnation uniting God and man, later on becomes a symbol of a summons to a higher form of the Christian life, when Count Maldolus[1] saw the white-robed monks of Saint Romuald, ascending and descending between heaven and earth, bringing God to man and man to God.

Centuries later, the ladder moved to the Camaldolese hermits, as they, through silence, penance and dedication opened the new highway to the mercies of God.

Now the Jacob's ladder has moved to the United States — one hermitage of Camaldolese in California; the other in Ohio. To the most active of nations has come the most contemplative of monks; to the land where togetherness is prized, the hermits have moved into a desert. In an atmosphere which is pragmatic and measures all things by utility, here are the new "angels" who believe that nothing becomes practical until we are saints.

Their silence will make atonement for vain verbiage where so many talk, but few listen; their lives as hermits will repair for those human alliances where men communize to be anti-God. And for those who always want to be "alone," these saintly men will prove that the only aloneness is being without God.

Naturally, they are looking for vocations — for men who want to be hermits; men who never again want to have a holiday, but to make every day a holy day; youths who want to return to their childhood when they liked to be playing alone, but in the way that God played with creation, *"Ludens in orbe terrarum"* ["Playing in the expanse of the earth" (Prv 8:31)]; youths who do not want so much to use time as a preparation for eternity, as to put the Eternal into time; former soldiers who once used to make more noise in order to forget noise, and who now want only that sweet repartee with Divinity in the peace that is called Silence.

The United States has been a land of skyscrapers — now the Camaldolese have built a ladder that does not scrape the sky but enters heaven.

Most Reverend Fulton J. Sheen (1960)

---

[1] *Camaldolese Spirituality*, p. 236.

Who are the Camaldolese? They are the elder of the two ancient, semi-eremitical orders of the Western Church, the junior being the Carthusians.[2] Saint Romuald founded the Hermitage of Camaldoli at a place by that name near the center of a wooded mountain chain of Arezzo, Italy, in 1023 or a little later. Saint Bruno (of Cologne) instituted the Carthusians in the French Alps in 1084, two kilometers above where the Grande Chartreuse is now located. There are today two autonomous Camaldolese congregations. The Camaldolese Benedictines, who retain Camaldoli, have both monasteries and hermitages, whereas the Camaldolese Hermits of Montecorona, founded as a reform by Blessed Paul Giustiniani in 1520, have hermitages only. The latter, who are the sponsors of this book, have three houses in Italy, two in Poland, and one each in Spain, the United States, and Colombia, as well as a new foundation in Venezuela. Paul (born Thomas) Giustiniani, never formally beatified, is Blessed only by acclaim.

From the very beginning of the Church, the contemplative life of Mary was present beside the active life of Martha (Lk 10:38-41 and Jn 11:20). There were always some[3] who responded to the Master's summons to greater perfection[4] through a life of poverty (Mk 10:21), celibacy (Mt 19:11-12), and obedience (Lk 10:16; Heb 13:17). Of these, some imitated more intensely Jesus' going about doing good (Acts 10:38) and others more His persistent withdrawal into the wilderness to pray (Lk 5:16). These were known as virgins and ascetics in the early centuries, and Saint Paul alludes to them in 1 Cor 7. The newly converted Saint Anthony, for example, entrusted his little sister to a community of virgins and then lived as an ascetic not far from his house.[5] With the proverbial ebb and flow of "10 persecutions in 250

---

[2]   NCE 3:161-168 and CS 186; on hermits in general, consult CCC 920-921 and
       2687, and CCL 603.
[3]   CCC 918.
[4]   CCC 915.
[5]   ACW 10:20; cf. CS 189:32, n. 3.

3

years," it took more courage for the disciple of Christ to remain within society than to withdraw.

But at length, toward the beginning of the fourth century and especially after Constantine's victory in 312, the Church reached a new level of maturity. It expanded as persecution and martyrdom abated and it consequently became easier to be a Christian. The growing mustard seed began to put forth great branches, and the seed that had died began to bear much fruit (Mk 4:31-32; Jn 12:24). It was at this point that the Fathers of the Desert[6] withdrew to the wastes of Egypt and started monasticism. As Archbishop Fénelon observed, those ancient Christians were simple, austere, and more fearful of the newfound peace that might soften them than they had been of the cruelty of the pagan tyrants. The hermit life came first, pioneered by Saint Anthony, who became famous throughout the world through a biography by Saint Athanasius which is available even today in several English translations.[7] Later, cenobitical ("common life") monasticism was organized by Saint Pachomius. Cenobitism was to become more and more preponderant as the centuries passed, and yet eremitism never disappeared.

The monk is one consecrated, as was his Old Testament prototype the Nazirite, by separation (Nm 6:2-3a, literal translation). "Monk" etymologically signifies one who lives alone, so the name fits the hermit even better than the cenobite. And yet: *Nunquam minus solus, quam cum solus*, "Never less alone than when alone." Saint Peter Damian insisted that the hermit priest fittingly says, "*Dominus vobiscum*" ("The Lord be with you"), during his solitary Mass. For "although space divides him from the assembly of the faithful, the unity of faith associates him with all in charity. His brethren may be distant in body, but they are all present to him by the mystery of the unity of

---

[6] NCE 4:793 and CS 59.
[7] Such as NPNF II:4 and ACW 10.

the Church."[8] And centuries before, Evagrius had defined the monk as one "separated from all and united to all."[9]

Underlying this classic definition and helping to clarify the paradox it presents is that fundamental fact of Christian faith known as the Paschal mystery:[10] Jesus has passed over from death to life, and through Him and in Him believers must also die and rise to new life. They do this especially by receiving baptism and living in accordance with it (Rom 6).[11]

The Paschal mystery unfolds in the life of the monk in the following manner: He makes every effort to die to sin through renunciation and detachment, and his profession of vows[12] is a kind of "second baptism" unto this end,[13] being deeply rooted in the baptismal consecration and expressing it more fully. Profession "drives out sin" and is baptismal justification's "companion and helper."[14] The vows counteract "the triple concupiscence" (1Jn 2:16), seated in our fallen nature,[15] with chastity taming down the concupiscence of the flesh, poverty blunting the concupiscence of the eyes, and obedience subduing the pride of life. Now renunciation and detachment are not the end but the beginning. They bring about a separation from all, a separation that clears the way for the practice of the virtues and a deeper life with God in charity. As this loving union with the Creator grows, so does harmony with His creatures. And so separation according to the flesh leads to unity according to the spirit; the quelling of the passions (Evagrius' byword is *apatheia*,[16] dispassion) ends in compassion.

---

[8] *Camaldolese Spirituality*, p. 202.
[9] *On Prayer* 124; cf. CS 4:7.
[10] CCC 571 and 618.
[11] CCC 2017.
[12] CCC 2103.
[13] CCC 916 and Blum 2:92-93.
[14] Saint John Damascene, PG 96: 971.
[15] CCC 377, 404.
[16] CS 79:270-277.

The subject of this volume is a vividly concrete example of that passover whose development we have just followed in the abstract. His *solo Dio in Dio,* "God alone in God,"[17] bespoke a heart as capacious as the world itself. Little wonder that his life is summed up at the point of his death in this phrase: "ever famished for solitude but never consenting to isolation."[18]

Monasticism started in the East and "has always been the very soul of the Eastern Churches."[19] But it also was adopted in the West in both cenobitical and eremitical forms. And in the West, when the times had reached a certain fullness, the Holy Ghost raised up Saint Romuald (950 or 952-1027) and Blessed Paul (1476-1528).

Dom Jean Leclercq (1911-1993) mentions that Blessed Paul's first biographer called him a second Romuald. Some points of similarity and contrast between the two men are well worth considering. Both were of noble birth. Romuald was scion to one of the most illustrious ducal lines of Ravenna. Giustiniani translates into English as Justinian. That renowned family[20] had included the first patriarch of Venice, Saint Lawrence Justinian, so admired and imitated by the forty-third patriarch, Blessed John XXIII.

Both of our subjects fell victim to sins of the flesh in youth. Yet there was abundant evidence of good impulses (actual graces)[21] at work in their souls even then. Their conversions came about quite differently. Saint Romuald was suddenly moved to do penance after witnessing a duel in which his father killed a relative. Blessed Paul was drawn gradually to repentance, especially through study.

After their conversions, they both were taken up with the idea of not only living the eremitic life but also propagating it. Saint Romuald traveled on unwearyingly, making new foundations. Blessed Paul

---

[17] *Alone with God*, Part Five.
[18] *A Humanist Hermit* IV:2, last sentence.
[19] Pope John Paul II, *Orientale lumen* 9.
[20] NCE 6:500-502.
[21] CCC 2000.

often contemplated in his Rule the possibility of its being observed outside of Camaldoli, which at that time was the only hermitage in the Camaldolese order. The faculty he received from Leo X in a brief of February 1515, to leave Camaldoli for the sake of establishing other hermitages, was a dream come true. Saint Romuald and Blessed Paul shared a persistent craving, never to be fulfilled, for martyrdom. The first wanted to go to Eastern Europe to die for Christ; the second felt drawn to travel to the New World in order to establish there the solitary life. These aspirations would be achieved only by their followers.

Giustiniani was a brilliant Christian humanist[22] who left behind voluminous writings, whereas his spiritual forebear, barely able to read when young, wrote little, of which nothing survives. Nevertheless Saint Romuald's "Brief Rule," handed down by Saint Bruno of Querfurt (see the Supplement), is a masterpiece.

Ecclesia semper reformanda: The Church always stands in need of reform.[23] These two men were given to the Church as reformers during those two eras when, with the quite possible exception of the present, reform was most needed. The first lived in an iron age of all-too-many worldly popes, and the second alluded to "this miserable time of ours" in the preface to his Rule. Blessed Paul saw the pontificate of Alexander VI who, despite the fact that divine providence worked for good through him, was one of those concerning whom it is commanded: "What they say, do ye, but what they do, do ye not" (Mt 23:3). To say that Alexander and his ill-fated son Cesare Borgia roused the admiration of Machiavelli is enough. A basic problem at that time was that ecclesiastical office had become too bound up with earthly princedom.

Although the reform works of both saint and blessed were confined largely to the eremitical-monastic sphere, they sometimes passed beyond it. One thinks of how Saint Romuald combated simony and of the memorial that Blessed Paul and Peter Quirini sent to Pope

---

[22] Cf. NCE 7:215-225.
[23] Cf. CCC 827.

Leo X in 1513. This *Libellus* has been hailed by scholars such as Father Hubert Jedin. They see it as not only the boldest and most complete program for the reform of the Church before the Council of Trent, but also as a presage of the Second Vatican Council: It proposed the revision of canon law, missionaries for the developing world, a vernacular Bible and liturgy for the laity, and dialogue for reunion with separated Christians. It is one of the pleasanter ironies of ecclesiastical history that, in the wake of the hardening of the Byzantine schism by the sacrilegious Venetian pillage of Constantinople in 1204 (contrary to the command of Pope Innocent III and to his grief and horror), two patricians of the City Wedded to the Sea should show such zeal for reconciling East and West. But Leo paid the *Libellus* no heed. If he had, maybe the Lutheran crisis of 1517 would have been averted. Among Giustiniani's writings are also found proposals for a revised sanctoral calendar and for simplification of the Breviary for the benefit of the diocesan clergy and the laity. He loved simplicity and shunned any hint of Renaissance pomp.

Both Saint Romuald and Blessed Paul suffered persecution and were at times subject to violence, captivity, and danger of death. Yet both, like their Exemplar, were "meek and humble of heart" (Mt 11:29). Father Aldo Visentin has sketched the scene in which Blessed Paul confronted the rapacious Abbot Basil with much forbearance. Likewise, his letter of January 1518 reprimanding the prior of Florence is so courteous that it scarcely seems to be a reproof, reminding us of Jesus' calling to account the Samaritan woman (Jn 4:16-18). As for Saint Romuald, we need only remember the kindly wit he used when, as Saint Peter Damian narrates, they brought to him a burglar just caught in the act. Deriding the cruel punishments of the day and sympathizing with the want that may have occasioned the crime, he said,

> "I too, brethren, do not know what we should do with so wicked a fellow. Gouge his eyes? But then he would not be able to see. Lop off a hand? But then he would not be able to work and might even end up dying

of hunger. If we cut off a foot, he will not be able to walk. At any rate, while we are trying to make up our minds what to do with him, take him inside and give him something to eat." And so it was that the saint, exulting in the Lord, reproved and admonished the man with mildness and, after he had eaten, sent him on his way in peace.[24]

It was Saint Francis de Sales who perhaps said it best: "A saint who is sorry is a sorry sort of saint."

How do our subjects compare as founders? Saint Bruno of Querfurt calls Saint Romuald "the father of the rational hermits."[25] This signifies that he wanted hermits to live a judiciously regulated way of life, utilizing norms he found in Saint John Cassian and other Fathers of the Desert,[26] whose works were recommended by the *Rule of Saint Benedict* itself. This is, in fact, identical with Blessed Paul's own program, so the two were fundamentally in agreement. And yet Saint Romuald did much else that Blessed Paul never did, sending out missionaries in hope of martyrdom and, especially, establishing cenobitical monasteries for men and women. "Renewing the eremitic life"[27] is the only achievement of Saint Romuald mentioned in the collect of the Mass of his feast day. But, was the cenobitic life somehow bound up with this, so as to make Giustiniani's failure to include monasteries in his reform a betrayal of the authentic Romualdian ideal? Some would answer this question affirmatively. Yet we believe that a careful reading of, especially, the conclusion and appendix of *A Humanist Hermit* and the ninth selection from the Rule will make it clear that a negative answer is not unreasonable.[28]

We will now analyze Blessed Paul's doctrine on prayer as

---

[24] VR 36.
[25] VFr 2.
[26] VFr 2.
[27] RM, June 19, Latin text.
[28] Cf. *The Privilege of Love*, pp. 13-14.

9

found in Chapter X of *Alone With God* (AWG X) and selection 10 from the Rule (Rule 10). The hermit's principal ideal, aim, or task is continual prayer (Lk 18:1),[29] that is, constant union with God. There is no fixed time for mental prayer in the eremitic life, unlike other religious institutes, because prayer is to be unceasing, a kind of spiritual equivalent to breathing.[30] How can one enter into this prayer? A footnote to the Italian translation of the last paragraph of Rule 10 points out that Blessed Paul takes up again there the doctrine (then attributed to Saint Bernard) of Guigo II the Carthusian.[31] This commonly-accepted monastic approach to prayer, called *lectio divina* or "divine reading,"[32] can be explained as a ladder (Guigo's *Scala Claustralium*) of four rungs: (1) *lectio* (reading), (2) *meditatio* (meditation), (3) *oratio* (prayer), and (4) *contemplatio* (contemplation).

(1) **Lectio**, as the "initial and fundamental element" (Coronese Constitutions 31), gives the entire procedure of four steps its name analogically. This reading is called *divine* because its object is divine revelation, the Word of God heard in faith.[33] One seeks this Word either in the Bible (also heard read in its entirety each year in the liturgy) or in "some other devout book"[34] faithfully echoing Sacred Tradition and Sacred Scripture.[35]

(2) **Meditatio** or meditation[36] is a careful thinking over of what has been read and focuses on "very definite dogmatic and moral considerations."[37] One needs an appreciation of the basic standards of interpreting Scripture and of its various senses.[38] Meditation can

---

[29] CCC 2742-2745, 2757.
[30] CCC 2697.
[31] CS 48, cf. CCC 2654.
[32] CCC 1177 and 2708.
[33] CCC 144, 2656; cf. RB Prologue 1.
[34] Rule 10.
[35] Cf. CCC 97.
[36] CCC 2705-2708.
[37] AWG X.
[38] CCC 109-119.

also legitimately pass beyond what has just been read to other points gleaned outside the time of private prayer.

(3) **Oratio** makes use of the truths and sentiments found by meditation in any of an "infinite multitude"[39] of possible acts of affective prayer.[40] Ejaculatory prayer formulas could be used at this stage, such as the invocation of the name of Jesus as practiced in the Eastern Church,[41] which Eastern practice would reinforce in the body by the fingering of beads, bows, and the like. Even though prayer most narrowly defined means asking God for something, yet its wider and widest senses, namely the ascent of the mind to God and colloquy with God,[42] are equally relevant and ought not be neglected. Blessed Paul says he prayed, in the first place, by confession of his misery and unworthiness;[43] then by adoration, confession (of praise), thanksgiving, invocation, awaiting, and desire. These acts of prayer agree with the more compact typology of 1 Tim 2:1: supplications, prayers with praise,[44] intercessions, and thanksgivings.

(4) **Contemplatio** or contemplation[45] moves from the many acts of the previous step to a single act. Beginners may achieve this level seldom and but briefly. The starting point of contemplation will later be called "the prayer of simplicity" by Bishop Bossuet and subsequent theologians. In order to enter into this state, Giustiniani bids us to be empty for and towards God, *vacare Deo* (cf. the English cognates "vacuum" and "vacation"), disencumbered of all attachment to creatures and expectant like the hungry chick of Saint Romuald's Brief Rule. This is the adoring silence of *apophatism*,[46] which eventually can give birth to annihilation, an ecstatic absorption in God, and Blessed

[39] AWG X.
[40] Cf. NCE 11:676.
[41] CCC 435, 2666-2668.
[42] NCE 11:670-671 and CCC 2590-2591.
[43] Cf. CCC 2631.
[44] Cf. Origen, ACW 19:54, 55.
[45] CCC 2709-2719 and NCE 4:258-263.
[46] *Orientale lumen* 16; cf. CCC 41-43, 2628.

Paul's experience of these resembles that of other mystics. Saint John of the Cross tells us:[47] "...God...is incomprehensible and above all, and therefore it befits us to go to God by the negation of all." And Aquinas summarizes thus Pseudo-Dionysius' interpretation of Ex 20:21: "At the end of our knowledge, we know God precisely as unknown."[48]

To ascend through these stages is to proceed from a solid grounding of the mind in truth to a more precious exercise of the will in hope and love, for "character is in the *will*, not in the intellect."[49] The effort[50] this ascent requires must not be stinted, because, through the practice of the seven gifts (Is 11:1-2),[51] the divine movement of actual grace, which is the soul of prayer, comes to be received no longer violently, but connaturally.[52]

The foregoing analysis will help us understand better Blessed Paul's distinctive teaching on methodless prayer. The famous four grades — elaborated by Guigo II, noted by both Blessed Paul and the redactors of the CCC, and just expounded — do not constitute a method in the strict sense. They are, rather, moments in a movement of interiorization of the Word of God. And yet Giustiniani does admit of what Leclercq calls "the method of prior asceticism,"[53] that is, of remote and proximate preparation for prayer.[54] *Remote preparation* is living a holy life, which detaches the mind from worldly preoccupations and disposes it for that ascent to God which is, as we have seen, prayer's broader definition. This remote preparation includes the practice of the virtues, liturgical worship, and discipline of the senses (the "Camaldolese trinomium" is solitude, silence, and fasting). *Proximate preparation* comprises the

---

[47] *Ascent* II 24:9.

[48] Cited by Maritain, *The Degrees of Knowledge* V:23.

[49] Archbishop Sheen, quoted in Reeves' biography, p.144.

[50] CCC 2752 and CS 79: 177-178.

[51] Cf. CCC 1830-1831 and NCE 7:99-101.

[52] AWG X, last section; cf. NCE 8:228-229 and Ps 118 (119):32 at RB Prologue conclusion.

[53] AWG X.

[54] NCE 11:676.

first two rungs of Guigo's ladder, reading and meditation. Now beyond such somewhat methodical remote and proximate preparation, we must climb up to the third and even, if possible, to the fourth rung. At this point, Giustiniani's counsel to eschew method comes fully into force, and with evident wisdom. Human planning and effort have served their purpose and run their course. They must now give place to the subtle groanings of the Spirit (Rom 8:26-27). His influence must be sought reverently and clung to tranquilly for as long as it lasts. If Blessed Paul requires a daily half hour of stillness in prayer, with a reverent and vigilant posture and in a sacred place, this is to assure that our own actions are not so unremitting as to block the Spirit's initiatives. We should allow Him to lead us either to multiply acts of prayer, or to ascend to contemplation, or even to return to reading and meditation. And normally He will provide us with some word to hold fast patiently in our hearts (Lk 8:15), as Mary did (Lk 2:19, 51), to sustain what the Holy Fathers call the remembrance of God.[55] "The mouth of the just shall meditate wisdom...."(Ps 36 (37):30; cf. Ps 1:2 and Jos 1:8).

Our thanks to the following: The Very Reverend Father Lanfranco Longhi, E.C., Superior Major of the Camaldolese Hermits of Montecorona, Monte Porzio Catone, Italy, for his sage advice and permission to publish; Farrar, Straus and Giroux, Inc., the Camaldolese Benedictines of New Camaldoli Hermitage, and Mr. Raphael Brown (1912-2000), for granting us reprint permission; Mount Saviour Monastery, Pine City, New York, for allowing us to use the translation of Florence E. De Hart of the main body of *A Humanist Hermit*, copyrighted by *Monastic Studies* in 1964, as the working basis for our own; Professor Emeritus Alex Corriere, for yeoman service done helping with the new translations and for financial assistance; Mrs. Carol C. Nelson, for manuscript preparation and editorial assistance; Doctor Christopher Bergman, for help with the illustrations and the expenses;

---

55 CCC 2697; cf. CS 79:340-341 and 189:107-126.

and all those others who lent the support of their labors or their prayers. Above all, we present this volume as a thank-offering for the millennium this November 11 of the patronal martyrs of Bieniszew.

In an address of May 25, 2002, in Bulgaria, the Supreme Pontiff commented: "I am in fact convinced that the monastic experience constitutes the heart of the Christian life, so much so that it can be proposed as a point of reference for all the baptized." We are delighted to open up a chest of too-long-buried treasure, containing some of the more dramatic episodes of monastic history and some of the most edifying lessons in monastic spirituality, that will enrich the soul of the thoughtful reader of whatever walk of life. Our indexed compilation of books and essays, five years in the making, is unique in any language. We can only hope that our rendering allows the intelligent elegance of Dom Leclercq and the inspired eloquence of Blessed Paul to shine through. Anything with no author indicated is the work of the editors. May the message of this Camaldolese collection go forth both into communities of consecrated life and beyond them, "so that this world may never be without a ray of divine beauty to lighten the path of human existence."[56]

For Further Reading

Anson, Peter. *The Call of the Desert*. London: SPCK, 1964. Pp. 73-86.

—— *The Quest of Solitude*. New York: E.P. Dutton, 1932. Pp. 79-106.

Belisle, Peter-Damian. *Camaldolese Spirituality*. Bloomingdale: Ercam Editions, 2007. Presents translations of VFr, VR, Saint Peter Damian's Letter 28 (*The Lord Be with You*), and Blessed Rudolph's *Constitutions* and *Rule*.

—— *The Privilege of Love*: Camaldolese Benedictine Spirituality. Collegeville: Liturgical Press, 2002.

---

[56] Pope John Paul II, *Vita consecrata* 109.

Bowd, Stephen D. *Reform Before the Reformation*: Vincenzo Querini and the Religious Renaissance in Italy. Boston: Brill, 2002.

> On the *Libellus*, see page 261. A translation of the *Libellus* has been accepted for publication by Marquette University Press.

Bruno of Querfurt, Saint.: see Belisle, Matus.

Bujak, Adam. *The Mystery of Camaldolese (Tajemnica Kamedułó)*. Cracow: Biały Kruk, 2000.

> Color photographs of Bielany ("Silver Mountain").

Catholic Encyclopedia. New York: Appleton, 1908. 3: 204-209. NCE 2:1095-1097.

Hale, Robert, O.S.B. Cam. "Camaldolese Spirituality." *The New Dictionary of Catholic Spirituality*. Collegeville: Liturgical Press, 1993. Pp. 107-110.

> The statement on page 109 that Montecorona does not have reclusion will be corrected in future editions to indicate that it does.

—— *Love on the Mountain*: The Chronicle Journal of a Camaldolese Monk. Santa Ana: Source Books, 1999.

In Praise of Hiddenness: The Spirituality of the Camaldolese Hermits of Montecorona. Edited by Louis-Albert Lassus, O.P. Bloomingdale: Ercam Editions, 2007.

Leclercq, Jean. *Memoirs*: From Grace to Grace. Kalamazoo: Cistercian Publications, 2001. Pp. 82-83.

> The transferred confrere who invited Dom Leclercq to Frascati was the late Father Maurice, who subsequently was sent to found Holy Family Hermitage at McConnelsville, Ohio. His editorial work underlies our Sections I and II.

Matus, Thomas, O.S.B. Cam. *The Mystery of Romuald and The Five Brothers*: Stories from the Benedictines and Camaldolese. Santa Ana: Source Books, 1994.

> Contains translations of VFr, VR, and (p. 60) of Saint Bruno of Querfurt's letter to Saint Henry about his warm welcome as missionary archbishop at Kiev by Saint Vladimir, who was

appalled by a premonition of his guest's eventual martyrdom by the pagans. This fraternal encounter took place less than a half-century before the Eastern schism.

—— *Nazarena*: An American Anchoress. New York: Paulist, 1998.

McCormick, Ignatius, O.F.M. Cap., translator. *The Capuchin Reform*: 1528-1978. Pittsburgh: Saint Augustine Friary, 1978. Pp. 5, 20-24, 78, 81, 162, 164.

Merton, Thomas. *The Silent Life*. New York: Farrar, 1956. Pp. 144-171.

Peter Damian, Saint. *Letters*. Translated by Owen J. Blum, O.F.M. Washington: Catholic University of America, 1989-2005, six volumes.

—— *Saint Peter Damian*: Selected Writings on the Spiritual Life, translated by Patricia McNulty. New York: Harper, 1959.

—— See also: Belisle, Matus.

Vigilucci, Lino, O.S.B. Cam. *Camaldoli*: A Journey into its History and Spirituality, translated by Peter-Damian Belisle, O.S.B. Cam. Santa Ana: Source Books, 1995.

Wencel, Cornelius, E.C. *The Eremitic Life:* Encountering God in Silence and Solitude: Bloomingdale, Ercam Editions, 2007.

Monte Rua

Holy Family Hermitage

CORONESE HERMITAGES OF THE WORLD

1. Sacro Eremo Tuscolano
   Monte Porzio Catone (Rome), Italy
   > Founded in 1607 at Frascati on the Alban Hills, near ancient Tusculum. It is the ordinary residence of the father major (superior general) and the novitiate house for Italy.

2. Eremo di S. Girolamo (Monte Cucco)
   Pascelupo (Perugia), Italy
   > Founded in 1521 by Blessed Paul; closed in 1926; reconstructed, beginning in 1985, and reopened in 1991. It is situated in a charming and quite secluded spot in the Apennines, where a local tradition says Saint Jerome once lived as a hermit. It does not have the separate, solitary cells typical of the other Coronese Hermitages.

3. Eremo di Monte Rua
   Torreglia (Padua), Italy
   > Founded in 1537 on the summit of one of the Euganean Hills; suppressed in 1810; reopened in 1863. The community now includes a perpetual recluse. In the past, it was the center of various Coronese Hermitages extant in the Republic of Venice.

4. Pustelnia OO. Kamedułów (Bielany)
   Cracow, Poland
   > "Silver Mountain" has been in existence since 1609 without interruption. It is situated on the outskirts of Cracow (Kraków), on a hill above the Vistula, and is the first and principal Coronese foundation in Poland. Visited by Pope John Paul II August 19, 2002. It houses a novitiate.

5. Pustelnia OO. Kamedułów (Bieniszew)
   Kazimierz Biskupi, Poland
   > The Hermitage of the Five Martyrs was founded in 1663, suppressed in 1819, and reopened in 1937 and 1945 respectively.

It was perhaps built on the site where the first Polish saints were killed in 1003. The five were hermits, two of them direct disciples of Saint Romuald; Saint Bruno of Querfurt (VFr) tells their story. In 1941 the hermitage was suppressed by the Nazis; three hermits died in concentration camps.

6. Yermo N.S.de Herrera
   Miranda de Ebro (Burgos), Spain

   Founded in 1925 on the site of an ancient Cistercian abbey of which there are some remains. It is situated in a solitary valley, not far from the Ebro. It is a novitiate house.

7. Holy Family Hermitage
   Bloomingdale, Ohio, U.S.A.

   Founded September 8, 1959, at McConnelsville, it was transferred in 1966 to its present location at a high point in the same Diocese of Steubenville. The nine solitary cells stand, in original fashion, in a semicircle about the church, the true center of the hermitage. The church's octagonal shape recalls the eighth day of Christ's resurrection and of eternity.[57] It is a novitiate house.

8. Yermo Camaldulense de la Santa Cruz
   Santa Rosa de Osos (Antioquia), Colombia

   Founded in 1969 in the vicinity of Medellin, it has occupied its current, more solitary site since 1993. The desire of Blessed Paul to propagate the Romualdian eremitical life in the "Indies" was realized with this foundation. It is a novitiate house.

9. Yermo Camaldulense Santa Maria de Los Angeles
   Pregonero (Táchira), Venezuela

   Initiated in 1998, with the intention of expressing gratitude to God and participating in the new evangelization on the occasion of the millennial Jubilee. As construction progresses, the local people are extending a cordial welcome that bodes well for the future.

---

[57] CCC 349 and Pope John Paul II, *Dies Domini* 26.

Sample Timetable

A.M.:	3:30	rise
	4:00	Matins, Angelus, *lectio divina*
	6:00	Lauds, Mass, thanksgiving, Terce
	7:00	breakfast, free time
	9:30	work
	11:30	end of work
	11:50	Sext, Angelus, examen
	12:00	dinner, free time (rest)
P.M.:	2:00	None, Litany
	2:30	work
	4:00	end of work
	4:15	Rosary
	4:30	Vespers, Angelus, *lectio divina*
	6:15	supper
	7:00	reading in the chapter room, Compline, Ps 129(130) for deceased brethren

The canonical hours[58] cover the Psalter weekly and are chanted monotone (rectotone) in the vernacular in the church. Divine reading *(lectio divina)* and meals are normally in the cell.

---

[58] CCC 1174-1178.

CHRONOLOGY

Amplified according to the booklet *Il Beato Paolo Giustiniani: L'amante impenitente del deserto* by Father Louis-Albert Lassus, O.P. (Eremo di Monte Rua, 2002).

1476	Born Thomas Giustiniani, on June 15 at Venice, to Francis and Paula Malipiero Giustiniani, the last of 6 sisters and 2 brothers.
1494-1505	Student of philosophy and theology at the University of Padua.
1506	Retreat at the family house on the island of Murano.
1507	Pilgrimage to the Holy Land.
1508-1510	Vocational search, ending with a summer retreat at Camaldoli, winter entrance there, and investiture at Christmas as Brother Paul.
1512	Solemn profession of vows, together with Peter Quirini and his brother and servant, on Sunday, August 10, the Transfiguration that year.
1513-1514	He and Quirini reform the Camaldolese order through a general chapter. Afterwards, they send Pope Leo X a *libellus* on Churchwide renewal. Quirini goes to Rome to secure the results of the general chapter against opposition and meets an untimely death.
1518	Priestly ordination in December.
1519	Elected Major of Camaldoli June 28.
1520-1521	Resigns the Majorate and leaves the Hermitage of Camaldoli September 14, with papal permission and after more than 5 years deliberation. He remains a member of the Camaldolese order while making a new foundation. He is accompanied by Brother Oliver of Cortona. Stopovers on the way to the Grottoes of Massaccio include Fontebuono, the Franciscan friary at Alverna, Gubbio, and Monte Cucco. At Gubbio they

are joined by a Franciscan tertiary and a Dominican, and they meet Galeazzo Gabrielli, who will join them in 1524. They visit and gain the support of the Duchess of Urbino. By the summer, Camaldoli concedes the Grottoes, and Pope Leo X Monte Cucco, to the new Company of the Hermits of Saint Romuald.

1522 Incarcerated for several days, by order of the Bishop of Ancona, in the Franciscan friary at Macerata, until the Bishop realizes that he has been deceived by calumny. On July 2, investiture of the first four novices of the Company.

1524 First general chapter of the Company at the Hermitage of Saint Benedict, Monte Conero, in January. Elected Major, he remains in office two years before resigning. On Sunday, August 7, while celebrating Holy Mass in the beloved chapel of his cherished Monte Cucco, he experiences, at the moment of holy communion, mystical annihilation and a deep certitude of election.[59] This leads to the composition of his masterpiece *My Secret with Myself* (*Secretum Meum Mihi*).

1525 In May, the Camaldolese general chapter meets at Ravenna and decrees the autonomy of the Company. This autonomy will not actually take effect until May 7, 1529, after his death. Visits Camaldoli in August, to the joy of all. There, in September, he encounters his nephew Francis, who will later transfer to the Grottoes and finally leave after two years, to his uncle's regret.

1526 On March 21 at 8:00 p.m., two fugitive Franciscan Observants knock on the door of the Grottoes. He protects Louis and Raphael Tanaglia by clothing them with the eremitic habit and sending them off to

---

[59] Cf. CCC 2014, 2016 and NCE 4:151-152.

	Monte Cucco for safety. But the general chapter does not accept them. So they join the itinerant Franciscan hermit Matthew of Bascio as popular preachers — the first Capuchins.
1527	He goes to Rome on behalf of the brethren and lodges with Peter Carafa (later a cardinal and finally Pope Paul IV) and Saint Cajetan. The Neapolitan armies barbarously sack Rome and confine them in a clock tower. They are released and put, destitute, on a boat in the Tiber. He returns to the Grottoes.
1528	He journeys to Orvieto, whither Pope Clement VII has fled the Neapolitans with his curia. After his papal audience, he contracts the plague at Orvieto but seems to recover. Offered the ruined Benedictine priory of Saint Sylvester as the site of a new foundation, he travels there with Brother James of Gubbio. It is on the summit of Mount Soracte, which dominates the Roman tableland and was celebrated by Horace for its magnificence. He is scarcely installed amongst the ruins, when the plague flares up anew and with deadly force. He dies, assisted by his devoted friend in religion and hermit of Camaldoli Father Gregory of Bergamo, on June 28 at the age of 52.

A HUMANIST HERMIT
Blessed Paul Giustiniani
(1476-1528)

Dom Jean Leclercq
Benedictine of Clervaux

This book was first published
by Edizioni Camaldoli, Rome, 1951
under the title
Un Humaniste Ermite
le Bienheureux Paul Giustiniani

IMPRIMI POTEST: Ex S.Eremo Camald., die 7 feb. 1951
                       P. Damianus Buffadini

IMPRIMATUR: Aretii, die 29 feb. 1951
                       E. Mignone, Episc.

A few minor errors have been corrected. The Italian version (Frascati, 1975) has usually been followed for the quotations, and occasionally for the text as well. It is still available from the Sacro Eremo Tuscolano and can be consulted for what we have omitted: footnotes and the second appendix on Blessed Paul's legislative work. As for the inventory of his writings in the third appendix, it has been superseded by Professor E. Massa's *Beato Paulo Giustiniani, Trattati Lettere e Frammenti I: I Manoscritti Originali* (Rome, Edizioni di Storia e Letteratura, 1967).

*Tu, Domine Jesu Christe, nosti quod
solitudinem non propter se,
sed propter Te amavi.*

"Thou knowest, O Lord Jesus Christ,
that I have loved solitude, not for its own sake,
but for Thee."

B.P. Giustiniani, "Soliloquy" of June 29, 1519

IN

MEMORY

OF

DOM ANSELM STOLZ

INTRODUCTION

Blessed Paul Giustiniani founded the Congregation of the Camaldolese Hermits of Montecorona, which still lives by his spirit. But today he attracts interest well beyond the circle of his disciples and his sons. One notes, from various points of view, his epoch-making influence on the history of the Camaldolese order and on that of eremitism, on the history of spiritual doctrine and of theology. Scholars have begun to study his style, his family, and his relations with the great humanists of the Church. Friend of Quirini, of Cardinals Contarini, Carafa, and Peter Bembo, of Saint Cajetan and of the first Capuchins, this contemporary of Luther appears within the Catholic Church as the animating spirit of a movement of reform and piety that was bound to bear fruit in the next generation. But almost all of his writings have remained unpublished and have never been examined in their totality. The essay attempted here purports to be nothing else but an introduction to his vast and variegated works. It is of first importance to sketch the character of Giustiniani's profound personality and to draw out from the texts and facts that which secures the unity of his activity: zeal for the solitary life.

The sources that allow us to begin this investigation are of two kinds: biographies of Giustiniani and his own writings. The first, three in number, are due to certain hermits of Montecorona. The oldest one was composed in 1587 by Luke of Spain. It was printed in a volume in which the author recounted the history of the Camaldolese institute. But it has also been written up separately as a narrative of which the prologue, still unpublished, is important: the author gives there the guarantees for his information. He says that he has collected the testimony of the first companions and contemporaries of Giustiniani, and that of his nephew

Francis who, although well on in years, was still alive at the time that Luke of Spain wrote. He moreover declares that he intends to write an objective history, at the same time vindicating the Blessed's memory against those who calumniate it.

The second biographer of Giustiniani was John of Treviso at the end of the seventeenth century. He made use of Blessed Paul's writings and gave some excerpts from them. His work remains unpublished. It had the advantage over Luke of Spain's in profiting from the documents. But these had been used without first establishing their chronology, which leads to some inaccuracies and, at times, some errors. Furthermore the account already presented a somewhat legendary character on more points than one.

Finally, between 1721 and 1724, Augustine Fiori in turn undertook to tell the story of Giustiniani. His work was published. Although it is more developed than that of Luke of Spain, there is nevertheless nothing original about it: as he himself says several times, Fiori depends on John of Treviso. He has, at least, the merit of reproducing, translated into Italian, several passages that John of Treviso had extracted from Giustiniani's writings and which have only been printed, as of the present writing, in this form.

Forty years ago the basic information furnished by Luke of Spain and Fiori was gathered together by Dom Placid Lugano. He devoted some chapters of his *History of the Congregation of Montecorona* to the founder, profiting from the original texts and other works published, after Fiori, in the *Annales Camaldulenses* and elsewhere. This narrative of Dom Lugano provides the framework in which is situated what we might call the exterior life of Giustiniani. What remains for us to study is rather the progress of his interior life and the genesis of his work.

Moreover, the second category of sources which we have at our disposal is by far the more important: it consists in what Giustiniani tells us of himself. He has written much: treatises, prayers, letters, poems, outlines and hurried notes which fill twelve volumes preserved in the archives of the congregation of Montecorona at Frascati. [The volume division and designation are described in endnote 2 of the introduction of *Alone with God*. From a footnote at this point, we insert seven sentences:] Almost all the volumes are preceded by an index drawn up by Giustiniani's own hand. From the manuscripts of the [Sacro] Eremo Tuscolano [of Frascati], which come from Monte Corona, a few copies were made which are found, or were found, in various hermitages, especially that of Rua. They were designated by the word "copy" followed by the volume number. I made use of the Frascati manuscripts. I did research as well in the libraries of Arezzo, Camaldoli, Cupramontana, Padua, Poppi, Venice, and the Vatican Library. At Cupramontana, in the province of Ancona, is found the library of the Hermitage of [the Grottoes of] Massaccio.... Some of these volumes [incunables]...[date from] the time of the Blessed and bear an ex libris in his hand. In September of 1513 he took care to reclaim, by means of his nephew Francis, all the letters that he had sent to his relatives and friends in Venice. Before departing for Jerusalem in 1507, he had burned all his writings previous to that date except for some letters and a series of "daily thoughts," written in 1506 and saved thanks to a ruse of his friend Canali. But he retained and collected the rest, and he himself drew up the index of all the volumes of this collection. Although he did not write an autobiography, he has at least left numerous elements of one in those texts in which, so often, he spoke of himself. As vast as it is, this documentation remains only fragmentary and entails some gaps; yet it permits us to record the states of Blessed Paul's soul and to follow its development with precision and continuity.

The utilization of this documentary material presents a double difficulty. In the first place, there is a difficulty in reading. The Blessed wrote rapidly and formed his letters poorly; he knew it and at times apologized for it. For example, he wrote to Quirini on June 7, 1511: "Perhaps you were not able to read the Latin opuscule that I sent you." What did he owe to some "little notes taken from memory," by means of which he says he had prepared himself to draw up this opuscule? Besides, he regrets that his letters are "so long and so poorly written." What had already been an obstacle for his contemporaries who wanted to understand him is still one today. It is aggravated by the fact that the lower part of some pages had been mutilated or damaged either at the time of the binding of the collections or afterwards. So we ought not claim to interpret all the expressions which Giustiniani makes use of with absolute fidelity. But these gaps in details, which some conjectures allow us to remedy, never prevent the text from being intelligible, at least as a whole.

The other difficulty presented by Blessed Paul's works is due to his manner of writing. He is almost always prolix, and very often disordered — according to our way of thinking, at least — above all in his intimate letters and personal notes; he is aware of it, moreover, and sometimes confesses it to his correspondents. He puts down on paper all the thoughts that come to mind: a precious testimony, but one scarcely lending itself to analysis. So the quotations will inevitably be numerous and long in the pages that follow; often it will be necessary to abbreviate or to content ourselves with summarizing, yet without betraying the thought which the texts dictate.

There need be no question here of studying exhaustively the activity of the Blessed in all the spheres in which it was exercised. His work deserves to engage the attention of various specialists: historians, philosophers, and theologians. But before all else, Giustiniani was a hermit. He took part in Church reform, in theological and political controversies, in the literary movement, only within the framework of the solitary life or in so far as they prepared for it. That which we must bring to light is, therefore, the birth and the development of his eremitic vocation.

I

The Stoic
(1476-1509)

I. Pleasures and Games

Thomas Giustiniani, who was to receive in religion the name of Paul, was born in 1476. His family tree could boast of high-ranking dignitaries of the Republic of Venice and even of a saint, whom we know as Saint Lawrence Justinian, patriarch of Venice when he died twenty years earlier. Our only source of information concerning the first twenty-six years of Giustiniani's life is what he himself wrote about them much later. After his conversion, and especially as he grew older, he often recalled his youth in terms whose objective reality is difficult to measure. For, with the passing of time, he seems to have exaggerated, on the one hand, the seriousness of his past faults, and on the other, his attraction for solitude, which seemed to be the unifying factor of his life. He tended to simplify, by reducing to its major lines and principal stages, an evolution that, in reality, had been slow and turbulent. Yet who knew his soul better than he did? His memory was very accurate, and the numerous accounts that he left of his previous life are in agreement and sometimes very precise.

One of the earliest memories that he retained, and even embellished, was of the attraction he felt for solitude.

It is she that I have loved and desired, she that I have sought from my youth. I was smitten with her and wanted to make her my bride.... I used to seek her everywhere, eager to carry her off in order to rest beside her in my room. Because for those who love her, her company engenders neither bitterness nor boredom.... When I was a little lad in my mother's house, I used to flee from the company of other children, as well as that of my brothers and sisters, to stay with my dearest friend, solitude. But how could I enjoy the embraces of solitude in the midst of so many people?

Life offers other pleasures besides solitude. Little by little Thomas Giustiniani discovered them. He left some very clear statements concerning the pleasures and amusements of his youth, which we need not hesitate to quote, for they explain several of the frames of mind that he will tell us about subsequently. One of the most suggestive passages is a meditation on heavenly and earthly pleasures, in which he recounts the first stages of his psychological development:

When I was still a little child, I had lots of fun with a toy, with a ball and with some peach stones. Later when I reached adolescence, I began to enjoy masquerades, dances and games. Did I not also take delight in study or the company of friends, or was I affected by carnal pleasures? Not at all. I got the most fun out of playing to my heart's content with a ball or a toy, or following men in masquerade costumes, or watching dances. At almost the same time, however, I began to be taken up with the love of study, of friendship, and of pleasure in wretched carnal excitement. Then, all that formerly amused me lost its charm: my joy lay in books instead of toys, in writing instead of playing ball. My gaze turned from grotesque masks to the prettiest girls. I enjoyed the company of friends more than the spectacle of dancing. As I grew older, my pleasures had changed. As Saint Paul says: "When I was a child, I thought as a child." But once an adolescent, all that was childlike about me disappeared. I began to speak, to feel and to enjoy myself like an adolescent.

Even these joys, however, did not last long. With the coming of new pleasures, the older ones decreased and gradually disappeared. Desire for honor and praise (which I had not previously known) made me derive more enjoyment from receiving praise than from all the other delights that I had tasted up to that time. Later, seized by an inordinate desire for possessions, the property, houses, and wealth that my father had bequeathed to me became my passion, and I rejoiced more in them than in the trifling books that used to please me. No longer did I take great pleasure in the mere sight of the prettiest girls, but in their embraces and kisses. Disordered satisfaction in honor, avarice, and indecent pleasure drove out the more honest pleasures of former days. Reading, writing and the company of friends grew boring, as I turned from them to the gratification of glory, avarice and lust.

Thomas Giustiniani has left some details concerning certain phases of this development.

From birth to the age of seventeen, in my fatherland and my father's house, under my mother's care (for my father died when I was still very little), and attending grammar school, my life seems to have been very simple. But alas, it was not innocent. On the contrary, very sad to say, I started to sin before I knew what sin was. But even at that tender age, my sins left me disgusted. As a child, I often wept tears that were not those of a child; nevertheless, I did not stop sinning in many ways.

Although Thomas Giustiniani felt all the pleasure attached to sin, yet he did not abandon himself to it: his conscience was pricked. "Remember," he would say to himself,

that during your childhood years, you scarcely knew the meaning of sin. And yet, by God's grace, when you sinned, you were sorry about it. Weeping, you vowed never to commit that sin again, though you knew neither what a vow was nor that, even without a vow, one is obliged not to sin.... With childish, though not blameworthy, emotion, you sought to appease God by saying: "Lord, I regret having committed this sin. I swear and I vow never to commit it again. Pardon me for having committed it, and if I fall again, do not pardon me." And yet, you fell into worse sins of the same kind and into other sins, not only once or ten times, but a thousand and ten thousand times. And for years, you were mixed up in this same sin and many others.

In 1496, he leaves Venice in search of solitude. He was later to apply to himself, with regard to this move, the words which the Lord spoke to Abraham:

"I went forth from my father's house," I left my family and my native land. Eager to devote myself to study, I sought solitude more and more and did not find it. To avoid the center of the city, I dwelt on its outskirts. I took care to have but few friends; I refrained from familiarity with those who served me. Nevertheless, I was still unable to get enough of the company of solitude.

That was because his heart was still divided.

From the age of seventeen to twenty-eight, in a place not far from Padua, I devoted myself to the study of the masters of logic, philosophy, metaphysics, and finally, theology. I attended the public schools, but for the most part I studied privately, in the manner of a hermit, and with moderation. However, I did not live virtuously enough: I fell and rose again; I sinned and then repented; often, in spite of good resolutions, I did wrong.

Later, he calls to mind "his adulteries of every kind." He recalls the times "when he passed the nights writing about carnal love," he speaks "of the poems in which he sang of his fleshly loves." And he adds:

When I loved a corporeal beauty, I had it always before my eyes; the words uttered by the mouth that I loved ever re-echoed in my ears; wherever I was, my love consumed me. My every concern was to avoid doing anything she might not like. Whether she saw me or she saw me not, I refrained from anything that might displease her. My only concern was to do what she found agreeable.

Thomas Giustiniani's reason for destroying the poems and letters that dated from that period is doubtless that they contain references to these enjoyments. At any rate, the memory of his past made a deep impression upon him. At the beginning of his novitiate, he will reflect that those who have preserved their virginity can easily attain perfect detachment. "But a pig, defiled by all the lusts of the world, who for many years, has been a slave of his flesh, who has never raised himself from the ground, a heart hardened by countless vanities, wrapped in a chilly cloud of countless worldly, lascivious and sad thoughts — how can such a one attain this state of consolation?"

Thomas was to attain it. But the period of rectification was prolonged. We do not know in what year it began. Let us set down, at least, the description of his first steps:

By the grace of God, new pleasures replaced the former ones. I had begun my studies less for love of learning than prompted by the hope of achieving fame from them. My mind took pleasure in the songs of the poets and the declamations of the orators, in which the vices are condemned and the virtues are praised. My desire for wealth and fame was gradually decreasing, but the lusts of the flesh were not diminishing; quite the contrary, the pleasure I took in them increased daily. Already the love of virtue, rather than wealth or fame, began to fill me with joy. Gladness in generosity had overcome delight in avarice. The love of virtue made me to want to be virtuous rather than to appear virtuous. I thirsted for the satisfactions that rise from the witness of a clear conscience rather than from the praises of others. With all that, however, the shameful lusts of the flesh increased. As I grew older, I applied myself more seriously to study. The teaching of the philosophers filled me with a joy that was more intense than any other I had previously experienced. And so carnal pleasure, which deprived me of strength and time for study, attracted me less and less. Those base pleasures I had formerly sought so avidly, my mind now disdained when they were offered to it, for it began to take keener delight in the knowledge of the truth. Now and again, there were periods in which I was taken up anew with the love of philosophy and, at the same time, with the violence of lust, and my spirit scarcely entertained any but these two delights. The company of my friends did not amuse me much. On the contrary, when their visits snatched me away from the reading of books or the embraces of women, I derived more sadness than joy from them. There was a struggle between the impure delight in the pleasures of the flesh and the love of knowledge. It would have been difficult to say which of the two was stronger, for I often turned from women to books and from books to women.

Yet with the help of that divine clemency which does not refuse to aid even the unworthy, I was moved (I know not how) to read not only philosophical works but also Christian authors. And my mind was so pleased with them that I no longer considered all the rest as true joys, but as dreams and follies. Now the knowledge of God which is obtained from Christian books, the admiration for Christian virtue, and the desire for this virtue so satisfied me that the pleasures of carnal wretchedness began to lose all their attraction; the mere thought of them saddened me. My spirit had joined together the delight of pagan philosophy with that of Christian doctrine, and it became incapable of enjoying almost anything else. Day by day, I found greater delight in sacred letters, while that produced by the teachings of the pagans kept diminishing. As I realize now (but was unaware of then), these studies affected my habits. My spirit found greater satisfaction in a single moment of continence than it could have found in the endless satisfaction of the desires of the flesh.

2. Peace of Mind

The first of the extant letters of Giustiniani dates from 1503, when he was twenty-seven. We know almost nothing about the years immediately preceding this date, with the exception of this confidence, which he will let slip much later: "At the age of twenty-four, I intended to become a religious. But certain things arose on the day I was to enter the monastery which made me postpone the step. And following this decision, my desire for the religious state grew cold."

Giustiniani continues, then, to lead a life of study in Padua. He frequents the Benedictine abbey of Saint Justina, attends the Divine Office and sometimes goes to confession there. But his preoccupations remain those of a humanist enamored of philosophy. A letter to his friend, Nicholas Tiepolo, sets the tone of his correspondence during the year 1503. Relying on Petrarch's affirmations, Thomas recommends that his friend read Cicero's *Tusculan Disputations*, but he adds his personal opinion: "I derived not only great pleasure but also the greatest profit from this reading. These pages have roused and fortified me against death and pain, against the passions and, finally, against every possible turn of fortune, to such a degree that I hesitate to call the fever from which I am suffering an evil. There is no evil but vice, there is no good but virtue, as Cicero proves." Tiepolo prefers the Peripatetics. But Giustiniani asserts that Cicero is a model of serenity for him through his doctrine and through the peace of mind that emerges from his writings, especially from his letters, in which he is seen at grips with all of life's difficulties.

He does not lack reasons to be troubled. He is often ill. He tells one of his friends, Mark Anthony Discalcio, a physician, how another physician wanted to cure his fever by getting him drunk. Thomas never calls a physician: he is afraid that they will make him progress from quartan fever, in which one is still able to read and write, to tertian fever, which confines one to bed, unable to think of anything but eating and sleeping. A physician from Cologna

Veneta had come to examine one of his brother's servants, whose health gave cause for concern. Having been introduced to Thomas, he began to extol wine, alleging that Avicenna had discussed this issue at length. To hear him tell it, one would think that wine cured not only fevers but all illnesses. He spoke more like an orator than a physician and got carried away to the point of perspiring and getting hoarse. His conclusion was that if Thomas wanted to get well, he should drink not only until intoxicated but until feverish and overcome by sleep. Thereupon a discussion takes place in which the authority of Avicenna and Galen are debated. Thomas' principal argument is that a bodily defect cannot be cured by a spiritual fault, the spirit being more noble and perfect than the body. It is better to have a healthy spirit in a crippled body than a weak spirit in a healthy body. But drunkenness and the rousing of the passions that it induces are moral evils. Therefore Thomas refuses the physician's treatment in order to remain faithful to his master, Cicero.

He speaks in the same vein to his brother, James: the fever which prevents his visiting him does not at all lessen his affection for him: "If you were not my brother, I would want you for a friend." Like Seneca and Cicero, he extols friendship: "I believe that nothing is more pleasant or useful for mortals than mutual love and kindness." That day, Thomas suffers from a double quartan fever: he is exhausted from chills and high temperature, and during the intervals when the fever leaves him, he is weak and hardly feels any better. But he remains persuaded that the only evil is vice and the only good virtue. Equanimity is the means to control the worries and vexations by which fate seeks to test us. Scipio in exile, Metellus in widowerhood, Regulus tortured, Cato after his fall, Socrates poisoned: these have shown by their experience that adversity can be overcome. Likewise in sickness, one must remain calm and self-controlled: nothing can force the soul to lose its peace, and sickness is but an occasion for it to manifest its greatness.

In this period of moral crisis brought on by his vices, Thomas regained his taste for friendship. Several letters from this time give us the names of his friends: Victor, Bernard Monald, Mark Anthony Discalcio, Peter Campesano, George Alovisio, a certain John, and above all, Tiepolo and Vincent Quirini. His relations with them have two characteristics. First, he feels the need to see them and to converse with them. He explains to Victor that his sister's unexpected visit to Padua has forced him to go to the busiest sections of the city. His sister has just left, not without having made him lose still another day. Fearing that she might want to return, he accompanied her a considerable distance, as far as the river. Now he is free once again to meet his friends. Victor must come to see him, unless he prefers that Thomas visit him instead. After supper, the one in whose home they have eaten will accompany the other back to his lodgings, in keeping with their long-established custom.

The second characteristic of this friendship is that it requires intellectual exchanges. Thomas writes to Tiepolo about some difficult points in the doctrine of Aristotle and Averroës. He relates to Quirini that a hermit whom he visited gave him a dialogue of Pontano to read. But after having read it, Thomas does not believe that the text was written by Pontano. He conveys his own reaction to his correspondent and asks for his opinion on the matter. He presents an internal critique of the work: neither the style nor the ideas are consonant with those in Pontano's other writings. Could Pontano have written it in his youth? The differences are so great that this hypothesis is ruled out; there is for example, a word that Pontano never uses. The dialogue rather recalls Apuleius. Perhaps Pontano was imitating Apuleius? But this hardly seems likely.

Thomas Giustiniani is sometimes obliged to retire to a family estate to manage his property. It is doubtlessly this residence which he calls his "solitude." This retirement impels him to ask his friends for news of academic affairs in Padua. He implores Bernard Monald to send him an account of a disputation which he was not able to attend. The report should be so vivid and detailed so that, upon reading it, one would get the impression of actually being there. Thomas sends his first poems to a scholar for criticism and correction. He also mentions his poems to Quirini, whom he questions on an obscure passage of Themistius, and with whom he exchanges ideas on sensible and intellectual knowledge. Also dated in the year 1503 is a curious note "from Thomas Giustiniani to Thomas Giustiniani," urging himself to moderate his language in accordance with a maxim of Pythagoras. For thought does not remain in the realm of speculation for Giustiniani: Stoic philosophy was for him a way of life.

The year 1504 is almost entirely taken up by illness. But at the end of the year, a series of letters following a long silence reveals to us that further progress had taken place. On November 20, he informs his brother James that he has attained, thanks to his illness and his success in overcoming it, "knowledge of God and self." Two days later, he bares his soul to Quirini and indicates to him the point of his spiritual development:

> I suffered a very serious illness this year, to say nothing of lesser ailments. Never, however, was I conscious of my mind's losing its composure to the point that it did not function as well as when I was in good health.... In spite of all sorts of disturbances, my mind has not lost its power to make good use of both itself and my body. I feel better now than I have in three years in this respect. Then I was shaken by many disturbances that I no longer experience at all. I was really badly off then, for my mind behaved badly in itself and toward my body, which is, nevertheless, its companion.

And for the first time, the letter ends with an allusion to the Lord: "If I have reached this stage, it is not thanks to my efforts, but an effect of God's goodness, since I have followed your excellent and holy counsels."

The next day, he writes another letter to James: "I have decided to speak frankly to you. First, know that, through long reflection on good and evil and reading those books that contain the discipline of living well, I have subjected, insofar as I can, all of the operations and actions of my body to the governance and control of my mind." And quoting Euripides, he describes this victory over himself. He has endured fevers and pains without moaning or showing the slightest impatience; his mind now rules his mouth, tongue, and even every nerve, to the extent that every unseemly impulse is excluded. Daily thought on how to live and die well has enabled Thomas Giustiniani to reach this stage: adversity was able to bring him what prosperity could not: "knowledge of self and of God. This victory was brought about by God's goodness."

What are those "books which contain the discipline of living well?" Outstanding among them, he declares to Tiepolo, are the *Tusculan Disputations*: "I have just read this book with a greater spiritual rapture than any I have ever before experienced. This work is worthy of Cicero, but it suits my misfortune just the same. It teaches me not to fear death, to scorn pain, and not to consider sickness as an evil." In the same spirit, Thomas explains that there is no reason to be afraid during an earthquake: the masses were wrong to take fright at the sight of collapsing houses.

On November 24, Giustiniani learns that Soriano, the Carthusian who during his term as prior was Giustiniani's confessor, just became Patriarch of Venice. He is surprised that this rich nobleman who had renounced everything to retire to the Charterhouse, "where, without any doubt, solitude and peace of mind reign supreme," should have accepted the episcopacy, whose obligations are incompatible with solitude. So Thomas takes things seriously. In fact, a few days later, he reveals an important resolution. His friend John informed him of his decision to renounce all other disciplines in favor of Holy Scripture. Thomas rejoices to have him as companion and master and to converse with him henceforth on this subject which is dear to him. For he adds: "Having rejected Aristotle's philosophy, I made up my mind to turn to the same science that you are taken up with." Not that he wants to follow the lessons of those who teach theology at Padua. These are "only declamations, trivial questions, argumentations, and, to put it more truthfully, sophisms." "On the contrary, my intention is to draw from that true theology which is found in the Sacred Scriptures of the Old and New Testaments." He congratulates John for having retired into solitude to fulfill his plan: "Nothing can be more profitable than devoting oneself to study in order to put one's habits in order and acquire peace of mind."

Thomas too retires to the mountains. He so informs Bernard Monald, at the same time that he tells him about the illness which threatened his life, his recovery, and the change which took place in him. "I have made up my mind to live as a solitary.... I have chosen as a retreat a very pleasant and comfortable house, situated on one of my brother's estates. I will be at peace there and can devote myself to study and receiving my friends." Soon he is able to write: "I live apart from all human society and, insofar as I can, free from lewd pleasures and other passions of the soul." The result of this painful period, therefore, is this first step toward the solitary life.

3. The Desire for God

Toward the end of 1505, Thomas leaves Padua to return to Venice; he remains there until spring, reading, among other things, some extracts from the Greek commentary of John Grammaticos on the *Meteorology* of Aristotle. But he does not find his longed-for quietude in Venice.

> After completing my studies, I returned to my fatherland; I chose to reside in a suburb, hoping that I would more securely possess my well-beloved solitude there than in the city. But all my well-wishers came to see me, and I grew apart from my beloved. I then fled to the country, where I was told that the solitude which I loved delights to dwell. But scarcely had I rested for a few days with my sweet friend than I

was snatched from her embraces by the visits of my friends and the obligation of attending to my brother's affairs.

In fact on June 1, Giustiniani arrived at the island of Murano in the vicinity of Venice. He tells Tiepolo: "I retired today to Murano, where I am arranging my books, for I have come here to study." "I have come to refurbish my house in Murano," he writes to his brother, James, "with the end in mind of being able to concentrate a bit on study and on my soul. My love for good authors increases every day, especially those who treat of the discipline of living well." He explains to Jerome Acorombono, one of his old teachers at Padua, his reason for leaving that city:

Last year, I was suffering from a very serious quartan fever which made study almost impossible and, moreover, a terrible epidemic was sweeping through Padua, so that no one could remain there without endangering his life. So I left that city for good, and I no longer have a house there. Having finished my studies, as they say, I returned to my native country. I am in Venice, though this house which I own in Murano is, as you know, more outside of Venice than within Venice.

Then he tells of his desire to continue studying the natural and divine disciplines. Yet his health always leaves something to be desired. One day he will describe it in these terms:

I lived for thirty-four years in the world, and from the age of twenty to thirty-three (that is to say from 1496 to 1515) I had some serious illness almost every year. When I was well, maintaining my health was a heavy burden. I had to abstain from almost all foods: salads, pork, citrus fruits, vegetables, oil, from everything. And the slightest excess in quality or quantity, or the least change in the time of my meals, had the most deplorable consequences for me.

45

The summer of 1506 is marked by a kind of long retreat that gives us the first extant work of Giustiniani: *Daily Thoughts on the Love of God*. Under this title, he left us a series of sixty-three elevations, written "with flying pen" between April and September. This spiritual journal permits us to follow closely the development of an interior crisis which is one of the most important stages of his life.

Three years later, he would himself say why and under what circumstances he had written it. This declaration merits attention, for the same reasons that are given here explain the genesis of almost all of Giustiniani's subsequent writings. He seeks to concentrate his mind on the loving contemplation of God. But the occupations and cares that distract him hinder this. He forces himself to write, as a remedy for this dissipation.

> I considered it necessary to have recourse to the pen: not with the object of putting into writing what I was thinking about the love of God, but just to bring myself to think, at least a little bit, about this God whom we ought to love. It seemed to me that, with the help of the pen, I could fix my mind's attention. It is always tempted to wander out of weakness. Just as pronouncing the words of the Psalms and other prayers sustains the mind (which needs to express itself) in its contemplation, so the pen comes to the aid of my meditation. The pen, therefore, is not so much a herald charged to make known my thoughts as it is their companion and assistant.... After I had spent the whole day in taking care of the affairs of the house and the whole evening in reading philosophy, I would not have had any free time left for reflection if I had not made the decision to write at least something every day, even though it was sometimes necessary to steal time from the hours rightfully demanded by sleep. That is why in the final evening hours, when I already felt tired from other reading and thought and sleep was beckoning, I would take my pen in hand and confide to paper everything that came to mind on the subject of the love of God. There was no chance, therefore, to put these thoughts in order or to embellish

them. The pen brooked no delay and wanted to put them down just as they came to mind.

This accounts for the plan — or, more accurately, the absence of a plan — and the style of this work. One also understands better why Thomas alludes to his current reading. It gives direction to his meditation and nourishes his fervor. From the very first lines, it is evident that he is fed by Holy Scripture. He expresses himself in Biblical terms which he has made his own and assimilated into his language. An abundance of echoes reveals his assiduous contact, as far back as this time, with Holy Writ. During this period, he chose to read a series of texts and works on charity. He cites the *De diligendo Deo (On Loving God)* of Saint Bernard; he copies out passages from Plato, Plotinus, Saint Augustine, Marsilio Ficino, and Pico della Mirandola on the love of God; he studies the Canticle of Canticles and Origen's commentary on it. But he is not bookish: he speaks from the abundance of his heart and quotes from memory. He addresses himself to God in a tone reminiscent of that of the *Confessions* of Saint Augustine: to use a word with which he entitles many of the elevations, he engages in a soliloquy. He speaks in a Latin that is perfectly fluent and fully elegant and supple, by which he effortlessly expresses all the freshness and vivacity of his spirit. Some classical verses come to his mind; he also remembers some of Cicero and Aristotle and borrows his vocabulary and expressions from them time and again. But his thought moves on the plane of love. In his mystical flights, this humanist philosopher surpasses philosophy, even if he continues to make use of it.

He does not intend to compose a systematic exposition but takes advantage of daily events for reflection and prayer. Sometimes he carries on with a conversation that he has had with his friends about the degrees of the love of God. These conversations with fervent and cultured men do not lack subtlety, but their final appeal, when reason fails, is always to their personal experience of love. Their thoughts are tested in their lives, and their conversations end with the resolution to love God more by practicing what the Gospel says. Another time, a conversation with his brother or the illness or death of one of his relatives provides the subject for his meditation. From one day to the next, speculative expositions alternate with ardent supplications. His tone remains ever lofty. From time to time, in moments of more intense fervor, Thomas makes a first attempt, but in Italian this time, at short poems like those that he wrote not long ago to sing of his carnal loves.

He desires to abandon himself completely to the serene occupation of loving. In theological schools, they hold disputations and even fight in an attempt to ascertain whether love is seated in the intellect or will. He is not ignorant of these controversies and summarizes them with precision. But he no longer feels anything but distaste toward these discussions, which at first troubled him but now seem absolutely vain to him. Philosophy, no doubt, gives knowledge, but it does not lead to love. He speaks about this from experience: he went to the limits of knowledge, and he saw that it was necessary to go beyond science. He now realizes that love precedes knowledge and makes it grow to full measure, because it is a gift of God. If it remained proportioned to the knowledge man can have of God, it would always be very restricted. But when God gives someone the love of Him, He makes Himself known to him and to the same degree. The human disciplines, on the contrary, are unable to make God sufficiently known so as to be loved. So the love of God can only come from God: it cannot come from philosophy books or from one's own feelings. All man can do is desire Him, get ready for Him, and then cherish Him within himself by prayer, fasting, charity, and simplicity of spirit.

The major problem that bothers Giustiniani during this period concerns the place that he ought to give to philosophy in his new life. One senses that he is still completely penetrated by philosophy. He is already a mystic by the purity of his love, the intensity of his desire for God. But his entire psychology, his whole manner of expressing himself, is still that of the philosopher that he has been up to

48

this point. He still holds the authority of the thinkers of antiquity in high regard. He exalts their teachings or insists on their limitations in turn, but without despising them: he gives them their place in the hierarchy of means that lead to God. Philosophers and poets can give a certain peace of mind. Did his conversion not begin thus? But this is only a first step. Thomas only renounces philosophy to surpass it: he continues to esteem it now that love has made him overstep its bounds. Philosophy would deserve scorn only if it pretended to be sufficient: without charity, it is nothing: "If we possess all the science of the philosophers of Greece and Islam but do not love God, it profits us nothing." As for that friend of his who has just died, all his knowledge of ancient tongues, logic, and medicine would have been completely useless to him if he had not loved God. But having loved God, he was able to put that knowledge to profit, for it was not bad. Philosophy is an asceticism of the mind, a preparation to know and to love God. The time comes when it is necessary to renounce it in order to go further. Natural knowledge is like a ship's boat that brings us to shore, at which point we have to proceed on our own. "When it has enabled us to think something about God, when it has taken us to shore, let us abandon the sciences and run toward God with all the strength of our love."

Giustiniani sees clearly that love of God is inspired by holy reading rather than by secular literature. In spite of his resolutions, however, he admits that "his studies remain as they were, that is to say vain, Platonic and Aristotelian." He reacts to this, however. Instead of thinking, as he did at first, about the love of God in the abstract, he fixes his attention more and more on the concrete manifestations of this love: the life of Christ, the mystery of the Eucharist. He prays all the more, tells of his love and his desire to love, speaks of the Holy Ghost and of the Holy Trinity. He wants to be converted. "When Christ was thirty years old, he began to preach. Today, it is thirty years since I was born. It is time that I began to practice what Jesus preached." One day when his fever is more intense than usual, he envisages death. With this perspective, he discovers the vanity of all worldly things, including worldly science:

> I was confined to bed, prey to a double tertian fever. I had not a moment's respite; death itself stood at the foot of my bed. Of what use would the natural sciences have been to me then? Of what value the Aristotelian and Platonic opinions? Only my love for God, as weak as it was, consoled me. If I had been obliged to depart, I would have had nothing to take with me. I would have had to leave everything behind. Love alone would have followed me.

Once restored to health, Giustiniani decides to break definitively with the sins of his youth, the memory of which hounded him, and to spend the rest of his life being healed of them and doing penance. He has a hearty contempt for everything earthly, "pleasures, riches, honors, and the sciences that savor of the world." "As for us, let us account ourselves nothing. Let us love neither beauty, nor vigor, nor health."

Already he has renounced riches, honors, and sensual gratifications; he has broken with the pleasures of the flesh; he has distanced himself from public life. But the one tie that keeps him attached to the world is human science. Toward the end of this long retreat, he concentrates his effort on this matter. Henceforth, he will read only Holy Scripture and the writings that can help him to understand and live it. He cites Jerome, Ambrose, Gregory, and Bernard. It is the Gospel that is the true philosophy. "What further need would we have, then, to read the *Ethics*, the *Economics*, and the *Politics* of Aristotle? Do we dare to compare the *Dialogues* of Plato with divine Scripture or the letters of Cicero with those of Saint Paul? All the rules of eloquence have been observed in the Psalms. The knowledge that we seek and the rules of conduct that we need are found in Holy Scripture, and only there to the full." In comparison with "the ancient theology of the Fathers," the "new theology, that of Paris, proceeding by questions," is very much adulterated. It is only a series of disputations for the pleasure or glory of debating, a tissue of subtle and useless arguments. This knowledge has become, according to its proponents, a logic, a physics, a metaphysics more than a theology. "I will now conclude this discourse and this notebook with a sound maxim: let he who desires to love God renounce the vanity of all the other disciplines, let him read attentively the true theology of the Christians of antiquity. But one who devotes himself to the new theology in an effort to draw love from it is laboring, in my opinion, in vain." The discredit implied here with regard to Scholasticism does not extend to Saint Thomas. On many occasions, Giustiniani expresses his esteem for him and his indebtedness to him. But we see here an example of how a humanist, accustomed to going to the sources, to studying Plato, Plotinus, and Aristotle in their original texts, reacted in the face of a theology that was purely speculative and which had lost touch with patristics. In the writings of the Fathers, which spoke to him of sacred mysteries, Giustiniani found more motives for love than in abstract discussions saturated with philosophy.

A whole plan of life is contained in this opuscule on the love of God. These *Daily Thoughts* mark the culminating point of Giustiniani's conversion. The rest of his life is but their aftermath. He is past the stage when he thought he had found peace of mind in Cicero. The memory of his sins plagues and perturbs him. "A familiar and absolutely truthful witness bothers me: my conscience." He seeks and he prays: a slow and painful conversion, with periods of resolutions, of hesitation, and of renewed ardor, wherein his desire for God alternates with a vivid experience of his powerlessness to love. For love is a gift. Not even the very solitude that he has come to Murano to seek can give it to him.

> It now depends on You, Lord, that I may know You and love You, and not on me. If I were to love You more intensely in this solitude, I might be led to think that I could attribute this good fortune to myself and that I did not receive it from You. But You want me to realize, O Lord,

51

that love can only come from You. When I was in the midst of the noise and bustle of the city, I knew well that my love for You did not come from me. Now that I might be able to get the idea that I have done something to earn it, You take away Your love from me: not the love with which You love me, of course, but the love with which I ought to love You.

The retreat at Murano has been, then, but an occasion for renewed purification for Giustiniani. Yet it is not there where he will find the Lord — he must seek Him elsewhere.

4. In Search of Solitude

During the last months of the year 1506, Giustiniani travels, looks after himself, and reflects. At the beginning of 1507, he makes plans to go to Rome the following summer, where he wishes to take part in a disputation. He draws up his arguments, but illness and, as he says, "other causes of trouble and disturbance" prevent his completing them. As a matter of fact, he has made a new and important decision: to go to the Orient. He spends the spring of 1507 in preparing for this great pilgrimage, from which Giustiniani will perhaps never return. He seeks solitude, and since he has not found it in Italy, he will scour the wide world and especially those places where it is reported to exist, Syria and Palestine. His intention is clear: he has resolved "to renounce the study of all human disciplines to give himself entirely to that of Sacred Scripture and Christian philosophy." As a result, he burns all that he has previously written. He makes a vow to preserve chastity of body and spirit and procures a residence in Bethlehem in advance. The draft of his agreement with the Franciscans provides that, on condition that he pays them an allowance, he will be permitted to live in their monastery in Bethlehem for several years or even until his death without, however, entering their order. Thus prepared, he embarks on June 4. At the stopping places he puts down his impressions in writing.

This account of his route from Venice to Jerusalem reveals much about his state of mind at that time. This pilgrim remains a humanist. He is curious and inquires about everything. He disembarks at each port of call, even if only for a few hours. At Rovigno, he will venerate the relics of Saint Euphemia, whose legend he relates. At Pola, he finds out the explanation of the name of the city, called Chrysopolis in ancient times, and reports the story of its origins. He deciphers the Greek and Latin inscriptions that he encounters, admires an ancient theater, describes its architecture, gives its dimensions and measures its proportions. Something of the art lover persists in him, for as he views ruins, he compares them to those in Rome and examines the material and the system of construction. His visit to Ragusa, with its walls, fountains, and churches, fills him with admiration. He has not renounced the beautiful things of the world.

In several places he disembarks at monasteries or to see priests whom he knew during his studies in Padua. He venerates, without making any critical comment, such relics as the clothes that Simeon wore when he took Christ in his arms. He does remark, however, with regard to a crucifix in the Church of Saint Francis of Ragusa: "Every year, on Good Friday, some angels who take on flesh come to incense it with censers — something I consider an inept fiction rather than a fact that merits belief." He lists the islands that he catches sight of from the boat. He gets off at Crete and stays seven days at Candia: the monuments there offer nothing interesting. As for the customs, all that he has learned is that "the women do not go to Mass, and very few men go to confession." The city is dirty, but many Greek books are found in the monasteries as well as in the private homes, especially works of Aelian and some historians, also of Alexander of Aphrodisias and lastly of Origen. He visits Rhodes, then he sets foot on the coast of Palestine. He rides a donkey as far as Rama, where he sees some Arabic inscriptions "which he does not transcribe, not having the time and not knowing these characters." Finally on July 30, at the sixth hour, he enters "most holy Jerusalem, the city of God."

We know few details concerning his stay in the Orient. Only ten years later will he write these few lines.

Moved, or rather impelled, by the divine goodness to leave the world with its vanities and iniquities, I desired to lead a solitary religious life, and I sought for a long time in Italy a place that would lend itself to this intention of mine. Leaving Italy and Europe, I traveled through Greece and Syria and reached the solitary place in Bethlehem made famous by the memory of Saint Jerome. I also penetrated another solitude where formerly, not far from Jerusalem, twenty thousand monks lived under Saint Sabas. But since, my sins being in opposition, it was not God's will that I should find in these holy and venerable regions what I wanted, I returned to my native country, Italy.

Thomas Giustiniani received Holy Communion at the Cenacle. He prepared himself with a prayer that he preserved. In it he expresses sorrow for his sins, whose memory haunts him, especially those of his student life in Padua. "I beg You not to impute to me the times I went astray in childhood and the mistakes of my youth. But how can the graver faults that I committed during my more mature years fail to condemn me?" He bears their marks, admits them, and wants to be healed of them. Soon he will receive Holy Communion. After having confessed his unworthiness, he proclaims his hope. Now that he has seen the grotto where the Son of God deigned to become man, touched and kissed the manger where He lay, pressed his lips to the soil of Calvary, he has confidence. He seeks rest for his soul and he implores Christ to grant it to him with His body and blood which he is going to receive. He will set out again, but with renewed strength and determination, more than ever before, to live a good life.

Before leaving the Orient, while waiting in Cyprus for the Venetian triremes which are to carry him off, he composes a homily for Christmas at the request of a Franciscan who rendered him service. From the opening, he is pleased to recall that God is declared "admirable in His works" not only by Christians but also by philosophers and infidels. The benefit of the Incarnation, however, surpasses all that the intelligence or the genius of the greatest philosophers could possibly contrive. Here the Stoic gives place to the pilgrim who does not forget his former training or reject it, but who, in contemplating the place where the Word was made flesh, admires the transcendence of revelation in comparison with all human wisdom.

One of the elevations in which this same conviction is clearly expressed doubtlessly dates back to the same time and to this same stay in the Holy Land. During the Night Office, Thomas heard these words of the Lord read: "If anyone wants to be my disciple, let him renounce himself!" Back in his room, Thomas reflects on the meaning of self-renunciation. First he refers to the philosophy of the Academics, which ancient philosophy Saint Augustine claims to be most in harmony with Holy Scripture. Then, according to the definitions of man given by Plato and Cicero, he concludes that the man who gives in to the instincts of his body lowers himself to the level of the beasts. But no worldly philosophy, whatever its eloquence, is as profound as the teaching of Jesus Christ. By renouncing what is inferior to and unworthy of self, according to the philosophers, we return to ourselves, and enter again into ourselves. But the Lord says that we must renounce even ourselves, so that "it is no longer we, but Christ, who lives in us," as Saint Paul says. Thomas understands that this means renouncing all worldly pleasures with the help of Christ and living henceforth only for God, with an eye to heaven, our true abode. Such is, then, the philosophy hidden in this passage from the Gospel: Christ demands that we renounce not only our sensual pleasures, our vices, but ourselves. To do this, we must first renounce our bodies, which are part of ourselves, and also riches, which have been made for the body. Next we must become entirely spiritual, rejecting worldly standards. Thomas hears this call of the Lord as if it were addressed to him personally, inviting him to a complete conversion. And he soars to the greatest heights in speaking of these demands: let whoever understands this secret philosophy, which is higher and more intimate than any human discipline, go out of himself, abandon himself completely. The same call to exile which Abraham heard rings out for him, and he embraces it: *Exi de cognatione tua, obliviscere domum patris tui* ["Go forth from thy kindred, forget thy father's house," Gn 12:1 and Ps 44 (45):10]. To forget oneself means to unite oneself to God by thinking henceforth of Him alone.

With these dispositions, Thomas Giustiniani returns to Venice, toward the end of 1507. He will spend two years there, studying theology and reflecting on his vocation. He is not yet firmly decided to become a religious. He has already decided this, however: to leave the world. But where can he find solitude? He continues his search. Murano no longer suffices him, and one day he will write:

> I recall having wanted to try to live in a solitary villa, that is, in a house I had in Murano. But the experience showed me that such a life is rather that of a gentleman philosopher than of a Christian and religious soul. For there was neither renunciation of the world, nor mortification of one's own will, nor the virtue of obedience, nor real poverty, and there were countless dangers to chastity. But even if all other things had been present, it lacked the open confession of Jesus Christ and the example of one's neighbor.

So he seeks a monastery. He frequents that of the Camaldolese of Saint Michael in Murano. But before making a choice, he wants to come to an agreement with his two best friends, the priest John Baptist Egnazio and Vincent Quirini. In a letter, which is full of humor, he tries to make them get a feel for the misery of their daily lives. He pictures for them everything that a wealthy Venetian does from the time he arises until he retires. *Surgimus.... Eximus.... Pergimus....In ecclesia sumus.... In foro....* [We rise.... We go out.... We proceed.... We are in church.... In the square....] An agitated life, completely outward, continually dominated by ambition, the reason for all their worry. They are curious about anything new, about anything that could furnish a pretext for a conversation which, although it may be brilliant or useful, is always self-seeking, for they are always seeking their own glory or advantage. What a chore do they not impose on one another with their incessant greetings and responses to greetings! How much trouble do they not inflict upon themselves in their efforts to win everyone's favor! "If they are speaking with a young man, they assume a smiling countenance to give an impression of youth and freedom. But if they are conversing with an elderly person, they try to put on a serious visage, sterner than Cato's." The church itself is but a public drawing room where they go to greet one another. The conversation that ensues there is nothing but gossip, hypocrisy, flattery, and boasting. Do they frequent a monastery? They go to show off their devotion. The entire day of a Venetian nobleman is spent in the pursuit of honors and profit. All their intrigues reach their climax in the council chambers where public affairs are discussed; it is there that petitions are received and candidates are presented. "At one and the same time they fear, hope, shiver, and sweat. They are a prey to envy, annoyance, and greed." "If, then, a Stoic philosopher appeared to free their minds from all these disturbances, his efforts would be in vain, so completely does agitation dominate and enfetter their whole lives. How can one not feel disgust for such an empty existence?" Egnazio and Quirini seem to be as convinced of these things as Thomas is. All three apply for admission to the Benedictine abbey in Praglia, situated in the country at quite a distance from Padua, as oblates or *commissi*, but on condition of not taking the habit. Giustiniani will remark later to some monks of this observance: "We were afraid that if we made profession in your order that we would have to accept numerous transfers, take care of temporal goods, or occupy ourselves with others, especially adolescents, with whom every one of you is charged at one time or another, whether he wishes it or not. Our request was not granted." The three friends immediately look in another direction. But the entire year of 1509 constitutes a period of search and delay.

It is then that Thomas composes a commentary on Genesis. He states his intention in the preface. Of all the works that he has read, Genesis contains the most wisdom and eloquence, no matter what those who reserve these terms for the princes of worldly philosophy may think. There is not a character or letter in it that does not have a spiritual sense. He labors, therefore, by dint of reading far into the night, to draw out this sense. What method does he use? That one which is used in the study of worldly authors. When one wants to understand a philosopher, one explains his words by others that he has spoken elsewhere: Aristotle is his own best interpreter. Thus the word of God explains the word of God. The fruit of this study is peace of mind. One draws from it a discipline which is able to regulate habits and banish those indispositions of spirit called perturbations [passions], whether one eliminates them completely, as the Stoic school teaches, or moderates their excess through temperance, as the Peripatetics and the new Academy have thought in the matter. "We are convinced that there is no discipline better adapted for moderating or completely extirpating all disturbances of the spirit than Sacred Scripture.... This is what we have set out to achieve as a result of the effort which we have put forth in reading and in writing this work."

The commentary explains Genesis by the use of quotations from the Old and New Testaments and the Fathers of the Church. It is already positive exegesis, as it is called today, containing vast information and making opportune use of numerous works of Saint Augustine, Origen, Saint Jerome and Boethius, as well as some untranslated works of the Greek Fathers, in particular Gregory Nazianzen. The first treatise concludes with this postscript: "I have written this treatise in Venice on May 24, 1509. I, but a poor sinner, certainly not a man but the reproach of men, and who, although knowing the will of my Lord, does not fulfill it in anything." In the second treatise, Thomas deplores the corruption of the Church:

I cannot hold back my tears when I consider the state of the Church — or, to be more exact, her dissolution and ruin. Without saying anything further (for there are many scandals about which I say nothing, so as not to raise my voice against heaven — an expression, let it be said in passing, that is often used with reference to the pope and his court).... Without saying anything further, then, I am still unable to pass over in silence, or notice without weeping, that any kind of superstition finds acceptance in the Church of Christ.

The treatise closes with these words: "I have written this, I who am overwhelmed by the burden of my sins, who see and approve the better but do the worse."

In the following treatise, Thomas takes up again the theme of renunciation of self, and not only of vices, by which the Christian is raised above all the philosophers. At the end of each of the nine treatises, confessions similar to the following appear as a refrain: "Shaken by the storm of my anxieties, I see the port of my salvation and seek refuge there.... I detest my way of life, but I cannot but be what I detest.... I sigh for God's blessed promised land, but I do not run toward it, for I am constrained by the bonds of earthly pleasure.... Affected by a certain disgust for myself and the things of the world, I am not at all satisfied with what I write." The next to the last treatise is dated November 14, 1509. The last is unfinished.

II

THE HERMIT
(1510-1512)

1. The Departure

This great news spreads in the Camaldolese monasteries from the first days of January 1510: Thomas Giustiniani and two rich Venetian friends wish to embrace the solitary life in the order. Thomas himself, up to that time, had mentioned nothing of this in his correspondence or his personal notes. Yet everything readied him for this decision. The hermit existed in germ in the Stoic, and his past life was a rough sketch of the new existence which was to begin for him. "From your birth," he will later write, addressing himself,

> God gave you a nature inclined *ad otium magis quam ad negotium* [to leisure more than to business]. This inclination kept growing with you from your childhood so as to become second nature, as the philosophers call it. You preserved it not for just a few years, but even until your conversion at the age of thirty-four. Indeed, you spent this entire period reading if not studying, never desiring to involve yourself in any activity. Then you spontaneously chose the eremitical, solitary type of life, whose intrinsic law is the renunciation of business and cares, in order to devote yourself at leisure to the contemplation of divine truths. At your profession, you bound yourself by oath never to forsake this way of life.

At the start of 1510, Thomas is still far from this final stage. He will be professed within a shorter interval of time than that which has already elapsed. But the road to be traveled to the acceptance of a definitive commitment to the religious life is still hard and long. In order to ascend to solitude, it is first necessary to leave the world, and this break was, for Thomas Giustiniani, slow and difficult: it takes no less than a year. Only an objective review of the documents, which mark out his path, will enable us to follow his progress during this decisive year.

The superiors of the Camaldolese order yielded to the temptation to jump ahead. They believed too soon that the three new recruits had made a firm decision. This is understandable, for they expected much of them. The priest, Egnazio, was as distinguished a humanist as Thomas. As for Quirini, his birth, his culture and his high offices made him one of the first figures in Venice. Thomas will describe him one day like this: "He is one of the most learned masters in Padua. While still young, at the age of twenty-three, he disputed publicly in the presence of the cardinals and maintained more than four thousand theses. He is one of the most illustrious and sensible of all the Venetian senators, for the Republic entrusted him, in preference to all the others, with the most honorable and important missions to princes." Indeed, after the disputation of May 29, 1502, following which Alexander VI had given him the title of doctor, Quirini was appointed Venetian ambassador to King Philip I of Portugal in 1505 and later to Emperor Maximilian I. Novices of this caliber were a fortune to the Camaldolese order.

On January 7, 1510, the General of the order, Peter Delfino, writes to Paul Orlandini, Vicar General, that three young Venetians wish to become solitaries. Delfino sees here a promise of prosperity for his order. He expected nothing less from God. Did not Abraham hope against hope? Is God not able to bring forth sons of Abraham even from stones? This is the promise held in the vocation of these three men, concerning whom there is every reason to believe that they have given careful consideration to the supernatural character of the eremitical life and every reason to hope that they will persevere. From Orlandini's reply, Delfino understands that he, who resides at the monastery in Murano, is not unaware of their decision, for he has often conversed with them. Besides, Orlandini intends to spend the following Lent with them in order to fortify them if they still have any hesitation. Delfino is delighted; he "is as exultant as conquerors that have captured prey and are dividing the spoils." He adds: "Through your prudence and exhortations, you will easily compel them (*facile eos coges*) to lift their spirits and put aside their fears." And he gives instructions so that all three can come to spend Lent at the Hermitage of Camaldoli. Everything possible will be done to put them up, even if Orlandini has to stay at the monastery of Fontebuono, which is near the Hermitage where he can go every day.

On March 2, Delfino writes another letter in which he congratulates Orlandini for the care he is taking to see that the three recruits persevere in their intention. Orlandini must look after them persistently, *opportune et importune* ["in season and out of season," 2 Tim 4:2]. He must not forget to prepare them for the austerity that they will find at Camaldoli, so that they will not be scared off later. If they are tempted to back off, Orlandini should remind them of the eternal reward. In a word, he must do all in his power to ensure their becoming hermits. Orlandini passes on to Delfino the letters he is receiving from Giustiniani, who is the leader of the three friends. Delfino already regards him as one of their own. On March 26, Orlandini writes "to his three very dear friends, the priest, Egnazio, and the illustrious patricians of Venice, Giustiniani and Quirini" to tell them that he has sent their letter of March 15 to Delfino. He takes advantage of the occasion to praise the anchoritic life and to bring to their attention the distaste that men of their spiritual worth feel for worldly life. Let them come without delay; he awaits them at the Camaldolese monastery of the Angels at Florence and is counting the hours. Delfino informs Orlandini that he is postponing a journey that he had to make to Bologna. He is bent on being present to receive the new arrivals, for whom he has provided companions and transportation from Ravenna: "For I do not think we should reckon the vocation to the Hermitage of these three men together to be of little account." He says with regard to Giustiniani's letters: "Such contempt of the world can only be from God. For all three of them desire to be allowed to retire into solitude, a thing ordinarily granted from the beginning of their calling only to those who have been exercised under the cenobitic discipline for a long time."

The three friends do not demonstrate as much eagerness to come to Camaldoli as that shown in inviting them. The trip is postponed to the summer, and Giustiniani will come alone, delegated by the other two. Furthermore, they do not have the same idea about their retiring to the Hermitage as do the superiors of the order. In fact, on May 10 Giustiniani sends a memorandum to Delfino in which the following points are clarified: Thomas Giustiniani, John Baptist Egnazio and Vincent Quirini have decided to leave the world. However, they do not want to enter religious life just now, or take on the obligations and the habit of religious, for several reasons. First, because they do not yet know their strength. Next, so as not to be disturbed in any way by the cares which they would not lack if they were required to look after the temporal administration of the monastery or to govern the community spiritually. And finally, because they want always to be together in order to study better; they are not willing that obedience should one day oblige them to part. On the other hand, they want to live in a monastic institute in order to profit by the example and advice of experienced religious and to find there a confessor. They also wish that this monastic institute be far from the city. Consequently, they are asking whether they might be admitted to the Hermitage of Camaldoli on the following conditions: That they be given a cell, but not the status of hermits or monks or lay brothers, so as not to have the obligations of these states. And they ask that this arrangement be permanent. The three of them desire to live apart in eremitical surroundings according to a cenobitic Benedictine observance. They will not adopt the habit, schedule, diet, or Rule of the Camaldolese. Giustiniani enumerates the items from which he asks dispensations and exemptions: assistance at the Divine Office, silence, fasting, going out, etc., all for the purpose of devoting themselves to study under the best possible conditions. In return for this, they will pay a pension to be determined once and for all: for although they will not take a vow of poverty, they nevertheless intend to dispose of all their goods in advance. If this proposal is accepted, a contract can be drawn up to be approved by the general chapter and even by the pope.

Giustiniani set out on his journey. He received the following instructions en route from Quirini:

> When you arrive, make a detailed survey of everything that concerns the place, the climate, the construction, the way of life, and also the inhabitants, from both the corporal and spiritual point of view, to see whether we will find all the conveniences that we desire for body and soul. Look about, inquire from every possible source, and check one piece of information against the other. Make certain that, even though our conditions are accepted in writing, the environment is not unfavorable. Otherwise, we may be forced one day to renounce the liberty we require and instead take on the obligations of religious.

On July 3, Giustiniani arrives at Camaldoli, which includes the monastery called Fontebuono and the Hermitage at a short distance. Giustiniani spends the night at Fontebuono. On July 4, he ascends to the Hermitage, where Delfino has already gone before him. There the chapter is convened and Giustiniani is at once given a certificate in which all the conditions requested in the memorandum of May 10 are approved unreservedly and "with satisfaction." The reply to the three Venetians closes with these words: "If there is anything lacking in our reply, a fuller explanation will be supplied by Lord Thomas, your companion, who is present and residing with us in our holy Hermitage. And we pray that God will grant both you and him steadfast perseverance." The first thing the next morning, Delfino writes from Fontebuono to the abbot of Saint Michael of Murano: "Your Vicar, Orlandini, is at the Hermitage with Giustiniani, our patrician. May God confirm what He has begun in him so that others, prompted by his example, will walk in the steps of Christ. Thus may the house of God be filled with such men, who in the future will be strong pillars to sustain it."

It is obvious that Quirini's plans do not coincide with the hope cherished by Delfino. The latter, however, is right without knowing it. For at the same time that he writes to the abbot of Murano, Giustiniani addresses an unexpected letter to Quirini. After having told of his arrival at Camaldoli, he makes a major disclosure to his friend: he has completely changed in his plans. On July 1, while traveling across the Apennines, he had an accident: both he and his horse fell to the bottom of a ravine and in such a way that the horse was killed instantly. "I myself was beneath the horse. Not only did I live, but I escaped so safe and sound that I was able to ride twelve more miles until evening on another horse." He has to admit, therefore, that God worked a miracle in saving his life. And there is another miracle. He immediately felt the desire to withdraw from the world, but no longer merely in the manner in which he had decided with Quirini and Egnazio, but rather still more completely by becoming a monk and hermit. He desires above all something that he will never renounce, since he has promised it: to remain with his two friends. Next, he wishes to withdraw from his native country and from all participation in its government. These two conditions being guaranteed, here is what he would prefer: to live at Camaldoli as a religious hermit, with Quirini and Egnazio beside him under the conditions which they had set down, if, of course, they accept this solution. By way of advice, he suggests that it would be better for them, also, to become truly hermits and live under obedience. Then he gives them a general description of Camaldoli and its inhabitants, who make a very good impression on him. As for himself, he has made up his mind to enter religion without further delay.

On July 15, Quirini replies: "You have received the grace to desire to give yourself completely to the Lord. I congratulate you, or rather I give thanks to the Lord. As for me, I do not yet possess this grace, so pray that He will grant it to me. But have you never thought of becoming a Benedictine or Carthusian? Think it over.... If you persist in your intention to become a hermit, we will follow you, either as hermits or as nonreligious companions." But Quirini is afraid of the fasting; he asks Giustiniani to write him at the periods of the Ember weeks or of penance to let him know in what the fast consists, how he bears it, and what discomforts or temptations it occasions. And after asking about various "conveniences," he concludes: "If you get on well, I think that I will embrace the same life as you." On August 1, Quirini again asks him for details on the fasting, especially during Lent. He feels more inclined every day to imitate Giustiniani. He speaks to him of three young men who are visiting the Carthusians to get some idea of the life. Giustiniani has urged him to approach them in order to learn whether they might not prefer Camaldoli, far superior for recollection and austerity. The three friends hesitate: neither do they want to be separated from one another.

Giustiniani sets out to answer Quirini's questionnaire in detail. He does so in the form of a lengthy report with full particulars, which fills not less than sixty pages of close writing. He gives the topography of Camaldoli, a minute description of the buildings, an exact account of the daily routine, the observance (which turns out to be excellent), the fasts, disciplines and other penitential practices, which are austere. In addition to the hermits, there is a recluse in the Hermitage, Dom Michael Pini from Florence: an uneducated man but one by whom Giustiniani is deeply edified. The superior is called major. Giustiniani describes his stature, his complexion, his mannerisms in speaking. "Every few words, he says: '*Così a questo modo.*' ('So like this.') He administers temporal goods well. He has little culture and, although he reads well, he does not always understand what he reads. One day I had to explain to him the meaning of a papal bull he could not understand." He is a spiritual man, and he would like to be a recluse; all the religious are very pleased to have him as superior except a certain Dom Romualdino, who is not happy at the Hermitage and advises Giustiniani to become a Dominican. "I think he lacks intelligence and common sense." It seems that he himself may desire to found and promote a new Hermitage with a new form of life. All the inhabitants of the Hermitage, seven monks and five lay brothers, are thus passed over in review. All make a good impression. And yet Giustiniani neglects nothing that might help to enlighten him; he even makes use of his servant to learn certain things about the monks and lay brothers.

> All things considered, I think they would receive us well. We would have here all the conveniences desirable for recollection and study. There is a good library, and it would even be possible to borrow some Greek or Latin works from a monastery in Florence. We would be better off here than in a monastery: more separated from the world, less exposed to the cares of business, in the company of religious without culture, without learning, but full of charity, humility, kindness, and simplicity. They love their Hermitage and are full of saintly example.

After a month's stay, Giustiniani leaves Camaldoli on August 6. "He was satisfied and so were we," Delfino writes on August 14 to a monk in Murano. "He will return in September to take the habit. All here hope for his perseverance, especially if his two friends also come with him, as he does not doubt they will." At Venice, Giustiniani makes preparation for his final departure. He assigns Peter Campesano to buy him works of the Greek Fathers, especially Origen, Cyril, the two Eusebiuses, Gregory Nazianzen and Gregory of Nyssa, Athanasius, and Basil as well as the acts of the Councils. He also makes an engaging move toward his old domestic. Before his departure for the Orient, he had already written him: "Lawrence, although you have left me with the utmost baseness, on account of which I ought not to concern myself with you any more, I cannot refrain from wishing you well, you who lived in my house for so long. I am about to go...to Jerusalem. As I know that you always wanted very much to see the world, I would take you along in preference to a great number of others, who make me proposals, if you would like to come with me." This note received no response. Toward October 1510, Thomas Giustiniani wrote afresh to Lawrence, but this time at greater length. He told him in substance:

> When I was getting ready to leave for Jerusalem, I was not able to reach you. Since then, I made another long journey through all of Tuscany and Romagna, and I often thought of the pleasure you would have taken in making it, too. Now I am going to leave for a journey still further afar: it involves leaving the world and going as far as the heavenly Jerusalem. Do you want to accompany me? I am going to enter religious life. Will you not come with me? You are now in the army, in surroundings filled with vice. But I know that you have always been a good Christian. Would you not be happy to abide with me in a life that is austere, it is true, but peaceful and beautiful?

One final temptation arises to assail the vocation of Thomas Giustiniani. A religious, Paul of Modena, before setting out to dwell among the Maronites of Beirut or of Aleppo or in the solitudes of Lebanon, asks Giustiniani to go along with him. The latter replies on October 14 that his offer breaks his heart. But the decision has been made and he will not look back. It has been so long since he resolved to live in absolute solitude, far from the world, busy meditating day and night on the law of the Lord! He encourages his correspondent to go dwell among the Maronites, who have recently submitted their obedience to the Apostolic See. He takes an interest in everything that might favor the reunion of the Oriental Churches with Rome: he mentions the Abyssinians, Georgians, Maronites, and Armenians. He hopes that a large number of occidentals will learn their language. This letter overflows with the love of Christ and philosophy is not even mentioned.

Thomas' departure is delayed by matters that had to be cleared up. At last, all is ready. On December 14, Delfino sends him mounts, guides, and words of encouragement. On the seventeenth, he welcomes him to Fontebuono. "I have often stopped to think," he writes a few days later, "asking myself how something so unheard of could happen, that a noble patrician of Venice, breaking the bonds of his sins, should fall into the trap that our Apennines set for him...." This proves that the Spirit of God blows where He wills, all the more because Giustiniani comes of his own accord without anyone having pushed him. Delfino intends to give him the habit and tonsure for Christmas. Giustiniani prepares for this ceremony by a general confession. Filled with regrets for the sins which he has committed during thirty-four years, he is also filled with confidence; he prays fervently to be healed of his offenses.

Already on December 22 he sends a long report to Quirini and Egnazio. He tells them about his journey which, because of the season, was as heavy going by sea as across the mountains. At Ravenna, he conversed with a certain brother Francis of Piacenza:

> It will console you to know that, after having spent a long time in the study of Parisian theology without any benefit for his preaching and being at the point of discouragement, this religious began to read the Scriptures and the Fathers with so much profit that he no longer wants to stop preaching.... This will fill you with consolation and confound those who preach Aristotle or other human subtleties in the churches instead of the discipline of the Gospel and the Old Testament.

He gazed devoutly at Mount Alverna as he passed in view of it. The journey was dangerous and exhausting. "On the vigil of Saint Lucy, we arrived starving and dripping from the rain at an inferior inn where they had, nevertheless, some fresh eggs, pears, and chestnut soup. Consequently, so as not to embarrass my companions, we did not observe the vigil fast, which was not obligatory."

But these ups and downs are as nothing in comparison with the fighting that goes on in Giustiniani's soul throughout the entire trip. He had left his family without letting them know that he was leaving forever. He feels remorse about this and suffers from the thought that he will never see them again. All the memories of childhood and youth which attach him to his country come to mind: "Whenever I would turn my eyes toward Venice, I would find new difficulty in saying: 'This fatherland, as noble as any in Italy, where I was born neither obscurely nor basely, where I lived almost all the years of my life, where all my friends are — I will never see it again!'" The thought of Christ in His Passion consoles him. He knows that heaven is his true homeland. The only argument that is reassuring to him now is the example of Jesus Christ. But a real "battle" continues to be waged within him. In his imagination, he sees each one of his friends again, whom he names in turn. He hears their reproaches, answers them and promises to write often to each one of them. From now on, he meditates willingly on Abraham, whom God commanded to leave his native country. He foresees that his friends will malign his conduct, interpreting his departure from Venice as a betrayal: he accepts it all. He even goes so far as to be willing to see himself criticized and abandoned by his dear Quirini. For the love of Christ, he accepts the disappointments that may be in store for him at the Hermitage. All sorts of temptations beset him with regard to the fasting and the cold, but he is ready to give his life for Christ.

In this text, touching in its candor and revealing to the fullest his sensitive and richly endowed soul, he tells his friends of his new attitude regarding culture. One of the temptations that assail him on this journey is the prospect of the intellectual mediocrity of his future surroundings. But do his sins entitle him to anything else but penance? He accepts that, too.

> I was thinking that the true and beneficial study for a Christian and a monk is to occupy his mind with the contemplation of the mysteries, rather than with the subtle, human arguments of Aristotle, or the

investigations of Plato, which often fail, or other human subtleties. I believe that the Psalms are more beautiful than any other part of Scripture and are always capable of keeping the mind occupied.... All Scripture is an abyss of divine intelligence and sacred mysteries on which Christ gently feeds His servants...but it is in the Psalms more than in any other part of Scripture that the highest divine realities appear. And I recall that our good and saintly general is accustomed to say that the Psalms, in comparison with the other parts of Scripture, are like bread in comparison with other food: it is always good and nourishing, without it nothing else is tasty, and it alone never gets tiresome.

It is to Scripture, then, that Giustiniani now looks for all his nourishment:

The simplicity of these hermit monks began to delight me. I was thinking that the kingdom of heaven is made up of such simple ones; that the unlearned, simple as doves, come and seize the kingdom of heaven by their goodness, while the learned, with all their proud science, plunge headlong into hell. The end of all doctrine, of all science, is nothing other than goodness and simplicity of soul. Whoever studies and lives amidst books for another reason than to conduct his life in good works and holy simplicity is vain and does not himself know what he is doing.

Now that he has arrived, Giustiniani forewarns his two friends that they will undergo the same temptations as he and perhaps even more violent ones. He describes the Hermitage covered with snow. He speaks to them about the cold and the fast, comparing Camaldoli as he sees it to what he saw in the summer. He finds advantages in the present situation: it is not so hot and water is more abundant, and besides, the cold is almost always tolerable. The bread is good and also the wine; fruit is plentiful: a crate of figs, apples, chestnuts, walnuts, hazelnuts, and almonds has been given him, enough to last half a year.

In choir, he feels much devotion and consolation, and the time spent there does not seem long. But the marks of honor and charity that they shower on him make it difficult for him to master some impulses of pride. Each one says to him: "It is you who will do that, say that, be that." He has asked admission as a lay brother with permission to attend choir or as a monk without being a priest, leaving it to the decision of the superiors. If they want him to become a monk, he will not leave off rendering the more humble services of the lay brothers.

In a postscript to this letter dated December 29, he speaks in great detail of the cold weather they are having, and he reassures his friends on this point; he signs the whole thing: "Partly by Thomas Giustiniani and partly by Paul the Hermit." In fact, on the twenty-fifth, he started a long letter that begins by notifying Quirini that it is written no longer by Thomas Giustiniani but by the very lowly servant of Jesus Christ, Paul the Hermit. The general arrived on the Vigil of Christmas. He did not quite promise Giustiniani that he never would be obliged to become a priest. And that very evening, in the general's oratory, the new novice was tonsured, and his beard was cut off. This was a real sacrifice which he generously offered up after having resisted for a moment, thinking to be able to invoke the cold as an excuse for keeping his beard. But once it was cut, he felt great joy about it. On Christmas morning, he was given the white habit of the hermits. Several of the religious who were present at the ceremony had tears in their eyes. He describes the habit in minute detail. Then he returns to the beard which he sacrificed in order to do God's will. Once more he feels the desire to give his life for Christ: "Could I not die for love of Jesus Christ? ...O Lord Who has died for me, I want to die confessing Your name." He adds haphazardly some confidences:

> The flesh gives me more trouble than ever; nothing avails.... There is
> only one remedy, which I find most effective: calling on Jesus Christ
> for help and thinking on Him. My Lord hangs from the wood of the
> cross, and would I think about the pleasures of the flesh? ...Being all

alone as I am, eating alone, finding myself still alone in the evening, still and silent, sometimes gives me a certain tenderness of soul when I recall those with whom I used to live. But soon it goes away, and I find my soul filled with such contentment and satisfaction that I cannot express it. It is no burden to me to sweep my cell in the morning and to clean the bowl from which I eat. Likewise, to do other similar tasks like fetching wood from the woodshed and putting it on the hearth is my greatest pleasure.

He concludes by saying that nothing could be more painful to him than to see Quirini delay coming to his side by accepting an invitation to go to Jerusalem. And he signs this long letter: "Brother Paul the Hermit." But he adds as a postscript: "There is a bit of pride in this signature. If you think so too, chide me, so that I will not add Hermit any more."

And so he has become a hermit. He lets the abbot of Bagno and Julian de' Medici know, asking the latter to inform the Duchess of Urbino. He sends his family a letter of consolation and apology, asking them to have all his books sent to him, which will be his share in the inheritance, and some little things which are in his living quarters. Delfino, on his part, tells Dom Eusebius Priolo, a monk in Murano, that for the first time in the thirty years of his generalship in the Camaldolese order, he spent Christmas at the Hermitage, for Giustiniani's investiture. He was the only one who wanted to receive the habit that soon, but Delfino is delighted about it: his presence at Camaldoli is a godsend, as much for himself as for the Hermitage. The novice was given the name of Paul, so that he might imitate the conduct of the Apostle in the midst of the adversities and vicissitudes of the present age.

These vicissitudes are precisely what Thomas Giustiniani wanted to avoid by seeking refuge in Camaldoli. He would not lack them. But he had at least found his long-sought solitude. He bears witness to this later: "We requested admission to the Hermitage of Camaldoli under the same conditions with which we would have wanted to be received at Praglia. We were accepted and came here to see things. After having ascertained that no one is obliged to travel or be occupied with temporal things and that youth are not admitted (these things had made us suspicious of cenobitic life), we took the habit and made our profession."

Up to the time of his profession, Paul Giustiniani will enjoy the company of his beloved.

2. Solitude

The year 1511 is a year of formation for Paul Giustiniani. In this first and decisive experience of solitude, his whole future lies in germ and as though on trial. For solitude will be his exclusive master; he will attend no other school. He spends this novitiate year without Quirini, whose affairs keep him in Venice. But this separation gains for us a series of friendly letters written by Giustiniani, which enable us to read his inmost soul. On only one occasion, in the endless and almost daily reports that he writes for his friend, does he speak of the Hermitage and the community. On the other hand, he almost always describes his state of mind. It is not possible to follow him day by day. But these engaging texts at least show us his nature, his ideals, and how he reacted, under the action of grace, in contact with the realities of daily life.

On December 30, he begins a journal for Quirini in which he notes day by day, and even hour by hour, what he feels, does, suffers, and thinks; he says both what he likes and what he dislikes. It is a time of great consolation and joy. He considers his sins, not so much those of his youth as of his adulthood, for which he feels more responsible. He is detached from everything. He has no desire to become either procurator or prior. Venice is only a spot in Italy, and Italy only a small part of the world: "Paltry grandeur to take part in governing a little spot in a single corner of the earth!" Now it is not hard to attain this renunciation: a desire to overcome oneself suffices; it is only necessary to put one's mind to it. He tries to communicate his enthusiasm to his friends and inspire them to desire his new life. He wants to do so, nonetheless, in complete sincerity, and so he goes into all sorts of details. He is reading Saint Bernard just now. He is also doing some manual work: he has started to bind a book; he is learning other tasks "from a good old lay brother who works very well." He is happy that he has been assigned to help sweep the church every fortnight. He is pondering the mystery of the communion of saints with the help of the opuscule of Saint Thomas on the Creed.

Two elevations that he writes at the beginning of January verify that he really adopts, in the presence of God, the attitudes that his first letter to Quirini revealed. One has as its theme "the conversion of the soul to the Lord by penance." It opens with the triumphant song of one who has won solitude. But this victory is itself only a beginning: it is now necessary to gain the heavenly country. At all events, our point of departure is where the philosophers end. Their aim was to arrive at a knowledge of themselves. The Christian, from that point, goes on toward the knowledge of God. But he attains it according to the degree that he purifies his soul by penance. The first problem that confronts Giustiniani is posed by his past sins: he examines those that he has committed through each of his faculties. But he does not lose heart. He puts all his confidence in Jesus Christ, contemplating first His divinity and then His human nature. This song of hope and liberation is dated "January 10, in the very sweet peacefulness of the cell."

In another elevation, Paul Giustiniani lists all the intentions for which he wants to be sure to pray. First he names his nurse and his tutor, all those who have done good to him or to whom he is indebted for any reason, his confreres and his friends. The circle grows; everything enters in: all the material and spiritual woes of the whole world and all the great causes in which the Church takes an interest, especially the conversion of the Saracens and the union of the Churches.

But already Lent is drawing near. On January 29, brother Paul gives Quirini advice on how to spend it: to go to confession and to recite the

Psalms, attentive to their literal meaning. For it is important above all to understand "what good David," who surpasses all the philosophers and the poets, "wanted to say according to the very ring of the words." To arrive at this, Quirini must study the Psalms in the Hebrew text. In a long postscript the novice, after having told his friend of what he likes about his new life, states what he dislikes. The first thing is "that there is no clock in the Hermitage: you never know what time it is; the hardest thing is that you never know how long you have slept!" This clock which is lacking and which he will obtain with great effort will be one of his most constant concerns during his novitiate. He then enumerates fifteen other things that he does not like. Some are less important, like the untidiness of the path that leads from the cells to the Church. Others are more serious: "I am very sorry that the place is too rich and that everything is so abundant here. I would prefer a state of poverty, not only for each individual but for the community as a whole, and that it would sometimes be necessary to suffer for the lack of something and to tire oneself earning board and clothing. I am sorry that the lay brothers are so willing to serve the monks that they do not give them any opportunity to weary themselves...." He does not like it that the cells are so huge, and to substantiate this point he quotes a passage from Saint Bernard, which serves not only as a source of spiritual doctrine for him but as a guarantee of his desire to lead a life in increasing conformity with the eremitical ideal. But Giustiniani hastens to specify the meaning of his expressions of dissatisfaction: "When I say: 'I do not like that,' I mean that the contrary would be more satisfactory." This is hardly, therefore, a criticism, and certainly nothing that should discourage Quirini. Besides, each thing that he dislikes also offers some advantage: the wealth of the place, for example, eliminates the obligation to go out in search of necessities, which would be very regrettable. And so forth..."In short," he concludes, "I like everything they do, say, and use here."

An occasion soon arises for him to say what he thinks of study. Delfino sends him the works of Gregory Nazianzen. He thanks him immediately, expressing his admiration for this great Greek theologian. He adds that he has renounced worldly books: henceforth the divine Scriptures will be sufficient for him. He now has five guests in his cell: Saint Basil, Saint Cyprian, Saint Athanasius, Saint Gregory Nazianzen, and Saint Gregory of Nyssa. "As for the Psalter, it represents the most pleasant time that I spend. You cannot imagine how much this reading delights me." He explains to Quirini, whom he invites to come see him, that he is in no hurry to receive his books: he has too many already. Besides, he must now learn from a new book: "Jesus Christ crucified, man and God.... I value books less every day. Every day I think more of that passage and transformation of mine, in which I shall take with me the love of Jesus Christ and not be able to take any books." In all his letters to Quirini, however long, he never returns to the criticisms expressed once and for all. He always has the same enthusiasm for his new state of life.

His relations with Delfino are excellent. He loses no opportunity to repeat to him his admiration for Scripture, the nourishment of his soul. Yet about March 28, after having thanked the general for admitting him immediately to the Hermitage, he feels that he must reproach him for having recalled a certain brother Leonard to live at Fontebuono. Delfino answers that Leonard asked for this himself. Giustiniani then writes to Leonard to reprimand him for yielding to the temptation to leave solitude, which he eulogizes, and urges him to return to it and to persevere. He reminds him that the austerity which one finds there is a little thing in comparison with that of the Greek monks, as he saw when he visited the East. Leonard takes refuge behind the authority of the general, who recalled him to Fontebuono. But he also opposes Giustiniani's arguments with this common sense answer: all monks who live in monasteries do not lose their souls; therefore, one must be on guard against exaggerating the benefits of solitude. Meanwhile, in a letter to Michael, the recluse, Giustiniani accuses himself of perhaps having been the cause of Leonard's leaving so soon after his arrival. Could it have been his example? Actually, brother Leonard prefers the cenobitic life and is delighted that the general has recalled him to it. But one guesses that, from then on, Paul Giustiniani is a cause of edification for the majority, whereas he makes some few feel out of place in the Hermitage. Moreover, he will become more indulgent with Leonard and will even go so far as to write to Quirini: "Dom Leonard left with a legitimate excuse. Perhaps I might even say: it is not, after all, so bad as you might think."

He continues to work; at the request of a confrere, he explains the meaning of the Greek term *metanoia* (repentance). He feels well: "I am healthy and cheerful, and happier every day to be here." And he adds, recollecting a passage from Saint Benedict: "And if some temptation bothers me, I say to my wretched sensuality: *Filia babylonis, misera, beatus qui tenebit et allidet parvulos tuos ad petram*" ["O wretched daughter of Babylon, blessed is he who shall take and dash thy little ones against the rock," Ps 136 (137): 8-9 and RB Prologue 28]. He asks the recluse this question: "Do you sleep on your straw mattress or not? I do not think you do. In that case, I must not use mine either. If you who are aged thus tame your flesh which, as Scripture says of Abraham's, must already be numb, what must I not do — I whose blood still boils in all my veins, who every night am assailed by the thoughts that I have carried with me from the world?" Carnal temptations are not the most serious ones that he has to suffer. Besides, they have the advantage of reminding him of his past sins. But he is tempted in a more subtle way against faith, humility, and hope. He resists through prayer and confession.

One of the most valuable documents that Giustiniani wrote during his novitiate is the very long description that he gave of his first Lent in the Hermitage. He wrote it day by day in reply to Quirini's set of questions on Lenten practices. It enables one to become familiar with day to day life in Camaldoli down to its least detail, and with Giustiniani's interior dialogue with himself and with God. This text is admirable for its exquisite freshness and spontaneity. In it Blessed Paul reveals himself with pitiless lucidity about himself, and yet as how fervent and estimable! Fortunate the man who can think out loud in this manner and set down all his ideas and desires on paper! He had asked the major to impose on him in the presence of the full chapter perpetual silence this Lent and to forbid all to come and speak with him. Inspired by the rules set down by Saint Macarius, Saint Anthony and Cassian, he fixed the measure of his fast. He decided to live these forty-six days as though he were going to die on Easter day. It is a time of great fervor for him. On March 10, he writes: "My thoughts have never been less base nor more calm and serene than now. They have diminished to very few and almost to a single one: to prepare my soul to receive divine mercy in the next life." He peacefully enjoys God's creatures: "In the morning you can hear the birds singing sweetly among these firs. They invite us to praise the Creator with the intelligence that He has given us, just as they praise Him with that shred of life they have received from Him."

He speaks about his reading and the impressions he gets from it:

Today I read some things of Saint Bernard, a lot of him. I take delight in such reading, since it is about things not merely useful but necessary for a monk, and they have an effect.... During meals, I have the habit of keeping a book upon a bookrest on the table. Before, during and after the meal, I read a little. I have read the *Rule of Saint Benedict* and the entire first part of the *Lives of the Fathers* in this way.... But in reading these *Lives*, I was astonished several times that they do not cause you the scruple that I feel. For they contain too many obviously doubtful things. I regret not having jotted them down, but the truth of the matter is that I did not want to interrupt my meal. It was enough that I read without trying to write as well. Consider at least a few of them that caught my attention. One father claims to have learned from an angel that he has arrived within twenty miles of the spot where the sky joins the earth, and his whole *Life* is founded on just that. To me it seems madness, and consequently I wonder how much truth the whole tale can contain. Another holy man commands people to swear by him instead of by God.... several others, who are priests, receive a sealed note about sins and, without reading it, pardon the sins.... As for the rest, if you read their *Lives* you will find countless things which are admirable but are neither imitable nor desirable: miracle upon miracle, but not practical instruction for living. These miracles, then, afford little edification and great ruination to those who have not received the grace from God to know how to be content and not to go astray by desiring such things.

Giustiniani also mentions his confessions and fervent Communions. From time to time he relates a charming scene.

It had snowed all night. At the hour of Matins, three monks happened to be on the path that leads to the church: the two whose cells are next to mine, together with me, each of us with his lantern. One of the first two, stepping ahead of the others, said: *"Benedictus Deus, benedicite Deum, fratres."* ["Blessed be God; Bless God, brethren."] The response was made: *"Benedictus, benedictus sit Deus in omnibus operibus ejus et nunc et in saecula."* ["Blessed, blessed be God in all His works, both now and unto the ages to come."] And soon was added: *"Benedicant nives Domino, et nos cum nivibus benedicamus Domino."* ["Snow, bless the Lord; and with the snow let us bless the Lord."] The third, approaching the other two, said in a clearly audible voice: *"Succincti estote, fratres, et quasi ad opus parati."* ["Be girt, brethren, and, as it were, ready for work."] The other two responded with one voice: *"Succincti et parati et non conturbati."* ["Girt and ready and undisturbed."] And one continued: *"paratus non solum per nives, sed per ignem et aquam sequi Dominum, ut adducat me in refrigerium."* ["I am ready not only for snow, but to follow the Lord through fire and water so that He might bring me into refreshment."] The one who had spoken first replied: *"Ergo et in carcerem et in mortem ire."* ["Therefore one should be ready to go both to prison and to death."] And no longer speaking in Latin: "But let us be on guard lest before the cock crow we perchance deny the Lord." And so all three of us reached the church laughing, and I noticed that the lantern, which had gone out, was left behind in the snow, leaving me holding only the handle. I retraced my steps to look for it, but not finding it, I rejoined my companions. With a brush we whisked away the snow that was clinging to us and then covered ourselves again, they with their cowls and I with my mantle.

March 21 brought back the Feast of Saint Benedict:

For this day, a throng of monks and "monklings" had come up from Fontebuono and occupied the choir. I was so troubled about it that I am still repenting for my grave impatience. The Mass was very solemn, with singing, copes, and vestments, which increased my impatience even more. Then we went to dine in the refectory. Although it was Friday, they were not content with bread and water but prepared a dinner that was much too sumptuous and delicate. The major asked me whether I wanted to read at table or rather ordered me to do it, which delighted me. For although the day before I had fasted on bread and water, I did not feel hungry and was glad not to have to mingle with such a crowd. So I stationed myself to read, my back turned to the tables (as the disposition of the place requires), and I saw no one. It was as though I were somewhere else. Little by little my spirit became calm again, and I dined afterwards with the lay brothers. It was a sumptuous dinner: fish, fritters, cookies, sauce, flavorings, and new dishes, which I ate without much appetite in spite of the late hour. Those "monklings" went back and forth from the fire in the refectory. I heard them, but I did not see them. In short, I would have preferred to spend that day in cell like other Fridays, on bread and water but with peace of mind.

Everything about the daily life pleases him, including the inclement weather. "Today I liked best of all: it has not stopped snowing, but that was just fine with me. I like having to exert myself...." He reads the commentary of Bede on Saint Mark and admires the style. He follows an impulse to write some verses on the wind and the snow and the love of the Lord. He does not take himself seriously or attach any importance to his states of soul, reporting them without any solemnity: "These are follies of brother Paul, who writes you less to show you the thoughts that arise in these little cells than to beg you to kindly correct his shortcomings." With Holy Week, his fervor continues to mount, and he addresses many pages to the Lord. Finally Easter arrives, and the spiritual desire with which he has awaited this feast is satisfied by deep joy and recollection.

On May 6 he reproaches Quirini and Egnazio, who are putting off their entrance into religious life. Meanwhile, he advances in detachment. He satisfies his conscience by inviting them to come, but he now accepts their going to serve Christ elsewhere than in the Hermitage, if such is their vocation. From now on he will possess the peace of mind that he formerly sought in Stoic philosophy. However, it will no longer come from contempt of the world and himself, but rather from the confidence that he places in Jesus Christ. An earthquake has spread ruin in Venice. "But if it had happened here, we would not have been afraid. We fear only one thing, anything that can separate us from Jesus Christ. We are prepared to accept death as well as life with equanimity." A few days later another letter to Quirini is dated thus: "Here it is, the fourteenth of May, and the roses have not yet bloomed."

Giustiniani remains human and affectionate toward everyone. He writes, for example, to his nephew, Francis, to console him for being far away from his uncle. He too suffers from this separation but accepts it for the sake of Jesus Christ. "I would not ask you to come for a visit for my own pleasure, since the journey is long and hard. I do not want to seek this sort of human satisfaction in any way. Rather, I want to flee from it. However, if you come for your own enjoyment, my spirit cannot but rejoice."

He composes a treatise called *Divine Vocations*. He treats again of the problem of conversion with respect to the calls that God makes his creatures hear. He gives the lay brothers a conference on the prologue to the *Rule of Saint Benedict* and continues to fill entire notebooks for Quirini's benefit. He speaks to him about Delfino, whom he calls "our holy general." They are preparing for Quirini the cell which Saint Francis occupied when he stopped at the Hermitage on his way to Mount Alverna. Another cell, which Saint John Gualbert occupied, gives him occasion to recall that the relations of the Camaldolese with the Vallombrosans have always been as good as those of Saint Romuald with Saint John Gualbert: "When the Vallombrosans visit us, they wear our white cowl and join us in choir. The same holds when we visit them." Meanwhile, Giustiniani continues to bind books. He writes some elevations in thanksgiving for God's blessings, and he collates all the texts in the Psalms and the Prophets that refer to Jesus Christ. He begins his essay on the martyrdom of the monk. He reads Saint Leo and Saint Caesarius of Arles. As for the commentary of Venerable Bede on the Gospel, he not only reads it, he studies it. He has frequent contact with Dom Michael, the recluse, who is his confessor. Several of his relatives and friends want to come to see him with the intention of remaining, and he hopes that they will. He wants them to arrive in time to see the roses, now in bud, in bloom. He gives practical advice for the journey, maps out the route, and offers to send them mules.

In the midst of these varied and often charming particulars, he takes up with Quirini a more serious problem. The general, at the request of the monks of the Hermitage, wants to assign them a pension to assure their livelihood in any circumstance.

> It is almost an accomplished fact. In this allocation of goods and benefices, the major and the other monks would like the Hermitage to receive a great deal. The recluse and I are in agreement in preferring little, for love of greater poverty. We would be content with what is strictly necessary, and we would even prefer that something be lacking from time to time. The major and the others would like to have a large sum for building and to provide for the sick.

This disagreement, however, is not sufficient to discourage the novice. On June 10, Delfino writes to Dom Eusebius Priolo that Giustiniani is well and edifies everyone: "Yesterday, I visited the Hermitage; I found brother Paul exultant in the Lord.... I hope that others will join him soon in our solitude."

George, the brother of Vincent Quirini, speaks of marrying Blanche, one of the nieces of Giustiniani. The latter reminds him of the doctrine of Saint Paul that it is better not to marry, if one can do so without danger. But, in this case, it is almost necessary to leave the world to flee occasions of sin. If George wants to get married, Giustiniani could not recommend to him a better partner than his niece. He describes in detail her qualities of body and soul: she is young and beautiful of face and otherwise. Now choosing a pretty woman is the best way to avoid the temptation of seeking others later on. Above all, Blanche is intelligent and a fervent Christian.

Spring has finally arrived. Giustiniani describes its charms to Quirini, for he enjoys it to the full after having borne the brunt of the winter fogs.

Morning and evening, I recite my Psalms in the porch in front of my cell. There I see the garden smiling at me, presenting to me its thousand perfumed herbs. The roses are starting to try to come out. If I raise my eyes a little, I see the clear and serene atmosphere, the dazzling sun and the forest so beautiful that one would think it wholly renewed. On one side, I hear the water that falls into the channel by my cell and that which murmurs by the neighboring cells. On the other side the birds, especially the nightingales, vie with one another in singing. The danger of their enchanting concert is that it may be pleasing my exterior senses too much.... I am still waiting for the clock. It is about time it was here! You must know that in order to live here in an orderly manner, this clock is more vital than bread. Otherwise it can turn out that Prime and Vespers are rung only a few hours apart.

He is forming himself by drawing from the best sources: "I study the *Rule of Saint Benedict*, the *De Dispensatione* [*On Dispensation*] of

Saint Bernard, which is a treatise on the *Rule*, the *Speculum* [*Mirror*] of Bernard of Monte Cassino, the commentary of Remi on the *Rule*, the Institutes of the Camaldolese in five books, and the former and recent constitutions of our Hermitage."

Giustiniani fears that his letters may be causing Quirini to postpone entering the Hermitage. Nevertheless, this correspondence is of mutual benefit. It allows Giustiniani to request some favors from his friend. On June 10 he asks him: "The recluse begs and orders you, for the love of our Lord Jesus Christ, to do all you can to attract Dom Paul Orlandini here to become the master and light of our souls." A little later on, he charges Quirini to settle some urgent matters in his behalf with members of his family. Another day, he asks him to find out from the bishop of Cremona whether a monk who does not want to be a priest can be compelled to the priesthood by his superiors. If he is commanded under obedience, is it a sin to refuse? Can one include a clause in the profession which would exclude this possibility? "For my constant frame of mind is not to become a priest, if I can manage it in good conscience. Nor do I wish, on this one point alone, to bother about what others want." One further request:

> There is a monk here who wears spectacles. He told me to write you to ask you to be kind enough to bring him two pairs of spectacles, good for a man of sixty for seeing at a distance. The wait until you can come and bring the spectacles will seem like a thousand years to him. He also told me that he will not be able to pay you because he has nothing. But since he is a good calligrapher, he promises to copy willingly whatever you tell him. I advised him to obtain them sooner by another means, but he replied that he wants to get them only from you.

At the beginning of September, Giustiniani jots down "in a few hours and from a poor copy" some extracts from the first book of the *Peri archon* [*First Principles*] of Origen. A little later, he writes to Francis, nephew of Pico della Mirandola, and speaks highly of his uncle for having united in himself science and *zelum christianae religionis* [zeal for the Christian religion]. At this time a curious event takes place. A certain Dom Bernard Oricellario was writing a chronicle. He had prepared the prologue with particular care, and it has been conserved for us. It is a piece of pedantic literature in which all of mythology is invoked to glorify history. He sends it to Delfino with this request: "I understand that there are several Venetian gentlemen of great dignity at the Hermitage, and among them Lord Peter Bembo.... Would it not be possible for me to submit my prologue to them for evaluation? I would like to have their approval." Delfino forwarded the prologue to Giustiniani, who replied very courteously to him on September 27. He began with praises and then bashfully expressed reservations about the composition of this work that had been submitted to him. He especially regretted, seeing that sincerity obliged him to clearly state his opinion, that the prologue was filled with nothing but pagan nonsense, and that false gods took the place of the only true God, the master of history. Delfino transmitted this reply to Bernard, but he felt obliged to comment in these terms:

> I beg you not to take umbrage at your critic's reply. He is a hermit and scrupulous. He spends his days and nights praising God, constantly meditating on the divine law and reading the Greek and Latin manuscripts that he has brought with him. Disregarding pagan works, he devotes himself entirely to sacred literature. He no longer even deigns to look at the works of poets and philosophers which were formerly his constant fare. He has rejected the old Academy to put on the new man.... Accept the judgement of our hermit in good grace, then, and go on with your work.

One supposes that Bernard was not discouraged, but one would also guess that Giustiniani's sincerity would inevitably stir up some hostility against himself in the general's circle.

One of his confreres found him too fervent. Giustiniani felt constrained to justify himself for observing silence. His reason for entering the Hermitage was to put the works of the eremitic life into practice. Otherwise, it would have been better for him to remain in the world. "Therefore from now on, if you do not want to ask permission when you desire to speak to me, at least have the patience to wait while I go to ask for it. With permission I am ready to tell you everything I know, poor and ignorant though I am, not only during the day but even during the night." His fervor did not diminish. From afar he advises Quirini to submit humbly to the interdict which the pope has imposed upon the Republic of Venice. Toward the end of the summer he begins one of his letters with this triumphant cry: "The blessed clock has arrived at the Hermitage! But what good is it," Giustiniani hastened to add for Quirini, "but what good is it if the master craftsman who is supposed to get it going does not show up? Before the weather starts to get cold, please send John Charles here, or else someone he designates who is competent to put this blessed clock into operation." At last, the glad tidings resound: Quirini and his brother George, along with two servants, are on their way. Giustiniani sings a song of victory inspired by the theme of the Exodus and the Canticle of Moses: *"Cantemus Domino, gloriose enim magnificatus est!"* ["Let us sing to the Lord for He has been magnified gloriously!" (Ex 15:1)].

Again, on October 2 during their journey, Giustiniani sends them an encomium of the life which they come to embrace. However not all those on whom he had counted are coming to the Hermitage. Contarini, Tiepolo, and Egnazio are undecided. Quirini himself falls ill and has to take to his bed in Fontebuono, where his friend goes to embrace him. Time passes. It is now November. Soon it will be a year since brother Paul took the habit, and the day when he must make profession draws near.

3. Invitation to the Hermitage

Paul Giustiniani has left the world and found solitude. Yet scarcely has he tasted it when he undertakes a new task, that of peopling the solitude. He feels the need of it, or rather the duty. And for the rest of his life, half of his activity will be devoted to the satisfaction of this facet of his vocation. As early as his departure, he had addressed a call to solitude to his servant, Lawrence. Throughout the year 1511, he was constantly drawing Vincent and George Quirini to solitude solely by describing what it meant for him. His novitiate is now as good as completed. He enters a new period: he will be concerned henceforth less with his personal formation than with recruitment for the Hermitage. He is going to enter into this new function, which will determine the course of the rest of his life, during the few months which separate him from his profession. First, he must overcome Quirini's last objections. He knows sufficiently what solitude is from Giustiniani's letters, but his decision to embrace it is not yet final. His friend wants to help him to carry off this last victory over himself. The wear and tear of the winter journey has made Quirini take to his bed in Fontebuono. A short time later, he is taken to the Vineyard of the Musolea, a comfortable villa where the general resides, who visits him daily. Giustiniani sends a fervent letter to him there, filled with love for Jesus Christ, in which he depicts the religious state for him as a life of detachment from the world and of attachment to Christ. But Quirini is tormented by the thought of his grandmother, who is now in her eighties and is like a mother to him. Would it not be cruel to abandon her? Giustiniani replies that he has at least assured her a decent living and explains the demands of charity: love of Christ above all else is compatible with a love of neighbor which can cause him, as well as us, grief.

While convalescing, Quirini leaves for Florence, where he resides at the Camaldolese monastery of the Angels. On December 30, Giustiniani makes this request of him: "Try to find out about their customs, what they are and how they observe them. Also go to the Cistercian abbey of Cistello and see what their breviary is like. It is said that they recite it exactly as the *Rule of Saint Benedict* prescribes." On January 1, he resolves the final objections of Quirini regarding his grandmother, indicates to him the arrangements to be made to provide for her support in Venice, and alludes to the postponement of his profession. In a letter to his sisters, Giustiniani gives the reason for its postponement: the sole obstacle is the difficulty that he has encountered in settling his estate. He had charged Quirini to take care of it and he did so, but the problems raised by the distribution of his property and the formalities to fulfill to bequeath it to his heirs require more time than one would imagine. "You can clearly see how wretched it is to be obliged to take care of worldly affairs. You may not believe it, but nevertheless it is the truth: this, and this alone, has prevented my making profession at Christmas." And he draws a practical conclusion from this observation. Why do not his six sisters who are still at home imitate their sister who has become a religious and "this crazy monk Paul?" A little later, he again reminds his sister Malipiera that at least at times she has expressed the intention of becoming a religious. Why does she wait to answer this call? On February 1 it is his nephew Francis that Giustiniani addresses. He asks him to send back all his poems that he has lent him. In exchange, he offers to send him a collection of sonnets by a Florentine poet: "They speak of the love of God, but they are good, as good as those of Petrarch." Brother Paul even writes to none other than his former domestic, Lawrence, to invite him once more to become a religious.

Quirini likes it in Florence. He receives letters from his friends in Venice who reproach him for having left the Republic at the very time when it has been struck with an interdict issued by Pope Julius II. Has he not become guilty of treason? Giustiniani urges him not to let himself be shaken. He himself reproves Tiepolo and Contarini roundly. To defend the vocation of his friend and refute those who attack it, he consults the treatise of Saint Thomas, *Contra retrahentes ab ingressu religionis* [*Against Those Restraining from Entrance into Religion*]. Giustiniani does not want to make his will before Quirini has decided his future: "I do not want to decide such an insignificant matter until you have decided about your life." So his profession is postponed until Easter and, if necessary, for ten successive Easters. Quirini should feel free. He is getting along well at the abbey of the Angels. Let him remain there, if he wishes, but at least let him say so. Besides, Giustiniani is persuaded that if he experiences life at the Hermitage, he will prefer it to that at the abbey of the Angels. He asks him to bring the *Contra retrahentes* of Saint Thomas along with him when he comes. At long last, Quirini sets out, comes, and arrives. On February 22, he receives the name of Peter and takes the habit along with his brother George and their two servants. On the very eve of their clothing, their vocation sustains a new assault. Giustiniani faces it squarely. A certain Francis Boninterdotto of Florence has been instructed by someone whose name he does not give, and whom Giustiniani does not want to identify, to warn Quirini that he does not have the right to be admitted to the Hermitage before undergoing the test of cenobitic life, in conformity with the counsels of Saint Jerome, Saint Bernard, and Saint Romuald. Giustiniani defends the eremitic life at length. He begs his friend not to be bothered by the scruples of conscience which such persons, "perhaps out of good zeal, but not with due consideration," are trying to arouse in him. Quirini has foreseen the objection which they are making and has resolved it. He is old enough, has had enough experience, and is sufficiently informed to be able to make a decision with full knowledge of the facts. Thanks to the numerous and detailed letters which Giustiniani has written him, it is as though he himself has already been living in the Hermitage before coming there: "It may be said that through me he has already tried out this life."

Giustiniani and Quirini now unite in urging Egnazio to follow their example, and together they compose a letter for his benefit. The misfortunes of Venice and the premature death of Egnazio's brother ought to suffice to make him reflect on the vanity of this world. Without doubt, he will face up to the truth of the duty incumbent upon him to become a hermit. Is not leaving the world and coming to the Hermitage the surest way to obtain eternal life? A series of couplets promises him the joys which await him. "I promise you a pleasant spot.... I promise you a comfortable cell, filled with books: Aristotelian, Platonic, or better yet Christian.... I promise you the charitable company of twenty monks and lay brothers...." Then Giustiniani gives brother Peter's first impressions: "He is very calm, cheerful, and content." He adds the following argument, which appears to him decisive for a humanist like Egnazio: "If you would come and live with us for a while, you would get to be a philosopher and a true friend of wisdom which, pardon me for telling you, we have not yet begun to be after so many years of vain studies." A little later he speaks along the same lines for the benefit of Egnazio, Tiepolo, and Contarini. Henceforth Giustiniani's strongest argument is Quirini's very example: his slow consideration substitutes for that of his friends. A great man of letters, Mark Anthony Della Torre, has just died. Of what use is his learning to him now? Egnazio thanks him and promises to come at Easter but recommends to Giustiniani that he write with less vivacity to Contarini. Giustiniani hastens to send Tiepolo and Contarini a letter of apology, but he profits from the occasion to invite them once again to come to the Hermitage.

Giustiniani's relations with the general continue to be good despite a hint of strain, which does not, however, alter the cordiality of their correspondence. Giustiniani wonders whether he should offer to accompany Delfino to the Lateran Council which is to begin soon. He confides this idea to Quirini, for he feels somewhat scrupulous about it. He did not come to the Hermitage to go out. And yet, Delfino is old. He will offer to accompany him to the council, but without asking it, much less imposing himself. If the general calls upon him, he will go; if not, he will remain calmly and cheerfully in his cell. He would prefer the latter alternative, but he is ready to renounce his peace and quiet for a higher good. Delfino thanks him but fears reproach if he should make brother Paul leave the solitude in which he has expressed the desire to remain, and where he is needed besides to guide and advise the new arrivals.

Delfino is Venetian. To prevent his taking sides against the pope because of the interdict imposed on the Republic, Giustiniani warns him that if he does not submit to Julius II, the Camaldolese would not be able to remain under him. Apparently this possible disagreement concerns a schism and not the government of the order. Giustiniani goes only so far as to recommend to Delfino that he not lend an ear too readily to poor advisers. On May 1, Delfino replies courteously but firmly: he recalls Quirini and Giustiniani to silence and solitude, and he is astonished that these two novices are so well informed about what is taking place outside the Hermitage. As for himself, his mind is made up, and no one can make him change his decision. All the same, Orlandini had just written to Quirini to attest that all the hermits were in agreement to persevere in submission to the pope, the Vicar of Jesus Christ, in any event.

Meanwhile Quirini has begun to look after the interests of the Hermitage. Already toward the end of his stay in Florence, Giustiniani had informed him that one cell lacked window panes and had asked him to bring what was necessary to repair them. Another matter left a lot to be desired. The Hermitage was surrounded by a forest which isolated it. Now Delfino had delegated the entire responsibility for the maintenance of the property and grounds of Camaldoli to Basil Nardi, the abbot of the Camaldolese monastery of Saint Felix in Florence. Basil cleared land without ceasing under the pretext that he was having more trees planted than he had cut down. He was even threatening to extirpate the whole forest, which not only adorned the Hermitage but also assured its solitude. However on May 8 Cosimo Pazzi, archbishop of Florence, who had been on the best of terms with Quirini for a long time, wrote him that he had been appointed to judge the dispute occasioned by the cutting down of the forests of the Hermitage. He assured him: "I will do whatever the matter calls for without respect of persons, desirous only of satisfying all the hermits and especially Dom Paul." This letter shows that Quirini took the affairs of the Hermitage to heart, but counter to Basil and Delfino's circle.

The Hermitage lacked a wall of enclosure. This was one of the things that Giustiniani had pointed out to Quirini as regrettable from his entrance into the novitiate. Scarcely arrived, Quirini takes it upon himself to have a wall built. Giustiniani himself is constrained to moderate his zeal: he recognizes that it would be good to have a surrounding wall, but would it not be suitable first to obtain a brief which would forbid going out? Without this, it would be useless to incur the expense. Before building it, it is important that either the hermits accept the enclosure or at least that it will be imposed on them to remain shut up in it. Souls must be bound before enclosing bodies. And Giustiniani proposes to Quirini the terms of a brief, approving a formula by which each hermit would oblige himself to perpetual reclusion within the Hermitage. But these plans are not to everyone's liking. On June 13, Delfino writes to Giustiniani:

> Two of our novices, companions of yours, talked with me yesterday of your desire to make the eremitical life stricter. As you could tell from speaking with them, I am far from disapproving all that. What could be more normal than to confine the Hermitage with a wall? It is necessary to be prudent, however, and not to put the obligation to remain within the enclosure under penalty of apostolic anathema. All that glitters is not gold. Although the eremitical life has its advantages, it also presents some dangers, as Saint Jerome recognized, and after him Saint Bernard in several of the *Sermons on the Canticle of Canticles*.

Delfino reminds Giustiniani, therefore, that Saint Benedict counsels discretion: "Lest through wanting too much to scrape off the rust, the vessel be broken." The tone of this letter is extremely cordial.

At this time Giustiniani is reading Saint Ephrem in the Greek text. Neither his fervor nor his desire to populate the Hermitage slackens. He proclaims an invitation to the Hermitage, and its promises, to a priest named Jerome:

I invite you to this solitary life, in which I believe it will be much easier for you to serve the Lord in truth of spirit than in the hubbub of the towns.... I invite you to this solitude, where day and night we do nothing but desire and seek the mercy of Jesus Christ.... I invite you to a place, a life, a company which will help rather than hinder you in reaching that blessed happiness which is eternal.... I promise you in this place, within these modest cells, a much more quiet and restful life.... I promise you a sweet peace, a pleasant leisure, an agreeable silence....

The enthusiasm built up within Giustiniani during his novitiate now pours forth. He speaks from experience:

All that I was accustomed to reading in the world on the subject of the solitary life, whether in my blessed father Jerome or in other Fathers and Doctors, could not convey to me the sweetness I have experienced here during the last year and a half. Not because the solitary life has not been eloquently and copiously described and praised by the saints. It is just that there is no eloquence that can express the feelings of a soul seized by the love of God when it finds itself established in solitude.

Giustiniani, with the tone of one who has reached perfect detachment, has this to say about the dignitaries of the order: "Few in number and rare are those (if in fact they exist at all) who are content, I do not know whether to say to descend or to ascend, to the state of simple monk."

At last, the day approaches when Giustiniani and his companions are going to make profession. The constitutions of the Hermitage specify that only priests who are at least twenty-five years of age and who have spent three full years in the monastery may be admitted. The Venetian novices had to be dispensed from this prescription. Such a long delay would have been unbearable to them and also to Delfino, who longed to see these rich patricians definitively incorporated in his order. As of the day following Quirini's investiture, the general asked Cardinal de' Medici, protector of the order, to obtain from the pope that the requirement of spending three years in the monastery be abolished, not only for them but for all those who might want to imitate their example in the future. Quirini and Giustiniani, on their part, asked the Duchess of Urbino, sister-in-law of Julius II, to have them dispensed from holy orders by the pope. So it was done, and their profession took place on August 8, five and a half months after Quirini's arrival.

III

The Reformer
(1512-1520)

1. The Liberation of the Hermitage

Giustiniani's prolific correspondence and the interior life to which it gives expression betray an exceptionally strong personality. A man of this quality was bound to stand out immediately from the mediocre.

He could have become chief, although he did not desire it. But straightaway upon his profession, we see that he is prompted (or, to be more exact, led on) by his friend Quirini to demand that the Hermitage become what it ought to be. As early as September 14, 1512, Quirini writes to the Duchess of Urbino to obtain a brief from Pope Julius II modifying the organization of the Camaldolese order:

> I request that His Beatitude direct a brief to Dom Peter Delfino, general of the Camaldolese and prior of our order, an old man, very observant and of holy life, exhorting him and imposing on him all the things I am about to note. The tenor of the brief will surely need to be something like this: "I, Julius II, desiring that Holy Church be reformed in all its members...impose upon you with paternal love that, setting aside every other concern and furthermore leaving off coming personally to the Lateran Council now underway, you convoke the customary general

chapter of the Camaldolese order. You and the other hermits are to celebrate it for the entire upcoming octave of Easter...."

Quirini goes on to indicate all the measures which the chapter should take: "With the consent of the majority of the hermits, let the Hermitage and monastery of Camaldoli with all their income be united to the observant Congregation of Saint Michael of Murano, also of your order, which should, among other things, be in charge of administration of the incomes.... And let conditions be agreed upon so that, above all else, the eremitic customs will be firmly maintained in the Hermitage." Dom Peter Delfino will remain general for life with a guaranteed pension. Every three years, the hermits will elect a prior for a triennium who will be chosen from among them and who will live among them. His office is not to be confused with that of the general. The chapter will reform the constitutions of the Hermitage in view of a stricter observance, and the general will reform the monks, drawing his inspiration from the example of the hermits. If the general does not execute all the clauses of this brief, the hermits will be authorized to convoke the general chapter and proceed in his stead. The brief ought to be addressed "to the general and to the hermits" so that the latter may see to its immediate execution. Quirini assures the duchess that he makes this request in agreement with Giustiniani and the recluse, Michael Pini. He believes that Delfino will be delighted with this brief, thinking that the pope has sent him *motu proprio* [on his own initiative] to carry out his duty of reforming the Church.

The points of reform proposed by Quirini were not his own invention. The general chapter of 1474 had based itself on them in constituting the Camaldolese congregation of Saint Michael of Murano. These measures, which then had given good results, were now a must for the Hermitage, which ought to be the head of the whole order. In a memorandum written in September for a confrere, Giustiniani gives an account of the grounds for his present attitude and explains his intentions. He admits that he came to the Hermitage to be free from all business, including "chapters and processes among religious."

> But I must take cognizance that the Hermitage itself really needs to be reformed. The Hermitage, whose name signifies nothing other than a deep solitude, has ended up, in fact, as a public square, a fair, a house more frequented and noisy than those at the heart of town. We see its goods ill-administered and squandered. For all these reasons, to maintain a clear conscience and not to lose our soul, we are obliged, even forced, to renounce our long-held intention not to get involved in any business. It does not seem that we can let all this take place without sin, without very serious sin.

Another memorandum, dated November 3, which gives some very precise details on the abuses to be reformed, has the same ring. About this time, Giustiniani wrote a letter to Delfino. He never sent it, but it shows his deference and affection toward the general, who is allowing himself to be surrounded by dangerous advisers. "Perhaps you do not see that you are making all your intentions known among men of whom one, as you yourself have to admit, is a bad religious. He despises you, and you know where and how he lives. Another dissipates all your goods. As for the third, it is better I say nothing, for what would have to be said about him would not be to your liking." Then Giustiniani puts Delfino on guard against his weakness, which has some excuses, and tells him again how much he loves him. In a letter of November 20, Giustiniani denounces to Julian de' Medici, archbishop of Florence, the general's counselors, particularly the abbot Basil, who has been chosen as administrator of the goods of Camaldoli and who is squandering them. He characterizes Delfino as *vir simplex et rectus ac timens Deum* ["a simple, upright, God-fearing man", Jb 1:1]. If he and Quirini are appealing to the archbishop of Florence, this is in application of the *Rule of Saint Benedict* approved by the canons, which recommends recourse to the bishop of the diocese if the elected superior is unworthy of his office. Giustiniani asks the archbishop to intervene with mildness toward Delfino to get him to send this administrator away, but with threats toward the administrator himself, deposing him if necessary. On December 16, Delfino informs Quirini that Julian de' Medici, in the capacity of pontifical legate, approves the decision to hold a general chapter, and that it will take place after Easter.

Julius II dies soon afterward on February 20, 1513. However on March 31, his successor, Leo X, brother of Julian de' Medici, appoints the abbot Baptist de' Succhetti, Benedictine of the congregation of Monte Cassino, as president of the chapter; he designates Quirini and Giustiniani as definitors representing the hermits and having the full right of active and passive voice. The preparation for this chapter is pending. Giustiniani and Quirini intend to keep silence. They do not want to allow their role as definitors to impair their life as hermits. They exchange in writing the necessary memorandums. On February 9, Giustiniani submits to Quirini a plan for a rule of life to be observed during the chapter, with the intention of keeping the observances of the Hermitage insofar as possible. In particular, "let us flee vain arguments and discussions between ourselves and with others. This can be accomplished if one yields and willingly gives his consent to another." Quirini noted this in the margin: "Provided that we yield not just verbally, but sincerely." And he concludes his observations on this plan with these words: "Let us put our hope in God. He will give us strength and courage." The following is an addition: "On February 16, we left the Hermitage to come to Florence, where the general chapter of the order will be celebrated."

The long-awaited chapter opens at the end of April in the Monastery of the Angels. Two opposing camps very soon arise, Delfino on one side, and Quirini and Giustiniani on the other. Delfino is thrown into a minority position. The decrees are drafted by Quirini and Giustiniani, and they themselves bring them to Rome. "On May 10, we left Florence, sent to Rome by the fathers of the chapter. What was accomplished in Florence was sanctioned and confirmed by Leo X, who conceded numerous privileges to our order." "On August 10, we left Rome and arrived in Florence on the 13th. We stayed there a few days, and on the 19th we returned to the Hermitage, praising and blessing God, who brought us back safe and sound from the turmoil of the cities to the port of solitude after so long a journey."

In a letter to his nephew, Giustiniani gives vent to these words of relief: "Now I am back at the Hermitage, with deep desire and satisfaction. I intend never to leave it again." He takes up again his former activities. He composes a commentary on Psalm 72 (73), writes to Egnazio to invite him to become a monk, and starts a letter to the king of Portugal to congratulate him for having recovered Malaga and to urge him to promote the faith. He also starts a letter to "the emperor of the Turks" to advise him "to follow the example of Constantine rather than that of Alexander," and finishes up his commentary on Genesis. In collaboration with Quirini, he sends Pope Leo X a long memorial on the reform of the Church. He composes a *Treatise on the Twelve Degrees of Obedience*, copies the *Tome to Flavian* of Saint Leo and the decrees of the Council of Chalcedon, and writes a theological advisory report on the remission of sins. At the beginning of 1514, he sends some observations on Cassian to Orlandini, then prior of Florence. Although he likes and admires Cassian, some authorities are in opposition to Cassian on some points where he is not in conformity with the present doctrine of the Church. Toward March 24, he sends and recommends Saint Augustine's *The City of God* to a Cassinese monk who wants to become a hermit, which desire Giustiniani can only encourage.

Suddenly the storm broke that one could have sensed was brewing. From October to January, the general sojourned at Rome, was received twice by Leo X, and pleaded his cause. Giustiniani is upset by this. In a petition to Leo X in the name of all the hermits, he recalls that, through the negligence of Delfino, Camaldoli had become a den of the debauched, and that its possessions were being frittered away. The situation has been remedied. But the general, influenced by some very bad dispensers of advice, wants to return and hopes to obtain papal authorization. His return would cause the situation to revert to its state prior to the chapter. The monks and their superiors do not want to see him return at any price. As for the hermits, they recall being poisoned, beaten, insulted, and imprisoned under Delfino's regime. To avoid constraining men who have lived in a hermitage for thirty or forty years to abandon it, the general must be kept away from Camaldoli. If the pope should want to authorize him to live at Fontebuono, let him assign to the twenty hermits another solitude far from the Hermitage.

Quirini goes to Rome to look after the interests of the Hermitage. On May 31, Giustiniani informs him that he sent a petition from the hermits to the pope, to the cardinal protector, to Delfino, and also to the archbishop of Florence. He speaks to the latter even more clearly than to the pope:

> If the general reestablishes his residence here, the hermits are decided to a man not to remain in the Hermitage another day. They see clearly that if the general returns, *essent novissima peiora prioribus* [the new situation would be worse than the old]. For the general has always loathed the eremitical life and has never much liked the hermits themselves. Now presumably he will like them even less, for he has taken offense. He is minded to speak of forgiving, but he will not forget. I believe that if the general comes back to live around here, with or without administration, one day you will have fifteen or twenty hermits in your quarters for whom you will have to make provision. They say that they would be more at peace if you were to put them in the middle of Saint Peter's Square than here with the general. He would sow a thousand tares among those of the congregation and the hermits, between whom there is now peace like a veritable Garden of Eden.

Meanwhile, the rumor starts to spread that Quirini's head is now topped by a red hat, so great is the esteem that the pope has for him.

"I do not believe it," Giustiniani writes to him; "This is not the time for such things. Many accuse me of trying to dissuade you.... And they believe that it is my fault that you are not yet a cardinal." Giustiniani advises him to make up his mind freely. What he fears more is that the abbot Basil may be plotting against him and against Quirini:

> I beg you to watch out for yourself and be cautious in everything, so as not to fall victim to the sword or to poison.... I think it is a good thing we are separated, since if he harms one of us, he knows the other will still be around to make him pay for it.... The departure of Pucci, who is going to Portugal, increases my temptation to go to the Indies. Were it not for the deference that I have and ought to have for you, I would go with him or in his tracks.

From Rome, on June 14, Quirini informs Giustiniani that the Delfino affair is settled. The pope wanted to reach a compromise that would permit the general to remain in Camaldoli, but without exercising any authority. "Following your suggestions, I acted with a great deal of skill and maneuvering, honestly however, in order to avoid this." The general will be given a pension of 350 ducats, with which he is satisfied. He will no longer be in charge of the temporal or spiritual government of the Hermitage, Fontebuono, the monastery in Florence, or any other house of the congregation. "I asked the general's pardon in the presence of the Cardinals, and almost everyone wept. The general is content and praises the manner in which I acted toward him. The briefs will be framed in terms deferential toward him and useful for us." Quirini suffers from the active life to which he has been condemned: "Truly, I abhor this state of affairs more than anything." He would prefer to serve in the kitchen for as long as desired. Above all, he does not want to be a visitator for anything in the world: "Knowing the lapses of others and traveling about the monasteries is not for me. I could do no good in such an office." "I obtained a brief for Dom Paul (Orlandini) by which he can no longer be forced to take on a prelacy or be removed from the monastery of the Angels." Thus, two sides confront each other: on one side, Basil Nardi and Delfino's advisers, who think only of an easy life, and in opposition to them, Giustiniani and his friends, who live in the greatest detachment.

On June 15, Giustiniani reports to Quirini about the arguments that are advanced in favor of his cardinalate, and he puts him on guard against self-love, which would make him inclined to believe them.

> It does not seem to me to be the practice of the Roman court to make cardinals of hermits, nor does this Pontiff appear to me to be inclined to introduce such a custom. Judging from those he has appointed until now, ...the cardinals he will name will either be his relatives or else men great in the eyes of the world, and not of course, those of your condition.... So do not trust yourself and flee any occasion of being compromised. If, however, they impose the cardinalate in the name of holy obedience, then I tell you, almost certain of the will of God, that you must not stubbornly resist it. Rather you ought to accept it, not as a dignity but as a ministry: *in nomine Domini subire onus regiminis* [take upon yourself the burden of government in the name of the Lord]. The recluse thinks you will become cardinal in any case, and that you could accomplish great things for the reform of the Church. As for me, I do not believe that the pope would want to create a Venetian cardinal, or that the Venetians are asking for you, or that the pope's opinion of you is such that he would agree if they asked.

However, Quirini achieves complete success in the Delfino affair. The general will not be deposed but will no longer have any jurisdiction. Giustiniani rejoices over this solution: "As for titles, let him have them, and let them add a hundred and a hundred thousand others: Lordship, Reverend, Most Reverend whatever he likes."

On July 1, Quirini writes to Giustiniani that the rumor of his being made cardinal is getting more convincing every day. He is beside himself over it: "I hardly know what else I can say to you, since I am in a fluster. I see no end to all this. May God forgive you who have sent me packing to Rome. Patience! *Utinam non sit cum periculo* [may nothing happen with risk] to my soul. I greet the recluse. Tell him I do not believe the ideas he is getting." Quirini, living in Rome, feels that his fervor is evaporating. "I find myself deprived of grace, cold, and almost incapable of thinking of Jesus Christ or of promoting the good of souls. Honors, in the guise of good, are beginning to tempt me more than before." Soon afterward, he confides to Giustiniani: "What you write of your plans makes me stop and think. Suppose that even though I succeed in leaving Rome without taking on a prelacy...I return to the Hermitage and do not find you there any longer? ...At any rate, I have definitely decided to ask permission to withdraw for a while to a place where I will have no business obligations, whether to the Hermitage, if you judge that we can live there at liberty, or elsewhere." Above all, Quirini does not want to be charged with governing religious, for this is "the most tiresome activity there is, and perhaps the most dangerous as well."

The archbishop Julian de' Medici, brother of the pope, came to visit the Hermitage. "I requested two things of him," Giustiniani says:

> To beg the pope to let you return to the Hermitage and not to bend his efforts to see you promoted to any dignity. He replied that the Pontiff was quite pleased with your work...so he does not think that the pope would grant such permission...as for himself, nothing in the world would give him more pleasure and satisfaction than to see you promoted to the dignity of cardinal. However, since he knows how far you are from wishing any such thing and he loves you well, he will refrain from doing anything to bring about what you would regret. But if you should become cardinal, he hopes to receive your firm support. If you think it would do any good, all the hermits and I are ready to write to the Pontiff to ask him to allow you to return to us.

And always thoughtful, Giustiniani adds a friendly word for the lay brother who accompanies Quirini:

The Magnificent was here and spent an hour proclaiming your virtues. He spoke of a certain little room where you stayed when brother Peter was with him. All this indicates that he takes you for something of a saint. He is not aware, as I am, that you do not amount to so much. At any rate, he likes you a lot and admires you. Leaving the Hermitage, he passed in front of the "nook" of Saint Romuald and wanted to know its history. I told it to him and he wants to have a beautiful chapel with a nice little cell built for us there. "Brother Innocent," I told him, "will gladly stay there...." "In that case," he replied with animation, "I will by all means have it built. How much do you think it would cost?" "Not very much," I replied, so that he would go ahead and not be alarmed by the cost. He promised that he would leave an order about this before returning to Rome. So you see, the Magnificent himself prepares the place of your reclusion.

And he adds this good advice: "Bear your absence from the Hermitage patiently. Consider that I, poor brother Paul, even if at the Hermitage, have so many tasks that I need a lot of patience. I do not know if I can go on like this much longer."

The month of July passes, but Quirini does not return. He keeps repeating, seeing as he is still in Rome: "*Pazienza!*" ["Patience!"] Giustiniani calls his attention to a point that he has at heart. The draft of the brief that Quirini was awaiting contained a clause by which the general could demand by virtue of holy obedience to be received at Fontebuono or at the villa of the Musolea. "If he were aware of it, he would be there already with his mob of hangers-on." Now Giustiniani does not want this at any price: "Have this clause suppressed. If I did not hope for this, I would already be farther away from the Hermitage than you." And he lets slip this confidence, in which the word "alone" recurs with poignant insistence: "If it cannot be obtained, I will go off alone, alone,

alone, to a place where the general will not come to find me, and where perhaps no one in this country will know where I am." In his sorrow over his separation from Quirini, he turns once again to Abraham's example: "I recall that Abraham parted from Lot, that Barnabas took leave of Paul, and that the Apostles, according to Saint Jerome, '*salvis amicitiis, divisi sunt*' ['were, save by reason of their friendship, divided']. Even though it may be necessary for you to remain in Rome and for me to remain in the Hermitage, I will never cease to love you...."

On August 6, Quirini pleads with Giustiniani the cause of two monks of the monastery of the Angels, whom the last general chapter had punished with a sanction: "For love of me, restore their active and passive voice in chapter. This is of little consequence, and they will have regained their honor, which today's monks hold in such high regard. I promise to obtain some briefs under whose terms they will fear to form any cabals and make use of their voice." And he repeats to him his ardent desire for solitude. When one considers the attraction which the cardinalate has exercised at all times, especially on clerics living in Rome, one gauges the virtue of these two men, whose chief concern is that one of them does not become a cardinal. Julian de' Medici has revisited the Hermitage. He has promised not to take the initiative in favoring Quirini's election to the cardinalate. But if the pope asks his advice, he will not be able to refrain from recommending him warmly. "The Magnificent has more respect for you than for any other person in Italy."

At this point, however, their letters seem to have been intercepted. Giustiniani believes that it is the work of one of their enemies in Florence, one of those who fear that the monastery of the Angels will be enclosed by a wall. He bemoans such cares.

> Perhaps you think that I am at rest or that my spirit soars heavenward? I am probably more upset and troubled both in mind and body, my dear brother Peter, than you. This is not over big things, it is true, but over all the details involved in governing our houses.... As a result I have little

or no time left for prayer, recitation of the Psalms, or study. However I am putting up with all this, for the time being, for the love of God, until your situation is settled one way or the other. Then I will try to procure the means, either with or without you, to be at rest, free from all the employments of this world. Perhaps I will take my cue from our Dom Placid, who went into reclusion in the Saint Bartholomew cell this morning, or perhaps find another way.

The situation is this, therefore, in the month of August 1514: Quirini is absent and will probably become cardinal. Giustiniani remains at the Hermitage only in view of his return. If Quirini is appointed to the cardinalate and does not come back to the Hermitage, Giustiniani will either become a recluse or leave. In fact, Quirini will not return but will have been called to other joys than those of the cardinalate. At the Hermitage, there is a division of opinion: "Some would have you a cardinal, others a hermit!"

As for my opinion, you are already aware of it. I have not changed my mind in the matter. On the contrary, I urge you more than ever to flee from the court, when I see how it is governed. And so, brother Peter, you who have the pope's ear, you keep silent when you see that the generalship of Vallombrosa has been given to a secular priest! O God, what is all this? Counselor of the pope, you have a fine way of counseling him when this is the way things are going!

The brief excluding the general was to stipulate that he would be allowed to spend a fortnight in each of the monasteries of the congregation, except Fontebuono, the Musolea, and the Hermitage, unless the hermits consented to his coming. But the general's friends were endeavoring to have the words *nisi de licentia apostolicae sedis* [except by leave of the Apostolic See] substituted for the words *nisi de consensu eremitarum* [except by consent of the hermits]. Giustiniani insists, if it is not too late, that the original version be kept: "For the good general and his retinue, who know well that the Pontiff can be easily influenced as soon as you are no longer at his side, would use these words as grounds to obtain this permission and return here. Now I know, through one of his inner circle, that such is his intention." And Giustiniani closes this letter by exhorting Quirini once more:

> Love Jesus Christ and remember to still confess Him every day in all your actions, with heart, word and deed. Let the standard of your thoughts, words, and actions be none other than Jesus Christ, the Incarnate Word of God. Follow and imitate His holy evangelic doctrine. Flee the world. Do not seek your own interests or those of any other person, but only those of Jesus Christ. Seek the kingdom of God and His justice, and all the rest will be added unto you.

These words bore a prophetic character. The following day, August 28, Giustiniani writes this note to Quirini:

> Today at None, I learned of your illness. This very evening I am setting out to come to you.... I will travel easily, in order to be sure to arrive in good health, although my eagerness carries me away to the point of wanting not merely to run, but to fly. Take comfort in the Lord, and commit yourself into His hands, for you could not possibly come to other than a good end. Here special prayer is offered for you, both in private and in common. Prepare yourself to return to the Hermitage with me, for I am coming with the intention of making the Pontiff say "yes" and bringing you back. God be with you in any event.

These lines were to constitute the last note of a correspondence which had lasted for more than ten years. Quirini died on September 23. The day before he fell ill, he had written to Giustiniani:

> I already find myself, my dear brother Paul, in the midst of many

snares and tied up in a thousand knots. The Venetians have already begun to ask for me; they have already nominated me cardinal. The Board of Governors has written to Grimani, who has forwarded everything to the Pontiff.... Some praise me, others envy me, still others pity me. I am stunned and do not know what to say.... If I wish to go away, the Venetians at once beg me to stay. If I ask the pope's permission, he does not wish to grant it to me.... How confused I am! How much better it might be for me to leave this mad world completely! I feel well and fast on bread and water two days a week, not knowing how to restrict other foods, but avoiding meat, in any case. Pray for me, all of you!...

From then on, Giustiniani did not cease to live in the presence of him of whom he will one day say "that he had worn himself out with his efforts to free the Hermitage from the oppression of its heavy servitude." He begins to write his life but lacks time to complete it. But he was at least able to pay him this tribute:

He died either from his austerities, as is the opinion of many, or else, as a few suspect, from poison slipped to him by an envious hand. When it came time for him to leave this world, he surpassed himself in an admirable fashion. In an atmosphere of perfect patience and heavenly joy, his death shone with such sanctity that, in the eyes of all those present — and I had the grace to be in their number — his glorious passing was a more astounding sight than any miracle.

2. *Apostle of Eremitism*

Quirini's destiny seems to have been to bring Giustiniani to formulate his vocation. Before his conversion and during his novitiate, Giustiniani had been separated from him by affairs that kept his friend first outside of Italy and then in Venice. Therefore, he had had to describe his states of soul and his life in Camaldoli for him. After they had spent scarcely a few months together in the Hermitage, the two friends had again been separated by distance and then by death. This unforeseen trial had been an occasion of constant purification for both. During Quirini's sojourn in Rome, neither one had ceased to affirm his love for the solitary life, which Giustiniani had once again begun to praise in order to convince Quirini not to leave it. Quirini's death was heartbreaking for Giustiniani, but it was also the occasion of a new increase in his holiness of life, which authenticates and guarantees his work. After Quirini's death, Giustiniani's activity was to be an outgrowth of what Quirini had originally inspired. Giustiniani was going to continue to be an apostle of the eremitical life, and Quirini's example very often served as an argument for him.

Giustiniani's entire life is divided between two tendencies which seem to clash, but are really parallel: the need for solitude, and the need not to remain alone therein. To satisfy the first, he labors to restore the eremitical institution to the purity of its ancient traditions; to satisfy the second, he makes every effort to facilitate access to this institution for all those who feel attracted to it. Before his profession, and even before his entrance at Camaldoli, he had made an effort to draw his friends there. After his profession, he had extended an invitation to all those he loved to join him at the Hermitage. From the end of 1513 up to 1520, his activity as a reformer doubles with another function. He becomes the recruiter of the Hermitage, and all the more so as the observance flourishes again in all its purity. Vocations exist, but they must be enabled to become actual. Quirini had begun to exercise the same attraction as Giustiniani, who had written him: "Lord Bernard of Pesaro came to the Hermitage and stayed here six days. He is now free. His wife died and left him rich and with much property. He is awaiting your arrival to come and to live at your side. If he did not have this hope, he would have already remarried. I have already allowed him to be installed among us. As you see, we are selling the pelt of the bear before he is caught." But no longer are the relatives and friends of Quirini and Giustiniani the only ones who have the desire to come to live with them. Recruits show up from different regions and from several religious orders. First, there are the "black monks," that is, Benedictines. Soon afterward, a Carmelite and a secular priest ask for admission. Next it is a Dominican: "We have a Friar Preacher, who had already come a year ago but was not received because he was too young. Now, however, we have received him. He is learned and prudent, but because he is so young, he is lively, very lively! I do not know whether he will persevere."

But it is especially after Quirini's death, when the Hermitage has been liberated, that Giustiniani feels the need to make its benefits known and, when necessary, to come to its defense. He devotes all his letter writing, which until now he had engaged in for Quirini's benefit, to this end. He says clearly why he feels impelled toward this apostolate. He finds such happiness in being at the Hermitage that he considers it his duty to let others know about the happiness of such a life.

> Would that I were able to make others understand fully how much satisfaction the religious life gives the soul! I am certain they would abandon the world and embrace this agreeable state of life, with its lively hope for the beatitude to come. Do not think that I am trying to deceive others for my own satisfaction or to make them believe something that is not so. But for their own good, I would like to persuade all I love, that is all men, to follow my example by abandoning the world and entering an observant religious order. And it seems to me that I am so greatly obligated to speak about it to others that, if I did not do so, I would be culpable of endangering my salvation and that of others.

Giustiniani is aware of being an instrument of God to do good to others by reminding them of the vanity of the world. This contempt for the present age has as its correlative the attraction exerted by the solitary life. He develops this theme in a commentary on Haggai directed to Contarini.

The principle that he proposes as characteristic of the observance of the Hermitage is that which he will take as one of the goals of all his legislative and doctrinal work: the assertion that the role of Saint Romuald was to join together the advantages of the eremitic life with those of the cenobitic life. One of the phrases by which Giustiniani illustrates most aptly the benefits of the eremitical life thus conceived is this expression of Saint Jerome: *Mihi oppidum carcer est, eremus paradisus* [For me, the city is prison, the hermitage paradise]. The methods that he uses to win over his correspondents are diverse and always adapted to the spiritual state of those whom he addresses. Sometimes he appeals to his own experience:

> I tried out life in the world for many years and in various situations. For the past five years I have tried out religious life, and I can tell you that between these two states of life there is as much difference as between light and darkness or life and death. In the world, the cloud of occupations and affections is so great that a man seldom raises his eyes toward the sun of God's light. One walks among so many dangers and snares that it can be said that one passes continually through a thousand deadly perils, always tied by some fetter at the foot or neck. In religion, on the contrary, we are free to a very great extent from earthly occupations and affections. Free from such dangers and impediments, the soul turns toward its Creator and, enlightened by Him, it travels not only joyfully but securely along the path of this mortal life. It already has a foretaste, through affection and hope, of that blessed and eternal immortality that we await after this pilgrimage. Because of the great love that I have always had for you, and that I have for you now more than ever, I urge you to leave the world and become a religious in any observant order. If ours pleases you, if our Hermitage suits you, I offer myself as your inseparable companion, brother and servant through love.

Giustiniani is skilled in varying his language and the arguments he puts forward according to the individual. He usually writes in Italian.

But when he deals with a learned man and his son, "an intelligent young man," he speaks to them in Latin and quotes various authors. In the case of John Barberini, who has informed him of his desire to become a hermit, he warns him against disappointments. "Have no illusions: you will certainly find some imperfections even at the Hermitage." John Barberini desires to donate his possessions to the Hermitage, and he receives thanks for his offer.

> But it is you, whom we desire to receive among us as a brother, not your possessions, *te non tua*, that we seek. We do not have the end in mind of enriching ourselves with your wealth, for we want to remain poor always. Rather, our aim is that you also, having laid aside the weight of vain riches, can with us, in poverty and nakedness, follow in the footsteps of the poor and naked Christ. Bearing the yoke of holy religion, you can reach more easily eternal riches.

Giustiniani reminds another that although he may delay his vocation, he must not do away with it: *differre non auferre*. Sometimes he simply "invites," using a favorite phrase: "*Vi invito….*" ["I invite you…."]. When he must insist, this charming recruiter knows how:

> My love for you is not easily vanquished. I remember having the care of one of my nephews who was ill. He was subject to such prolonged and deep sleeping spells that he was in danger of death if he let himself be overcome by them. Therefore I had to call out to him frequently. When he did not answer me, I had to call more loudly and disturb him as much as I could, because he seemed to me in greater danger. At length, exasperated by my prodding, he would speak to me with unseemly rudeness and throw at my head everything that he had on his bed. Do you suppose that this made me leave off rousing him? Quite to the contrary, for several days and nights I did not close my eyes so that he might not sleep.

And so Giustiniani applies this parable to his persistence in fostering his correspondent's vocation.

As a matter of fact, his appeals sometimes met with the opposition of those whom he addressed, or more often of their superiors, if they were religious. This was true in particular in the case of some Carthusians and Benedictines. In November 1514, he had written to the prior of the Charterhouse of Florence, who found it difficult to accept that three of his religious had been received in the Hermitage. "The sacred canons permit whoever wishes to do so to pass to a more austere form of religious life. Undoubtedly you are aware of the privileges granted to our order precisely because of our stricter discipline, by virtue of which we can receive among us Carthusian monks even without the consent of their superiors." But the three Carthusians, after spending several weeks in the Hermitage, left during an absence of Giustiniani. He reminds them of the charity with which they were received. When the community began to wonder whether or not they would stay, everyone was saddened at the thought of their departure. Then suddenly they left, without waiting for Giustiniani to return and without leaving any word for him. He was not offended by this offhand behavior; yet he suffers in his great sensitivity because he took a liking to them. Now not only is his affection for them involved, but his zeal for their salvation also makes him very anxious. In fact, he believed that they had returned to the Charterhouse in Florence, and he was thinking of going to see them for a final exchange of views, which had not taken place by letter. Now he hears that they are in Rome at Holy Cross at Jerusalem. Their departure from Camaldoli grieves him, but he cannot blame them for it. He cannot, however, refrain from reproaching them for having gone to Rome:

Living in Rome, my brothers, is not a thing that good religious customarily do.... I have sometimes thought you would want to go to the Grande Chartreuse, which would have been much better than staying in Rome. If you have chosen Rome as your place of residence, I

seriously doubt your salvation.... If you want to return to us, you should
not feel held back by reason of any embarrassment or shame. For when
you return, we will receive you with full and perfect charity, just as the
father in the Gospel received the son who returned to him. I want you
to know that the Lord God has compensated for our loss of you by
giving us some good and holy fathers of the Order of Preachers from
the monastery of Saint Mark in Florence. One of these is very learned,
as erudite in Greek, Latin, and Hebrew and as noble in explaining Holy
Scripture as anyone in that order.

A little later, Giustiniani sends another letter to the three Carthusians. At least ten new vocations have been received since their
departure. As for them, they should beware of Rome: morals are so
corrupt there that one is in constant danger. Giustiniani replies to the
reasons which they might offer to justify their departure. "Some think
you were vexed by our lax manner of life and our many imperfections.
Others instead suspect, with greater foundation, that you could no
longer bear the strict observance of the eremitic life, the poverty and
the austerity in which we live." They are certainly not ignorant of the
meaning and the object of imperfections. These are an occasion for
practicing mutual charity. As for poverty, must we not perhaps imitate
Jesus Christ, the Apostles, and the martyrs? "Although our observance
is strict, we are not for all that bears, or tigers, or frightful monsters,
but only poor fellows like you, nor do we have more robust bodies than
you do." Then he breaks out into a hymn in praise of charity:

O great power of charity, O supreme violence of love! Not taking into
account her proper rights or the demands of nature, she does not get
angry even if abused. Instead, she sets out in search of those who scorn
her. When she is injured, she does not think of revenge, but rather
offers her caresses and tries to call back those who have struck her.
When abandoned, she does not give up, but with loving anxiety does
everything to win back those who have turned their backs on her. If she

believes herself a victim of injustice, she does not for that reason press charges. Rather it is she who prostrates herself to ask pardon, as though she were the guilty one! She does not wait to be begged but entreats those who ought to entreat her. She does not fear humiliations, is not jealous of her proper dignity, is not concerned about what others think. Careless of her proper rank, she ignores moderation in order to recover those she weeps for as lost. She tries everything, makes every effort by all means, until there is nothing left to do.

And so for many pages, Giustiniani expresses the most unselfish devotion along these lines to the Carthusians. In a postscript, he asks them to give him some news of their health, if only a word, for it appears that they have fallen ill. If they would like to return, mounts and guides will be sent to them. If not, they will not be bothered any further by letter. They are yet to receive, however, one last note from Giustiniani. For the burning letters that he sent to them in Rome have come back to him. How this pains him! He closes with these words: "Since in leaving, you did not remember to leave any word for me, at least remember now to pray for me, as I, dearest brethren, pray for you each day as for myself. I do so especially since I know that you are in Rome and not in good health, which puts you in danger in both body and soul."

Giustiniani has good relations with Dom Augustine, Benedictine of the Cassinese congregation of Saint Justina of Padua. This noble Paduan, who was still a layman when Giustiniani was a student, is now the abbot of Saint Paul-outside-the-Walls. He comes to see his friend at the Hermitage, and their letters are always marked by frank cordiality. Giustiniani writes the following to him:

O most pure and holy soul (I can say so without any flattery), I wanted to salute you in Christ, the sole true health. I do not write Reverend or Most Reverend, for these are titles of worldly dignity and ambitious exaltation.... I do not admire all these outward grandeurs, which the world has not found more apt words for honoring, as well as for flattering, than *Reverend, Most Reverend, Most Honorable, Monsignor.*

Two monks called Peter and Justinian, from the abbey of Saint Justina in Padua, have entered the Hermitage. A third, Bartholomew, from the abbey of Saint Flora in Arezzo, notifies them that he would like to join them. Giustiniani immediately writes him: "I have never seen you or received any letter from you. Yet I love you with the same charity as Peter and Justinian.... If you come, you will meet Dom Peter, the Major of the Hermitage." But the abbot of Saint Flora does not see things the same way. He is not content to tell Giustiniani but tries to discourage Bartholomew by describing the austerities of the Hermitage to him. Giustiniani replies to him: "I have the greatest respect for the Cassinese congregation, not only for its abbots but for all the monks as well.... It does seem to me, however, that before being able to speak about the austerities of the Hermitage, one would have to have experienced them, a thing you have not done."

On their part, the Cassinese monks in Padua, irked by the departure of Peter and Justinian, attack the hermits and the eremitical life. Giustiniani protests at length. He recalls his good relations with Saint Justina when he was a student in Padua. Now he hears that the Cassinese, not only in private conversations but in public meetings to which laymen are sometimes admitted, condemn the eremitical life, the transfer from the cenobitical observance to the solitary life, the manner of life of the Hermitage, as well as of the entire Camaldolese congregation, and finally their two confreres, and Giustiniani, who is supposed to have attracted them. He proceeds to reply to each objection. He writes the history of the eremitical life in the Church, shows that the role of Saint Romuald was to perfect the *Rule of Saint Benedict* on one point, and recalls the good relations which existed of old between Monte Cassino and Saint Romuald and his first disciples. This dissertation is unfinished and was probably not sent. Giustiniani did not like futile controversies. However he did send a lengthy *Disputatio* [*Argumentation*] to Pope Leo X, in which he established that it is permissible for cenobites to transfer to the eremitical life and, in general, for all religious to transfer to a stricter observance after asking, even if not obtaining, the permission of their superiors.

Moreover, Giustiniani did not engage in any misplaced propaganda against the Cassinese. We have as proof a letter dated the night of Saint Maur, 1518, to a Benedictine novice whose vocation he had encouraged. He tells him how much he respects the Cassinese congregation and especially the monastery in Padua; he judges from the two religious who came to the Hermitage that the observance is excellent. He rejoices that his young friend has taken his advice to enter and that he has lasted. He predicts temptations and urges him to resist them: "John Cassian warns the new religious to be blind, deaf, dumb, and stupid, so as not to see, hear, speak of or judge anything but himself. And I tell you that you should open wide your eyes and ears, not be tongue-tied, and strive to be the most sensible of all. Open your eyes, I tell you, to see the saints, and the admirable example of the religious observance of our fathers, so that you can imitate it...." This great spiritual personage is, then, a man of common sense. He is also very charitable, for he is delighted that his friend has entered Saint Justina, and he multiplies courtesies toward this novice and all the religious of this monastery that is attacking him. This is how he takes revenge.

Nevertheless, Giustiniani had to settle the issue of clothing. The Cassinese monks accused the Camaldolese of being clothed in white, whereas Saint Benedict wore black. Giustiniani takes up his pen, not in obstinate defense of the Camaldolese viewpoint, but rather so that the Cassinese will know that their position is not incontrovertible. In fact, Saint Benedict forestalled arguments about the color of the habit and prescribed that the material found where one is be used. The habit made from this undyed fabric would be, then, neither entirely white nor completely black.

The vocation which gives Giustiniani the most grief is that of his friend John Baptist Egnazio. He had remained in Venice when Quirini had entered the Hermitage. He always claimed to desire to join him, yet he could not bring himself to leave his parents alone. He asked that his friends not abandon him and that they help him to live in the world. Giustiniani could not agree to this: "Only if he wants to become a religious will we help him, so that he can take this step and to leave his elderly parents settled and well provided for." From time to time, Egnazio wrote that he had not forgotten his plan to come and be a hermit. One day he even declared that he was ready to leave Venice with two friends and requested information and help for the journey. But he did make up his mind. On August 4, 1516, he admitted that he was falling short of Giustiniani's hopes and begged him not to withdraw his affection. "Although we are now of different opinions, we must not change our dispositions and affection." So this old friend never stopped offering Giustiniani the occasion to exercise his zeal for recruitment, and bearing out how ineffectual that zeal could sometimes prove to be. He regretted that he was not able to be present at Quirini's death and asked for the details of his last moments. But he himself was soon to leave this world, without passing through Camaldoli. Giustiniani speaks of this new bereavement in a letter to Tiepolo and Contarini. This time he weeps, although he did not weep for Quirini.

> I neither weep nor feel any pain at all that our dear friend has left this miserable earthly pilgrimage. But I am pained beyond all measure and weep without restraint that the world and its vanities kept his mind occupied to the very end, that he let himself be overtaken by death before responding to God's call. Do not think that I am pained simply by the death of my friend, because I consider death in itself to be the best thing that can happen to a man. But I am heartily sorry, and always will be, at the thought that, deluded by the deceitful world, my friend Egnazio closed his ears to the continual call of the Lord. He scorned

the loving-kindness with which God drew him to religious life.... I do not judge, nor do I speak of the next life, for *inscrutabilia sunt omnia judicia Dei* [all God's judgments are unsearchable, cf. Rom 11:33]. But concerning this present life, I cannot help thinking that our Egnazio was torn from our midst and his life taken away because of his hardness of heart.... God knows that I have been living in dread of this, which has now happened, for over a year an half, and how bitter is my sadness.

Giustiniani's plaint is an exhortation to the two recipients of the letter not to follow Egnazio's example.

A canon regular, Constant Hieroteo, made known to his two Cassinese friends his desire to become a hermit with them. Giustiniani assures him that everything possible will be done to find the best available cell for him. And yet it will not be comfortable: "You will live here a solitary life that is very poor, rustic and austere, but at the same time very tranquil, glad, and pleasant." More and more, the invitation to the Hermitage takes the form of an apology, necessitated by the attacks on Camaldoli which its very attraction has earned. A Venetian priest named Thomas expressed his intention to come to the Hermitage along with a companion. Giustiniani fears that he will be held back by the calumnies brought against himself, and in his letters he expresses his anguish. None of these calumnies affects him personally, but they run counter to his deeply felt need to make the Hermitage known and loved and to enable others to profit from it. Solitude is a blessing which he does not want to enjoy alone. Now the two Venetians appear to have made up their minds to renounce the world, but they put off their resolution to embrace the solitary life. Each of these situations causes him much anxiety. He weighs the seriousness of being unfaithful to a calling from God and writes many pages against it. "We have here," he states in an effort to overcome the indecision of his two correspondents, "Dominicans, Augustinians, and black monks, including the abbot of Saint Faustinus in Brescia." Giustiniani hears that Thomas and his companion wanted to go to

Monte di Ancona. He can hardly believe it, for he has seen the hermits of Monte di Ancona and has written them what he thinks of their life: they have no vows, no superior, and no rule, and they practice neither obedience nor poverty.

Giustiniani knows that he is being calumniated and is not surprised. He is not the first person to whom this has happened. He retraces the history of calumny against religious from the first monks, whom Chrysostom had to uphold, down to the mendicant orders, which Saint Thomas defended. And here he denounces (and this revelation sheds much light on this period of his life) one of the sources of opposition with which he clashes.

The very monks of our Camaldolese order fear that, as the number of hermits grows, we will gradually bring back their cenobitic life to a stricter observance (as it seems to them has already been done in part). Or they fear that the hermits, if their number increases, will come to occupy the monasteries of the cenobites. And, to some of our monks who do not wish to lead so carefully regulated a life, it seems that the hermits are hindering them from living as they wish.... I urge each and every one of you...come here, not to change over to our way of life, but to see, experience, examine and discuss our life and customs. In this regard, we desire nothing except that you come here to stay for one, two, four, or six months, or a year, or else as long as you please. And so you can observe closely, touch, and examine everything that is ours, both in general and in particular, the life and customs of each one of us.... We are not, after all, in Egypt, nor in Thebaid, nor so far away that it would be greatly inconvenient to come here. The greatest distance is between Venice and Ravenna. There you will find good lodgings in our monastery of Classe, and the abbot will provide you with some mounts and guides.... Recall how many philosophers undertook very long and wearisome journeys to see the various customs and ways of life among men. For this reason, they called Ulysses the wisest of the Greeks, because he had seen the customs of many men and of various cities.

This letter to the Venetian Thomas is of great importance, for it clarifies the full situation that will orient Giustiniani's future. Thanks to this letter, we now know that the cenobites, who were far more numerous in the Camaldolese order, suffered from an inferiority complex and adopted a defensive attitude at the sight of the Hermitage in full fervor and growth. The Hermitage became the refuge of the most fervent among them. The rest could not forgive Giustiniani for attracting the best individuals. But as they were the stronger, it was Giustiniani who would one day have to yield before their opposition. From this point on he was forced to defend the eremitical life even within the order. In October 1519, he sends some news of the Hermitage to Delfino on the occasion of the clothing of two Genoese. He takes this opportunity to discreetly ask the general not to oppose the recruiting activity of the Hermitage:

> I beg you, Father, since there is so great an abundance of big fish in the lagoon of Venice, that you stop trying to allure into your nets those you see taken by ours. It is true that we are both fishing for the selfsame Lord, and that it is not for ourselves that we are trying to catch fish, but rather for the Father of the family. Yet for the glory of God, to whom all our effort is directed, it makes a great deal of difference whether somebody contents himself with the common life of the cenoby or embraces the austere life of the Hermitage. And you are not unaware what a shining example of love for Christ those offer to the world who, not content with having abandoned the pleasures of the world, renounce the conveniences of the cenobitic life to follow henceforth the hard and rugged observance of the eremitic life.

In his reply, Delfino expressed gratitude for the news received from the Hermitage but made no allusion to the lesson which he had just been given.

From this point on, it was evident that the Hermitage was getting to be too small. On March 9, 1518, Giustiniani had reminded the priest, Mark Favilla of Florence, that a bishop named Marcel (he did not remember what see he held) had promised to put a provision in his will to have a cell built in the Hermitage. The bishop has now died. Giustiniani hopes that the promise will be carried out. "It is essential," he states, "especially at this time when those who truly seek God are flocking from all sides to the Hermitage, so that we are lacking cells rather than occupants." Such was the situation at that time. Eremitical vocations were numerous, yet Giustiniani did not seek out prospective new recruits. He waited to be informed of their desire. But as soon as he was made aware of it, he did not cease to extend an invitation to these fervent souls, to justify and defend their vocation, and to help them to render it actual. More and more, one of his anxieties came to be just this: how should he respond to this grand aspiration so many souls had toward the solitary life?

3. Toward a New Departure

Another anxiety preyed on Giustiniani's mind: how could he himself lead the eremitical life in all its fullness? Without doubt, he was living at the Hermitage and could write in September of 1517: "By now, I have spent seven years in this solitude and never left it except because of obedience, or business, or the demands of charity. It is for such reasons that I had to go to Rome twice and to Florence three or four times." But even at the Hermitage, he was continually at grips with problems of organization, finance, and administration. He did his best to solve them, and he succeeded. This spiritual man had both feet on the ground. He did not lack the qualities of a man of action. But he desired more and more to flee from temporal affairs, not certainly because of incapacity, but to respond to a higher calling. His profound need for solitude and the contemplative life was constantly hindered from the time of his profession, and especially after Quirini's death in 1514. An interior crisis resulted from the excessive activity that overwhelmed Giustiniani and the violence of the opposition that he encountered in his reform work. This crisis was not to be resolved until September 1520, and we must now relate its development.

The exercises of the contemplative life were sufficient to occupy a man like Giustiniani. They were, to his mind, as entirely absorbing as the activities of a man of action. "Know that I do not believe I am any less busy than you," he remarked to Contarini.

> The difference between you and me is that you are perhaps occupied with many outward things and I am for now, thanks be to God, entirely occupied with my soul. Perhaps you consider reciting the Psalms, reading, meditation, prayer, examination of conscience, confession, receiving Communion, and similar exercises, to be idleness rather than occupation. But be sure that these are tasks which, far more than all the other, exterior works, require man's all.

That this part of his life given to leisure was his true life is confirmed in some of the spiritual texts which express his fervor: commentaries on the Psalms, elevations, and examinations of conscience. Their form varies as poems, soliloquies, dialogues, paradoxes, or parables. Some of these intimate writings, in which he gives his imagination and culture free rein, are little literary masterpieces. Nevertheless, they have almost all been written in one go on his return from the Night Office. "I do not know whether I wrote this when I was asleep or awake, whether conscious or not of what I was doing. But I do know that I wrote it in an hour in one fell swoop, while weeping profusely." Often fatigue prevented Giustiniani from completing something that he had begun to write.

But he did not write only thus, absorbed in God and for himself alone. He did not refuse to put his intelligence and pen at the service of others. The chapter of 1513 had stipulated that new constitutions were to be drawn up within three years. Giustiniani got down to work. After laboriously studying all the major authorities of monastic tradition, he completed in 1516 the *Regula vitae eremiticae* [*Rule of the Eremitic Life*]. Two years later, he will supplement it with the *De perfectiori reclusionis institutione* [statutes for reclusion]. In this period, preoccupied with the instruction of untutored religious, he undertakes the first of a series of translations that he will continue to make: he renders the treatise of Saint Ambrose, *On Naboth of Jezreel*, into Italian. A confrere questioned him on the discrepancies in the Gospels regarding Christ's childhood; he makes reply, without concealing from him the difficulties that the diverse chronologies raise. On another occasion he explains the nature of true friendship. He refutes the *Liber novae apocalypsis* [*The Book of the New Apocalypse*] of Amadeus. The archbishop of Florence consults him with regard to the errors of the "pseudo-angelic pastor," Theophilus. He asks him to intervene in the legal proceedings with regard to Savonarola in the metropolitan synod which he intends to convoke. In order to acquit himself of this duty, Giustiniani borrows from Delfino the latter's *Dialogue on Savonarola*. He himself reads all of the controverted works, since he has copies of them, and the dissertation that he writes evidences a personal acquaintance with Savonarola's writings.

To the same council of Florence, he gives a report on the errors of Meletius relative to the coming of Christ. He sets forth the doctrine of this heretic as it is found in his writings, which he has read, but does not wish to give a verdict on his way of life, of which he is ignorant. Dom Paul Orlandini had already requested his opinion on Meletius and had submitted a memorandum to him on the subject, but Giustiniani hardly had had the time to skim through it. The duties of his office keep him so busy that he can no longer take time for writing without remorse of conscience. He must, he says, "steal time from his sleep" to read what is sent him.

In fact, Giustiniani is the true head, the animating spirit, and the organizer, not only of the Hermitage but of the entire congregation. He is superior without title even before he becomes superior in spite of himself in 1519. As far back as 1514, he was able to write: "I am consulted in every matter and everything is referred to me to such an extent that, if I did not have the slavery of Jesus Christ before my eyes, I would be overcome with impatience." "I will write again when my mind is more at rest. Just now, I am quite confused."

> Unfortunately, everything passes through my hands, even though I flee from this and attempt to avoid it. Brother Paul has to hear about, give advice on, and discuss everything, whether temporal or spiritual, concerning the Hermitage, Fontebuono, and the whole congregation. I have reached the point that, if there were no hope to arrange things of this sort so that I would no longer have to be taken up with them, I would be very dissatisfied. I still hope, however, for I see good beginnings, and I notice daily that things are improving. Therefore, I am hoping to recover my calm soon.

In reality, even if the observance does improve, for him the occupations do not diminish. First of all, he has great monetary worries. He has the responsibility of restoring the economic situation of the congregation, of paying the general's debts, and of assuring his pension. The increase in new candidates poses the problem of housing and maintenance. The conflicts which are arising in the monasteries in Ravenna and Siena must be examined. But above all, he has at heart the interests of the Hermitage. "The affairs of the Hermitage concern me more than those of the whole congregation." Whence the complaint that escapes him: "I have an endless number of things to do, and I have been changed from a solitary into a businessman. But *ad tempus* [only for the time being]."

One of his rare diversions is the pilgrimage that he makes in 1516 to the tomb of Saint Romuald. Moreover, in a letter to Contarini he feels compelled to justify himself for making it. "It strikes me as not only appropriate but necessary to let you know, first of all, why I made a pilgrimage of this sort. Perhaps you think that I made it by chance and for no reason, or worse, out of boredom with the Hermitage. While

I believe myself to have observed my profession of the eremitical life, perhaps you think that I am a sarabaite or gyrovague." Not so. Dom Elias attended the chapter which was held at Ravenna; this virtuous priest lived with a companion in the Grottoes of Massaccio, which belonged to the Camaldolese order. Giustiniani was about to make the regular visitation of that hermitage. It was on this occasion, accompanied by Dom Elias and Brother Benedict, lay brother novice, he made a detour to go to Fabriano. He has left an account of this journey for the benefit of his confreres in the Hermitage. He tells in it how he went on foot without any other mount than "the hermit's staff." Although Brother Benedict was not a priest, he too recited the Divine Office. The first day, they devoutly crossed Mount Alverna, passed near a monastery of Camaldolese nuns ("we were not aware of their existence"), arrived at Città di Castello, and lodged with the Franciscans. In spite of weariness, one of the three travelers — unnamed, but he can only be Giustiniani — "rose that night out of devotion to assist at the Franciscan Matins. Then, upon returning to cell, he woke up his companions and they recited their monastic Matins." On the evening of the next day, the three were put up at the Olivetan monastery in Campo Rossano. They finally reached Fabriano, where the body of Saint Romuald rests in the Church of Saint Blaise. There they obtained a relic and returned singing hymns and canticles in honor of Saint Romuald. On the way back, they stopped at the Grottoes of Massaccio, Monte di Ancona, and Fonte Avellana.

These beautiful days were rare. More often, the weight of everyday occupations was made still heavier by the struggles which he had to endure. Giustiniani sensed that he was the target of a veiled opposition. He would have preferred that it openly declare itself. On June 2, 1517, he sends a cordial letter to Delfino, whom he recently met at Murano. Giustiniani had evidently returned for a few days to Venice. Delfino replies with a very friendly note. But at the same time that he addresses him thus, he writes to others along different lines. For this reason Giustiniani draws up for his benefit a courageous declaration, saying in substance:

If you have something against me, let me know about it in a face to face conversation. You know that I always treat you with deference. You know that I do nothing important without informing you. Now I understand that you have spoken and written against me in extremely harsh terms, and that you see to it that everyone reads these letters. I ask to read them also, not in order to reply in my own defense, but to know of what I am accused in order to mend my ways.

This letter was not sent. But a few months later, Giustiniani had to write to Delfino to notify him of the insults and slander to which he had just been subjected in Florence. He would not have said anything to him about it if the general had not already been informed by a letter from the major. Some petty tyrants were laying down the law at the abbey in Florence, and Giustiniani had pitted himself against them. Delfino replied by congratulating him. On the fifth of the following January, Giustiniani had to take up his pen again to soundly reprimand the prior of Florence. But he does it so tactfully that one would not suspect that the prior was at fault if one did not otherwise know it.

Such is indeed the attitude which Giustiniani adopts in the face of opposition: he does not get annoyed, but he humbles himself and forgives. He composes *De servanda etiam cum inimicis caritate libellus* [*A Plea to Observe Charity Even Toward Enemies*] for himself and the Major, Peter of Brescia, a former Cassinese. He develops five examples in it: those of Abraham, Isaac, Jacob, Joseph, and Jesus Christ. The question is a living one for him:

> Preserving toward all, even those who detest us, not only peace but a whole and unbroken charity, is a great virtue. It is necessary for all Christians, but especially for us, Peter, in these days. When I reflect and make an effort to acquire this virtue, by reading Scripture and the examples of the saints, my cell becomes like a gymnasium in which I exercise myself for the approaching struggle. In cell I am preparing myself for what I do not doubt will assail us from without.

In this very beautiful treatise one admires how Giustiniani repeatedly rectifies his intention. He concludes: "If, then, we find it necessary to displease our neighbor through a just action, let us show him later all the more, by our respect and good deeds, that we really and truly love him."

As for the hermits, the slander to which they give occasion must be for them only a stimulus to fervor. On January 20, 1518, Giustiniani comments on these words from the Psalter for them: "*Non erubescant in me qui quaerunt te Deus Israel....*" ["Let not those that seek Thee blush because of me, O God of Israel...." Ps 68 (69):7]. They must be as much the more generous as their state is the loftier and more austere. It is of them that the most is asked, for more is required of the clergy than of the laity, of religious than of seculars, and of hermits than of all others. And Giustiniani pays tribute indirectly to his confreres by saying to them:

> Although many have come to us during these recent years, attracted by the perfection of our state of life, yet others slander us. It is therefore of greatest importance that those who are attracted by the perfection of our state not be put off by our personal imperfection, and not one of those who leave us ought to be able to allege this motive. A Cassinese abbot, learned, devout, and prudent, has just asked to be admitted. This is a good sign, for fervor favors recruitment and recruitment gives proof of fervor.

And to confirm them in love and esteem for their vocation, Giustiniani quotes for them from a letter this abbot wrote after his first visit: "In your cells, you live the life of Anthony and of Macarius. In your community practices, I have not seen anything that did not conform exactly to the teachings of our blessed father Saint Benedict. In all sincerity, I do not think that there is a spot in all of Italy whose setting looks wilder but whose observance offers more joy to religious souls than the Hermitage of Camaldoli...." The Cassinese abbot adds:

"In looking for a solitude where nothing befitting a perfect monk is lacking, I do not stray from my vows, nor do I modify my monastic profession." Giustiniani draws from this testimony this practical lesson for his hermits: "Answer by your deeds the opinion which certain people have of you, and give no pretext to the attacks of our detractors."

He encourages the others by pointing out their virtues to them. On his part, he humbles himself. If he is the butt of contradictions, it is clear to him that his sins have deserved them. When he is tempted to despair in the face of adversity, he puts his confidence in Christ. He understands that the difficulties which he meets have an expiatory value for him, and he recovers his joy. He keeps a nostalgia for solitude in his heart. He speaks to solitude as a person and he writes her letters. She is his spouse, his Lady, as poverty had been for Saint Francis. And he asks God for the gift of solitude: "I beg You, grant me solitude, let me enjoy the embraces of my dearly beloved solitude. Grant that, comforted and aided by her, and inflamed by her conversation, I may tend toward You, my Lord, Who are the life of my spirit."

Now that he has forgiven, humbled himself, and prayed, nothing more remains for him but to be reconciled with his adversaries. And this he endeavors to do, to the extent, however, that the peace of the Hermitage is not at risk. In April 1518, he invites Delfino to make a visit to the Hermitage, to Fontebuono, or to the villa of the Musolea. In October he expresses regret that Delfino has not been able to come as yet; he advises him to profit from the season of autumn to make this journey without prejudice to his health. Delfino replies that only illness has prevented him from going to the Hermitage. As soon as he is feeling better, Giustiniani congratulates him on his recovery. He declares that he is ready to send him the lay brother whom he has requested, and he reassures him on the subject of his pension. Only an unforeseen pontifical tithe has prevented its full payment on the appointed day. He tells him the state of the Hermitage: twenty-seven hermits, of whom fifteen priests are *aperti*, that is, not in reclusion, seven lay brothers, and finally five recluses, with a lay brother among them. But sometime afterward, he feels compelled to write another letter in which we see how the general is responding to these advances. Giustiniani expected a peaceable visit. Now he learns that Delfino is going to come to Tuscany and to the Hermitage, not because he has been invited by the hermits, but because he is being egged on by Basil, Theophilus, and all their accomplices, who want to bring in the same accusations that they have sown everywhere along their path. Giustiniani can hardly believe it. But if somehow it is true, he begs Delfino to rid himself of his advisers:

> Otherwise, I am ready to resist you unto blood. And not only to resist you, but to stir up against you the fiercest struggles that I can. I will turn heaven and earth topsy-turvy and leave nothing untried, so that the war you will have provoked will be your ruin. I will spare no effort, nor even life itself. You want to disturb our peace, and I will know how to repay you in the same coin. I have a pen: I will write in Latin and in the vernacular, without regard for your dignity. I want to be your friend and son. But if you spurn my friendship and submission, know that you will find in me a bitter adversary, the likes of which you have never met all your livelong days.

This forceful letter was neither sent nor even finished. But it shows us Giustiniani's state of soul, haunted by the specter of Delfino and his entourage. What can he do? Should he leave the Hermitage, as Saint Benedict left Subiaco in face of the threats of the priest Florent?

He has been asking himself this question since 1515. Since then he has examined his conscience quite lucidly on this point. Before making up his mind to leave in search of solitude, he weighs the reasons that could hold him back and those that could spur him on. On the one hand, Saint Augustine and Saint Benedict condemned gyrovagues. On the other hand, if Saint Anthony, Saint Hilarion, Saint Benedict, Saint Maur, and Saint Romuald had not freely moved from place to place, the monastic order would not have spread. From the examples of the saints and from their writings, he concludes that a monk can travel not only without fault, but with a sense of complete security, in the following cases: when in the place where he has made profession of the solitary life he suffers, for whatever reason, a persecution that robs him of even a modicum of peace; when he realizes that he is too honored there and given too much importance; when he is charged with a prelacy or a function which he cannot discharge without endangering his salvation; when he is exposed to the envy and snares of those who wish to harm him. Even if his life is not endangered, it is his duty to withdraw in order to remove from his enemies this occasion of losing their souls. And this is the situation in which Giustiniani finds himself. He calls to mind his past life. He took refuge in the religious state, did not want to take the religious habit in his native country, and refused to enter a monastery located in a city.

> Far from my fatherland and far from my friends, in a country where I had never been, in a vast solitude, I made profession of the eremitical life.... Now that all the things that can authorize a monk to flee and to travel (I do not say to play the gyrovague) have happened to me, and since the supreme Pontiff (inspired, surely, by God) has given me full permission, I do not see why I should not decide to take flight and begin my pilgrimage. All the more since, from the age of twenty-four to the present, I have always had the idea to go to confess Jesus Christ, true God and true man, among the infidel nations (if not by my words, at least by my deeds). And it is for this reason that, before entering religion, I made a pilgrimage to Jerusalem.

As early as 1515, then, he had obtained authorization from Leo X to depart. He was not to make use of it until 1520. For five years, he kept asking himself whether he could do so in conscience. During the night of Christmas 1515, he examines the question anew under the form of a dialogue between Peter and Paul, that is to say, Quirini and

Giustiniani. He does not know what he ought to do, whether to depart or to remain. Quirini emphasizes all the reasons that common sense can bring to bear for remaining. He puts him on guard against subtle egotism and makes him heed the call of charity and of dedication to his neighbor. Giustiniani recognizes that all these reasons have their value, but his own experience tells him otherwise: "Your reasoning convinces me of one thing, *the testimony of my conscience* proves to me another, and reason can take me no further." Then Peter distinguishes between the outward man, who is upset, and the inward man, who remains recollected, and says: "*Secretum meum mihi....*" ["My secret is my own...." Is 24:16 Vulg.], a classic solution and a sage doctrine which Giustiniani would have himself proposed to anyone who had consulted him in the same situation. But he feels compelled by an instinct which escapes all reasoning. He realizes that his vocation is unshakeable, and he points out that the reasonable solution is without value for him. Peter reminds him of the texts of Saint Gregory and Saint John Chrysostom which Giustiniani himself often cited formerly. And Paul feels deeply the anguish of this conflict: "*Dura certe conditio!*" ["A hard condition to be sure!"] At any rate, he has weighed up everything. He knows that all the good reasons are against his departure, and yet he does not give in. Five years later, he will take up the same dialogue once again to continue it, after having spent a fortnight in tears. This interior crisis was his most constant source of suffering.

More and more, he reflects on how to know and to do God's will. He asks for light. In the treatise that he writes, *De divina exequenda voluntate* [*On Fulfilling the Divine Will*], he not only tackles a speculative problem, but he seeks to illuminate his own conscience in the light of theology. Applying a verse of the Psalms to the duty of prelates, he observes that he was not made to govern others. Several times, he complains of imitating neither Martha nor Mary, neither Lia nor Rachel. He has a kind of vision of two young men who appear to him. One is leisure, *otium*, the other is its negation, *negotium*, and he is divided between them. His sorrow bursts forth suddenly during the

summer of 1519. From August 15 to November 17, he writes a series
of *Soliloquies,* similar to the *Daily Thoughts on the Love of God* and
just as important. This retreat of sorts will be as decisive for him as
was that of 1506, for it is now a question of taking a new step along
the way of the conversion then entered upon. Giustiniani begins with
a vigorous invective against his cell. Its whole development rests on a
play of words. The "cell," even by its name, should have "concealed"
him, but on the contrary, it has brought him forth into the public eye.
"Cella, cella, ad te confugi ut me celares.... et non celasti...." ["O cell, cell,
I fled to you for refuge, that you might conceal me...and yet you did not
conceal me...."]. Giustiniani reproaches it as the cause of his immense
disappointment, for at the Hermitage he has not found the solitude
that he desired. He wanted to look after himself alone, and here he is
responsible for others. Ironically, he draws a conclusion. According to
the advice of physicians and logicians, an evil must be opposed by its
contrary. Now since the cell has not succeeded in hiding him, he has
only one remedy left, namely, beginning to travel and undertaking
a long pilgrimage. Perhaps just such a pilgrimage, which would put
others before the public, will hide him. If nothing else, it will at least
take away the innumerable vexations which have invaded his cell. And
when he leaves, he will put this inscription on his door: "Paul, in public, in the city, was able to lead a solitary life. He took refuge here to
live still more hidden. But this cell put him on display as a public
figure and overburdened him with worldly troubles. Then, brought
to his senses by such dangers and after untold harm, he abandoned the
one that had betrayed him. And you, whoever you are, who enter here,
watch out that the same misfortune does not befall you."

He wrote this on August 15, 1519. Later on, he adds a postscript:
"On September 15 of the following year, I left the Hermitage,
abandoning the cell." Still another full year was therefore to pass by
before this new departure, a year of reflection during which his plan
was brought to maturity. We have as proof of this the continuation
of the *Soliloquies.* In them, he recalls all the efforts that he has made

to find solitude and declares they have been in vain. Nevertheless, he is clearly conscious of his proper vocation. His need for solitude does not come from himself. Rather, it is a response to a call from on high. *"Seduxisti me, Domine, et seductus sum"* ["You deceived me, O Lord, and I was deceived" Jer 20:7]. I know I did not in any way deserve that solitude that I had gone in search of, that separation from all temporal affairs and peace and quiet of both body and spirit. It is You, Lord, who led me to the Hermitage, and not, to be sure, the dictates of reason." What now is the result of an entire life of seeking?

> I do not see how I can be called a hermit except that I dwell in a cell (which, however, does not at all conceal me), and I have a long beard. I am a hermit and a solitary in name only. In reality, I am a businessman, more troubled about many things than any Martha. They now not only speak but also write against me. And even this is still not enough. Since I have become superior, they arm themselves against me with clubs and swords. My cell is surrounded by a multitude of peasants, assembled here without provocation. When at daybreak I want to leave it, I find myself in the midst of armed men who want to chase me away from the Hermitage or to bind me and drag me off.
>
> Eight months have gone by since, in spite of myself and from obedience, I became a priest, after having refused to become one for eight or nine years. Now these eight months have been filled with so many afflictions and such bitterness that they have seemed to me like eight years, not to say eighty centuries! Scarcely seven months after I was ordained to the priesthood, I was already making preparations to leave the Hermitage. I had already decided to go to the Indies and had set out. And there you have it, to my misery they added this further misery: a month ago today, while I was fleeing, having already left the Hermitage, they elected me superior, pastor, major of the hermits. I had already been elected to this office three times, but I had always refused my consent. However this time I have had to place my miserable neck under the heavy yoke (and You see, Lord Jesus, with how many tears I

write all this). But what would be the point of reporting all that I had to undergo this month, which seemed like a century, while I see that they are preparing even worse tribulations?

"Lord Jesus Christ, You who have wanted me to be monk and hermit, grant me the grace to really be such, not exteriorly, by habit, ceremony, or appearance, but interiorly, by the intimate sentiments of my soul. Never let me stray far from the true and perfect institution of the monastic and eremitical life, but rather may I progress in it day by day." In September of 1519, he has a kind of vision foreboding all that he will have to undergo:

I see, and I know that what I see is not seen with the eyes of the body or of human reason.... And what do you see, Paul? I see that great evils threaten me, and that persecutions more serious than those that I have undergone until now are being prepared for me.... Here I am, Lord, Your slave. Even if the worst sufferings are to come upon me, may Your holy will be done in everything.... I ask only two things: that my tribulations will not harm others, and that they will never separate me from You.

IV

THE FOUNDER
(1520 - 1528)

1. Second Conversion

Paul Giustiniani had found the formula for solitary life that he felt himself called to restore. He had put it down on paper in the *Rule of the Eremitic Life* of 1516. But two things were still lacking: the possibility of fully realizing that formula and the means of enabling all those with this vocation to share in its benefits. In order to attain these goals, he took the risk of a new departure.

On September 15, 1520, he left the Hermitage. He wrote of this thus: "Brother Paul the hermit, when he left the Hermitage of Camaldoli, in which he had resided for ten years, was impelled, it seemed to him, by the sole desire of serving God in greater tranquillity." He remained a few days at Fontebuono. On September 20, he departed from there. Although he had prepared the minds of others for his decision, he knew that many regretted it. He himself suffered from this separation which, however, he believed to be necessary. To avoid grieving his confreres, he had not told them that he would never come back. In a long, touching letter, he put them face to face with the accomplished fact and excused and justified himself. He knew well where he was going. He told them about this journey and described the setting that he had chosen for his new life.

Out of desire for solitude, which I had always loved and desired, and for the solitary life, which I had never possessed as much as I would have wished, I gave up the care and burden of the prelacy of my own accord. Leaving the aforementioned Hermitage, I made my way to this place in the Marches of Ancona where, in a hidden valley, a brooklet runs between two crags. In these crags, there are grottoes or caverns which have been begun by nature and completed by human labor, fashioned in the manner of hermit cells. Matthew and John, both from Massaccio [formerly, and today, called Cupramontana], a village situated about two miles away, lived there long ago. Both of them, because of the many miracles which they worked in life and in death, and which the whole country acknowledged, are considered and venerated as saints. But after them, for perhaps two hundred years, the place was abandoned. There Brother Anthony of Ancona, a resolute man of uncommon prudence, took up his abode ten or twelve years ago after leaving the world for the eremitic life. When I first learned of him, he had stayed there for about six years, either alone or with some companion and without any rule, although adopting a type of eremitical habit. I urged him to submit himself to a rule and to holy obedience. He therefore united this place, called the Grottoes, to the Hermitage of Camaldoli. He received the Camaldolese habit and submitted himself to the rule, institutions and government of the same Hermitage. From then until now, brother Elias, a Camaldolese hermit, has been given him to share his poor and religious way of living. Now I came to this place, as I had intended upon leaving the Hermitage. We embraced and conversed as those customarily do who love one another in religious life and meet again after a long separation. Then I explained to Dom Elias and Brother Anthony the cause of my departure from the Hermitage, although it was already well known to them. Among other reasons, I began by saying that I had left the Hermitage of Camaldoli and made for these grottoes simply out of the desire that I had for true solitude, which I had always loved and sought in various ways since early adolescence but had never found. I added that I had gone to the Hermitage of Camaldoli in the hope of possessing true solitude there, and that I had remained there for ten years, hoping from year to year to be able to live there as a true solitary. But just the opposite happened to me. From day to day cares, occupations, and visits, things quite contrary to the solitary life, kept increasing for me.

The step had been taken. Three weeks after his arrival at the Grottoes, reflecting on these words of a disciple to Jesus, "I will follow You, wherever You may go," Giustiniani understood that there is no limit to God's demands. He desired more and more to forsake everything — honors, conveniences and homeland — to proclaim Christ more by example than by words. And he wrote on this occasion a treatise in Italian, more widely used than Latin, for the benefit of those unable to understand clearly the Gospel texts concerning vocation. A little later on, establishing a parallel between the "confession of Peter:" "You are Christ, the Son of the living God," and the "confession of Thomas:" "My Lord and my God," he concluded that it is necessary to confess Jesus Christ with both mouth and heart. On January 6, 1521, it is the example of Saint Mary Magdalen that impels him to renounce everything, as she gave all her possessions for the perfume that she bought, in order to remain at the feet of the Savior. He does not yet know where his generosity will lead him. In one of his elevations (composed now more and more frequently) he meditates on the "one thing necessary" with regard to the words: "Be converted, be converted, my soul, to the Lord Your God." He desires to be united to the Lord. "But I do not yet see with sufficient clarity in what manner to unite myself to Him *as perfectly as possible.* I desired in the past and desire now more than ever to rest sweetly in my Lord, free from all solicitude. At the same time, I feel ready to work incessantly for the Lord my God, subjecting myself to all sorts of hardships and toil...." That great soul Peter Quirini used to say: "It is either through excess or through lack of application to work that many are disturbed and lose, either partly or entirely, serene peace of mind."

Giustiniani is ready for whatever alternative the Lord will indicate to him. Once again, he examines the pros and cons. There are some good reasons in favor of toil: he knows and highlights them. But he is aware that God is summoning him insistently to peace and quiet. *"Deo quidem te a negotiis ad otium revocante."* ["God is surely calling you back from occupations to leisure."] It is a command: God's call is pressing. *"Deus ipse vacare te iubet."* ["God Himself orders you to be empty."] At the same time, he would like to give his life, to expose himself to martyrdom. The Lord replies to him that this desire is good, but that his own vocation is not to go forth: "Be very careful not to reverse the right order of things. You have professed the solitary life. If now you wish to work for the salvation of your neighbor or for the glory of God, instead of procuring the salvation of many, you will be their ruin. Many are scandalized at seeing a hermit give himself over to exterior works." So in the end, Giustiniani abandons himself to the Lord, to serve Him in the way that pleases Him, in action or repose. From now on, he will be settled in this calm abandonment. On August 8, 1523, the anniversary of his profession, before renewing his vows during Mass, he writes: "I desire to serve my Lord Jesus Christ. However, I blindly entrust the manner of service to His decision: in action or in contemplation, in peace and quiet or in suffering and tribulation, in the quiet of the cell or else in wearisome wanderings. So long as I am serving Him, I have no preference or taste of my own."

His generosity was not disappointed. He had offered everything, and the Lord took everything. He is now in extreme poverty and austerity. Eight months after his departure from Camaldoli, he writes to his sisters that he is now in a place "more solitary, more abject, and poorer than before." He has not forgotten his sisters, sends them all his affection and gives them some news of himself: "I am healthy in body, glad in spirit, and more at peace than ever before." He asks them to pray that he may know God's will: "I say this because I am very hesitant. I do not know whether I ought to remain in Italy or go on to Spain and from there go as far as the Indies, where there are new Christians." This intimate letter contains moving evidence of his poverty:

While I was at the Hermitage, I would not have cared to get anything from you. For the place was rich, and I would not have been able to take what you would have given me as alms given for the love of Christ, but as inspired by human, brotherly love. Now I am in a place which has nothing, nothing, and anything that is given to me would be, I believe, alms pleasing to God. He likes to see His servants supported, even if they do not deserve it. I wanted to write you this not to ask you for anything, for God provides me, through the hands of good people, with every necessity, but so that if one of you wanted to have some merit in the eyes of God, she might know that she can now give the smallest thing to her brother, Paul the hermit, not as to a brother in the flesh, but as to a poor servant of Jesus Christ who is now sustained in all things, whether as to food and clothing or in the things necessary for divine worship and the celebration of Holy Mass, only by the daily alms of devout persons. And it seems to me that I am now richer than ever, because my wealth is God alone and not earthly goods. Even though it is something that could seem either impossible or marvelous, I have nothing either privately or in common, and yet I do not lack anything. I am as content with this rich poverty and poor richness as if I had a world of wealth.

He speaks along the same lines in a letter to Cardinal Bembo:

I have renounced the majorate of the Hermitage with the firm intention of never governing again. I did so especially because in the Hermitage, even when I was not major, I would have to busy myself with either all or the greater part of the governance and care of things. Therefore I left the Hermitage never to return, or in any case not before ten years, if I live as long as that. And I have reduced my residence to a tiny place (I am writing you from there) where in the tuff and the stone there are two very small grottoes serving as cells. The place belongs to the Hermitage and two of our hermits have been here for some years already. I intend, if it pleases my father hermits, to settle down here and to arrange to live here in poverty. If it is not pleasing to them, I intend to undertake the journey to the Indies about which I have already spoken so many times.

He asks Bembo to obtain the pope's permission for him to make a general confession to a priest of his choice, even outside the Camaldolese order, to receive absolution from him for all the irregularities that he may possibly have incurred. Then he speaks again of the extreme poverty of the place: "There are two grottoes here and four of us, two hermits who were here already and I with the lay brother who followed me into this poverty." He regrets that the hermits are living together by twos. He recalls that Bembo had promised to make a donation to the Hermitage and asks him to make the Grottoes the beneficiary of it. "I assure you that at Camaldoli the donkeys of the Hermitage are better housed than we are.... The latrines in the Hermitage are bigger, nicer, more comfortable and pleasant than the places in which we sleep, eat, recite the Office, and celebrate Mass. The refuse of the Hermitage would be delicious fare for us." For the first time in his life, Giustiniani begs and apologizes for doing so. "God knows that extreme poverty and discomfort oblige me (listen to this) to write to you on my knees, not even having a stool."

See where "his second conversion," as he calls it, has taken him. Leaving Camaldoli was more distressing to him, and not less "necessary," than leaving the world the first time. Just as he had left the world and its ease to lead an austere life, so he had had to renounce the dignity of major to serve the Lord in a life still more austere.

At the Grottoes, he leads the life that he has dreamed of for a long time. His time is rarely taken up by the administration of temporal goods. He can at last follow the particular rule of life which he judges in conformity with his vocation and whose main points he now sets down in writing:

> To take part in the Divine Office and to recite half of the Psalter in private; to read, to write, to meditate, to choose the most tranquil hour of the day to consecrate to prayer, to celebrate Holy Mass every day; to examine one's conscience each day, to speak little and to read while eating, to sleep enough before the Night Office so as not to have to go back to bed after it; to do manual labor according to one's strength, and as much as possible for the benefit of others.

The letters that he writes are intended to console a hermit on the death of his mother, to discuss with Saint Cajetan of Thiene the virtues of Saint John the Baptist, and to make the hesitant hear the call of the Hermitage. Jerome the Spaniard, confessor of Saint Cajetan, does not know whether to remain in the world or become a religious, nor whether, if he becomes a religious, to take up the active or the solitary life. Since he is frail, he is not sure that he can endure the eremitic observances, and he consults Giustiniani. The latter assures him that he has much esteem and respect for Lord Cajetan, but he has not yet understood why he has chosen secular rather than solitary life. He is certainly performing good works in the world, but in a state inferior to that of the solitary life. If Jerome's health prevents his coming to the Hermitage, he can at least lead the religious life in the world by desire.

> In any case, according to Saint Thomas, we need only ask for advice and deliberate about the type of religious life and the place, because it is certainly a better thing to enter religious life than to remain in the world. And on this point I can say absolutely, with a certitude based on past experience, that for somebody wanting the eremitic and solitary religious life, there is no institution or place in Italy more

appropriate than the Hermitage of Camaldoli. All the other hermits are without rule, vows, or discipline, and I believe that they are more disapproved than approved by Holy Church and the sacred ecclesiastical canons. Besides, not having any vows, they are not religious. As for the Carthusian life, which also seems to be solitary, I will tell you that it is much less solitary than that of the Hermitage of Camaldoli, and John Gerson disputes at length about its liceity. Although they have the vows of religion, they do not have an approved rule but live according to their constitutions. I would certainly have entered there if I had not heard of the Hermitage of Camaldoli. But since it was a question of my salvation, it did not seem prudent to me to enter an institute whose approval is open to dispute. I do not know of another mode of solitary life in Italy.... If you so desire, you could come to see some solitary places which, under the Camaldolese institute, we have acquired recently in the Province of the Marches and in which we now number about twenty hermits. These places are poorer and more solitary than the Hermitage of Camaldoli itself but are not yet fully put in order. Anyway, in the name of my companions and me, I offer you these places and our company with all alacrity. And we invite you to desire together with us to serve God and to strive for the spread and growth in numbers of this eremitical life in Italy.

At the Grottoes, Giustiniani remains the apostle of eremitism. The more he is separated from the world, the more he enlarges the field of his apostolate. In an opuscule in which he proves that the solitary life is not an idle life, against the slander of those who maintain the contrary, he states that he can judge by experience both the active life, because he has been superior, and the solitary life which he is leading. On this occasion he indicates his occupations: he has undertaken to translate the whole Bible into Italian, or at least its most frequently read sections, like the Psalms, the Gospels, and the Epistles; he has also started an abridgment of all the ecclesiastical canonical collections for the utility of others; he has begun to write to all the hermits who live without profession, vows, or rule, to tell them what he thinks of their state and to urge them to seek one that is more secure, more perfect, and approved; he would like to relate the life of Quirini and that of their master, Canali. He is translating the treatise of Saint Bonaventure, *On the Five Feasts of the Child Jesus*. He is copying out an entire volume of Saint Peter Damian's writings. He is composing the treatise, *On the Great Number of the Elect*. For this very austere man is not a pessimist: he reacts against those who frighten men by telling them that very few are saved; he tries to prove the contrary to encourage them.

Even at the Grottoes, Giustiniani does not have undisturbed peace and quiet. He has dispersed his hermits in several places. One of these hermitages, that of Saint Jerome, has a chapel which depends on the parish of Pascelupo. He asks the pope's authorization to remain there. But Giustiniani now comes up against opposition of a new kind. After having been exposed to the oppression of the cenobites, Camaldolese and Cassinese, he now sees that the hermits without a rule are rising up against him. He urges hermits of this sort to embrace the religious state. It would be much better for them, he writes one of them, to embrace any approved form of religious life, cenobitic or eremitic. He himself maintains that he would not hesitate to part with his own companions, however virtuous, if they intended to lead the eremitical life without being religious. "Because the Sacred Canons," as he says, "forbid living eremitically without rule, without vows, and without profession." He also composes a theological treatise on the great value of the vows. He addresses it, in his capacity of "regular hermit," to a "secular hermit" by the name of Nicholas. In order to get him to accept it, he accompanies it by a charming introductory letter in which he tells him:

Dearly beloved brother, if I knew how to braid rushes, weave palm fiber, or work a lathe, then through these brethren of mine whom I am dispatching I would have sent you a gift of rush matting, or of baskets,

145

or of a chaplet of beads for counting the paters. Such are, in fact, the trifling gifts that hermits are wont to exchange among themselves. Since I do not have such things made with my hands and, on the other hand, my affection for you does not allow me to let these brethren go without bringing you a gift from me, I have thought to dedicate to you these three poor opuscules, fruit of my very poor reflections, and I send them to you as a brotherly present.

However certain hermits rise up against him, denounce him, and force him to abandon the Hermitage of Saint Benedict. In July of 1522, he will explain the matter to the cardinal protector of his order. The bishop of Ancona has been misinformed by certain hermits who were living on Monte di Ancona, a mile from the Hermitage of Saint Benedict. They are trying to expel all the hermits by force, without even listening to them and in defiance of their privilege of exemption. As for Giustiniani, they have driven him away with violence. And yet the Hermitage belonged to those who had built it with their hands and who were in peaceful possession of it for eight years. Giustiniani seeks the justice which ought not be refused to anyone. In order to obtain it, he invokes the remembrance of Quirini to the cardinals who formerly knew him.

They bring him to the monastery of Saint Francis of Macerata, forbidding him to leave it. He falls ill there. For all this, he gives thanks: "If all the members of my body were as many tongues, I could by no means thank You as I would wish, O Lord Jesus. If I am not mistaken, You have begun to make this useless servant of Yours participate, although in a small measure, in the sorrows of Your Passion and the sufferings of Your holy disciples." He expresses his joy. He accepts the fact that his captivity is prolonged and aggravated, just as he will also accept death if necessary. He understands that the vision he had before leaving Camaldoli is coming true. Great sufferings were foretold to him, so he is not surprised that they have now come upon him. He does not lose peace of soul and recommends that his hermits do likewise. While waiting for justice to be done, and while he is still a prisoner for Jesus Christ, *"Paulus vinctus Jesu Christi,"* he gives these instructions to the prior of the Hermitage of Saint Benedict:

> More for the sake of your peace than for anything else, it seems to me that you ought to get your things together and return to the Grottoes of Massaccio.... Take my things, too, especially the book of Saint Peter Damian with the other books that you find.... I hope in the Lord to see you again soon, and that we will later be able to enjoy lasting peace in this world, so as to pass later to the eternal rest that God will grant us in heaven. I have been assailed by a high fever these last few days.... Pray, all of you, that the Lord may deliver me from this prison, which is tolerable enough in any case.

And he adds in a postscript: "If, however, you prefer to remain there where you are, I give permission. I have only your tranquillity in mind in writing you all this." He is liberated a little before the Feast of Pentecost and, upon his return to the Grottoes, he composes a long prayer to the Holy Spirit. But he reproaches himself for not always having had perfect patience in adversity. He always feels himself far from the purity of conscience to which he aspires with all his might.

In 1522, he obtains permanent concession of the hermitages in the Marches of Ancona from the Hermitage of Camaldoli. In 1523, he obtains the official erection of his new foundation, which receives the name of "Company of the Hermits of Saint Romuald," from the superiors of the Congregation of Camaldoli and of Saint Michael of Murano. These negotiations oblige him to make a journey in the summer of 1523. He comes back sick and wondering whether he is going to die. Since his conversion, he has no longer been troubled with fevers. But now they recur, perhaps as a result of the extreme discomfort in which he lived during his first days at the Grottoes. Memories of his studies return to him along with the fevers. Like the Stoics, he wishes neither to fear nor to desire death. He repeats the words of the Psalm: "*Paratum cor meum Deus, paratum cor meum*" ["My heart is ready, O God, my heart is ready," Ps 107 (108):1 and Ps 56 (57):7]. He is torn between the desire to go to meet God and to go on living with his brothers. But he is ready for everything; he offers and he accepts everything.

He gets suggestions from various sources to write an apologia for his departure from Camaldoli. But what would be the use? He would not be able to do so without attacking others or justifying himself. He prefers to refrain from all this, leaving everything to God, and he transforms Psalm 108 (109), which is replete with curses, into a canticle of blessings: "*Deus laudem meam ne tacueris, quia os recti cordis et os justi super me apertum est. Locuti sunt pro me lingua veritatis et sermonibus dilectionis circumdederunt me*" ["O God, my praise, be not silent, for they have opened a right-hearted and just mouth about me. They have spoken for me with true tongues and with words of love they have encompassed me"].

Instead of going back over the past, he describes the present existence of his companions. This testimony to their way of living is worth more than any refutation. We quote here a letter of Giustiniani on this subject, although it is in part a repetition of what has already been said:

> In your last letters you ask me to send you a description of my way of life as an example for you to imitate. But my miserable negligence and tepidity in spiritual things would certainly not give edification, but could rather occasion scandal and ruin. I will instead narrate for you the fervent and devout life lived by these my father and brother hermits. From hearing about what I see all day long and do not succeed in imitating, may you derive not only consolation but even edification.
>
> As I see it, even though admonitions and exhortations do move men to the exercise of virtue, examples much more effectively impel them. They draw even the negligent to imitate them, especially when they are the examples of our contemporaries. For when we hear about

the wonderful perfection of the ancient Desert Fathers, our weakness and negligence finds a thousand excuses and tries to make us believe that, in those times, constitutions were stronger than in our day. But when we hear and see the examples of our fellow countrymen today, no excuse remains for our miserable negligence. There is nothing that so greatly hinders the perfection of the men and women who serve God than pusillanimity, indiscreet fear of incapacity, overcautious discretion, or better, too much tender care for oneself.

I know well that if these fathers of mine knew that I intended to describe their way of life, they would in no way allow it. However I will not identify anyone by name, so that when they also become aware of what I have written, they will not be bothered much, each one thinking that I am recounting, not his own virtues, but those of the other brethren.

But in the first place, permit me to describe, insofar as I can, the solitary places in which they dwell. If you were to see these places, they would not strike you as in any way inferior to the ancient solitudes of Egypt or the Thebaid. You should know, therefore, that these our father and brother hermits number about twenty-five, and they have four hermitages in this province of the Marches and the surrounding territory, in each one of which they live by five, six, or seven. When opportune, they change residence and go from one to the other, but that rarely, except for me who am without a permanent dwelling in any of these places. To my misfortune, it is rare that I succeed in remaining four months in one place. This would prove to be intolerable if it were not for the fact that the places are no more than twenty-five or thirty miles apart.

The first of these places is called the Grottoes of Massaccio. Thirteen or fourteen years ago a gentleman went to live there, of noble blood but nobler still by reason of virtue. Brother Anthony, as he was called, dwelt there alone, wearing the habit of the Third Order of Saint Francis. Six years ago, exhorted by me to the true religious life, he took our habit and Rule. In the first years of his conversion, the Lord showed him in many ways what good care divine providence takes of his servants. Among other things, there is one of them that is known to the whole village. He had confidently begun to have excavated that grotto that we now use as a church, having been persuaded to do so by a gentleman who promised to pay the workers. The work was almost finished, when suddenly the one who had pressed for the enterprise with his promise made it openly understood that nothing should be expected from him, since he did not have the wherewithal to pay. Then the good brother resorted to the garrison of holy prayer. So having prayed fervently Friday night, the next day, which was Saturday, the work was finished and he needed to pay the workmen. About the hour of Vespers as the excavation continued, the workers discovered a little cavity in the tuff where there was no hole or crack. It was full of ancient coins of Ancona, sufficient in amount to pay those laborers.

When he took our habit the Hermitage gave him as his companion a father hermit, a priest, who has dwelt with him ever since. In the first days of his living in this place he was sick and lacked bread. He was administered a fresh and good loaf by a raven sent, I believe, by the Lord. Every year now this raven makes his nest beside that father's cell. He and his mate have become so tame that they are always around us and come to eat from our hands. And if someone shows them some bread while they are flying, they come to eat it at once, a thing that affords me no little recreation.

Then Giustiniani speaks of the three other hermitages: Saint Jerome of Pascelupo, Saint Leonard of Volubrio, and Saint Benedict of Monte Conero.

There is a monastery near the summit on Monte Conero called Saint Peter's, in which some servants of God have lived for four or five years wearing the habit of secular priests. The members of this new religious institute, without vows and without profession of an approved rule, live as hermits for the edification of their neighbor. This place had been granted to our Company and to me by that Benedictine monk who had the site of the community and who built the cells there. All last year I had to bear a harsh persecution because of this property. Finally I went away with the intention of contending no longer. But the Lord God, as is His wont, struck the principal author of this persecution with a very serious sickness and all his accomplices with death, dangers, and adversities. Through their oppression He made them understand their guilt so that, when I was no longer expecting it, they sent messengers to ask my pardon. I was sorry about the sickness, prayed to God, and made a votive offering for their life and health and, as I had already done, cheerfully forgave them.

After having thus described the Hermitages, Blessed Paul speaks about the observances: the fasts, the timetable, and the habit. Unfortunately, this valuable document is incomplete. At least what he tells us clearly shows that the foundation, sanctioned by the Roman Pontiff and the authorities of the Camaldolese order, had immediately proved itself vital. The new congregation was prospering and growing in numbers.

2. Solitude Regained

Giustiniani could now die. He was only forty-eight, but he had accomplished the work which was his task and fulfilled his mission. He would remain on earth for four more years. In the course of his life, this last period is the response of the Lord, before his great departure for eternal joy. It is the reward of a lifelong quest, the approval of a string of renunciations, the confirmation of a vocation faithfully discerned and generously followed. The time of distress had passed. When he had left Camaldoli, wondering whether the Lord wanted him to go to the Indies, he had looked for a sign. He had foreseen that if his brothers in Camaldoli allowed him to live in the Marches of Ancona, he would not go on any farther. The sign had been given.

The religious of the Hermitage and the authorities of the Camaldolese order had not only not blocked his foundation but had contributed to it, granting him permanently the sites he occupied and including his Company in the Congregation of Murano without taking away any of its autonomy.

Abiding in peace of mind, Blessed Paul could at last devote himself entirely to the care of his hermits and to the eremitical life, just as he had always desired to do. He still must travel, but he no longer complains of this. Moreover, he notes that difficulties are little by little being resolved. During the pontificate of Adrian VI, he had encountered some obstacles in Rome. But in the summer of 1523, Cardinal Pucci, the protector of his Company, had encouraged him by saying: "Be of good courage, brother Paul, and believe me that I know what I am talking about. Soon you will get what you want and much more, even more than you are asking." Giustiniani and the others who had heard these words had not understood what they meant. They understood them very soon, however. In autumn, Pope Adrian VI died. His successor was the archbishop of Florence, Julian de' Medici. On the 19th of the following February, Giustiniani could write from Rome:

> Our business affairs are off to a good start, and I hope they will have as good a conclusion. We are in favor, as though back in the time of Pope Leo X. Many of our old friends have returned to their offices.... I am staying in the Borgo, behind Adrian's Palace, in the house of Lord John Francis Valerio. I am very well taken care of and almost without expenses.... Do pray for our business, and for many other religious affairs that are in my hands, so that they may have a good outcome.

A little later, he again sent the new pope Clement VII a report on the state of his Company. The hermits were 35, and another hermitage, Saint Mary of the Holy Spirit, had been added to the first four.

Relations with Camaldoli remained excellent. On August 16, 1524, he begged the major to assure all the brothers of his undiminished love for the Hermitage. He requested that they permit Father Justinian of Bergamo to come to help the new Company. He also asked for some books, a copy of the Koran in particular. He announced that he would visit them as soon as possible. As a matter of fact, a year later he sends a letter from the Hermitage of Camaldoli in which he can say that he has had the good fortune to have finally gained, or rather regained, solitude: "I am at the Hermitage in perfect disposition of body and soul. I feel as though I have returned to the time of my novitiate." It is only at the end of his stay that he must write: "Yesterday evening I had things to do with these fathers until four o'clock. Tonight I wrote more than ten or twelve letters. It is now the hour of Prime, and I have not yet said Matins, and I must leave just now on horseback for Ravenna.... " But he does not give way to complaining: he has found interior solitude. Passing through Val di Castro, he venerates there the cell in which Saint Romuald died. Ordinarily, his trips are limited to Monte di Ancona and the surrounding territory. He now has only a small society to administer and minor business affairs: pieces of cloth to buy, grain to be garnered, and easy dealings with Cardinal Pucci, benevolent protector of the Company.

He devotes more effort and time to directing the souls of his hermits than to increasing their worldly goods. In reply to a question from brother Peter Gabrielli on the manner in which to spend the day, he gives instructions which are full of moderation. He enumerates all the daily practices that he recommends but adds that one must take into consideration the time, the place, the person, and the length of day in the different seasons. To the superiors, he sends instructions that are at the same time firm and broad:

I have had in these last days the idea to write you, offering you the opportunity to come here for your comfort and, if you wish, to make your profession at this Hermitage.... Afterwards it occurred to me that this might be good neither for you nor for your Hermitage, and it could give the others reason for complaint. Therefore if you strongly desire it and it seems the Grottoes can get along without you, I would not want to hinder your coming here, but do think the matter over very carefully.... Please do as best you can, without me, whatever God will inspire.

In a long letter to Dom Francis, prior of Saint Jerome of Pascelupo, he gently and forcefully gives advice and permissions. After having spoken about a vineyard to be planted, he takes up the construction of new cells. He wants each to consist not only in a single room, but in several together, such as a bedroom, a chapel, a study, and a loggia, but all of these small. "I believe you understand my thinking. But since I am not present, proceed according to what I have just told you concerning the form and the size of the cells. I leave the rest to your judgment, always, however, consulting the brethren." A novice, brother Prosper, wants to leave:

> My intention is that he not be given permission to leave before the chapter, but that you bear with him with goodness and patience, and treat him with gentleness, without in any way exasperating him. The chapter will determine what to do about him. If he asks to leave beforehand, which I do not expect, I would like you to persuade him with good words to wait for the visit I will come to make before the chapter.... I would not want to have to render an account to God for this soul on Judgment Day, for if he leaves us, I am afraid that he will be in great danger. Do then, as I have told you. If you do otherwise, you will act against my will, and it will be a scruple for your conscience. I bore with brother Prosper for a long time at the Grottoes; you, also, bear with him for a while.

Giustiniani is a leader. He knows how to assert himself. "I beg you to be content to do this thing that I am ordering with sweet patience and charity.... Do not do otherwise than I have ordered, because I would be very displeased and you would act contrary to conscience." But he knows as well how to share the initiative with those who must carry out his orders. He especially insists that the local superior decide nothing without consulting the brethren. There is a scarcity of personnel and he has to deprive the hermitage of some members. In closing this letter to the prior of Saint Jerome, he writes: "Have much patience. God will help us and will send us enough members to supply all our needs." He has, finally, an obliging thought for the superior, by which he mitigates the peremptory orders he has had to give. "When I return from Venice, I will therefore do some favors for you. And at the chapter, I will try to obtain from the Hermitage of Camaldoli a fine panel or altarpiece, depicting a crucifix with Saint Jerome at the foot of the cross, for your church."

Another letter written in the same period is filled with practical instructions on the upbuilding and governance of the hermitages. Perfect harmony reigns among the hermits. For the new Company, it is a happy and heroic period, filled with suffering and privation, but also with grace and virtue. Consciences are delicate, as these few words show: "As for your scruples, I beg you, for the love of God, to banish them from your mind, for they are surely vain. I can tell you that in the Hermitage of Camaldoli my confessor, Dom Christopher, did not want to allow me to repeat the hour of Prime, which I thought I had recited poorly. Imagine, then, how he would deal with you."

Now that he has reached the culmination of his life, Giustiniani lets his contemplation range freely in writing very lofty expositions of mystical theology. Such are the "six argumentations" which he has entitled, *Secretum Meum Mihi* [*My Secret with Myself*], as well as the treatise *On the True and Perfect Way of Salvation*, also on the love of God, written in 1526 at the Franciscan monastery in Spoleto. A *Soliloquy on the Continual Struggle Between the Flesh and the Spirit* and an elucidation *On Delights in Prayer* were also written during the same stay in Spoleto. In spite of his age and experience, Blessed Paul does not consider himself to be excused from intellectual work.

With regard to a verse from the Psalms in which Naphtali, Benjamin, Gilead, and Manasseh are named, he studies the Biblical genealogies in depth in order to identify these personages. He always draws his doctrine from Holy Scripture. He extracts from the Gospels *The Doctrine of Our Lord on Maintaining Charity Toward All*. He always lives in the presence of Quirini, and certain of his writings take on the guise of a dialogue with him, as though there were two men within him. "Holy soul, I feel you near me very often. And yet, since you left your mortal remains, I have never had the grace to see you with my eyes or to hear your voice."

More and more, Giustiniani feels obligated to write for the benefit of others, and first of all for his hermits. From Rome, where he lives with Saint Cajetan of Thiene, he sends on request a sermon on the resurrection of Christ for Easter 1524. He reanimates his hermits from afar and sustains their fervor. But he also thinks of those who are ignorant of Christian mysteries and wants to enlighten them. For their benefit, he composes the treatise *On the Evangelical Precepts and Counsels*. To profit a greater number of readers, he now writes almost always in the vernacular. He justifies this as follows:

> I have always considered it something monstrous and incongruous to speak all day long in one language, in public and in private, with familiars and strangers, and then, upon picking up a pen in my study, to become another man, assuming another language, foreign and not native. This is especially clear since all the books which we read daily, for pleasure and utility, were written by their authors in the language they spoke familiarly. If they are translated into another language, they degenerate from their natural decorum and ornamentation in such a way that more sensitive readers are never as satisfied to read a book translated into another language as in the language in which it was originally written. The Hebrews wrote in Hebrew, the Greeks in Greek, the Latins in Latin, and we, although we have a common mother tongue for all Italy, do not deign to write in it. Rather we want to write in Latin,

supposing that there is more wisdom in this strange tongue that we learn with difficulty than in our own that we drink in with infant milk. As for me, who am as unlearned in the one as in the other, I followed the common error and wrote some things in Latin. However it is now my preference to write in the vernacular, which is more suitable and more commonly used, not only these opuscules for instruction in the eremitic life but everything that in the future I will get the idea to write. Being in this solitude, far from all human society and occupation, I think that I will be able to write many things, unless a premature old age interrupts my life.

Many reasons confirm that it is more suitable for one who has been born and brought up in Italy to write in a tongue which I would call, not vulgar, but Italian. But in the first place it is necessary to say, to satisfy those who consider themselves scholars, that at the time when the authors who are read today wrote in Latin, the Latin language was common to all Italians and to the most ordinary people. This is proved by many statements of Ambrose, Jerome, Augustine, and Gregory. Besides, Saint Benedict orders in chapter 48 of his *Rule* that during Lent all monks must take a book from the library and read it, at certain hours, from beginning to end. Let those who would have it that not everyone understood Latin tell us, then: What books did the monks read? They were not in the vernacular, since none such were to be had then. So they were in Latin, and yet everyone understood them. It is certainly not astonishing, as Saint Jerome says in his prologue to the Epistles, that Saint Paul seemed more eloquent in his own language, that is in Hebrew, than in a foreign language, that is in Greek.

Italian is the language in which Giustiniani describes the persecution by the Franciscans of two religious who were to later start the Capuchin Order. When a lay brother asks him to compose an invitation to one of his childhood friends to become a hermit, this tactful humanist goes so far as to adopt the style of the sender and the recipient. He speaks of those things that are at the same time the simplest and the truest: "So know, dearest brother, that since I entered holy religion, I am more satisfied and consoled every day. It seems to me that I have discovered the terrestrial paradise, so consoled am I in soul and so healthy in body. I live very cheerfully and contentedly, and I would not exchange my state with that of any secular person for all the world."

Giustiniani expresses himself in an entirely different manner to his friend Mark Anthony Flaminio. This man is a philosopher, and he is still at the stage in which Giustiniani was before his conversion. Giustiniani adapts himself to his condition, speaks to him as philosopher to philosopher, and writes for him a kind of treatise on the life of the blessed "comprehensors" in heaven. We quote some passages:

This beatitude can only be a participation in the boundless divine Beatitude, and a likeness of that beatitude that we consider to be found in all those heavenly creatures whom we hold for certain to be blessed. Now the divine Beatitude consists in nothing other than that most perfect understanding and that utter fullness of love which God has of Himself. And so, descending from the divine beatitude to the angelic, one could affirm that only all those heavenly spirits or intelligences are blessed, because they all know and love God. Among those, then, each one is more or less blessed insofar as each one knows and loves God more or less.

We therefore should believe that our happiness or beatitude has the character of a participation in the divine beatitude and a likeness to the angelic beatitude, and that that happiness, which we await in the heavenly fatherland, ought to have its beginning in us here below. Now such happiness can only consist in the knowledge and love of God. To Him, as to the supreme Truth, are referred back all those truths that our intellect extends itself to encompass; and in Him, as in the supreme Good, are gathered up all the goods that our will can be both moved and drawn to love.

So happiness is constituted by the exercise of the intellect and of the will, and it is the operation of the will that is more loved, easier, gladder, better suited to raise one to the supreme Good and supreme Happiness, and more unitive with its subject. Therefore it seems to me that whoever seeks with the operation of the intellect alone, rather than with that of the will, to arrive at being united with that supreme and unique Good that is God, deviates far from the true path and from common sense.

Besides, the intellect has received not only one, but diverse lights from God. Now to seek Him, not with the brighter and clearer light, but with one quite dim, is an inferior manner of proceeding. It wearies the intellect and never comes to that knowledge which, with less effort, would be easily arrived at by searching for it with the true light. To me it appears incontrovertible that, above the light and discourse of reason, there is another light. It is clearer and more evident, given by God to those human minds that do not refuse to receive it, and by means of it God can be properly understood. Therefore worthy of condemnation are those who, not wanting to receive this clearer and shining light, want to know God, supreme Truth, with the light of the intellect and of reason.

I know that to many it could appear to be something new when I say the following: There can be in man, above reason and its discourse, another, more perfect light, a clearer and higher light for knowing God and divine things, and with it alone the human mind can see God and those things that are of God. This is the light of faith. It incomparably exceeds any other, rational light; it alone can guide us to some measure of the true and solid knowledge of God; without it all discourse, all studies, can only give us as much perception of God and of divine things as the light of the senses can lead us to as demonstrable and natural conclusions. With this light of faith, and not solely with that of reason, it is possible for us, by the operation of the intellect, to attain in some degree to the supreme Truth and, consequently, to human happiness.

Let us not forget that he is writing to a Renaissance philosopher and humanist who overestimated the power of reason. Therefore he insists upon and reaffirms his thought:

> I say, then, that it certainly seems to me to be little less than manifest insanity and blindness to seek the knowledge of God and divine things amongst the books of the gentile philosophers, employing only the light and the discourse of reason. And here I think I ought to say that, although it is quite true that this light of faith is given by God and that not all have it, still no one is excused if he does not have it, for God is always ready to give it to all.
>
> Now there are two exercises by means of which one can hope to receive the clear light of faith: In the first place, the purification of the soul from all its passions and from all its disordered affections. In the second place, the continual reading not, of course, of Morgante or Petrarch or Boccaccio, through whom many intelligent people go astray, and not even of Cicero or Virgil, nor (this you may be sorrier about) of Aristotle and Averroës, or of Plato or Plotinus, but rather of the holy Gospel of Christ, of the most admirable Epistles of the apostle Paul, in a word, so as not to mention the books one by one, of all divinely inspired Holy Scripture.

He has come a long way, this humanist turned hermit, toward the end of his life. He testifies that through contemplation one arrives at such a clear knowledge of divine realities, at such a certainty of future beatitude, that it is as though instead of merely knowing, one already possessed these realities.

A holy old man, Dom Michael of Florence, was a recluse for thirty-five years in a little cell at the Hermitage of Camaldoli, uneducated in the eyes of the world, but very proficient in spiritual things and divine contemplation. He used to say with regard to the sacrament of the altar (in which there is certainly God, Christ ever blessed, whether inasmuch as He is eternal deity or inasmuch as He has an assumed humanity):

"Not only do I already see Him, but my faith has given way, and there has succeeded it and grown up in its place true and certain knowledge." Now it was not the study of the gentile philosophers that led him to this, but the inestimable ardor of his love of God and neighbor in which, as in two flaming furnaces, his whole heart was ever burning.

Following this preamble, Giustiniani draws the practical conclusion he was evidently driving at: "What marvel, then, dearly beloved Lord Mark Anthony, if I, desiring for you (as a friend would) true and solid happiness, invite, exhort, and spur you on to the solitary religious life as the way most apt to lead you to this happiness?" And then he resumes with greater insistence:

When you do not wish or do not feel able to reply to these and similar arguments, you always have ready the pretext of delicate health. Now although the example of others might fail to convince you, surely my example should not. In the world, besides being assailed every year by some illness which brought me to the point of death and sometimes made me take to my bed for over a year, even health itself was for me a continual infirmity. Now, I find myself robust even though sixteen years older, and I fast for seven or eight continuous months each year. I would not have been able to make a mile a day then, and the way seemed very long to me when I was making the indulgenced church visits in Padua. Now, instead, I do easily twenty-five or even thirty-five miles a day, up hill and down dale, and do not feel worn out. Finally, then, if you want to find the peace of mind that you desire, and if you would gain, at the same time, a healthy body, you ought to become a religious. Otherwise, you might be resisting until death the urgings of God, a thing not only very hard but, even more, most impious.

For several years, as already indicated, Blessed Paul had been fostering the eremitic vocation of his nephew Francis. But Francis kept hesitating. One last time, his uncle sends him a pressing entreaty:

I write you this letter although I do not know whether I can hope for it to bear fruit. However, the awareness that I have sought your perfection and salvation will benefit me in this life and on the day of judgment. If you do not receive it willingly, you will have a double grief. In this world, when more mature, you will regret in vain time and opportunities lost. And in the future life, you will not be able to make use before God of the excuse: "I did not know." I greatly desire that this letter of mine should be useful to you, and that is why I write it. But even if it is not useful to you, it will certainly be imputed to my credit.

And now listen, my Francis, to what your old brother Paul wants to propose to you in this letter. I want to depict for you, or rather roughly represent, a Francis such as he will be remaining in the world and a Francis such as he would be following Christ in religious life. You yourself know and have often told me that upon spending only a couple of days, or even a single evening, conversing with mean, base, or worldly people, you become mean-spirited, base, and inferior to your usual self. But conversing with people who are more high-minded, your own mind is filled with lofty and noble thoughts, and you surpass yourself. And so it truly happens, because you are still tender and susceptible to the influence of those with whom you talk. Now, if you remain in the world, you will have to deal most of the time with ignorant, servile, and base people. I do not speak so much of our housemaids, menservants, boatmen, and our tenants, however, but precisely of your gentlemen peers, who know no other world than that of the Rialto. And you too will become, like them, a tomfool whose main concern will be to ask: "What is new this morning?" and "What do I still have to pay?" And you will waste your life in paltry and base business of this kind, as do not only most but almost all our Venetian gentlemen. You will lose your adolescence and youth without realizing it.

Later you will be an old fool, ignorant and silly. You will sit all day long on some bench with your fellows and together fritter away your old age, as one sees happening on every side. And yet all this would still be bearable, compared to something worse. This something worse is the effect on your habits of dealing with very corrupt and vicious men. Our city, more than any other, is filled with them. And especially now that you are young, you will become an inveterate gambler. Or rather, I understand that you are already beginning to become one. You know well whether or not you are also beginning to scorn and offend your neighbor, and maybe even to blaspheme the saints and God. Vain, immersed in all the vanities of the world, vainly dressed up, you already take a fancy to velvet-trimmed stockings. Little by little, you will find the desire for fashions and pleasures growing in you. You will pamper your body with good food, choice wines, baths and perfumes. And so you will become lustful and given over to carnal pleasures, as are 90 per cent of the men of your age in our region.

The letter is unfinished. Blessed Paul did not have time to describe, in contrast, the happiness of one who follows Christ in the religious life. We do not know for certain what he would have said. But Francis heard his voice: in September 1525, he had arrived at the Hermitage of Camaldoli, where his uncle saw him. Returning from Ravenna to the Grottoes, Blessed Paul writes to his brother, Anthony, the father of Francis: "I will take more care of his body and soul than if he were my son a hundred times over. Since he is so amiable and quiet, I love him as my own soul.... No doubt about it, Francis will never lack anything, and of this you can be sure."

Souls were responding, then, to the invitation of Blessed Paul. In a letter to Galeazzo Gabrielli, the last one of these letters we possess, Giustiniani speaks of new hermitages that he is being offered in the province of Verona.

As one who puts his hope in God's help, I am bolder than I am strong. So having to come to these parts, I could not be satisfied with acquiring one or two places. Rather I would wish if possible to establish at once enough Hermitages in that region so that we could hold a chapter in that province without coming as far as the Marches.... There are so many of us here that we could also fill those places if we could have them.... Just as here in the Marches of Ancona, we have already gotten several places and almost constitute a province, so I would desire that we could live eremitically in those places that have been offered us in the area of Verona from the time that Brother Jerome started to bring our kind of life to those parts. I would like to take as many as six or eight places, not only in the regions of Brescia but also in the surrounding territory, and form another province. Exterior circumstances, and the fruit I hope such efforts will bear, move me to do this....

Galeazzo had asked him for a copy of the memorial he had at one time sent to Pope Leo X on the reform of the Church.

I agree with you and the others that it would be necessary to correct it. But do not imagine that at my age, grown cold in body and spirit, I could apply myself to see if there are some errors in the Latin or if some non-Latin words have crept in. The one thing I want you to know is that I made every effort in this writing to set forth the ideal and the desire that I felt then in my soul, since I had no other aim in writing, as I believe I said in the preface, than to put before Pope Leo what I was daily asking the Lord God in my prayers.... I do not think that it is out of place to desire the conversion of the Jews and of idolaters to the faith, the conversion of the Mohammedans, the reunion of all Christian peoples with the Roman Church, and worldwide reform, and these are the main topics treated. This is just what I felt I had to submit to Pope Leo X for his consideration. At the beginning of his elevation to the pontifical throne, I hoped for reform in the world as did many others, who were as mistaken as I was. In case it really ought to be printed, that should not be done without subtle examination and with the judgment of our reverend bishops of Bagieca and Thiene, whom I consider to be the wisest and most sharp-sighted judges in Italy. And I do not say that to flatter, but because I am convinced of it.... Moreover, I believe someone like Lord Peter Bembo would counsel no other correction than casting it into the fire.... To sum up, my style in this treatise is monastic, as one of my friends says, and that is all I can say.

This time, also, the letter is unfinished. But we can discern, from these last confidences, the level of humility on which Blessed Paul lived.

The last lines written in his hand are in the form of a pretty sonnet in Italian, perfectly constructed, perfectly rhymed. The humanist still remains beneath the hermit and saint, and he keeps his good humor. With an irony free of bitterness, a calm sincerity, this detached man confesses that he still loves life:

> From this earthly prison wherein I have been
> A constant recluse for fifty-two years,
> I long to go forth when the way is barred,
> Yet long to stay when the way is clear.
>
> I know well that this is a miserable state,
> Yet I accept my lasting confinement.
> Long use has made it such a habit
> That I fear deliverance from my affliction.
>
> Thus I both hate and love my flesh,
> Its society I both like and loathe.
> I wish for an escape that I would refuse.
>
> And so I long to flee this misery,
> Yet I regret having to leave the Company.
> I am just as sorry to stay as to leave.

He did not have to make a choice. Providence had chosen for him. In June 1528, he had left Rome for Mount Soracte, where he was to found a Hermitage. He was overcome with fever. At the end of the journey, he felt that his end was near. But it happened that a hermit of Camaldoli, Gregory of Bergamo, was in the region. He heard that there was a sick confrere on the Soracte. He hastened to climb up to him. And so Paul Giustiniani, ever famished for solitude but never consenting to isolation, had the grace of dying, on the twenty-eighth of June, in the arms of a friend.

BLESSED PAUL GIUSTINIANI IN THE HISTORY OF THE EREMITIC LIFE

A great work is always the reflection of an intense personality. In order to understand the role of Blessed Paul Giustiniani in the development of the institutions of the eremitic life, it was therefore necessary to have him recount his life himself and to cite the innumerable texts in which he has spoken to us of his personal vocation. His life explains his work: it is the illustration and the manifestation of his ideal, the projection and the realization of it.

He himself interpreted his existence as a search for solitude. Toward the end of his life, when as from a summit he looks upon the stages he has traversed, he grasps the meaning. He sees the detours on the road, but he discerns the direction where the Lord was leading him. He penetrates better than anyone the logic of his existence, guided by God, marked out by His signs. Now, the dominant idea that secures the unity of all his activity, exterior or private, the continuity of all his steps in the midst of vicissitudes, is that he cannot gain salvation without solitude: his life is an incessant flight toward solitude, a series of departures toward that goal which escapes him and which, at last, he attains.

His love and, so to speak, his instinct for solitude, push him irresistibly toward two kinds of effort: to seek solitude, and to people it. He wishes to lead the solitary life, but he does not wish to lead it by himself, for he feels called to help other souls, who also seek it, to enjoy its benefits. To fulfill this double task that his vocation imposes upon him, he is induced, on the one hand, to reform the Hermitage of Camaldoli, and on the other, to enlarge its dimensions more and more. This double undertaking overwhelms him with cares. As he wishes to plunge further into solitude, occupations pursue him, dignities try to take possession of him. At the same time, his labor to restore the eremitic life and to gather to it those who are taking refuge in it draws the opposition of all those who share neither his ideal nor his zeal. And so his life is no longer just a search for solitude, but it becomes, little by little, a struggle for solitude.

His soul is continually vexed by this sort of contradiction between that to which he aspires and the means he is obliged to employ to attain it. He tends toward quietness of spirit from his youth. The Hermitage of Camaldoli allows him to enjoy it during his noviceship. But as soon as he is professed, a parenthesis of seven years of imperfect solitude begins in his life: his friend Quirini, more a man of action than he, pushes him to take in hand the reform of the Hermitage and of the entire Camaldolese order. From reformer in spite of himself, Paul Giustiniani next becomes head of an order and superior without title, while expecting to be nominated superior in spite of himself. One solution remains for him: he leaves Camaldoli. This sacrifice — for his departure was not a complete break — at first only launches him toward some new battles. But little by little, the storms are calmed. And in extreme poverty, in the midst of a joy that nothing can anymore alter, his life draws to a close in a kind of sorrowful and tranquil blaze of glory.

The first biographer of Blessed Giustiniani called him a second Romuald. It is always hard to compare two figures who lived many centuries apart. In the present instance the comparison is rendered still more difficult by the fact that the first of these personages is still little known: the sources are neither very numerous nor very explicit and they have not yet been studied with all the critical rigor necessary. Therefore it is only with reserve, in view of the points that new researches will bring to bear, that after having related the life of

Blessed Giustiniani, we can attempt to situate his work in the history of monastic and eremitic institutions.

Saint Romuald had entered a cenobitic monastery. He spent three years there, after which he definitively embraced the eremitic life. The holiness of his life was not slow in attracting to him a multitude of disciples. For them, he founded or reformed a great number of hermitages and also of monasteries. He knew that not all monks are called to the eremitic life, this vocation being by far the less frequent. The characteristic of Saint Romuald's hermitages is that one leads there a life in which the properly eremitic observances, inspired by the life of the Fathers of the Desert, are united harmoniously to certain cenobitic observances inspired by the *Rule of Saint Benedict*. So although this is not a purely eremitic life, yet it merits to be called eremitic because all its observances are ordered to the perfection of the eremitic life. Thus it is accessible to those who come directly from the world, and passage through a monastery is no longer strictly necessary for all.

The characteristic of Saint Romuald's monasteries is the almost eremitic kind of life that he imposes on abbots. Romuald never ceases advising them to live an austere life and to leave their cells as little as possible. They ought to visit the brethren only once a week. When the monastery is near a hermitage, which frequently happens, Romuald wishes the abbot to fix his residence there; likewise he desires that the monastery have no other superior than that of the hermitage. As for the brethren, he untiringly recommends the strict observance of the *Rule of Saint Benedict* to them. When one reflects upon the wholly secular life that abbots then lived, and upon the consequences for monastic discipline that resulted from this, one easily understands why Saint Romuald sought to place the cenobites in contact with the hermits. These latter, actually, could not but exercise a salutary influence on the cenobites by their life, more withdrawn from the world and more austere, and stimulate their generosity by recalling to them the essential duties of their state.

Among the numerous foundations of Saint Romuald, that of Camaldoli occupies a privileged place. Camaldoli had been in the beginning only a little hermitage consisting of five cells, grouped around a chapel, and a hospice to receive the poor and pilgrims. But the fervor of the first hermits was not slow to attract vocations. Camaldoli developed rapidly and ended by becoming the center of a congregation made up not only of hermitages, but of monasteries as well. In this, Camaldoli prolonged the work of Saint Romuald. Between the hermits and the cenobites, there was but little difference. In fact, all abstained from meat, all rose at night for prayer, fasts were frequent, silence habitual, spiritual reading, meditation, and prayer occupied an important place in the life of all. Finally, all obeyed the prior of Camaldoli, who was the superior general of the congregation. As in the time of Saint Romuald, the hermits exercised a beneficent influence upon the cenobites.

But these latter soon became by far the more numerous, and their influence began to substitute itself for that of the hermits. Some important decisions were taken at the general chapter of 1273, which revealed the transformation that had taken place in spirits. The prior of Camaldoli ceased to be the superior general of the congregation, and admission to the Hermitage was put under these two conditions: one must be at least twenty-five years of age and have spent three years in a monastery. These decisions reversed the roles. Now it was the cenobites who became the masters of the situation. Moreover, the cenobites organized studies in the manner of the great orders of the thirteenth century. They likewise brought in professors from the outside whenever it seemed necessary to them. Certain monasteries, such as that of Florence, became centers of humanism. The care of souls became one of the principal occupations of the cenobites.

The hermits continued to live the contemplative life in their solitude, whereas in the monasteries the cenobites lived, quite near to men, what was called the active life. Now action, which is easier than contemplation, becomes a temptation for the contemplative as soon as he finds the means of giving himself over to it in the very setting in which his life unfolds. Thus it was that the "better part" was no longer cultivated except by a small number, the active life having become the portion of the majority in the Camaldolese order.

Such was the situation Blessed Paul Giustiniani found himself presented with. His whole work consisted in bringing in remedies, following an impulse that came to him from far beyond himself. Rather than consent to an institutional state contrary to its original purpose, he was forced to provoke a crisis in the order. It broke out, and he exerted himself to resolve it. He was quite fortunate to restore the Hermitage of Camaldoli. But when he wanted to enlarge it and multiply it, so as to procure for all those God called to the eremitic life the possibility to realize their vocation, he ran into the opposition of the totality of the order, organized in accordance with cenobitism. In addition, he who had come to seek solitude at Camaldoli was unceasingly overwhelmed by business. He bided his time for several years, then he made up his mind to leave. He withdrew to a little hermitage dependent on Camaldoli in hope of finding there solitude at last, stoutly determined to flee, if necessary, as far as the Indies. He lived there with three companions, in extreme poverty, happy to have found solitude at last. But, as formerly at Camaldoli, the vocations were not slow to present themselves; the hermitage became too small and it was necessary to found new ones. Finally, he asked and obtained from the superiors of the congregation of Camaldoli and of Saint Michael of Murano the official erection of his new foundation, which received the name "Company of the Hermits of Saint Romuald." On the occasion of the first general chapter, he drafted new constitutions, which only differed from those of the hermitage of Camaldoli by greater poverty and austerity. For all that is not specified, he refers explicitly to the *Rule of the Eremitic Life*. Some years after the death of Blessed Paul, his sons will be seen raising up the hermitage of Monte Corona, modeled on that of Camaldoli and including a hospice. Therefore, nothing is changed in the new foundation. It is precisely such an eremitic life as Saint Romuald organized and as Blessed Paul himself restored at Camaldoli.

Must we reproach Blessed Giustiniani for not having founded monasteries also, as Saint Romuald did? No text of his permits us to affirm that he systematically suppressed them. Their absence, on the contrary, is easily explained. Blessed Paul judged with reason that he could receive novices directly; in this he only takes up again a tradition interrupted in 1273. All those who presented themselves to him were religious or secular priests, fitted consequently to enter the hermitage straight off. In addition, given his relations with his cenobitic confreres, the foundation of a new monastery would have certainly given rise to a good number of difficulties for him.

As soon as one admits that the hermitage of Saint Romuald does not require a monastery for the formation of future hermits, there is no longer any difficulty in admitting that Blessed Paul was not obliged in the least to found them beside his hermitages if he wanted to remain faithful to the ideal of Saint Romuald. Blessed Giustiniani is essentially the restorer of the eremitic work of Saint Romuald. By uniting his hermitages in a congregation, he has furthermore given his reform a stability that has enabled it to last until our days and, it is to be hoped, will enable it to last for a long time yet for the good of the Church.

Appendix

The Reform of 1513
and the Departure of 1520

The work of Blessed Paul Giustiniani was quite justly characterized, in the beginning of the eighteenth century, by Dom Edward Baroncini [Vigilucci, pp. 99-100]. This hermit lived at the Hermitage of Camaldoli, where his grave is held in veneration because of the example of lofty virtue that he left. A recluse, he had all the documents in the archives brought to his cell, and it was thus that he drew up, according to actual sources, his *Chronicle of Camaldoli from the Year 1012 to the Year 1712*. His account is free of bias and of passion. For the period when Giustiniani lived, his witness is even more precious in that Dom Baroncini says several times that he has used the notes and manuscripts of Gregory of Bergamo, major of the Hermitage at the time of Blessed Paul.

The expressions that the chronicler employs several times to characterize the work of Giustiniani coincide with those of the Blessed himself: the work of Giustiniani consisted in "liberating" the Hermitage. In order to liberate the Hermitage from the ascendancy of the cenobites, it was necessary, as Blessed Paul says, "to liberate it from the general-for-life," who lent himself to the domination of the cenobites over the Hermitage; it was less a question of a tyranny exercised by Delfino in person than an influence surrendered, through weakness, to cenobites opposed to the Hermitage and to the eremitic life. The reform accomplished in 1513 by Quirini and Giustiniani only tended to make the Hermitage regain its rights and its independence and, as Baroncini says, "its freedom and its privileges." Originally Fontebuono had to be dependent upon the Hermitage and to come to the aid of the hermits. In fact, the Hermitage found itself subject to Fontebuono. According to Baroncini, Fontebuono was not supposed to be a monastery, but a simple hostelry for the servants of the Hermitage; in fact, Fontebuono was a monastery and had become the center of attraction: the primitive equilibrium had been upset, the order had been reversed. This is the situation that the reform of 1513 attempted to remedy.

> For Giustiniani indeed accomplished and obtained many things for the freedom and advantage of the Hermitage, by the favor and intervention of Lord Julian de' Medici. Among these is certainly included the shaking off of the long-standing servitude, the abasement of the General Delfino himself, and the removal of all the monks from the goods and places of Camaldoli....
>
> The prior and all the monks were banished from the monastery of Fontebuono, and it was reduced, as of old, to a simple hospice of the Hermitage, only its servants dwelling there.

The attempt at reform of 1513 failed partially in this sense, that Blessed Paul did not succeed in reforming the cenobites, nor in reestablishing the beneficial relations between them and the hermits that had characterized the early stages of the congregation of Camaldoli. The peace between the Hermitage on the one hand, and Fontebuono and the other monasteries of the order on the other, was only maintained during the following years by the presence of Giustiniani at the Hermitage. And then, after 1520, it was preserved by his influence and the action that he did not cease to exercise, thanks to his connections with those of high station, in favor of the Hermitage that he had left. But shortly after his death, in 1528, other conflicts rendered necessary a new separation between the hermitage and the monasteries. The whole subsequent history of the Camaldolese order is merely that of conflicts between the hermits of the Hermitage of Camaldoli and the cenobites of seventeen monasteries: unions and divisions that brought on disputes without end. These are the disturbances that Giustiniani had cut short by refraining from founding new monasteries. Therefore, the foundation of 1520 is a prolongation of the reform of 1513. This latter had aimed at reestablishing good relations between the Hermitage and the monasteries; confronted with the failure of this attempt, the solution that Giustiniani chose was a must. In fact, for some centuries the "Hermitage-monasteries" duality no longer was, and no longer could become once more, a source of benefits for the cenobites, but it remained for the hermits a source of continual trouble. Dom Baroncini has placed the work of Giustiniani back into this whole historical context; some excerpts from his chronicle will spare us from reading a lengthy account:

Then for the first time the Camaldolese monks, long distinguished in reality by their manner of life, were set apart by the name of cenobites and conventuals. In fact, at the beginning of the order, they dwelt at the Hermitage of Camaldoli itself, observing the food, dress, customs, and laws handed down by the prior Rudolph from the year 1080. And they were distinguished from the other monks, who inhabited places and monasteries given to or associated with the Hermitage, by unwritten usages and institutions, militating however under the same prior general of the order. Little by little, certain monasteries with special usages and laws elected their own superiors and prelates, whom the general of the order used to confirm. On account of this, they were called cenobites, to distinguish them from the others. And so in the year 1252 rules were prescribed for all of them, whether cenobites or others, by the Prior General Martin, and they were observed by them for a long time together with the decrees and statutes of the general chapters. But when those grew in number who dwelt in the many monasteries and in the temporal benefices (whether of the Hermitage itself or of the principal monasteries), they caused their monasteries to fall under commendam [NCE 4:9], since they gave themselves over more and more to ownership, a lax way of life, and ambition. Accordingly many, roaming through the order and outside of it, were serving at secular business and also in ecclesiastical offices. But to remove the just-mentioned commendam, our major superiors ordered unions and congregations of certain monasteries, first of Romandiola in the year 1444, then Murano and Lombardy in 1488, with fixed rules and chapters that they furnished with apostolic approval.

Meanwhile, those monks multiplied who at their pleasure were living temporarily in various places of the order with the leave of their prelates, bound neither to the monastery of their profession nor to any particular laws. Besides, Peter Delfino showed easy compliance in admitting anyone whomsoever to profession at Fontebuono, so that many, sojourning here and there throughout the order, acquired the name of conventuals by antiphrasis. In fact, the number of these conventuals far exceeded that of the cenobites. Wherefore decrees of reform were prescribed by privilege of Pope Leo X and imposed on the cenobitical and on the observant and especially on the conventual monks. It was commanded that the conventual prelates, whether perpetual or temporary, confer the religious habit upon no one in the future nor admit anyone to profession....

Next, Baroncini summarizes Pope Leo X's bull of July 4, 1513, reforming Camaldoli and uniting the Hermitage to the congregation of Murano. Then he gives the following historical commentary on that union:

But there soon arose so many big disagreements from this congregation of the Holy Hermitage and Saint Michael of Murano that they were disputed until 1530, as is recorded in their annals. And so the disunion that had become necessary was obtained by the entreaties of the hermits in 1531, so that they might be more at leisure for quiet and solitude. And so it was decreed and prescribed by an apostolic brief given in the sixth year of Pope Clement VII. But the following year, 1532, an act of reunion was negotiated through the intervention of the cardinal protector, Lord Anthony Pucci, with many agreements between the Lord General Paul of Lodi and the visitators of the order and the Lord Prior Stephen of Venice, major, on the one side, and representatives of the Hermitage on the other, by the hand of the cameral notary Francis of Attavantis. This document was confirmed by an apostolic bull of May 18 in the ninth year of Pope Clement and approved in 1546 by the general chapter held on the island of Martana under the presidency of the Lord Cardinal Protector Robert Pucci. Since none the less some of the monks did not cease to disturb the Holy Hermitage and the hospice of greater Camaldoli, that is, Fontebuono, they were warned under pain of censure by a *motu proprio* of 1550. Finally the hermits, taught by long experience how union with such monks could harm the hermitage and their quiet and bring damage to their property, assembled in chapter in 1606, decreed that entire separation and disunion ought to be obtained. Three hermits were delegated to protest to the chapter of Classe because the points agreed upon in the union had not been kept. But this separation was not decreed until 1616, by the apostolic visitator Jerome Ferretti.

In fact, union was newly proposed to the chapter of the hermits in 1623, and some were deputed to present the articles of union to them. But the Lord Cardinal Protector de Rivarola was not pleased. Still the very major of the Hermitage, Dom Anthony Bonaventuri, together with the general of the order, Dom Egidio Romano, came to mutual agreement on certain points and restored the brief of union on April 30, 1626. The same day, they convened the chapter of the hermits and promised by oath, with one accord, the liberty of the Hermitage itself.... But the union proved to be in vain and was revoked in 1629.... Once again in 1636, the monks and abbots of the province of Tuscany proposed a union with the Holy Hermitage.... Some articles for the union of monks with the Holy Hermitage were also proposed in 1646, but together with the new form of union, they came to nothing.

After this historical commentary on the reform of 1513, Baroncini takes up again the story of the events of 1513 and the following years:

On November 28 (1513), it was agreed and established for the future by Dom Paul Orlandini of Florence, vicar of the Camaldolese congregation, and the visitators, in lieu and in the name of the diet of the congregation, and Dom John Baptist de Lucca, major, and Peter Quirini and Paul Giustiniani, hermits, in the name of the hermits' chapter of the Holy Hermitage, that the monastery of Fontebuono should be considered for the future as one of the seventeen principal monasteries of the order. The prior however, being also cellarer, will be subject to the chapter of the Hermitage, which can remove him whenever it seems right. He will have voice in the general chapter also, as do the other prelates of the order. But whenever it seems good to the chapter of the Hermitage, the same monastery of Fontebuono can be reduced to a simple hospice of the Hermitage, inhabited only by its attendants....

But it was decreed in the chapter of Classe in 1515, on account of the many and burdensome expenses, whether for the pension of the General Peter Delfino or other outlays, that the monastery of Fontebuono should be reduced to a simple hospice for the Hermitage and its servants, both prior and monks being wholly removed.... Likewise it had already been ordered a little while before in 1512 that, following the exclusion of all the servants of Peter Delfino, the monastery was to be reduced to a simple hospice of the Hermitage and for the future would be provided with servants at the bidding of the hermits.

Although Peter Delfino himself had certainly been excluded from the Hermitage, from Fontebuono, and from the Musolea, as much by the above-mentioned brief as by a special one for him, yet moved by the counsel of the conventuals or by some malcontents of the congregation (as Fr. Gregory of Bergamo notes in his memoirs), he came to Fontebuono in 1521. This was under the pretext of convoking the general chapter or of zeal for reforming religion, but really with a mind to resume the former regime and administration. The hermit fathers replied to him that the manner of convoking the chapter was regulated by privilege of Pope Leo, and that without the consent of the congregation it would be utterly invalid and void. Having ascertained, therefore, that the minds of the hermits were contrary to him, beyond what he had decided and premeditated, he departed from Florence a little later and returned to Venice.

After having spoken of the decree of Leo X of February 2, 1515, forbidding the crowd to invade the Hermitage on the feast of Saint Romuald and on other occasions and stipulating that they no longer be given hospitality, Baroncini adds:

> It charged that the duty of hospitality, ordered by the ancient Fathers and kept down to the present, be exercised in the hospice of Fontebuono toward men of whatever condition and rank. While it indeed prohibited women of whatever age from entering the enclosure of the monastery, it granted, however, that they be served food and other necessary things outside of the monastery.

There follows the account of the difficulties encountered by the Hermitage due to the cenobites and their accomplices:

> 1525. As soon as the death of the General Peter Delfino became known (who, as was reported, died at Saint Michael of Murano on January 17th), the hermits of Camaldoli gathered in chapter on the 19th and, according to the prescribed privileges of the Hermitage, elected Dom John Baptist de Lucca (who was prior of the Holy Hermitage) and commanded that there be conferred upon him the firm possession of the priorship itself. And thereupon, to defend the freedom of the Hermitage against any sort of disturbance on the part of the villagers and neighbors (who were very much in favor of the prior of the monks and his government), they stationed some men of Anghiari to guard Camaldoli....

For in fact there arose a little later at the Hermitage of Camaldoli another conflict, provoked by the chapter of the monks of Classe because of the supporters of the general Paul of Lodi.... The hermits, forestalling the action, had sent letters to the aforementioned chapter, protesting the nullity of any acts contrary to the liberty and privileges of the Hermitage....

1527. The sack of Fontebuono by the abbot Basil and his recall and condemnation.

1528. The general chapter of the congregation took place at Ravenna in the month of May...and it was established that for the future the residence of the general would be at Fontebuono. As soon as the hermits found out about this...considering this sort of statute to be gravely prejudicial to the liberty and the privileges of the Hermitage itself, they drew up letters of protest....

The experiences reported by these texts make one think that it was no longer possible to unite the cenobites and the hermits. The situation that Giustiniani wanted to remedy was not brought about by a fleeting crisis; it had existed for a long time and was bound to prolong itself for quite a long time after him. But he had found peace for his hermits, he had secured their freedom in the face of all the intrigues of the cenobites, by admitting only hermitages in his foundation. The stages of his work for the liberation of the eremitic life were, therefore, the following:

1. At the general chapter of 1513 at Florence, the independence of the Hermitage regarding Fontebuono had been affirmed; Fontebuono had been made dependent once again upon the Hermitage.
2. By the capitular decision of November 28, 1513, Fontebuono had been reduced to being merely one of the seventeen monasteries of the congregation.
3. By the decision of the general chapter at Ravenna in 1515 and

by the brief of Leo X of February 6, 1515, Fontebuono had been reduced to being no longer a monastery, but only a hospice.

4. The foundation of 1520 definitively sanctioned the independence of the hermitages, which could henceforth freely grow and multiply.

BEA: SERVVS DEI PAVLVS IVSTINIANVS PATR: VEN
EREM: CAM: EIVSDĒ ORD: PROPAG ET MONTIS CORONÆ FVNDATOR

Blessed Paul Giustiniani

+ In nomine Dñi nri Jesu Christi

INCIPIT EREMITICE VITE REGVLA

Sicut extra christiane fidei pietatem nulla est uiuendi ratio que ad eterna ualeat producere beatitudine, ita in numerosa christi fidelium uniuersitate multi sunt ordines plurimeque uiuendi institutiones quibus ad celestem patriam tendere et ad uere felicitatis immortale gloriam possumus peruenire. Inter omnes autem nulla est christiane uite regula que facilius ac perfectius et presentis uite suauissima tranquilitate et future optatissima felicitate quam solitarie et eremitice uite recta institutione suis prestare possit sectatoribus. Hec enim ceteris omnibus semitis artis facilius ad celestis regni ipsam beatitudinem que se concomitantur dirigit gressus et tantum interest quod se eius gradientibus mortalibus huius uite presentis tranquilitate ut ceteris alibi degentibus non quaquam celestem delitiarum exhibeat portionem. Nam et ab his omnibus que in hac mortali tahs peregrinatione humanas mentes commouere ac perturbare solent quam maxime homines alienos facit et occasiones omnes adimens delinquenti bonis operibus insistendi ui quodammodo necessitatis imponit onde et mortales interea homines non multum angelis ipares efficit et ad angelicam illos comprehenso tramite prouehit sublimitatem. Habuit singularis hec conuersatio pretereuntis felicioribus seculis multifarios institutores preclaros laudatores sectatores

Sacro Eremo Tuscolano

Monte Cucco

Bielany

Bieniszew

Herrera

Canonical Visitation in Colombia, 2000

El Greco, *Alegoría de la Orden Camaldulense*

Saint Romuald presenting Monte Corona
(Detail; 16th century, artist unknown)

Monte Corona today

ALONE WITH GOD

Dom Jean Leclercq

Preface

by Thomas Merton

Just as the Church of God can never be without martyrs, so too she can never be without solitaries, for the hermit, like the martyr, is the most eloquent witness of the Risen Christ. It was on the night of Easter that the Risen Savior breathed upon His Apostles, that they might receive of His Spirit, Who had not been given before because Christ was not yet glorified. Saint Paul has told us that all who are sons of God are activated and moved by the Spirit of God. They have the Spirit of Christ because they belong to Christ. Having His Spirit, they live no longer according to the flesh but according to the Spirit. *Qui vero secundum Spiritum sunt, quae sunt Spiritus sentiunt.*[1] Therefore they are of one mind and one Spirit with Jesus Christ.

Now at the beginning of His public life, Jesus was led into the desert by the Spirit, that He might engage in single combat with the devil. The struggle in the desert was the prelude to the struggle in the Garden of the Agony. This last was the exemplar and meritorious cause of the charity of all the martyrs and all the hermits who would be tested, like Christ himself, in the furnace of tribulation because they were pleasing to God. The Church of God, triumphing in her martyrs and ascetics, would thus be able to declare with Christ Himself: "The prince of this world indeed comes, and he has no part in me: but he comes that the world may know that I love the Father!"[2]

There must, therefore, be hermits. Nor is this only because there will always be men who desire solitude. The Christian hermit is one

---

[1] Rom 8:5. "To live the life of the Spirit is to think the thoughts of the Spirit."
[2] Jn 14:30-31.

who is led into the desert by the Spirit, not by the flesh, even though he may well have a natural inclination to live alone. Our own time has seen hermits like the Dominican, Père Vayssière, who entered the Order of Preachers knowing that he wanted to preach the Gospel, and completely unaware that he would spend most of his life in solitude at La Sainte Baume. Nor must there always be hermits, merely because there are always contemplative souls, or because the contemplative naturally seeks physical solitude (for without the efficacious desire of exterior solitude, interior solitude will always remain a fantasy or an illusion). The true reason for the persistence of hermits even in ages which are most hostile to the solitary ideal is that the exigencies of Christian life *demand* that there be hermits. The Kingdom of God would be incomplete without them, for they are the men who seek God alone with the most absolute and undaunted and uncompromising singleness of heart. If we have forgotten that the Fathers of the Church assigned to the hermit a high, even the highest place among all Christian vocations, a modern theologian, Dom Anselm Stolz, is there to remind us of the fact.[3] And now another Benedictine, Dom Jean Leclercq, has added an important volume to the slowly growing collection of works on the solitary life appearing in our own time.

This book is all the more important because it introduces us to a hermit as interesting as he is unknown: a surprising figure, rising up almost unaccountably in the Italy of Raphael and Machiavelli, Castiglione and Michelangelo Buonarotti. Paul Giustiniani, as we learn from the brief note on his life which opens the author's introduction, became a novice at Camaldoli in 1510 — that is to say that he entered the most ancient of the eremitical orders that have survived in the Western Church. Camaldoli goes back to the tenth century and Saint Romuald. Less famous than the Chartreuse, Camaldoli nevertheless has retained more of the aspect of an ancient "*laura*" than we would find in any Chartreuse. The Camaldolese idea is simply to apply the

---

[3] In *L'ascèse chrétienne*. Chevetogne: 1948.

Rule of Saint Benedict to the eremitical life. Saint Benedict declared, of course, that his *Rule* was written for cenobites, but he also holds the solitary life in high honor, and suggests that certain monks, after a long probation in the monastery, may be called by God to a hermitage. Saint Romuald made it possible for monks to have solitude without losing anything of the *bonum obedientiae*, that blessing of obedience which is the treasure of monastic life, and without departing from that life in common, the life of fraternal charity, which is the security of all who do not feel themselves equal to the heroism of another Anthony. The *Sacro Eremo* of Camaldoli is, therefore, a community of hermits, a village of ancient cells hidden in a pine forest several thousand feet above sea level in the Apennines behind Arezzo.

Paul Giustiniani entered Camaldoli at a time when the fervor had lost some of its ancient heat, and he left it for a stricter solitude. Eventually he was to start a new eremitical congregation of his own, the hermits of Montecorona, who still have a community at Frascati outside Rome, and several others in Italy, Spain, Poland, and the United States.[4] Giustiniani thus bears the same relation to Camaldoli as the Abbé de Rancé does to the Order of Cîteaux, and, in another sense, as Dom Innocent Le Masson does to the Chartreuse. Like each of these great men, Paul Giustiniani seeks to rekindle the ancient fire that is burning low in an age that has no love for asceticism, for contemplation, or for solitude. It is therefore of the greatest interest to have at our disposal a volume that brings together from his various works, most of which are inaccessible, a complete doctrine of the solitary life.

Let us now turn to the doctrine of Blessed Paul, whose name recalls to our minds the half-legendary figure of the "first hermit" whom Saint Anthony is supposed to have discovered in the cave where he had lived for over a hundred years unknown to men. The eremitical

---

[4] A new foundation, which is located near McConnelsville, Ohio, was established in September, 1959.

life is above all solitary. Saint Romuald chose to settle in the once inviolable forests of Camaldoli and to seek God in a solitude that was *sacred*, that is to say entirely consecrated to Him. The inviolable character of "holy solitude" is a witness to the infinite transcendence of Him whose holiness elevates Him above all things. In order to seek Him Who is inaccessible the hermit himself becomes inaccessible. But within the little village of cells centered about the Church of the *Eremo* is a yet more perfect solitude — that of each hermit's own cell. Within the cell is the hermit himself, in the solitude of his own soul. But — and this is the ultimate test of solitude — the hermit is not alone with himself — for that would not be a sacred loneliness. Holiness is life. Holy solitude is nourished with the Bread of Life and drinks deep at the very Fountain of all Life. The solitude of a soul enclosed within itself is death. And so the authentic, the really sacred solitude is the infinite solitude of God Himself, Alone, in Whom the hermits are alone.

From this obligation to seek interior solitude flow all the other demands made upon the hermit, the other essential obligations of his state: silence, stability, recollection, mortification, labor, fasting, vigils, and prayer. These detach the soul from all that is not God. They are not peculiar to the hermit. They belong to the monastic life wherever it is found. But the hermit has a very special obligation to practice them, without, however, departing from discretion which is one of the most important virtues of the solitary. After all, it is discretion which teaches us to live by the interior guidance of the Holy Spirit. It is discretion which teaches us to distinguish between the voice of the Spirit and the voice of the flesh or of the evil one. Discretion does not permit us to be cowards, but neither does it allow us to fall headlong into the abyss of vanity, pride, or presumption. Without discretion, the solitary life ends fatally in disaster. In the true spirit of Saint Benedict, Paul Giustiniani declares that even in the hermitage the best mortifications are those which are not of our own choice, and that even the hermit should seek to please God more by great fidelity in his ordinary duties than by extraordinary feats of ascetic heroism. The life of the solitary will be a continual warfare, in which the flesh fights not only against the spirit but against the flesh itself and in which the spirit also fights not only against flesh but even against the spirit. It is here, in this inexpressible rending of his own poverty, that the hermit enters, like Christ, into the arena where he wages the combat that can never be told to anyone. This is the battle that is seen by no one except God, and whose vicissitudes are so terrible that when victory comes at last, the total poverty and emptiness of the victor are so absolute that there is no longer any place in his heart for pride.

Such is the *eremitica puritas*, the hermit's purity, which opens the way for contemplation. Without this "annihilation" the solitary might perhaps be tempted to seek rest in the consolations of God for their own sake. He might enjoy a selfish and self-complacent solitude in which he was delivered from responsibilities and inundated with supernatural favors. In words that remind us of Saint John of the Cross, Paul Giustiniani speaks of the false contemplatives who "are displeased by everything that deprives them of the rest they think they have found in God but which they seek, really, in themselves. Their only care is to seek after peace, not in things below them, not in themselves, but in God; however they desire this peace not for the glory of God, but out of love for themselves."

Nor does the sacredness of solitude and the true eremitic purity allow the hermit to become absorbed in a zeal that does not extend beyond the welfare or reputation of his own monastery and his own order, still less beyond his own progress and his own virtues. A life alone with God is something too vast to include such limited objectives within its range. It reaches up to God Himself, and in doing so, embraces the whole Church of God. Meanwhile, the hermit supports this interior poverty of spirit with the greatest exterior poverty. He must live like the poorest of the poor. *Eremitica puritas* is the peace of one who is content with bare necessities. Such peace is impossible where poverty is a mere matter of exterior form. The hermit is not one who, though deprived of the right to possess them, actually has the use of better objects and enjoys more plentiful comforts than could ever be afforded by the materially poor. The eremitical community itself must be a poor community. And although this simplicity guarantees the hermit a high place in the Church, he himself will remember that his elevation is in reality a matter of humility and abjection. He takes no part in the active affairs of the Church because he is too poor to merit a place in them. For him to accept prelacy would be an infidelity because it would be an act of presumption. Paul Giustiniani pursues this subject of poverty into the most remote corners of the hermit's soul. The solitary will not even pride himself on his strict observances, or compare himself with religious of other orders. He will avoid the supreme folly of those who, having nothing in the world but their humility, lose even that by boasting of it! By this perfect forgetfulness of himself, the hermit merits to be called the successor of the martyrs.

There is a positive side to all this. Solitude is not sought for its own sake. If the eremitical life is the highest form of Christianity it is because the hermit aspires more than anyone else to perfect union with Christ. Jesus Himself is the living rule of the hermit, just as He is the model of every religious. It is Christ Himself Who calls us into solitude, exacting of us a clean break with the world and with our past, just as He did of Saint Anthony. Perhaps more than any other the solitary life demands the presence of the Man Christ Who lives and suffers in us. Even if we worshiped the one true God in the desert, without the Incarnate Word our solitude would be less than human and therefore far short of the divine: without Him no one comes to the Father. Without Jesus we all too easily fulfil the words of Pascal — "*qui veut faire l'ange, fait la bête*" ["He who would play the angel ends by playing the beast"]. Solitude therefore must translate itself into the three words: *cum Christo vivere* — to live with Christ. Solitude is a fortress that protects the heart against all that is not Christ, and its only function is to allow Christ to live in us. Solitude spiritualizes the whole man, transforms him, body and soul, from a carnal to a spiritual being. It can only do so in the Spirit of Christ Who elevates our whole being in God, and does not divide man's personality against itself like those false asceticisms which Saint Paul knew to be enemies of the Cross of Christ.

In a hymn to this solitude which is "too unknown," Giustiniani says: "It is thou that announcest the coming of the Holy Spirit: and not only announcest Him, but bringest Him into the human heart just as the dawn, which announces the day, brings to our eyes the brightness of the sun."

This brings us to the mystical doctrine of Paul Giustiniani who, like the Fathers of the Church, believed that the eremitical life was ordered exclusively for contemplation and was the only purely contemplative life. Like the Fathers, also, when he speaks of contemplation he means mystical contemplation. This is without doubt the most interesting and important part of the book. In pages that remind us now of Saint Catherine of Genoa, now of Saint Bernard, now even of John Ruysbroeck, Paul Giustiniani teaches us a doctrine elevated but sure, since his whole emphasis is on the coincidence of humility and greatness in the experience of union. The way of contemplation is never exalted, and the hermit must aspire to be "lifted up" in no other way than on the Cross, with Christ. He does not reach the Father except through the abjection of Christ, Who lives again in the hermit that *exinanivit semetipsum* ["He emptied Himself," Phil 2:7] by which He merited for us a share in His sonship and in His divine glory. Reading the pages of Giustiniani on annihilation, we are reminded of Saint John of the Cross, who describes the soul that is purified and ready for union with God in these terms: "In this detachment the spiritual soul finds its quiet and repose; for, since it covets nothing, nothing wearies it when it is lifted up, and nothing oppresses it when it is cast down, because it is in the center of its humility; but when it covets anything, at that very moment it becomes wearied."[5]

---

[5]   *The Ascent of Mount Carmel*. I, Chapter 13, in *The Complete Works of Saint John of the Cross*, translated by Allison Peers. Burns and Oates, 1935. I, p. 60.

The whole purpose of the solitary life is to bring the soul into "the center of her humility" and to keep it there. The hermit does not pretend to have acquired any esoteric secret or any exalted technique by which he penetrates into the mystery of God. His only secret is the humility and poverty of Christ and the knowledge that God lifts up those who have fallen: *Dominus erigit elisos.* Without this humility, the contemplative can be a prey to "all the illusions." For "the true servants of Christ love God with all their being, and do not love themselves at all. They keep themselves so perfectly under the guardianship of humility as to be known by God alone, but unknown to men."

But once he is perfectly united with the poverty and humility of Christ crucified, the solitary lives entirely by the life and Spirit of Christ. He can therefore be transformed and elevated to the perfection of selfless love for God, that love in which he no longer knows himself or anything else, but only God alone. This is the culmination of mystical love in which the contemplative "loves God in God." It is here that we detect interesting resonances from the doctrine of Ruysbroeck. Whether or not Giustiniani knew the Flemish mystic, a comparison between them might be interesting. This is not the place for it. What is more important here is to notice that this love for God in God, which is the highest perfection of the solitary and contemplative life, is also the perfect justification of the hermit's utility to the rest of the Church.

The hermit is not to be considered a "dynamo" of apostolic power in the crude sense of a machine actively producing a great quantity of prayers and works of penance for the salvation of souls. We have seen that quantity becomes a negligible factor in the life of *eremitica puritas.* The solitary should not seek to replace his lost possessions by merely numerical accumulation of prayers and good works over which he can gloat like a happy miser at the end of each day. In praying to God for souls, he realizes it is not so important to know the souls for whom he is praying, as *Him to Whom* he is praying. But the perfect love of God teaches him to find souls in God Himself. He discovers that the soul which is on fire with love for God actually loves herself and other men more in proportion as she thinks about herself and them less. Hence the paradox that the less the contemplative seems to love others and himself, the more he forgets them in order to direct all his love to God, the more he actually loves them and the better he serves their spiritual interests. Loving God in God, the solitary is perfectly united to that infinite Love with which God loves all things in Himself. Loving all things in Him, the hermit powerfully cooperates with the action of His love, drawing them to Himself. Thus he fulfils most efficaciously the purpose of his divine vocation which is to restore all things in Christ. Consequently the fruitfulness of the hermit in the Church of God depends on his fidelity to the call to solitude, obscurity, and abjection in Christ.

The doctrine of Paul Giustiniani is, therefore, a striking testimony to the primacy of contemplation and of the contemplative life in the Church. It does not follow from this that everyone who aspires to perfection should therefore seek to become a hermit. The eremitical life is a charism reserved for few. Most monks will remain in the cenobium. Nevertheless, the fact that the cenobitic life is safer and of wider appeal does not imply that the eremitical life is unsafe and has no appeal. The cenobium and the hermitage complete each other. If the cenobium disdains and repudiates the hermitage, it dooms itself to mediocrity. When the windows of the monastery no longer open out upon the vast horizons of the desert, the monastic community inevitably becomes immersed in vanity. All that is accidental, trivial, and accessory tends to assume a rank of high importance and to become the sole end of the monastic life. It is where monks have forgotten their potential destiny to solitude, that they allow themselves to run to seed in bickering about curiosities, or squandering their contemplative leisure in material cares.

This book should do something to remind us all of the monk's true destiny as a man of God. True, Paul Giustiniani lacks the freshness of Cassian and the Desert Fathers, the luminous simplicity of Saint

Benedict or Saint Gregory, even more the sober enthusiasm of Saint Bernard or the Greek Fathers. There is something in him of dryness which he contracted from the Stoics and from Scholastic philosophy. But the genuine spirit of the desert is there, and the contemplation which brightens his pages is unmistakably true.

In closing this preface, I might observe that it is perhaps something altogether new and unusual for a book on an Italian hermit to appear, written by a Benedictine in Luxemburg and prefaced by a Cistercian in the Southern United States. This joining together of Camaldoli, Monte Corona, Clervaux, and Gethsemani is surely significant. I dare to hope that it speaks very well for the union of the sons of Saint Benedict with one another in our time — a union in prayer and deep charity and mutual understanding. If it be true, as I think it is, then our monasticism indeed has a function in the world. And it proclaims to all who will hear it the solemn affirmation of Christ Who said: "Behold I am with you all days, even to the consummation of the world."[6]

FR. M. LOUIS MERTON
Abbey of Gethsemani

---

[6] Mt 28:20.

I

INTRODUCTION

The Life and Doctrine of Paul Giustiniani

Blessed Paul Giustiniani is one of those men of God who, in the Italian Renaissance, steadfastly upheld the primacy of the spiritual life over all the other forms of human culture. He was born in Venice in 1476 of a patrician family. Study absorbed him for many years, first in his own city, then at the University of Padua, and finally on the Island of Murano, where he sought a leisure entirely free of distraction. As a humanist imbued with Stoic doctrine, he renounced the pleasures of the flesh and turned increasingly towards God. Without forgetting Seneca and Cicero, whose books led to his conversion, he nourished his soul on the Bible, the Fathers of the Church, the monastic writers of the Middle Ages, and the great Scholastics. In 1510 at the age of thirty-four, he entered the Hermitage of Camaldoli as a novice. A year and a half later, shortly after he had pronounced his vows, he was drawn to reform the whole Camaldolese order. In 1520, after ten years of trouble and effort, he left the Hermitage of Camaldoli to seek out a still more solitary life in absolute indigence. Disciples came to him, with whom he founded the Company of the Hermits of Saint Romuald, which continues to exist under the name of the

Congregation of the Camaldolese Hermits of Montecorona. Since his death in 1528, his sons have called him Blessed. [1]

His many writings, which are almost entirely unpublished, [2] contain testimony of great historical value on many problems, as well as original and sound teaching. But in the midst of all other concerns, at the heart of Paul Giustiniani's teaching, are his convictions about the realities of the spiritual life. These give unity to his thought, and we must now examine them, having completed the sketch of his life. [3] Giustiniani was primarily a monk and a hermit: his spiritual doctrine, therefore, explains his whole work, reflects his education, and is connected with the experiences of his life. This doctrine is a source of nourishment for the Congregation that he founded and developed. To pick out the main themes of his spiritual doctrine will in no way exhaust the treasure but will merely offer samples of its value.

Paul Giustiniani's writings contain the elements of a complete doctrine on the eremitic life. His open-minded attitude, his wide culture, his extensive philosophical, literary, and theological formation that was typical of the highly developed civilization of his day — all this enabled him to view the whole panorama of diverse problems involved in the organization of an eremitic order. Because of thorough instruction in tradition, he was familiar with examples and texts of classical times as well as those of the Middle Ages. [4] We could hardly

---

[1] It is for this reason only, and not to anticipate the judgment of the Church, that he is called Blessed in this volume. On the history of this title, consult the texts collected by Dom N. A. Giustiniani in the Introduction to his edition of Paul Giustiniani's *Trattato dell'ubbidienza*. Padua: 1753.

[2] An inventory of Giustiniani's writings is found in Dom Leclercq's earlier book *Un humaniste ermite. Le bienheureux Paul Giustiniani* (henceforth: HE). Rome: Ed. Camaldoli, 1951. Appendix III, pp. 147-176. The references in the present volume are based on that inventory, which lists the titles of all the writings. The letters F and Q refer to the folio and quarto series of autograph manuscripts preserved in the Sacro Eremo Tuscolano of Frascati. The number following each letter is the number of the folio that contains the beginning of the quoted passage.

[3] I recounted Paul Giustiniani's life in a previous volume, cf. HE.

[4] Cf. Appendix I: The Sources of Paul Giustiniani.

claim that he has said everything on the subject of the hermit life, but at least he has said something on its every aspect, considered all its questions, and given his opinion on them. However, he left no systematic treatise presenting his doctrine organically: his ideas are found scattered in a multitude of texts of quite diverse types. Moreover, his chief purpose in writing was to sustain his attention, to express his own fervor, or to stir up that of his friends. His letters and elevations are usually long and unsystematic. Hence the necessity — but also the difficulty — of gathering together these scattered elements and condensing their contents. The synthesis we attempt here is little more than a mosaic of quotations translated and abridged.[5]

One of the principal sources will be the series of rules written by Giustiniani: the first redaction done in 1516, the *Regula vitae eremiticae* [*Rule of the Eremitic Life*] of 1520,[6] and finally the Constitutions of 1524 for the Company of Hermits of Saint Romuald.[7] Even the first redaction contains the whole essence of Giustiniani's thought. In the revision of 1520 he merely developed and specified the same material, while adding detailed regulations concerning the cenobitic monasteries to which the Hermitage of Camaldoli was joined. Thus he improved the organization of the eremitic institution, but his fundamental ideas remained unchanged. The Constitutions of 1524 were another recasting of the Rule of 1520 regarding the hermitage and reclusion. They retained the practical regulations, often scarcely modified, but omitted the accompanying commentary. The successive rules are, then, in continuity. The *Regula vitae eremiticae* is certainly the one richest in content. It relies on earlier sources: some of its chapters are

---

[5] Passages that are translations, or in some cases summaries, of Giustiniani's texts, are placed between quotation marks or indented. Because of the very nature of the sources, we cannot always avoid repetitions and long-windedness.

[6] In footnotes this will be indicated by the abbreviation RVE. The Camaldoli edition of 1520 has been used.

[7] Concerning these texts, see Appendix II of HE on "Giustiniani as Lawgiver," pp. 143-146.

merely compilations of texts borrowed from the writings of Saint Peter Damian, from the Camaldolese Constitutions of Blessed Rudolph (1080 and 1085), of Blessed Martin (1249 and 1253), and of Gerard the Prior (1278). But all these traditional elements were distinguished, selected, and assimilated by Giustiniani in such a personal way that they became truly his own and belong to his doctrine.

In general we need not take into account the chronology of the texts: while this was important in relating the history of Blessed Paul and his works, it is quite secondary to the task of assembling his views on the eremitic life. The Company of Hermits of Saint Romuald, though the final realization of his eremitic ideal, included almost all the elements of doctrine and organization already found in the Hermitage of Camaldoli. What Giustiniani says about Camaldoli already presents the gist of his definitive ideal.[8] In this present book we are not concerned with the *coenobia*, which continued to play an important role in the Rule of 1520. The actual details on how life in the hermitages was regulated will be treated only insofar as they reveal lasting ideas.

Thus reduced to its basic lines, Giustiniani's spiritual doctrine displays an astonishing cohesion. His principal theme, from which all else develops and which constantly emerges from the texts, is the basic notion of the whole hermit life: "Live alone with God, and live for God alone." His teaching is perfectly balanced, presenting not just an ascetic doctrine or a psychology of the spiritual life, but a real theology. Nor is it only an abstract theology: it is all centered upon and controlled by the mystery of Christ and the realities of sacramental life. Moreover, far from being a purely personal or even individual teaching, it takes a comprehensive view of the world's redemption, wholly animated by the mind of the Church.

Underlying Giustiniani the theologian and the spiritual master, we

---

[8] This fact has been clearly proved by the Camaldolese hermit, Dom S. Razzi, in his introduction to the Italian translation of the RVE published at Florence in 1575 under the title, *Regola della vita eremitica*.

still have Giustiniani the humanist. His rich personality, his culture, his experience of life's sorrows give his texts a human flavor which enhances their evocative power. In several aspects his doctrine might appear too demanding. To follow it completely requires an exceptional vocation and a particular grace which constitute the eremitic charism. However, the ideal of perfection that he presents, as well as at least some of his means to the end, have universal value and can be helpful to any monk and to any Christian.

PART ONE

THE HERMIT'S VOCATION

II

THE HERMIT'S ROLE IN THE CHURCH

At the beginning of his first Rule, Paul Giustiniani presents a general idea of the eremitic life which all his other texts clarify. He first shows the place of the hermit within the whole Church. The Church's goal is the heavenly Jerusalem; every form of Christian life leads to that end. But there is one way of life that not only leads there but even anticipates it. In the hermit life, men are free of matters that often estrange them from heaven and, for that reason, become like angels and live in the company of angels.[1]

To compare the eremitic life to other forms of Christian life, Giustiniani considers the life of the Church, past and present. He notes first that there are diverse vocations within the unity of the Church. "Some are given contemplation alone, that is, the soul's repose in God; others are given action only, which consists of toiling for God in external affairs; some are granted now one, then the other: contemplation for a time and action for a time, but never

---

[1] F A: 3.

both together."[2] Another fact, therefore, becomes immediately self-evident: within the unity of Christian life there are many states of life differing in form and activity, but all animated by the same principle, that divine life bestowed and communicated by Jesus Christ in His Church. Their common foundation is the duties of the Christian life. They can be understood in terms of this suggestive triad: *christiana vita, religiosa vita*, and *eremitica vita* — the Christian life, the religious life, and the hermit life. Each extends the previous: the second and the third are superimposed, so to speak, upon the first and must never depart from it. Before being a religious and in order to be one, before being a hermit and in order to be one, a man must first be a Christian — truly and not merely in name.[3] The holiness common to all the states of life derives from the fact that they all share in the same life of Christ within the one Holy Church. Without faith and the practice of Christian duties, without submission to the Church, no way of life, however sublime it may appear, leads to salvation.

The states of life that *do* lead to salvation, since they are various, are of unequal value. But before emphasizing the degrees of perfection that distinguish them, we must recall that the personal perfection of the Christian depends primarily on his faithful response to his vocation, whatever it may be.

It is one thing to speak of men and another of their state of life. When we say that religious life is more perfect than secular life, we compare one state of life to another. But we do not mean that every religious is more perfect than all seculars. For we do not doubt that in a less perfect state there are men more perfect than those who live in a more perfect state. We believe that many married persons are more perfect than some who are widowed, and yet the state of widowhood is superior to that of marriage.[4]

---

[2]   Q II: 24.
[3]   Q II : 146.
[4]   Q III: 191.

What, then, is the place of hermit life among the various Christian vocations? It is one form of the religious state and therefore differs basically from secular life. Its essential excellence stems not from its being the solitary life as such, but from the fact that it is the *religious* life. A man may be a solitary without being a religious, and consequently without being in a higher state of life. In Giustiniani's time there were in fact two kinds of Christians leading a secular life in the world: men immersed in tasks of an active life, living with their families and moving in society; then again, other men who were living as hermits without truly being such. As their way of life was not backed by the authority of the Church, it was fraught with danger. The Fathers and the Councils of the Church are unanimous in maintaining that religious life, in comparison with secular life, is a surer way of reaching heaven.[5] Religious life itself assumes two general forms: active and contemplative. Active life is the religious life as led in communities other than hermitages. To accept such a definition, we must remember the historical fact that in Giustiniani's time, the monasteries were centers of active life. They were generally situated in cities where the monks were busy with the education of children, with preaching, with parish ministry, and with other occupations outside the sphere of the religious life itself. Hence this observation that Giustiniani never ceased to make throughout his life and which in his time was indeed valid: the contemplative life requires the hermit life and is bound up with it.

These notions and distinctions will become clarified as we examine the texts. The following passage introduces and summarizes them:

> We must consider religious life on the one hand, and secular life on the other hand; then contemplative life in contrast with active life.... If we compare first religious life to secular life, we can easily find that the holy doctors and Holy Church have defined that religious life is

---

[5] Giustiniani has collected their witness on this point. Cf. Q III: 191.

more perfect and safer. To differ from their opinion would be not only imprudent, but impious.... If now we wish to compare the active life and the contemplative life, we may be sure that, in spite of all the controversy on this subject, the final word is still Our Lord's dictum: "Mary has chosen the better part and it shall not be taken away from her."[6] As to activity, there is no doubt that works of spiritual mercy, as they are commonly called, should be preferred to all works of corporal mercy. Thus in the secular state, among the various ways of life for serving God, it is more perfect to be occupied in spiritual affairs than in corporal affairs. Nevertheless this state of life is still very imperfect, principally because the secular state in itself is a great obstacle to the works of spiritual mercy. Similarly in the religious state: those who practice the works of corporal mercy are in a state of perfection, but their works are imperfect, especially because such works hinder the perfection of their state. Whence I conclude that pure contemplative life would be most perfect, if our fragile nature were capable of it. But since the human mind, particularly in those who have lived too long in a worldly way, cannot remain always in a state of contemplation, the perfect life is found among those who, in the religious state, devote themselves to contemplation as much as possible and who, during the intervals when they descend from this lofty state, perform works of spiritual mercy.[7]

Such is the hermit's way of life. Because it is a form of religious life, it stands apart at the outset from all secular life, whether the latter be solitary or not. Its essential value derives, not from its particular form, but from the fact that it is a state of life approved by the Church. Like all forms of religious life, it implies these three inseparable elements: the vows, a rule approved by the Church, and an authority established in accordance with this rule and which all are expected to obey. Giustiniani often had to insist upon these three elements, as he

---

[6] Lk 10:42.
[7] Q II: 178.

reacted against the drawbacks of what he called "secular eremitism." At almost all periods, there have been Christians who have renounced the world without wishing (and often without being able) to adopt a style of life determined by a rule. Some of them have attained sanctity in this path: in the first days of Oriental monasticism, for instance, various ascetics achieved great virtue under guise of, and sometimes by means of, eccentric behavior. In more recent times Benedict Joseph Labre has demonstrated that it is possible to become a saint without belonging to any "state of perfection."[8] But these instances were always considered exceptions. Monastic reformers and lawgivers warned against the dangers of any solitary life that lacked the safeguard of a rule and a legitimate superior. There were solitaries of this kind in Giustiniani's day, and he often exhorted them to enter religious life. In his first Rule he declared his intention of making a place for them in the Church.

> Eremitic life was of old considered the fairest glory of the Christian religion and of the religious state; but in our day it has declined even more than other forms of religious life and has almost disappeared. In fact only the twenty or more Camaldolese hermits who follow the *Rule of Saint Benedict* and their own constitutions are legitimately leading a true religious life as hermits. All others who, wearing whatever habit, live in solitude or in any way enjoy the title of "hermits" are in fact neither hermits nor religious, because they lack the first requisites of religious life: they pronounce no vows of religion, profess no approved rule, and do not obey any superior. Their deplorable conduct must be censured, for they do not serve God but their own desires, contravening the sacred canons.[9]

The vows of religion are important in more than one respect:

---

[8] This vagabond hermit's particular form of sanctity is well described in Dom P. Doyère's book, *Saint Benôit-Joseph Labre, ermite pèlerin, 1748-1783*. Paris: 1948.
[9] F A: 3. Unpublished prologue to the Rule of 1516.

they admit a Christian to a state of life approved by the Church; they stamp his whole existence with the seal of obedience, the only escape from illusion. Moreover, they constitute a noble act of the virtue of religion, a consecration that enhances the value and increases the merit of whatever acts of virtue a Christian voluntarily binds himself to perform.

> Even if one who has not taken the vows observes obedience, poverty, and chastity perfectly, even if he seems to proceed along an arduous path, nevertheless he cannot achieve the yet more sublime merit of the religious life. As the Church teaches through her saints, all good works become better and more meritorious when offered to God by a vow, particularly a solemn and public vow. In fact, to make a vow is an act of latria: the worship which is due to God alone, which is most pleasing to Him, and which raises all subsequent actions to a sublime level of perfection.[10]

Whoever makes a vow offers God not only his actions but himself. He consecrates to the Lord once and for all not only the good use of his liberty, but that liberty itself. He commits himself to an entirely new relationship with respect to the Lord, so that the vows truly resemble a second baptism.

But religious life has two principal forms: active and contemplative. We must first define them exactly in order that we may grasp the distinction and the connection between them.

> By "contemplative life" I do not mean the life we await in the world to come, when we participate in the true life and perfect contemplation, seeing God and enjoying perpetual bliss. Nor do I mean the ecstasy of spirit that is occasionally granted during this earthly life to certain men of great perfection, a sort of vision of divine realities, bestowed as a special

---

[10] Q II: 155. This text summarizes the classical theology regarding the vows of religion.

grace beyond the conditions of human nature. I call the contemplative life the manner of life of those who have renounced all temporal and spiritual cares in order to be occupied with only God and themselves — *sibi soli et Deo vacat.* They strive, as constantly as human frailty permits, to unite themselves to God by holy reading, by meditating on the eternal realities, and by assiduous prayer. By "active life" I do not refer to the state of those who are taken up with the vain cares of the world or with secular business, but I mean that way of life which makes room for the care and direction of souls, as well as various other activities that pious men may undertake for the honor and the service of religion.[11]

In comparing these two forms of religious life, the active and the contemplative, we must judge their value by their proper acts:

We can easily collect texts by various doctors proving that the totally contemplative life (insofar as human frailty permits it) is more perfect, since it is ordained to the act of loving and knowing God, which is the most perfect and also the most useful to one's neighbor, even though its usefulness may not be apparent.... According to the doctrine of Saint Thomas, who in a way prefers active to contemplative religious life, there are two acts of the religious life, the first antecedent to contemplation, the second springing from the root of contemplation. Now even those who somewhat prefer action to contemplation agree that the action which precedes contemplation is less perfect than contemplation itself. The action proceeding from contemplation is likewise less perfect. I personally have always deemed both these actions less perfect than contemplation. Regarding action which leads to contemplation, there is no doubt. As for that which follows it, one generally does not undertake such action as if he were climbing up to a more perfect level, but rather he descends to action more necessary to his neighbor and unobtainable from others. To turn from God's love and the act of loving God which

---

[11] Q I: 41.

is contemplation to the act of loving one's neighbor is not an upward but a downward movement. For we do not love God for the sake of our neighbor, but our neighbor for the sake of God.... If our neighbor needs help in order to save his soul, and if there be none other to care for him, we may, without relinquishing our own salvation, consent to lose something of our perfection, or a bit of unnecessary consolation, in order that we may attend to his neglected urgent needs. Similarly the doctors teach that Christians, and priests in particular, have no right to take flight and hide in times of persecution if this deprives the Christian people of the necessary means of salvation. They should rather stay and face the persecution. So I believe that when others are available, contemplatives may be excused from good works for the benefit of their neighbor. But if there is a lack of such persons, then the contemplatives should interrupt and relinquish the act of contemplation to devote themselves to actions necessary to the salvation of their neighbor. And so they pass from the contemplative to the active life, not as to a more perfect life, but as to one more necessary. They do not then advance upward, but stoop downward. They should not do this through mere love of neighbor, for they should never abandon the act of the love of God for the act of the love of neighbor. I say that their motive should not be love of the neighbor for himself, but only for the love of God and to serve God through service of neighbor.... At the present time those who practice works of spiritual mercy on behalf of their neighbor, far from being wanting, are most plentiful.[12]

An "entirely contemplative" life is, then, legitimate and objectively the most perfect. In Giustiniani's time this coincided with eremitic life, being realized only in hermitages. These, he held, had and continued to have the providential role of maintaining that perfect life in the Church. In his general introduction to the 1520 edition of

---

[12] Q II: 178.

the Rule, he traced the general outline of monastic history in order to situate the Camaldolese hermit life therein.

Among the numerous forms of monastic life, only two are admirable and pleasing to God: the cenobitic and the eremitic. They were instituted in the East in the blessed times of the ancient Fathers, the first founded by Saint Anthony, the second by Saint Paul. According to Saint Jerome, Paul was the first to live alone in the desert, while Anthony was the first to train disciples in the monastic life. As leader and originator of the hermit life, Paul must be forever honored as the first hermit. Anthony is acknowledged as founder of the cenobitic life because he was the first to teach many monks to live together in a common dwelling, sharing the wherewithal for sustaining their human frailty. These monks, therefore, were called "cenobites," which means "living in common." Anthony was likewise the first to receive the title of abbot, that is, father of many brothers living together.

In the West the establishment of the monastic life, as well as many other things related to Christian faith, occurred only much later. There too however, as in the East, it claims two equally renowned and holy founders: Benedict and Romuald. For the blessed Benedict is called patriarch of Western cenobites, not because that life was not practiced before him, but because he was the first in the Western Church to establish the rules of the cenobitic life. And though he himself, as Saint Gregory relates, adopted the hermit life at the beginning of his conversion when he spent three years in a cramped cave unknown to all men but the monk Romanus, yet later he passed to the cenobitic life. As leader and founder of the cenobitic institution, he wrote his rule of life for cenobites alone, disregarding other kinds of monks. And though he always preferred what Saint Gregory called "the place of his beloved solitude," yet for the benefit of the majority he lived as a cenobite, as father and abbot of numerous cenobites at his monastery of Monte Cassino, until his blessed and glorious departure to Christ.

In the meantime, while the hermit life doubtless claimed adherents in the Western Church, no one had actually organized it yet. Its first founder was a man of radiant holiness and wholly admirable life, Romuald. He was the first to transmit to his contemporaries and to bequeath to future generations the institutions and rules of the eremitic life, not in written form, but by the example of his life and teaching. In this he imitated Christ our Lord, who did not put into writing the ideal that He practiced and taught, but left it to others to write down afterwards. As Saint Romuald's biographer Saint Peter Damian tells us, the blessed Romuald first embraced the cenobitic life and led it for three years in the then famous monastery of Classe in Ravenna. But afterwards, when he became more eager for greater perfection, he transferred to the hermit life and, just like Saint Paul the Hermit, he persevered in it until death.... He founded many hermitages in different regions, not only in Italy but beyond the Alps and overseas. Countless men flocked to him from every direction, and he trained them in the hermit life. Even within his own lifetime several of his disciples achieved the palm of martyrdom.

But if we seek the origin of these two modes of life in more remote antiquity, we find that in the Old Testament, Elias observed the solitary way of life, while his disciple, Eliseus, in company with many followers, practiced the cenobitic life. Whoever ponders on these facts will understand that these two modes of monastic sanctity were not invented by men but were given to the human race by God, who governs all things wisely, and who loves human beings supremely. Even in Old Testament days He providentially willed to show in Elias and Eliseus these two modes of religious life, these two ways to easily arrive at eternal bliss, to the men whom He wished to save. Later, when the Gospel had been proclaimed, these ways were more clearly and openly shown in the East by Saint Paul and Saint Anthony and in the West by Saint Benedict and Saint Romuald. With their help men could journey as on two royal roads and thus safely reach the unutterable delights of the heavenly Jerusalem, prepared for those who fear and love God. And if we examine the origin and progress of these two modes of life, we can easily perceive that they are like two sisters showing a close resemblance, though wearing different clothing.

Moreover, if we consider carefully not only their origin, but also their respective institutions, it becomes evident that they are linked by such a close relationship and intimate bond that the fullness of cenobitic life is impossible without some participation in the hermit life, and the latter cannot be perfect without some form of support from the cenobites. It is undeniable that anyone who has any experience of either one or the other life knows that each needs the help of the other, and that both have many important features in common. For truly a monk — if we think of the proper meaning of the word — is none other than one who lives in solitude.[13] But the word is rightly applied to cenobites living together in a monastery, as well as to hermits dwelling in the same solitude and following the same vocation. The word *monastery* has rightly come to mean the home of several living together. Both the hermit and the cenobite are known as solitaries because, in so far as human weakness permits, they withdraw from the exterior and the interior multitude, that is, they remove themselves externally from the throngs of other men whose lives differ from theirs. At the same time, by their interior discipline and unceasing practice of virtue, they strive to expel from their souls the many passions and impulses disturbing them, in order that divine love alone might dwell in their hearts. Therefore one who wishes to live without companions cannot be more truly called a *monk* on that account than one who shares the company of others as a way of more perfectly devoting himself to God alone. The latter truly escapes both physically and spiritually from the common throngs, sharing a common purpose with many brothers in a monastery or in a hermitage....

When the cenobites learn of the rules of eremitic life, they may either persevere humbly in their own life, while applying some elements of the eremitic ideal within their own monastery, or else they may transfer from the monastery to the hermitage, from battle in the ranks to single

---

[13] Monk is from the Greek *monachos*, from *monos*: alone.

combat, from a perfect way of life to a more perfect way of life. This is not forbidden in any cenobitic rule nor by any pronouncement of Saint Benedict. More than once he declared in his *Rule* for cenobites that those most ardent in the quest of perfection might well advance from the gentle initiation of cenobitic life to the more robust institutions of the hermit's way. Thus progress takes place from the good to the better, from virtue to virtue, by a direct path of ascent towards the perfection unto which we all should tend. On the other hand when hermits read the rule governing cenobites, they should blush for shame and amend their ways if they perceive that they, who have professed the higher and more perfect duties of the eremitic life, do not fully observe the lower and easier precepts of the cenobitic life. Thus they can see more clearly what a singular purity of life and consummate perfection of all virtue is required of them, if already the institutions of the cenobitic life are themselves perfect. To fall short of *that* ideal would be blameworthy and shameful on the part of those whose profession (if they are true hermits) binds them to a still higher and more perfect discipline....

But especially in our day it is important that the rule and the practices of eremitic life be made known, in particular to those who desire to serve God.... For in other times, all who decided to lead the monastic life sought out solitary places. The Councils and the holy canons forbade monks to live in cities or even to enter them. But now the monks have come down from their holy solitude and have mingled with the worldly throngs of city streets, either to flee from the disturbances caused by wars or because they wished to help Christians in secular life to save their souls. They have forsaken the paradise of all delight for a wretched prison. But it has come about now that city-dwellers are more upset by wars than those inhabiting the deserts, while the conduct of monks no longer proves helpful to the salvation of laymen.... It is time, therefore, for the monks to leave the monasteries located within city walls and to go back to the greater freedom and hiddenness of solitary places.[14]

---

14 RVE f.II-V.

III

CHRIST'S CALL

The hermit life, then, does exist, and in Giustiniani's time it is the refuge of contemplatives. But who can be admitted to it? Being more perfect and more difficult than any other life, a vocation to it must be all the more evident.

There must be a vocation. To recognize it, we must know what it is not. The illusion of false vocations is by no means unreal.

Some men who experience neither spiritual devotion, nor desire to reform their lives, nor zeal for God's glory nevertheless wish to enter religious life. And why? Because they hope that religious life will give them some particular advantage which they prize: perhaps physical rest or leisure for reading and study. In some cases they want to be fed and clothed and cared for in sickness and old age. Sometimes the motive is vainglory — the wish to be admired, to acquire a reputation for virtue, to live in a better situation and on a higher plane than they can reach as laymen. But such desires must be discouraged. A candidate showing such dispositions must be reminded of the Sage's remark: "My son, if you enter God's service prepare your soul, not for delights, honor, or rank, but for temptation."[1] We must point out to such a one, as Saint Benedict directs, all the hard and difficult things through which anybody who desires to follow Christ must pass. Such warnings will

---

[1] Si 2:1.

induce these aspirants either to refrain from entering religious life, or to rectify their intention. The Lord did the same when a certain man promised to follow Him everywhere. Jesus answered him: "The foxes have holes, and the birds of the air nests; but the Son of Man hath not where to lay his head."[2] It is as if He had said to that man: "You say that you will follow me, but perhaps you are hoping for an easier life or seeking fame and a high position in the world. Know that you will be disappointed." Know that Jesus Christ provides for His followers not ease but trouble; not honor but contempt, insults, dishonor, calumny; not rank, but utter subjection. In God's service even rank itself means service and subjection.

If anyone seek to enter religion to be served rather than to serve, to relax rather than to become wearied, he should be told outright: "Depart, my brother, depart. You think you will find rest in religious life? You will find anxiety. You expect to be praised, taken for good and holy? You will be blamed and insulted; more often than not even your good deeds will be repaid with scorn. You seek high rank? I tell you that to enter religious life means to enter into constant servitude, perpetual subjection. Even if you are promoted to a position of rank, the yoke will become still heavier, for you will become the servant of servants."[3]

One should enter religion to follow Christ, and Him alone.

Saint Dominic and Saint Francis were men subject to error. But Christ is the Son of God: it is Him they followed. We truly imitate Dominic and Francis, Augustine and Benedict, when we follow Christ, for they themselves strove to imitate Him. Christ is the true leader, the way and the end. With Francis and Dominic and all Christ's followers, let us run along His fragrant path, running after Him. Let us run towards Christ with the holy founders, not towards them. Christ is the target at

---

[2] Lk 9:58.
[3] F VII:28 and 138.

which the arrows of our desires should be aimed. Dominic and Francis shot their arrows at that mark; let us shoot ours toward the same mark. This in nowise lessens the respect due to these saints: we simply wish to follow the leader whom they followed. Do Saint Francis' humility and poverty preach to us anything else but to follow the humble and poor Christ? Do Saint Dominic, Saint Benedict, or Saint Augustine do anything else in their *Rules* but turn us towards Christ? They show the way for us to follow Christ; they do not offer themselves as leaders. There is only one leader, for them as for us.

Let our rule of life be the life of Christ; let our written rule be the Gospel, having it always in our hands, taking care never to stray from the very rules of Christ. Therein lies true religious life, the norm of all perfection. What is there in the *Rules* of Saint Dominic or of Saint Francis that is not in the Gospel? Since we are Christians, let us renew ourselves, as by a new baptism, so as to follow Christ alone. What Saint Paul told the Corinthians applies to us: Did Dominic and Francis redeem us in their blood? Have we put on Dominic or Francis? Christ is the font of living water; all these saints are but tributary streams. Let us drink from the source. Let us follow along the royal road, as they did, the One who has called us.[4]

A vocation then is not a call like those issued by the world. It is a call from the Lord, an invitation that must be received quite humbly, without any presumption. For if Jesus Himself does not supply the means of complying with His demands, man is powerless to do so. Christ calls us and He attracts us. As soon as a man hears that voice, he should not only say: "Guide me, lead me, and teach me to follow You," but, like the bride of the Canticle, "Draw me. *Trahe me*, that is: Force me, do violence to me that I may walk after You. For not only can I not follow You of my own accord, but even if You call me, even if

---

[4] F+ :96.

You show me the path, if You do not draw me, if You do not use Your strength, I shall never succeed in following You."

A vocation is a grace of election. It implies a choice on God's side; man's role is only to consent.

"You have not chosen me, but I have chosen you," says the Lord.[5] It is certain that a man cannot enter religious life if God has not chosen him for it. The call to follow Christ must come from God, not from oneself. God chooses whom He will, and those He chooses, He calls. But all do not answer this divine call. Some say: "I have bought a farm, and I must needs go out and see it."[6] What is really needed? God must draw us. "No man can come to me, except the Father draw him."[7] God must force us to leave the world, to enter into the feast of the religious life, to Christ's table, to take up the cross to follow Him. Do we not read that Lot refused to leave Sodom, though invited by angels? He had to be forced. Does not Scripture say: "And they forced him to leave?"[8] The Lord must speak to us with authority. He must overcome our impotence, our resistance and that of the world, and He must force us to follow Him. He tells us that we do not follow Him because we have chosen Him, but because He has chosen us. If human choice does not coincide with God's choice, it is worth nothing. If God does not call you, choose you, draw you into religious life, do not imagine that human judgment or human prudence or human exhortation can have any effect.

But how does God make His call heard?

He calls His servants to religious life in various ways: some by an inner inspiration, some by the silent example of other men, some by human

---

[5] Jn 15:16.
[6] Lk 14:18.
[7] Jn 6:44.
[8] Cf. Gn 19:16.

exhortations; some by prosperity, others by adversity. But however the call comes, blessed is he who is not indocile to the divine vocation.[9]

God's call resounds in the soul by the voice of Holy Scripture. It rouses the soul and kindles a desire that is the most obvious sign of a vocation.

God called you when He put into your heart the desire to leave the world and to take refuge in poverty and nakedness, bearing the yoke of Christ. Such aspirations cannot arise from human weakness.... If you have heard this call, do not be deaf to it, and do not refuse to answer. Otherwise it is to be feared that you will have no right to mercy at the Last Judgment. Those who were not called, who were not privileged to feel such a desire, will all have an excuse. But you whom divine grace deigned to rouse from lethargic sleep and to open your eyes to eternal truth, you have been called to observe the religious life. By desire you have put your hand to the plough: do not look back.[10]

A vocation is imperative. It respects liberty but creates an obligation. When the Lord has made His call heard, He must be followed without delay. One need not "wander about visiting every religious house in search of the one place where God can be served in perfect serenity." No need to expect some extraordinary sign or divine miracle to point out the way. You must seek God, that is, hasten to search for Him, not wait for Him with arms crossed. You must act decisively, set out without fearing criticism, run the risk of being misunderstood by good men and likewise of scandalizing evil men.

For in proportion as good men are edified by a holy way of life, so are bad men scandalized by it. Indeed often the more perfect a way of life is,

---

[9] F VII: 28 and 138.
[10] FVII:87.

the more the bad blush and are abashed to see others correct their vices, and the worse are the insults and calumnies they spread against it. But in the Gospel our Lord, when speaking of the Pharisees, taught us to pay no attention to their opinions.... Saint Paul said that the good odor of Christ is an odor of life for some men and of death for others.[11]

A man who has begun to follow Christ should not be divided between Christ and the world. Having put his hand to the plough, he should not look back.

In the first fervor of conversion, he should flee and utterly despise all worldly things, all obstacles to his free and cheerful following of Christ. If he looks back towards those whom he has left at home, if he is anxious about anything worldly, then he will be all the less able later to restrain his desires to see, to help, to console those whom he has left behind. How many there are who have been inspired by Christ to follow Him and to become religious, but who first wish to provide their families not only with the necessities of life, but with superfluities. They want to find husbands for their nieces and wives for their nephews! Of course they wish to become religious; but they want to stay in their own region, enter a monastery where they will be allowed to write often to their parents and their nephews, see them, and receive their visits. Receive visits, yes indeed! Why, they even want to go and visit them in their own homes and dine with them!

A vocation demands a courageous break. He who wishes to become a religious should not immediately tell his household, his father, mother, brothers, and sisters, for he can expect from them many hindrances and difficulties. They may induce him to change his mind. Let him rather think of these words of the Lord: "No one who puts his hand to the plough and looks back is fit for the Kingdom

---

[11] Q IV: 345. Mt 15:14; 2 Cor 2:15-16.

of God."[12] "Fearing lest he be hampered, let him abandon the world and enter religious life without raising up countless obstacles ahead of time by forewarning his relatives. Soon enough for them to know once the thing has been done."[13]

As a vocation is a gift from God, it confers the required strength. God is wise, and if He really calls a Christian to the life of solitude, He gives also whatever aptitudes and health are necessary.

> If I saw a physician buying a sickly slave to serve him, I would think that the physician knew about the illness and could cure the slave so that he would be able to serve his master. Similarly if God calls you to the solitary religious life, I think that you must have the necessary health, or if you lack it, God will make you robust enough to bear the wear and tear of the life. According to some doctors, if the soul is weak, God gives proportionate help through the practices of religious life and by the good example and exhortations received there which, by the grace of God, can strengthen the weak. It is evident that the same principle applies to physical weakness. Experience proves it as well. Among many others, I have seen a man enter eremitic life at forty years of age, so apparently incapable of fasting that he had never fasted for even one day, not even on Good Friday, because he was sure that he could not do so. Either he *could* do it, but thought he could not, or being really unable to do it previously, he received the necessary strength from God: in any case I have seen him observe fully, without any impairment of health, all the fasts and abstinences of the Hermitage of Camaldoli: the daily fast from September 13 to Easter, the Lenten fast twice a year (with three days a week on bread and water), the simple fast of bread, water, and fruit on Fridays throughout the year, as well as other abstinences. He is amazed at himself.
>
> Recently a man came to me who had been a physician in secular life

---

[12] Lk 9:62.
[13] F VII:28 and 138.

and who was, or appeared to be, of such delicate health that, though he tried his best to observe Lent, he hardly ever could persevere to the end: fasting seemed extremely difficult for him. Now that he has become a religious he fasts more than the common eremitic rule requires, and it seems nothing to him. On the contrary, he feels as if he were leading a pampered life, and he is healthier and stronger than ever before. But why speak only of the example of others? *"Iste pauper clamavit et Dominus exaudivit eum."*[14] I myself lived a secular life for thirty-four years, and from the age of twenty until thirty-three I suffered a serious illness almost every year. Even when I was well, the price of health was very high. There was almost nothing that I could eat: no salads, salty food, tart fruits, vegetables, oil, etc. The slightest excess in quality or quantity, the slightest change in the time of my meals, had a distressing effect. If I fasted, I could not sleep. To conceal nothing of my weakness, I even considered myself so weak and incapable of keeping Lent that I thought I committed no sin by not observing it. If by chance I wished to keep the Lenten fast, all my relatives objected and caused me qualms of conscience, saying that I was trying to become ill by doing what experience had proved to be beyond my strength. In short, I was constantly sick, and everyone supposed that I had no more than two years to live.

Well the truth is that, since my conversion to religious life, I have always observed, at the very minimum, all the fasts of the Hermitage of Camaldoli without any ill effects. Not only "without ill effects," but I really am cured and in much better health. Nothing in our customary diet disagrees with me. To delay or advance the time for eating does not bother me. I get no stomachache or headache. I have as much sleep as my body needs. In fact I sometimes have said that I have the impression that these twelve or thirteen years of eremitic life have not aged me, but have actually rejuvenated me by many years.

It would be presumptuous to expect extraordinary help from God.

---

[14] Ps. 33:7 (34:6). "This poor man cried, and the Lord heard him."

That He confers very rarely. But the help I am talking about has been given to many, and that is quite understandable. If a man chooses an approved rule and a life that others are also leading, he is praiseworthy if he trust in God. The Lord does not abandon those who trust Him. *"Quis confisus est in Domino, et Dominus dereliquit eum?"*[15] As long as we trust ourselves, as long as we gauge our strength by the standard of human prudence, which is vain and deceptive, we are always frail, disabled, and timid. But if we commend ourselves into God's hands, we shall straightway feel strong and fearless.[16]

---

[15] Si 2:10 (11). "Who ever trusted in the Lord and was forsaken by Him?"
[16] Q II: 178.

IV

WORDLESS PREACHING

The hermit life exists in the Church, and some Christians are called to it. But at the same time that we note these two facts, a question arises in our mind. What is the hermit's role? Sometimes the question is put in the form of an objection:

> It is often believed that within the whole framework of Christian society, the solitary life is either entirely useless or is the least useful organ of the mystical body of the Holy Catholic Church. It is almost a common opinion that a hermit can be useful only to himself. Therefore, some condemn that way of life or retire from it, fearing the fate of the servant who hid the talent entrusted him instead of making it bear fruit.[1]

This objection, while easy to formulate, is difficult to refute. To do so, we must in the first place recall certain principles.

> All Christ's servants should seek their neighbors' salvation and God's glory, but in different ways. Each man, by carrying on his own proper activity and function, without usurping the role of others, should seek God's glory and, in view of God's glory, his neighbor's salvation. It would be ridiculous and pitiable if one single member of the body of which Christ is head were to try to usurp the functions of all the other

---

[1] Q IV bis: 103. Mt 25:28.

members. You, who are a hermit, not a bishop or a pastor but a sheep of the flock, you should seek God's glory and your neighbors' salvation not by restless activity, but by prayer and entreaty, for this is the hermit's proper role. Why should you rashly try to swing your scythe in another man's field? Why do you try to do another's duty? That is not your task. It is not for you to become immersed in the turmoil of worldly affairs. Not for that purpose did God intend that you be born, that you grow in the desire for solitude and be called to conversion. It was to allow you the leisure to devote yourself to prayer: for that He attracted you, withdrew you, as it were evicted you from the realm of worldly concerns.[2]

The fruitfulness of the life of every Christian and of every religious depends upon his fidelity to his personal vocation.

Like all who follow Christ, the hermit has heard that call which the Lord issues in the Gospel: "Go and announce the kingdom of God."[3] To follow Christ is to announce the kingdom of God. What truly does it mean to announce the kingdom of heaven? It means to scorn the kingdom of the world. How then does one *announce the kingdom of heaven*? Oh surely, surely the kingdom of heaven is most effectively announced by all who can say with Christ: "My kingdom is not of this world."[4] He who with all his heart truly renounces the pleasures and honors and dignities of this world announces the Kingdom of God more than if he preached it in a thousand languages, but did not practice what he preached. He shouts out not only with his mouth but with all his members: "I have no lasting city in this world. Here I wish neither father, mother, friend, nor relative because I look forward to another city in heaven, a kingdom not built by human hands. I aspire, I hope, and I run towards the kingdom of heaven, the kingdom of God." This

---

2   Q III:4r.
3   Lk 9:60.
4   Jn 18:36.

kingdom is announced by any man who testifies that this mortal life is a pilgrimage tending towards the fatherland, any man who shows that on earth we are not in our homeland, but that we await our native country in the celestial kingdom.

The kingdom of God was announced by the Apostles, the martyrs, the virgins, the doctors, and the hermits. The Apostles preached and performed miracles in the name of Jesus. The martyrs joyfully faced death and torture to confess that they awaited the kingdom of heaven. The virgins rejected earthly delights and carnal pleasures in exchange for the chaste delights of heaven. The doctors defended the truth by dint of ceaseless study and in announcing the future judgment, the eternal beatitude of Christ's servants, and the perpetual punishment of those who love this world. The hermits of old renounced all things, left everything, and fled from all the joys, honors, and dignities of the world. They, it is evident, announced the kingdom of heaven not just by words, but through all their works their whole life long and with all their members.

For to leave country, wealth, honor, and position in order to go and live in the desert, poor and despised, to practice the eremitical austerities in eating and drinking, to sleep on the ground, to wear a rough habit, and to endure all the other rigors of eremitic life: what is all this but a cry to worldlings: how foolish and how blind you are—intoxicated by worldly delights and honors, you forget the delights of heaven and the honors of the celestial realm. Do you think we are so foolish as to miss reaching a better life because we refuse to renounce the pleasures that prevent our arriving there? We renounce voluntarily all that causes pleasure in this life, because the gaze of our soul is ever fixed on the kingdom of heaven. God's kingdom is more easily accessible to those who more truly despise the world and follow after the cross of Christ, prepared to crucify their concupiscences and their very selves with Christ.

I claim that in our time there is no truer or more effective way to announce the kingdom of God than to become a religious. Do you not believe that men who know you and consider you sensible and prudent, when they see you leave your country, your house and your abundant wealth, will say: "Surely that prudent, educated, intelligent man would not abandon all that were he not sure that after this life he would reach a nobler and truer homeland, a grander house, more substantial wealth, keener pleasures, higher honors, a more exalted position." So though your tongue be mute, your whole life, all your actions, and your entire person announce the kingdom of God.... He who preaches the kingdom of God in the way most calculated to help his neighbor is the man who, to follow Christ, renounces the most wealth, honor, and dignity. For he most clearly shows how wretched is all else compared to the kingdom of heaven.[5]

From this point of view religious profession acquires a new value. The vows are a consecration to God, but they are also an effective example because they are a public testimony.

To teach or to correct others or to perform any other spiritual works of mercy are fruitless tasks if the teacher or reformer does not first himself achieve fully what he urges on others. Nor can he help his neighbor if his achievement be merely interior, for human minds cannot perceive what is hidden in another man's heart. The man who would be useful to others must accomplish openly and outwardly what he wants to teach. Scripture says: "*Coepit Jesus facere et docere....*"[6] Therefore the very act of leaving and despising all worldly things in order to devote oneself to God's service and to religious life by a public act of profession, that act by itself is a spiritual work of mercy that is more perfect, more pleasing to God, and more fruitful for one's neighbor than all that a man could do throughout his whole life while remaining in the secular state. A man remaining in the world may help one particular neighbor to correct one vice, or he may instruct another in one virtue. But if he openly renounce all vice

---

5   F VII:28 and 138.
6   Acts 1:1. "Jesus began both to do and to teach...."

and all occasion of vice, if he embraces the state of life that best fosters virtue, if he enlists forever as a humble servant of God, then he offers the clearest sermon on virtue, the clearest repudiation of vice, the most effective demonstration of what it means to despise the world and to love and serve God. And so by a single deed he preaches on every virtue and arouses hatred of every vice. This lesson reaches not only the ten or the hundred persons whom he knows personally, or even to a thousand, but to all the living and to all who will come after him. To them he points out, inasmuch as he can, the path they should follow in fleeing from vice, loving virtue, and seeking wholeheartedly their salvation and God's glory.[7]

The hermit's way of serving his neighbor is to remain true to his vocation as a hermit. His very responsibility towards his neighbor obliges him to *be* perfectly what he should be.

Woe to us if we provide no edification to those who expect it of us, if the perfection of our life does not encourage the hesitant and attract the seekers.... For men expect more from clergy and priests than from laymen. Of those who have left all things and have "become eunuchs"[8] for the sake of the kingdom of heaven, of the followers of the Lord, much more is demanded than of those who try to keep the Christian faith in the midst of marriage and wealth. And we above all who, with God's help, have embraced the solitary life, which is so perfect, so sublime, so very austere, we must offer only what is great and only what is perfect. Woe to us if those who seek the Lord must blush for our conduct! Woe to us if our light does not shine before men so that, seeing our good works, they may glorify the Father in heaven![9] Let us take care then that through our good works and the splendor of our virtues, our existence in the midst of the nations on this peak of the Apennines, may

---

[7] Q II: 178.
[8] Mt 19:12.
[9] Mt 5:16.

force even those who do not wish to know God to confess this: that to serve Almighty God sincerely and in truth brings the only real life and happiness possible in this world.[10]

The more we strive for personal perfection, the more we help our neighbor.

Mary's leisure is not less fruitful than Martha's work. For that leisure is not inert, idle, and drowsy (as happens all too often with prelates whose honors contribute more to their own relaxation than to the welfare of their subjects). Mary's leisure is busier than all work, and it is as much more useful to herself and to others as action is more useful than talk, as giving an example is more useful than preaching. In this private leisure more help is given to oneself and to others than in absorbing work. And if I may quote the example of the pagans, I believe that what was written of Cicero can truly be said of us: that in a short time of leisure he rendered greater service to his fellow citizens, as well as to all posterity, than by many years' work.... The soul at rest is more serene and free: therefore, a hidden life is better than public life. Active life reaches a high level, according to the opinion of the Peripatetics, if it succeeds even in moderating and restraining the passions, thus preventing their overstepping the bounds restraining them from vice and blame. The life of leisure, on the other hand, according to the Stoics, accomplishes nothing unless it frees men entirely from all their passions, leaving no room for them, banishing them afar.[11]

The fruitfulness of a life is measured less by immediate results than by the fruitfulness of the being to whom it is dedicated. A life wholly given to God is more useful than a life divided between God and what is not God.

---

[10] Q IV: 345.
[11] Q IV bis: 252v.

The man most useful to the human race is the one who can help the greatest number of people in the most ways and for the longest time, not in bodily things but in those of the soul. He serves them not for this short life, but for the future life. He directs them, by a shorter and a quicker path, to the goal of all desire, eternal beatitude. Such is the case with the solitary. Matters of the soul and eternal life are more important than matters of the body and earthly life. Now with respect to the former, there are three ways of helping men: by eloquent exhortation in doctrine, by the attraction of example, and by imploring divine help in prayer and in other meritorious works. Teaching is accomplished by speaking or by writing: these are similar, for what is speech but transient writing and what is writing but abiding speech? Men can give good example by particular virtuous actions or by their whole manner of life. The third way of help is given by those who think of others in their vocal or mental prayers, or by those whose good works are so meritorious that, for love of them, God grants His help to others besides themselves. Thus we read that God set Lot free for the love of Abraham[12] and did not do so because Abraham prayed for it, but because of his holy life. All these means of help are available to the solitary, who, all other things being equal, is more useful to the human race than the man who is not a solitary.[13]

The contemplative helps his neighbor more than others, just as a subject who gains a prince's favor helps his family more than the man who tries to amass riches by working. For a prince's patronage brings greater benefit at one stroke than all the exertions of many years. Imagine someone who knows nothing of the art of navigation, but who wishes to cross the sea with his whole family: he will take better care of himself and all his family by trusting an expert sailor than by trying to steer the ship himself. It is similar for he who knows that God is the reliable, wise, and infinitely good guide of the human race. He is more useful to himself and to all other men if he commits to God all care

---

[12] Gn 19:29.
[13] Q IV bis: 103.

of himself and of his neighbor, commending himself to Him without ceasing in order to acquire and retain His grace.[14]

Thus good deeds and prayer are the two very efficacious means by which the solitary proves himself useful to Christian society. But here is the ultimate explanation of this usefulness.

In the Credo we say each day that we believe in the Communion of Saints. What do these few words imply? That all prayers and all good deeds, all the merits of all the saints, are common to all Christ's good servants.... It is not I who thus explain these words, but the very learned Saint Thomas. Commenting on this article of the Creed, he says that all Christians are members of the body of which Jesus Christ is the head. And just as the food which the body receives is common to all its members, so the good accomplished in this body, of which the saints in heaven are equally members, is common to all its members. Excluded, however, are those separated from the body, or cut off by excommunication, and thus no longer in any condition to receive its nourishment.[15]

To justify the hermit's way of life in the Church, Paul Giustiniani refers more often to the example given *to* others, than to prayer *for* others. We might be surprised that, after his strong presentation of the dogma of the Communion of Saints, he does not stress more the role of intercession. But we must admit that in this he is in conformity with the most authentic monastic tradition. He cannot be refuted from the theological point of view. He emphasizes the transcendence of God and the value of a life wholly taken up with God. Because God *is* God, it is fitting that some Christians should dedicate their whole existence to seeking Him, to living in His presence, to offering Him their constant

---

[14] Q IV bis: 128.
[15] F I: 175.

homage of adoration, thanksgiving, and supplication. When a hermit asks for pardon and for grace, he thinks first of himself, realizing that he is a sinner — *sibi soli et Deo vacat* [he is empty for himself and God alone]. But at the same time he confesses in his person the wretchedness of all humanity, so that all sinful humanity profits by his humility and by the grace which it draws down.

The hermit serves his neighbor by prayer, it is true, but not necessarily by praying for his intention. Prayer contains a value in itself, regardless of its object or occasion. Its effectiveness derives from the fact that it is addressed to God. It has been said that "it matters not that we know *for what* we pray, but rather *to Whom* we pray."[16] To formulate particular intentions may be a psychological device to sustain fervor; but this fervor ought to spring, in the first place, from a conviction that the Lord is almighty and worthy of our adoration, that He is Love and wishes to be loved.[17] To fix our prayer on special objects which, however numerous, are always limited, is to reduce its universal range. God is the common Father of all men; by praying to Him, we necessarily help all men.

---

[16] Louis Bouyer. *The Meaning of the Monastic Life*. New York: P.J. Kenedy and Sons, 1955.

[17] Cf. *Alone with God*, Chapter 10.

PART TWO

THE HERMIT LIFE

V

FORMS OF THE HERMIT LIFE

The term *eremitic life* designates all the ways of living in solitude. We must now define it more closely by describing the form under which it is realized, particularly in the Camaldolese order.

The many kinds of hermits may be divided into three groups. The first consists of men who, without vows of poverty, chastity, and obedience, without a rule, or profession, or a superior, live in solitary places wearing a religious habit. Saint Benedict says that these are the worst brood of monks. They are censured in Church law and are called acephalous, that is headless.

The second kind of hermits are those who, after probation in the cenobitic life, after pronouncing the three principal vows and being professed under an approved rule, leave the monastery and withdraw to live all alone in solitude, as the Fathers of Egypt did of old. Such a life, as Saint Jerome affirms, is more perfect than the cenobitic but also much more perilous. It permits no companionship but requires that each be self-sufficient. Therefore it is no longer permitted in our day, as Holy

Church now orders us to hear Mass often, to make our confession, and to receive Communion. None of those things can be done alone.

There remains the third kind of hermit life: ours. It combines cenobitic and eremitic life. We make the vows of poverty, chastity, and obedience; we follow the *Rule of Saint Benedict*, oftentimes approved; we live under a superior, as a united community, in constant obedience. Our discipline is in every way stricter and more austere than that of the cenobitic life. This hermit life, because it comprises the vows, the profession, and the rule, is not condemned as is the first kind of religious solitude. Because it gathers together a group of hermits for the same purpose, it is neither dangerous nor illicit like the second kind.[18]

Giustiniani describes in some detail this Camaldolese eremitic life.

The third form of eremitic life is that of men who go out either from the world or from a monastery and withdraw from all cities. They separate themselves, as far as possible, from all association with men who live otherwise than they. They go to places absolutely solitary and remote: to the top of mountains that are steep and difficult to climb, or to the bottom of deep and almost inaccessible valleys, to grottoes unknown to men, to the secrecy of well-hidden caves, to dense forests. Each lives there in a separate cell, but subject to a rule and to a superior and bound by the three vows. Though they are in solitude, they are not absolutely alone, deprived of the help of their brethren. Even in the desert they are at home as in the Lord's house, and each profits by the society of all. For if one falls, the other lifts him up; if one is defeated by an enemy, that enemy is overpowered by many others; they all stimulate each other by their good works. They can provide for each other all the services which Holy Church prescribes as necessary to salvation. They escape entirely all the hindrances which endangered the salvation of the second kind of hermits. Their way of life is well-balanced: they enjoy the advantages of

---

[18] Q I:211.

a life of submission and a life in common, but without the diverse tasks and manifold distractions of a monastery; they relish the sweet and happy tranquillity of solitude, but they escape the dangers of solitary life.

This third kind of eremitic life was devised, under the inspiration of the Holy Spirit, by Saint Romuald, patriarch of all the hermits of the West. In his day the Charterhouse had not yet been founded by Saint Bruno, nor Vallombrosa by Saint John Gualbert, nor Cîteaux by Saint Robert, nor Clairvaux by Saint Bernard, as dwelling places for monks. And it was long before Saint Francis and Saint Dominic founded the orders of Friars Minor and Preachers, in which now militate an almost countless multitude of men and women. At that time the Western Church seemed no longer to have any religious life. Only a small number of abbots observed the *Rule of Saint Benedict*. With no monks or very few under them and without the regular life, they occupied their monasteries rather than governed them.

Then, like a light breaking through the clouds, Saint Romuald appeared. He was the first to restore cenobitic life itself, for through him or after him the Lord stirred up the zeal of all those who undertook the reform of the monastic life. In the desert of Camaldoli he instituted this form of eremitic life, exempt from the multiple activities found in monasteries, free of the harmful distractions occasioned by business matters and by association with laymen. It is both a pure cenobitic life (that is, purified from all hindrances) and a total eremitic life. It preserves all the advantages and precludes the disadvantages of both ways of life.[19]

In such an existence certain points of Saint Benedict's *Rule* cannot be practiced: some points of detail or observances are rendered impossible by the fact of living alone (such as the common dormitory), while certain prescriptions are not sufficiently severe for

---

[19] RVE f. 40-41v.

the hermit life, such as the regulations on food and drink.[20] But all the essentials of Benedictine life are safeguarded. We may even say that the Camaldolese hermit life is closer to community life than to solitary life.[21] Thus the question of determining if one can enter the hermit life directly, or of deciding the conditions necessary for passing from cenobitic to eremitic life — such questions need not be asked, since the hermitage itself is cenobitic.[22]

Are there, then, no degrees of progress within the Camaldolese life? Does it offer no prospect of a yet more perfect life? This need is fulfilled by an institution that is proper to it and extremely important: reclusion.

After having been put to the proof for a long time in the practice of obedience and austerities, one can ascend to a more perfect life and become more truly a hermit. This happens without losing the treasure of holy obedience, which is the monk's wealth, without the presumption of living according to one's own lights, and without leaving this ring of firs. And this is the usual practice: Some of the monks are allowed to withdraw from the others and to confine themselves in a cell from which they never again emerge, in order that they may contemplate heavenly realities in greater tranquillity. They must first have undergone a long period of testing and have attained the mature age of forty or forty-five years. Then, if they request it insistently, the permission is granted after serious consideration. Always in our midst there are some such recluses, good fathers who stir up the fervor of the younger monks. In such reclusion their life is noticeably stricter as to fasting, psalmody, silence and other observances. But even so, they are not at liberty to follow their own judgment, ideas, or desires without the express authorization of the

---

[20] Q I: 106.

[21] F + : 145. This long text develops this idea, clarifies it by examples, and lists the advantages assured and the disadvantages avoided by the Camaldolese hermit life.

[22] Giustiniani deals with this question, but from a more speculative viewpoint and for the sake of its traditional antecedents, in Q IV: 312.

superior. These recluse or secluded hermits — *inclusi* — are served by all the other hermits, who are called open — *aperti* — to distinguish them from the first. The superior provides for all their necessities, so that they need not concern themselves with anything earthly.[23]

Reclusion indeed is the Camaldolese hermit life brought to its ultimate perfection.

It is proper to those who crave more freedom for contemplation and has been devised by God rather than by men. One under the sway of this craving ceases to associate with other men or even to see them: he cuts himself off from contact even with his fellow hermits. He is exempt from all human affairs. But he is not released from either the rule or the superior, nor is he deprived of help from others or of the usages of the Church which he cannot supply for himself. A cell with a little garden is assigned to him, either for a definite, prearranged time or even, if he keenly desires it, for always. There he is shut away, free of all care; there he can occupy himself with God alone — *soli Deo vacare*.[24]

The purpose of the hermits is to live with Christ — *cum Christo vivere*. Though the whole organism of the Hermitage of Camaldoli aims at this goal, and because it aims at it, Saint Romuald, inspired by the Holy Ghost, presented a still more perfect way of life. In it the advantages of the two ways, cenobitic and eremitic, are realized more fully, and their perils avoided more securely. In the happy ages of antiquity, this way of life had been adopted by a host of cenobites, hermits, and anchorites in the deserts of Egypt and in other regions of the East. But it remained almost unknown amongst us. However, just as all regions and all seasons of the year are not embellished by the same fruits, so the divine Spirit does not confer the same gifts on each age. Religious who longed for the blessings of solitude either had to miss the benefit of obedience,

---

23 F+:145.
24 RVE f. 40v-41.

attend to their daily needs and other necessities by themselves, and draw up their own individual rule of life — or else they had to renounce the tranquillity of solitude in order to preserve the treasures of obedience and poverty. Enlightened by the Holy Ghost, Saint Romuald devised for our Western Church this admirable institution of reclusion. Ever since that time there have always been Camaldolese hermits who, after leading the common life in the hermitage — *communis vita in eremo* — keenly desire freer contemplation and more perfect peace of soul and ardently long to give their continual attention to God alone. With the consent of the major and of their co-hermits, they are shut up in a cell with a garden, where they continue as always to bear the yoke of the constitutions and where they endeavor all the more to converse with God in heaven. It would be hard to imagine any happier life for those who are filled with zeal for prayer and for divine contemplation.[25]

Reclusion, thus, is not only a means whereby certain hermits carry out their personal vocation, but it is also a masterpiece of the eremitic institution as such. It offers an example and inspires emulation, keeping within the hermitage the ideal of a more perfect life. Just as cenobitic life should stay open to the vista of hermit life, so the eremitic life in its "open" form should retain the possibility of something stricter. Without reclusion, the rule of the hermitage seems a maximum that cannot be surpassed and the hermit life closed upon itself; rejecting all possibility of progress, it runs the risk of regression. By reclusion we are reminded that open eremitism is only a minimum; it can be surpassed by an existence even more remote from other men, having its only outlook on heaven itself.

---

[25] RVE f. 130 v-131.

VI

The Requirements
of the Hermit Life

To remain in solitude is the first condition of the hermit life. But to fulfil this condition truly, one must first be convinced of its importance: practice will result from conviction.

Solitude has but one aim: to allow Christ to abide in us. Because the Lord dwells in us, our hearts must not make room for Christ's enemies. Solitude is the fortress surrounding us to prevent their entry.[1] Solitude delivers us, and once we possess ourselves, we can realize the true worth of all things.

> By staying ever in my cell I am enabled to see a shadow, a remote but clear image, of a life which is true life. Then do I scorn this life, which is death rather than life, for this earthly life I love only insofar as it can help me to acquire the only true life. This is just what I could never do — and I think that no one finds it easy — while I was surrounded physically and mentally by busy throngs, distracted by conversations, immersed in the swirling thoughts which in one way or another enter our hearts.[2]

To understand what solitude means for us, it is enough to recall its role in the history of salvation. Let us hear its voice:

---

[1] F I: 155.
[2] F I: 47.

I am that solitary life which makes earthly men heavenly and carnal men spiritual. It is I who gathered together the dispersed children of Israel, the men for whom the Son of God, exalted above all the heights of heaven and exempt of all sin, willed to come down to the secret and hidden dwelling of the Virgin's womb. It is I who shut the door on the secret oratory of that recluse, the solitary Mary, when the angel came to greet her. I am that solitary life that makes all things and by which all things that are made have that life without which there is no life. I am the one that often separated the true Life which was made flesh from the crowds. Thanks to me He spent nights in prayer, multiplied bread in the desert, overcame the devil in the desert, fasted, lived alone among the wild animals, and yet at the same time enjoyed the presence of the angels who served Him when He had no human company. When He wanted to show the glory of His Transfiguration, He left all others and took away three Apostles alone with Him to the mountain. And finally they, raising their eyes, saw no one, but only Jesus, for contemplation sees nothing but Him. Again alone, separated from His closest Apostles, he prayed at length to His Father three times in His agony. He sweat blood and was comforted by an angel appearing from heaven, not because He needed help, but because He wanted to teach us that those who pray alone for a long time may hope for the comfort of an angel, even though the angel may not appear to us visibly.

What can we say of that blessed first man, Adam, who was safe as long as he was alone, before his wife, his helpmate, drove him out into miserable exile. He had been put into that solitude of the terrestrial paradise in order that evil should not pervert his heart.... Abraham also was seated alone beneath the oak of Mambre when he saw three men and adored one.... He was alone when he received the promise of the Savior.... When John the Baptist was a child, who gave him a sweet and vast wilderness? Who instructed him in the desert? Who revealed to him the mystery of baptism? I, of course, I was with him in all things. Neither parents nor nurse helped him; wine did not warm him; pleasant and delicate garments did not clothe him. But I alone was with him in all these things. I was adequate to all his needs.[3]

This beneficial action of solitude continues among us.

O blessed solitude, which teaches human spirits to return to themselves and to desire to see, as much as men can, the Majesty of God. O solitude, giving a foretaste of heaven's delight, a bit of divine pleasure granted to men living in the flesh! When holy souls weep as they wait in this exile, you alone, amiable solitude, show the ideal of that eternal joy that we desire and hope to obtain in the fatherland. O solitude, too little known by those who have not known you by experience! O solitude, never sufficiently praised: you change human misery to angelic happiness. If I understand rightly, you make angels of men. Though their bodies are detained here in this valley of woe, you make their spirits dwell in heaven. You make the soul adhere always to God the Creator, all good and almighty, who caresses the soul like a cherished bride. You delight it with divine words, as sweet as the kisses of a bridegroom. You it is who announce the coming of the Holy Spirit — you not only announce Him, but you bring Him into the human heart just as the dawn announces the day and also brings to our eyes the brightness of the sun.... Truly until I was alone, I never really lived. Until I was alone, I was not with myself. Until I was alone, I never drew near to my Creator.[4]

But how can such an exalted ideal be realized? The hermitage makes it concrete.

"For solitary places have always greatly helped true solitude of the soul...." Saint Romuald chose the desert of Camaldoli because it was remote from all towns and human dwellings, because the vast area of forests around it hid it completely and made it almost inaccessible.

---

[3] Q III: 208.
[4] F VII: 101.

Since then, settlements have appeared in the district. If, therefore, the hermits truly wish to safeguard their solitude, they should exert all their efforts on the task of seeing that the forests around the hermitage belonging to them should not be thinned out, but should be kept intact and developed. Permission to cut down pine trees for the needs of the hermitage should never be granted except with the express consent of the whole chapter. We should take care that the saplings are not injured by either men or animals. The grove enclosing the hermitage should be inviolable. Each year four or five thousand fir saplings should be planted to replace those that have withered or that have had to be cut down. We should strive in every way to avoid contact with laymen, even under the pretext of offering alms or hospitality: this is not through lack of kindness, but as a safeguard of solitude. In the hermitage no craft requiring the help of laymen will be carried on. We must remove all animals except those that are needed; these should not be allowed to graze either by day or by night within the hermitage grounds, nor should they remain there for long. No one, of whatever rank, will be authorized to enter the hermitage on horseback; arms must be left at the gate, for the hermitage is sacred: it is not fitting that men enter the Lord's house armed, nor should they trouble the peace of its inhabitants by speaking in loud voices.[5] All the territory within the grove of trees surrounding the cells, as well as the paths leading from the cells to the church, will be considered a cloister.[6] "And hidden in each separate cell, the hermit will be able to taste the deep tranquillity of holy solitude."[7]

But he must not forget that "no physical solitude can give peace of mind, without the help of the true solitude which is interior.... Perfection is not conferred by place or time. The Lord has condemned those who believe that the Sabbath sanctifies man because the Sabbath

---

[5] RVE f. 44v-47; F A: 19-21v.

[6] RVE f. 97.

[7] RVE f. 41v.

is holy: it is man who sanctifies the Sabbath. Similarly, places do not sanctify men, but rather it is they who sanctify places."[8]

There is, then, no solitude without recollection and silence. Silence is the "principal adornment of solitude."[9] It must not be confused with mere absence of speech and noise, for it must be full of the divine presence.

> The solitary enclosed in a narrow cell cuts himself off from human conversations only to speak with the Creator in prayer, or with himself in meditation. Otherwise man, who alone of all animals has received the gifts of intelligence and speech, becomes a mute animal and misuses the holiness of silence. The silence of religious solitary life was not instituted to make us dumb animals, but so that, putting an end to external conversations, we might not cease speaking to God in prayer or usefully to ourselves in meditation. For that is how religious silence is rightly observed: never to cease praying and meditating. The solitary may also write, either to sustain his attention or help his memory, or else to exhort his neighbor.[10]

If, then, the silence is filled with the thought of God, it becomes

> a very sweet food, much desired by the spirit.... Sweet, solitary silence lifts my soul closer to God and renders more translucent the obscurity through which I glimpse the Redeemer's infinite sublimity than the study of Plato or Aristotle or all the other authors I used to read could ever do. I find that silence teaches more than many conversations. Never did I perceive as clearly as now the Lord's kindnesses towards us. How grateful we should be to God, who created us from nothing, created us in His image, created us with an intelligence and a will capable of making

---

8 Q I: 37v, cf. Mk 2:27.
9 Constitutions of 1524. Ed. P. Lugano. *La Congregazione camaldolese degli eremiti di Montecorona*. Frascati, 1908. P.161.
10 Q III:79.

their way towards Him, created us nobler than all other creatures, all of which He made for us. Never did I realize all this as keenly in the world as I do in this solitude and silence.[11]

In practice, eremitic silence comprises two degrees. All conversation with laymen will be avoided, but among themselves the hermits will not be so severely bound to silence. Silence is the condition of true solitude. Like the remote location, it is a way to remove whatever disturbs peace of mind. Without silence, there is no solitude. One could withdraw to the most hidden places and the most unknown to men: but without silence, one will have nothing but the appearance of solitude.[12] We should not inquire about, talk about, or care to hear of wars and other happenings in the world, especially the dealings of princes.[13] "To hear news of the world and of the town is a greater hindrance to spiritual progress than we think. So true is this that Saint Benedict, who is the origin of so many religious congregations, strictly enjoined those who go out on monastery business not to report on their return what they have seen or heard."[14] To retire from the world is of no use if the noise of the world invades the hermitage.

The hermits are allowed to have spiritual conversations among themselves. At certain times the superior will break the silence, so that the brothers may speak of necessary matters. There are recreation periods when they may walk about together on the outskirts of the hermitage. The days and the hours for all this are indicated in the constitutions.[15]

It is even permitted to talk with the recluses.

During the great week before Lent, on the days and at the hours

---

[11] F I:47.

[12] F A: 22v.

[13] RVE f. 42v.

[14] F+ :145.

[15] RVE f. 97-97v, 104-105, 107.

when silence is broken, this is granted to whichever hermits wish it, only once for each. Each separately may approach each recluse and, without entering his cell, speak with him through the window, moderately and briefly, unless a recluse should spontaneously refuse such visits because of his preference for silence and tranquillity.[16]

So we see that silence is not absolute for anyone. Besides "temperance in speech,"[17] another guarantee of interior solitude is stability. It too is primarily a state of mind.

A change of place is sure to disturb the mind and cause many distractions. For a man does not move from place to place unless his mind changes from one purpose to another. The mind first begins to feel a slight change of this kind, which little by little induces the hermit to move to another place. Then the change of place, far from relieving the mind's inclination to change, only intensifies it. This need of change, at first so hidden as to be barely conscious, becomes so strong, once a man consents to it by physical change of place, that it disturbs his whole life and likewise becomes evident to others. Thus fraudulently and secretly we first persuade ourselves to change only our place but not our purpose. But the change of place in turn persuades us, and this time obviously, to change our manner of life. We must, therefore, avoid not only any change from the more perfect to the less perfect, or even to the equally perfect, but also any change that is not very clearly in favor of greater perfection. The monk who changes place, like the farmer who often transplants his trees, is cheated by the enemy of the fruits of the religious life. For a tree transplanted to a new field, even if the second spot be as good as or better than the first, easily dies and withers up unless it can thrust down its roots there. In any case, it bears fruit that is sour and inferior to that which it previously bore. So also most certainly with the monk whose roots

---

[16] RVE f. 98.
[17] F A: 22.

have already reached deep into the ground. If, persuaded by the enemy, he lets himself be transported to ground which he thinks better, he dies there miserably or, giving in to frequent changes and assailed by worldly cares, he becomes worse than laymen. If indeed the desire of heavenly realities still clings to his heart, the fruits of perfection that he produces are no longer as sweet or abundant as before the change. Wine, however good it may be, loses its sweetness and turns into vinegar when it is often transferred from one container to another, even if both containers are flawless. Material things are not easily marred merely by being changed: but our souls thus suffer corruption, as they are like hot wax that retains the slightest change.[18]

One of the motives which suggests a change of place is the imperfection of the environment in which one lives. But to wish to avoid every imperfection is a temptation.

Wherever there are men, there are imperfections which must be borne. In absolutely every community, however small it may be, each member has much to endure from the others, while they have to endure even more from him. Whenever men are together, even if it be only two of them, there are many grounds for mutual hurt. He who refuses the virtue of mutual forbearance, so necessary to all human society, dissolves all social life. He becomes worse than the wildest savages, for even they would derive no benefit from gathering together unless they managed to bear with each other to a certain extent. We must be convinced that every man is subject to some imperfection; but the most harmful imperfection of all is to resent too much others' imperfections and to be unable to bear with them always serenely. For such a one is himself very imperfect, at least in this respect, whatever great virtues he otherwise may have. What could be farther removed from the divine goodness than to fail to bear, imperfect as we are, with the imperfections of our

---

[18] F I: 155.

brothers, when the infinitely perfect Lord patiently tolerates the vices and affronts of so many thousands of men. A monk who considered himself more perfect than the others was pained by their imperfections. He traveled to the desert with but one disciple. But he could not long bear the imperfection of even this one companion, and he decided, therefore, to live entirely alone and thus avoid all imperfection. But as soon as he was alone, he stumbled against a jug and broke it with a gesture of anger. Immediately he understood that the imperfection that needed correction was not in the habits of others, but in his own heart.... I recall having once read, in pagan authors treating of the duties of husbands, that a man should either tolerate or correct the faults of his wife: if he corrects them, he improves his wife; if he supports them, he himself becomes better. And it is always preferable to bear with others than to make them bear with us.[19]

The hermit will rarely have occasion to go out.

When we are here, we can say: *haec requies mea in saeculum saeculi, hic habitabo quoniam elegi eam.*[20] By quietude of the body, we can acquire quietude of spirit. The monks who live in cities often go out of the monastery enclosure to mingle in the hustle and bustle of the city. And seeing certain things, or hearing certain rumors, they return, I fear, weaker and sometimes more troubled than when they left, bringing back with them some worldly thing which will long trouble their minds. The solitary monk does not have this danger to face. If we leave our little cells, it is to enter a vast forest of very high fir trees. The forest breeze and shade, the variegated flowers covering the ground, the springs and brooks that rise and run everywhere, the sweet singing of a host of birds: nothing in all that can disturb a tranquil soul. If one is sad, he recovers

---

[19] Q IV: 257.
[20] Ps 131 (132):14. "This is my rest for ever; here will I dwell, for I have chosen it."

his joy. All these creatures invite us to pray, to praise the Creator of all things. Then we return to our cells deeply serene.[21]

When a journey proves inevitable, we must learn to remain hermits even when traveling.

Hermits are not forbidden to mount horseback, any more than cenobites. But if anyone prefer to go on foot, either to practice humility or to mortify his body, he should not be obliged to take a horse, unless delay is harmful to the business at hand. On the contrary, all who are not impeded by age or weak health should make an effort to go on foot if the journey required of them take only one day. Those who profess the eremitic life should always practice what is harder and more perfect. Above all, when two hermits travel together, particularly for a rather long distance, let them avoid that one go on horseback and the other on foot, even if one be a priest and the other a lay brother. They should both go on foot or both on horseback, unless they are forced to do otherwise because of the weakness of one of them or because of the lack of horses. Brothers should be equal in all things.

If a monk, as soon as he has gotten clear of the enclosure of the hermitage, hastens to cast off the severe life he led therein, it is a bad sign and reveals paltry observance. Such a hermit shows that in practicing austerities, he was not so much inspired by love of the rule as forced by the necessity of the place. To avoid this, hermits who for any reason leave the hermitage should, as far as conditions allow, preserve the customs of eremitic life. Where that is impossible, they should at least observe those of the cenobitic life according to the *Rule of Saint Benedict*.... They should flee as from a conflagration monasteries of nuns, of whatever order they may be, even Camaldolese....[22] They should carry a little Bible.... Unless they have to cross vast tracts of uninhabited land, they

---

[21] F+ :145.
[22] RVE f. 106, 106v.

should never consent to take food for more than one day; if more is offered to them, they should give the surplus to the poor.... Their whole conduct should be marked more by simplicity rather than by prudence.... They will not associate with the great or eat at their tables.... They will avoid long conversations with their hosts or companions and will strive to speak serenely of God, not through vainglory, but for the benefit of their neighbors. Above all they must ever praise God and bless Him and ask His help for their benefactors. They should not become too familiar with anyone: *Solus esse, solus jubilare, gaudere* — they must be alone, exult and rejoice alone.[23]

Those who are not lovers of solitude ("*solitudinis amatores*")[24] have no right to the title of hermits. There must be a kind of devotion to the hermitage in order to justify the traditional title of *eremi cultores*, cultivators of solitude.[25] In order to love solitude one must stay there. "The hermits should be glad to dwell in the hermitage through love of solitude, which is so lovable and pleasing to holy souls."[26] Little by little it will reveal all its sweetness to them. "They should learn to keep to themselves, to abstain from human conversations, and to speak of God. Then they will begin to taste the very sweet tranquillity of solitary life, and once they have absorbed this, they will find no difficulty but rather great joy in persevering there until death."[27]

They must strive to maintain constant stability in the hermitage and in the cell, in order that by God's grace their unremitting faithfulness will make it pleasant to stay there. If they get into the habit of leaving

---

[23] F+ :217 v.

[24] F A: 19.

[25] This title is used, for instance, in the *Chronicle of Saint Benignus*, PL 162,825. It is applied to Saint John the Baptist in the hymn of first Vespers for his feast on June 24, in the Roman Breviary. The same title is found inscribed at the gate of the Sacro Eremo Tuscolano of Frascati.

[26] FA: 21.

[27] F A: 22c.

it, their cell will soon become a prison for them: he who often leaves it, spontaneously and without good reason, quickly forgets it and comes to detest it. But he who rarely leaves it, and then for but a short time and by order of the superior, returns ever more eagerly and finds it ever sweeter.[28]

To observe stability, it is not enough merely to refrain from going out. Even within the cell instability must be avoided.

Hermits should so completely cut off the vice of rambling about that, even within the cell, they should prefer to stay firm and steady in the same spot at the same occupation. Those who have less taste for stability might be stirred up by a spirit of wandering and, spurred by some devil or other, spend the whole day wandering from one room to another of their cell, taking up several tasks at once only to drop them as quickly. On the contrary, they should strive to be ever in the same place at the same task, not yielding easily to boredom or the need for change. Our fathers in the eremitic life have always declared this: for the fretful, restless hermit, the cell is a prison and a torture chamber, occasioning great agony. But for the hermit who is calm and mindful of stability, the cell and the silence offer a safe refuge from all temptations, a place of refreshment, a beginning of paradise.[29]

---

[28] RVE f. 102, 102v.
[29] RVE f. 102v.

VII

THE OCCUPATIONS OF THE HERMIT

The hermit in his solitude is free from all the ordinary occupations of other men. In this sense the solitary life is a life of leisure. Contrary to what one might think, however, it is a leisure full of work, the most laborious of leisures: *negotiosissimum otium*.[1] It must be so: otherwise eremitic life would be worthless rather than useful. The Rule, therefore, formally expresses the obligation to fill all hours with real occupations.

> All must keep busy at manual work during the proper and prescribed time for it. Then they must devote other definite hours to reading, prayer, and other spiritual exercises, so that the whole length of the day and night may seem short and insufficient. There should always be more to do than there is time for. Woe to him who begins to find the days too long.[2]

How, in practice, should the use of time be organized? Giustiniani has left us two individual timetables, the first addressed to one of his hermits, the other written in the form of a soliloquy. They are characterized by a perfect equilibrium between all the needs of the body and those of the spirit. With winning naturalness the author

---

[1] F+ :218.
[2] RVE f. 102.

passes from the most concrete details to sublime considerations. We can see this in a few examples:

When you go to bed, before falling asleep, read a book of history, preferably the life of a saint or some other easy and devout subject. Never cover more than one octavo page, because short and easy reading best suits that time of night.... Your confessions should be brief, pure, and without repetitions: just tell your sins simply without entering into details of when and how; do not seek or give advice; do not discuss any other matter; do not return to past confessions.... Never fail to set the table for meals, for you should never eat in a negligent way. If you have no table or bowl, or if they are dirty, ask for clean ones, and always eat in an orderly and gentlemanly way.... After Vespers spend the time until Compline at manual work in common, or if there is no common work, do then all the tasks that you can save for that time: washing linen, fetching wood or water, sweeping the cell or the Church, and so on. Get all these jobs done ahead of time for the next day.... Each time you return to the cell after the Office, genuflect and say a short prayer, at least a Pater or an Ave, or else: *Domine Jesu, adoro te, miserere mei et adjuva me* — "O Lord Jesus, I adore Thee, have mercy on me and help me." Always keep your cell very tidy and well swept (when I say "cell," I mean also the garden and the fountain, etc., that are in front of it). Keep your body and your clothes clean; take every precaution against lice, which are a hindrance to the spiritual life. Be humble enough to ask the lay brothers to help you in such tasks as the laundry. But we should not *order* but rather humbly *request* others to do what we cannot do or do not know how to do for ourselves. Often it is as great an act of charity to receive a service as to render one. To avoid falling asleep at prayer, lean little or not at all.[3]

You should always keep a balance in favor of spiritual activity.

---

[3]   Q III: 187; Q III: 52.

Do manual work of that kind and to that extent that either serves practical needs, or keeps you healthy, or makes you humble, or provides necessary relaxation. Prefer the more modest and menial tasks, those which help your brothers more than yourself. If there is no need for such work or if your health does not require it, then concentrate on spiritual, rather than physical exercises. Just as the soul is not for the sake of the body, but the body for the soul, so spiritual occupations are not subordinated to the body, but bodily works are ordained to those of the spirit.[4]

But what are these spiritual occupations? They are innumerable and each is endless. The most enlightening explanation of how a contemplative soul keeps busy attending to "itself alone and God" is a long elevation which we quote in part:

Those who have never practiced the occupations of religious leisure imagine that a solitary is constantly overwhelmed by inactivity and idleness, bored stiff, full of regrets, like a sleepy man or an irrational animal that lets the time pass doing nothing.

But, my Lord God, I in my solitude speak to You. How it enchants me to speak to You, and when I speak to You I cannot lie. I declare that long years of experience have proved that the more I am solitary, the less I am idle. Only when I am not solitary am I inert, subject to boredom and regret. Never do the days seem so short, the nights so brief, the passage of time so rapid, as when I can enjoy amiable solitude, free of all outside occupation and far from men. It seems to me that in this, more than in any other way of life, occupations are both lacking and superabundant. No indeed, the life of solitaries is not what some may imagine, inactive and idle. More than any other life, it is active and laborious. Is it idleness to read, to study, to compose, to write? Is it idleness to examine our conscience, to regulate the soul's affections, to recall our past life, to put in order carefully our present life, to provide prudently for the future?

---

[4]   Q III: 52.

Is it idleness to repent our past misdeeds, to combat temptation and inordinate desires, to arm ourselves in advance against the near occasions of disturbance and downfall, to think of death and to place it before our eyes so that it may not catch us unawares? Is it idleness to meditate on human and divine realities worthy of ceaselessly occupying noble minds, and to ponder these, not in haphazard daydreams, but with order and concentration? Is it idleness to raise our voice frequently by day and by night in Psalms, canticles, and hymns, praising God the Creator, and thanking Him for all His benefits? Or with a voice still more ringing and effective to ascend by mental prayer toward the divine Majesty insofar as mortal man can? Thus may we, as it were, leave this world insofar as our mortal state allows and converse in heaven with the blessed spirits, with the holy angels, and with their divine Creator and ours. Thus may we in some way contemplate the ineffable and inexpressible perfections of God, as in a mirror and by analogy. Is it idleness to arouse and exhort others to such a life and to such exercises, by speech to those present and by letter to those absent? Is it idleness to wear cheap, rough garments, to eat poorly and meagerly, to keep long vigils, to do hard and menial work? By these means we can tame the pride of life and curb the desires of the flesh, training the body to submit to and obey the soul and reason in everything. Do you maintain that all these activities and many other similar practices of hermits are mere inertia, boredom, lethargy? Instead you must admit that the solitary life is more active and laborious than any other, busy not at external corporal tasks or worldly business, but at those nobler and more fruitful interior and spiritual exercises as best suit the part of ourselves that is immortal.

How it is with other solitaries, I do not know. But I can easily believe that each of them manages the leisure of his solitude better than I. As for me, You know, Lord, and You can see that the more solitary I am, the more tasks occur that I ought to do and want to do. But unfortunately through lack of time I must put aside some projects, as if I wanted to save them for another occasion. Those that I do undertake must often, alas, be left uncompleted, because I lack time to finish them as I should, or at least as best I could with God's help. How often in the leisure of solitude I have postponed prayer because I desired and took pleasure in reading! My application to prayer, weak and cold as it is, keeps me from reading. How often the effort to write down a few thoughts for my own sake or that of others has hindered me from giving due time to prayer and reading! How often, because of one of these occupations, I have put off my next meal or deprived my body, as right now, of the hours of needed rest! I would like to do more; each task seems necessary, each attracts me strongly. Yet I do none perfectly, or even as well as I might with divine help, if I had enough time and if I thought of only one at a time.

Some may believe and say that solitaries are inactive and idle, but I shall never cease thinking and saying that no other life is as active and toilsome as that of God's servant, the hermit. For a time, longer than I would have wished, I experienced worldly affairs and the worries of governing a congregation. In these matters I always seemed impeded more by lack of ability, solicitude, and diligence than by lack of time. With the business of the active life, the more I do, the less there is to do. But in matters of the solitary life, the more ability, solicitude, and diligence I muster, the more I always find to do and the less time to do it. In the exercises of solitary leisure, that is, the contemplative life, the more I do, the more I see to be done. In the active life it is generally enough to prepare and arrange matters well, and then to entrust the execution to others. But the business of the solitary life must all, with God's help, be arranged and executed by ourselves. The former can, for the most part, be arranged and executed while eating or walking about. The latter is of such nature that each matter requires an entirely free mind and absorbs the whole self.

To express what I mean, I will make use of an example. To discharge worldly duties, however numerous they may be, one soul suffices. Yet it seems to me that even a hundred souls would not suffice for the exercises of the life of leisure. In any case I am sure that all the hundred could be occupied worthily and fruitfully. Men who are engaged in secular service, especially those who govern worldly affairs, need only one soul and have plenty of time at their disposal. Sometimes they know neither how to keep their mind occupied nor how to spend their time without boredom. So they even take up games, music, and all sorts of inanities characteristic of ludicrous and deliberately senseless persons. A hermit finds that one soul alone does not suffice him to serve God as he would like, and ought, and perhaps could. He would like to have a hundred souls, and if he had them, he is sure that he could put them all to work: he even doubts if that many would be sufficient. He takes great care in regulating his time. He keeps vigil, eats only once a day, and avoids all extraneous occupations, in order to make his days and nights longer than they are for other men. In spite of all this he has too little time and too much work. On the other hand, men who are occupied in base worldly activities, in sleep, in debauchery, in laughter, in dissolute talk, loathe as if it were death itself the idea of being alone and recollected, of thinking about themselves. These are the very men, oddly enough, who are bold enough to call solitaries inactive, useless, and sterile, who style them "breadbaskets." We must not only pardon such men, but pity them, for they are fooling themselves. They stray from the way of truth by thus judging and condemning others, while they themselves are wandering off into still greater peril by their own conduct. Lord God, deign to pardon them, and by paths known only to Your Majesty, lead them to eternal light, so that they may be delivered from the darkness of this world and may know this truth and many others that are still hidden from them.

But returning to myself: now that by Your grace, Lord, I am more solitary than ever before, I know that I cannot find time to do all I should do and would like to do in Your service.... Oh, how much reading I would like to do, were it not for lack of time and the demands of other duties! Not that I yearn to reread the books of pagan philosophers and poets, for I regret and repent having devoted more time than I should have to such study. But I would like to read many writings that would reveal the hidden and spiritual sense of Your holy Scriptures, many works that might spur my soul to devotion and compunction, much that would help me to distinguish, so to speak, one leprosy from another, one sin from another. Oh, how I wish I could carry Your holy Gospels ever in my hand next to my heart, as we read of the holy virgin Saint Cecilia, that I might never interrupt day or night that divine reading! You know, Lord, that I have often intended to do so; but either I lacked time or my soul was occupied with other things. Not only would I like to read, but I need to apply myself earnestly to understand what is read, to commit to memory the meaning rather than the words, to compare the opinions of several doctors, or several passages of one of them, and to do other similar things, that only those who study can understand....

To read and to write are truly the easiest tasks, the least absorbing and the most imperfect of the solitary's life.... But he must also meditate, pray, and ascend as much as possible to the contemplation of heavenly realities; think over with bitter regret the ill-used days of his life; examine, describe, dispose, regulate, moderate the passions of the present day; commit the future to God's service; think of death and prepare for it. After such meditation on visible and created things, what can we say of the quest of the invisible reality of God, of prayer? We must thank You, Lord, for Your favors, thank You for having created us, and for us having created the whole visible world. We praise You and thank You for the benefit of the Redemption that You accomplished, You who became incarnate, who lived among men, who taught them by example and doctrine, who died and was raised to life for them. We must thank You for the countless marvelous benefits that You have granted to all humanity, for the particular benefits that You granted us and that You continue to grant each day. We must praise You, adore You, offer You the homage of latria or adoration that is due to You alone. Our intellects and our wills must unite to invoke You, to offer ourselves and to consecrate ourselves to Your service, to submit and conform ourselves to Your will, to desire You alone and Your glory, to strive to know You ever better, to love You, to raise ourselves towards You, to make friends with You, to unite ourselves to You, to be transformed in You, to disappear and to be annihilated in You. Oh, how many acts are involved in the practice of prayer, the contemplation of Your invisible and ineffable perfections: Your eternity, omnipotence, immensity, wisdom, ineffable charity, and the justice that is inseparable from Your mercy. You alone, Lord, are an endless abyss, immense, capable of absorbing forever the attention of a countless multitude of souls, as You engross the countless multitudes of heavenly spirits.

Men occupied with worldly affairs should not say that solitaries are inactive or idle. If by *idle* they mean that hermits neither buy, nor sell, nor build, nor navigate, nor engage in lawsuits, nor raise children, then such a condemnation would likewise apply to the holy angels of God, who could be termed idle, inactive, and useless. According to his own manner and degree, the solitary undertakes the same activities as the blessed spirits. With the Seraphim, he loves his Creator without ceasing; with the Cherubim, his intelligence is ever occupied with Him; with the Thrones, he strives to make himself a temple of His Supreme Creator. And likewise for all the other angelic functions: in all things he endeavors to act like the angels. Moreover, since the solitary is a man, he performs all sorts of corporal actions...which the angelic spirits do not. So it is that a human solitary could be considered even less idle than an angel, since the hermit devotes to God's service not only the operations of his spirit but also his exterior actions: He lifts his voice to praise Your divine Majesty by day and by night; gives an example of humility, patience, and all the virtues; celebrates the sacred mysteries of the Mass, offering the saving Sacrifice of the Sacred Body and Precious Blood of Jesus, as well as receiving that Body as his food often, almost daily; prepares himself for this mystery, contemplating the divine clemency, offering thanks for so divine a gift, such an extraordinary boon.

In addition, since the solitary, as religious as his life is, still treads the slippery and dusty path of our human pilgrimage, he must admit how often his feet, that is, his affections, are sullied by the mud of some vain and harmful concupiscence or by the dust of human praise. He must then undertake a laborious task unknown to the angelic spirits, who are free of this necessity. At every step, that is in every action, in every desire, the hermit must watch with a great caution to avoid stepping into the mud or the dust. In spite of all this effort, so frail is human nature and so numerous are the perils of this life that he must frequently be purified, washed by contrition, penance, and confession. He must be strengthened in his purpose to watch over himself with greater caution in the future. I need hardly mention, as it proves little or nothing, the hermit's tears, as he weeps through sorrow at having offended God or because of the sweetness of the divine graces and heavenly visitations he experiences within himself. Perhaps he weeps in his impatient longing for the heavenly fatherland, or in his burning ardor to see You, my Lord Jesus Christ, and to enjoy the beatific vision of Your presence. I shall not describe the spiritual colloquies of the hermit with his Guardian angel, with the other blessed, and with the souls of those whom he loved in this world and whom he now loves more than ever since they have left him, especially those whose virtue was so great that he may suppose them already blessed in heaven.

If in the midst of actions so numerous and so great anyone can pass for idle, inactive, and subject to boredom, I confess that I am content to be, and even choose to be idle and inactive in that way rather than to be active in the manner of those who love the world. Of this I am not ashamed. Rather I am proud of being chosen to be in Your service, Lord Jesus Christ, and to be disdained and taken for inactive and useless. Being a religious and a solitary, I leave to others the worldly and civil affairs in which they suppose themselves to be so active, so nobly employed, so important. In return for their opinion of us, I consider *them* to be like those children who fashion little houses of straw and mud and play all day with pebbles as if with precious gems, a laughingstock in their simplicity. When I see worldlings engrossed and busy all day long with earthly matters, which are nothing but pieces of straw, when I see them place such a high value on the treasures of this earth, which are but mud and pebbles, then I cannot say that I laugh, but I feel a great pity. Knowing that this world passes away and that nothing in it can endure, I am a stranger to it as much as I can be by leading a religious life in solitude. All my thoughts and desires are to direct my steps to the true homeland in heaven. Weak as I am, as much as I can I spur on and invite others to the same destination. On this path, which to me seems nowise idle or inactive but rather active and laborious, I ever praise You, my Lord, and strive to know and to love You always, until through Your clemency alone, I may reach that land where I can endlessly and perfectly know You, and love You, and eternally praise You. There may I sleep and rest in peace with You, rest in the peace that is not inactive and idle but is more laborious than any other occupation, the peace which You enjoy, and with You all the blessed spirits. Amen.[5]

There have been several references to the angels in this text which details the hermit's occupations. Because angels adore God constantly, they offer the ideal of a life wholly consecrated to His praise. But the hermit must do more than adore. Unlike the angels, he belongs to this sinful world, and he must do penance. Moreover, he still lives by faith, not by vision. In this double aspect he has other models: the prophets and the penitents. Elias was "the first to introduce eremitic life."[6] John the Baptist "fled from cities and from men."[7] Both these prophets awaited the revelation of the Lord. But perhaps even better than them, Mary Magdalen is the perfect type of the eremitic life, if we admit that the Gospels refer to her in telling of the woman who wept for her sins and then lived near the Lord. She was at His feet at the time of the banquet in the home of the Pharisee, at His feet when He hung on the cross, and she again threw herself at His feet after His resurrection.[8]

"Mary of Magdala is my longtime patron. I meet up with her

---

[5] Q IV bis: 92.
[6] Q II: 103. This theme is developed at length.
[7] Q I: 192.
[8] F VIII:30.

everywhere with Jesus: on His journeys, at His meals, near the cross, at the tomb, at the resurrection."[9]

By her entire life, therefore, and by her very constancy in following the Lord everywhere, she is a model for the hermit. "If you wish to lead the solitary life, imitate Mary Magdalen in everything. In her are ascertained all the elements of the solitary life." By what the Gospels tell of her and by what is reported of her subsequent life, Mary Magdalen teaches the hermit all his duties. "Do not be satisfied to kiss the feet of Christ, but hold them in your embrace.... Do not abandon solitude for the active life.... Withdraw from everything and everyone, and live perfectly alone with Christ, with no other solace, no other love. Await the dissolution of the body, knowing naught but yourself and Christ, or rather, Christ alone, and yourself in Christ."[10]

---

[9] Q I: 130. The life and deeds of Mary Magdalen are treated here at length. She is called *quella incomparabile amatrice di Gesù*, "that incomparable lover of Jesus." At the end of the text (f.158ᵛ-159ᵛ) Giustiniani tries to establish that the same person is involved in all the actions which would come to be ascribed to Mary Magdalen.

[10] F VII: 140v; further development in Q II: 134.

PART THREE

THE HERMIT'S PRAYER

VIII

THE HERMIT'S ONLY TEACHER

Among the hermit's occupations, spiritual exercises are divided into three kinds, which the rule clearly sets forth: "Whenever the hermits are not engaged in manual work, their whole time is allotted to study, psalmody, and prayer."[1] Such is the total program: *study,* which really means careful attention given to Holy Scripture; *psalmody,* in its various forms; *prayer,* both public and private. These three activities complement each other and should aim at the same union with God. All three are equally necessary.

Study is justified only to that degree–a great degree–that it prepares for the other two activities. In this regard it is absolutely necessary to the hermit. Once the hermit understands the precise object of his study, that will in turn determine his method.

Giustiniani repeats several times this important principle:

He who believes that Jesus Christ is true God and true man need not

---

[1]   RVE f. 84V.

look elsewhere for moral discipline or for doctrine, nor for examples of philosophers or outstanding men. It is sufficient that he read and reread the holy Gospels, which openly propose to everyone the doctrine and example of Jesus Christ. He who believes that Jesus Christ is true God and true man need not seek to learn from any other master the meaning of virtue and life, good and evil, truth and falsehood. He has in Christ the ineffable divine wisdom, teaching all we need to know of these matters. He need not wish for any other illustrious and excellent man to teach him by the example of his life. In Jesus Christ, true man as well as being at the same time true God, he has at hand all the most brilliant examples of the highest virtues, gathered together more perfectly in Him than in any man who is nothing more than a man, and devoid of any flaw or defect. And so he should not seek any other teacher or master.[2]

Christ is the only master and the only book, the book that contains all divine wisdom. My book should be Jesus Christ on the Cross: a book entirely written with His precious Blood that is the price of my soul and the redemption of the world. The five chapters of this book are the five sacred wounds. I want to study that one book alone, and other books only insofar as they comment on it. Did not Saint Paul say that he no longer knew anything but Jesus Christ, Jesus Christ crucified? It is vain to wish to know anything else at all. But this book must be read in silence.[3]

Those Christians are blind who, believing in Jesus Christ, think they can learn the truth in another school than His or from another author than Christ and His holy Gospels.[4]

All other true doctrine derives from His, and in particular, all that the doctors have written in the Church is inspired by Him and should lead to Him.

---

[2]   Q II: 52.
[3]   F I: 49.
[4]   F I: 47.

Christian authors have produced numerous and varied writings. Some have studied in detail one particular mystery of Christianity, others some other, using different methods and displaying more or less subtlety. They have also spoken of the examples furnished by the saints of the times before Christ or after His coming. But the most salutary doctrine is that which sets before us the very mystery of Christ, our glorious Redeemer. In fact we are called *Christians* on account of Christ, and Christ is the blessed Son of God, the uncreated Word, the divine Truth, who could not be mistaken in His teaching. On the other hand, He took on our human nature, without any of the stains of original sin or of our actual sins. His doctrine, therefore, is necessarily the holiest, more perfect than that of all other men who have ever lived, live now, or will live in the future. No teaching can surpass that which sets before our eyes Our Lord and Redeemer Jesus, as the light, the guide, the mirror, the infallible rule, the one true tutor.

We should always go to the sources: but all that has been said or written in Christianity has its source in Him.

Jesus Christ is a book in which is summed up, for those who know how to read the writing, all doctrine, all discipline, all controversy, all treatises, all exhortations which have been or will be done in conformity with God from the beginning to the end of the world. The sacred writers have never conveyed more than a particle of the total doctrine contained in this book; they have been little streams in which flow the water of that inexhaustible fountain. Each of them writes only a chapter, a short paragraph of the blessed book that is Jesus Christ, the abyss and source of all intellectual and moral doctrine.[5]

This conviction determines the method to employ to acquire knowledge in Jesus Christ. After stating the general principles, the

---

[5] Q III: 172.

Rule then descends to the practical details that the regulation of study requires.

> The hermits are allowed to undertake any study that is not forbidden by the Church. They should always take care to avoid banned or superstitious books. Everything else may be read by each according to his capacity. Undoubtedly those who study Holy Scripture rather than profane works have chosen the better part, for the latter are as nothing compared to the former. Those, therefore, who have made sufficient progress so as to find their delight in the continual study of Holy Scripture without the help of any secular books, should abstain from reading the latter. But those who, either to improve their Latin or to acquire other useful knowledge, need to study other matters, may do so, but without forgetting that their goal should ever remain to gain a better knowledge of Holy Scripture. Moreover during the days and hours when silence may be broken, two or more hermits together may discuss some point of their studies, give each other lessons, or explain authors, especially Christian ones.... When religious who are in the habit of preaching visit the hermitage, the superior will ask them to speak to the hermits as a means of exhortation.... All the hermits may, without any special permission, enter the library of the hermitage, where the books must be arranged in good order. A catalogue of all the books will be kept, and any hermit may with the superior's permission take to his cell whatever volumes he may need, provided he furnish the library with a written record of the books he has taken.... Each year new books should be bought, whichever seem the best and the most useful: no year should pass without at least ten gold crowns being spent on books.... All this is arranged because experience has proved that for religious souls study stimulates all the virtues.[6]

The Rule of 1524 goes a step further by providing a new office:

---

[6] RVE f. 84V-85.

To encourage the brothers to study, the general chapter will each year designate one or more lectors, chosen from among the most competent hermits. Every day they should read and explain to the others a passage of Holy Scripture. The father definitors should also take care to send to the lectors those hermits who are more studious and better able to learn.[7]

Throughout his life as a religious, Giustiniani preached by example what he ordered regarding study. He never ceased this work, especially in the domain of the sacred sciences. He certainly continued to write on philosophical subjects:[8] he drew up a list of the writings of Aristotle, Plato, and Plotinus, as well as a list of the names of Platonic and Peripatetic philosophers.[9] He took notes on the classical authors,[10] but above all on the Fathers of the Church: Origen, Rufinus, Eusebius of Caesarea,[11] Saint Augustine, Cassian, Saint Gregory the Great, Cassiodorus, Pseudo-Dionysius, and Saint Bernard. He read Saint Thomas, Saint Albert the Great, and Dante.[12] He translated into Italian some opuscules attributed to Saint Basil, to Saint Bernard, and to Richard of Saint Victor.[13] He did not neglect either canon law or Church history. He began a treatise on interdiction,[14] and he made a summary of Sozomen's *Ecclesiastical History*.[15] He took notes on the history of monasticism[16] and of what he called "the Camaldolese republic."[17] He made a list of all those who had written against the

---

7   Ed. Lugano, p. 156.
8   F VII: 201.
9   F VII: 168-169.
10   F VII:170.
11   Q I:3, 15, 16.
12   F II, Q I, F VII, passim.
13   Q I: 181, 187.
14   F VII: 197V.
15   F VII: 163-166V.
16   F VII: 198V.
17   F VII:110V.

Koran since Peter the Venerable.[18] In an opuscule against superstition he appealed to history, law, the Fathers of the Church, and Saint Thomas.[19] But on the other hand, to be within reach of all men, he composed for the novices who were illiterate a summary of Christ's teaching according to the Gospels.[20]

Thus we see that he is a model of vast culture — vast, but not diffuse, for it remains centered on the incarnate Son of God. It is nourished above all on Holy Scripture, on which most of his writings comment. The Bible can resolve all problems much better than any other book.[21]

> The Bible possesses a special power to glorify God's Name and to attract men towards the knowledge and the love of God. To hear it read is always profitable, for it cannot fail to affect the souls of those listening. But of course they must understand it. Therefore it is desirable that good translations be made in every country and that these be read in the Churches in the language that the people understand.[22]

> The source of all perfection in the Bible is the Gospel, for the reasons that we have already stated. As Christ is both God and man, His teaching possesses divine authority and is addressed to every man. He offers both doctrine and example at the same time.[23] Never, then, should we tire of reading the Gospels.

> It is reported that Arcesilas loved Homer so much that he read him before falling asleep, resumed the book on awaking, and took care that nothing could prevent his reading it. But the supreme philosophy of

---

[18] F+ :220.

[19] F+ : 182.

[20] F VIII:22.

[21] Q II: 19 — with reference to Job and the problem of evil.

[22] F I: 184. Giustiniani states that he intends to present such a plan to Pope Leo X.

[23] Q IV: 166; cf. Q III: 104V.

Christ is contained in the Gospels. Let us, therefore, follow Arcesilas; let us read a few pages on the life and teaching of Christ each morning and again in the evening. Let us likewise hear Saint Paul teaching us about Christ. Let us love Christ and do what He loves. Did He not say: "He who loves me keeps my words"? Let us fill our memory with them. Those who do not read the Gospel find it difficult to love Christ.[24]

The conclusion of the Rule is an invitation to have recourse constantly to the Gospel. "If a man wishes to win through to the interior perfection of the eremitic religious life, he must first of all read the Gospel and the best commentaries on it, that is, the Epistles of the Holy Apostles, for they do no more than explain the Gospel teaching."[25] The Fathers of the Church should be read because they speak of Jesus and set forth His teaching. Blessed Giustiniani rejoiced to live in their company.[26] He especially exalted the one whom he named "our Christian Sallust and our Christian Cicero, Pope Saint Leo the Great."[27] Why? Because "in all his writings this great Doctor teaches and proves but one thing: Jesus Christ is true God and true man. This is a truth that contains all the mysteries and all the sacraments of evangelical perfection."[28] The authority of the Gospels is based on the Incarnation,[29] and reading them directs the mind toward this mystery by which "the Lord God became a recluse in the womb of the Virgin Mary."[30] The Incarnation is continued in the Eucharist, and this mystery also inspired Giustiniani with ardent elevations.[31]

But why does this hermit write so copiously? He himself tells us: "I write less what I have learned than what I want to learn by writing. I

---

[24] F + :96, Jn 14:23.
[25] RVE f. 140V.
[26] F I: 224; cf. HE, p. 56.
[27] Q II:51.
[28] Q II:51. In F II :107 there are notes on Saint Leo's writings about the Incarnation.
[29] RVE f. 141.
[30] F I:47.
[31] F II:100.

am one of those, I confess, who make progress by writing. I have often noticed that by writing I have come to understand what I could not grasp by reading, meditating, or praying."[32] Thus he does not study for the sake of study but for the sake of contemplation, though the possibility of usefulness to others is not excluded. In the two timetables which he drew up, one for himself, the other for one of his hermits, he provided for this activity: "*utilis scriptio*: each day write something of use to yourself or to your neighbor. Once you have begun writing something, finish it and do not drop it easily."[33] "Write something for the common good or for your own consolation."[34] Study is an obligation of the eremitic life. While the hermit's object is not to write for the benefit of others, yet that may become one of the fruits of his contemplation, the result and the expression of a culture that is entirely orientated toward God.

---

[32] Q III: 104V.
[33] Q III:52.
[34] Q III: 187.

IX

THE DIVINE CANTICLES

As in study, so the hermit's spiritual life also nourishes and expresses itself in psalmody, in the traditional sense of the term. By psalmody we mean both the celebration of the Divine Office, where the Psalms play such an important role, and the private recitation of the Psalter.

Eremitic liturgy should be marked by the simplicity and austerity characteristic of the solitary life. In Giustiniani this need is accentuated by his determination to react against the pomp so prevalent at the time of the Renaissance. These two motives affect every detail and the whole tenor of the liturgy.

> In choir we remember that the monk's function is to weep for himself and for the world; we do not sing, except very rarely: we should not seek to please men.[1]...You must not take pleasure in the pomp of processions.[2]...A single bell will announce the time for the Divine Office. In cities the superfluous chiming of sets of several different bells may serve a good purpose by stirring up the people's piety and by summoning crowds: the cenobites, therefore, tolerate them. But they are quite contrary to eremitic serenity and purity.[3] ...In accord with tradition, the hermits never sing: they celebrate the work of God with modulation,

---

[1] F+:145.
[2] RVE f. 42.
[3] RVE f. 61.

in voices neither too low, nor too high, nor too loud, but devoutly, and yet with virile joy. The hermit's function is not to sing and exult, but to weep and to do penance.[4]

"The psalmody must be calm: neither too slow nor too fast, avoiding haste and confusion, so as to pronounce everything distinctly and clearly. One choir must never begin before the other has finished. Always pause in the middle of each verse.... On solemn feasts the chant should be slower and clearer. The same for the Night Office during winter, taking advantage of the longer nights."[5] Numerous points further regulate the psalmody, which by itself is the object of more recommendations than all the rest of the Office, being indeed its most important part. The Psalter must be kept in mind in drawing up the calendar or in classifying solemnities: "We must reduce the number of saints' feasts to prevent the monotony of saying the same Psalms all year long. Two principles must govern the allocation of Scriptural texts in the liturgy: the whole Bible should be read each year, and the whole Psalter should be recited in common each week."[6]

In addition to the liturgical psalmody, one of the traditional eremitic practices is "to rejoice each day in the private recitation of Psalms."[7] This psalmody also has its complete legislation. The number of Psalms to recite varies according to the seasons and according to the time remaining after the recitation of the Divine Office. It is greater during certain periods, such as Lent, and for the recluses, but it must never be lacking.[8] It must not, however, become a chore. The Rule of 1524 reduced the assignment to fifty Psalms a day in order to allow more free time for prayer. Moreover, of these fifty Psalms, half could be replaced by reading. "And it is understood that these Psalms may

---

[4] RVE f. 67V.
[5] RVE f. 68r.
[6] RVE f. 70V -71V.
[7] RVE f. 42V.
[8] RVE f. 81-82.

be said either by pronouncing the words or by going through them mentally."[9] What is essential is never to lose sight of the purpose of these instructions: "Carry out this psalmody so as to draw from it some fruit of piety or of spiritual understanding."[10]

Giustiniani often eulogized what he called "the divine canticles,"[11] which so far surpass all the science of the philosophers.[12] But he insisted that they must be studied to be appreciated. He himself did so. He translated and explained from the Greek certain verses that had a different meaning in the Vulgate.[13] To attain a deeper insight into the meaning of the Psalms, he wished he knew Hebrew, and he consulted those who did know it. "I greatly desire a commentary on Psalm 144 (145), which in Hebrew is alphabetic. Study it in the Hebrew so that you can tell me something. I seem to recall that Pico della Mirandola explained it, but I do not have his books here."[14] Giustiniani recommended paying attention in the first place to the literal sense.

> In reciting the Psalms, I would like you, if possible, to curb your high intelligence and turn aside for a while from all mystical or allegorical senses to consider purely and simply the literal meaning, that is, what good David meant at the moment he composed the Psalms. Then you will see that Scripture is beyond compare with any poet or philosopher. David is truly a great philosopher, as he contemplates in the Psalms God's lofty mysteries, the creatures of His hands, and the qualities of our soul!...[15]

Now that you have a tutor to teach you Hebrew, have him read you

---

[9] Ed. Lugano, p. 157.
[10] Q III:52.
[11] Q IV bis 229.
[12] F II: 122V.
[13] F I:205, 211. There are notes on the Psalms in F I:207V, Q II:10-15, etc.
[14] Q IV:459.
[15] F 1: 49.

the Psalms, the most obscure part of Holy Scripture, but also the most useful, the most pleasing, the most necessary for the interpretation of all the rest of the Bible. Take a close look at the Psalms according to the Hebrew, if not for your own sake, then in order to help me. If you devote intense effort to it at first, you will be spared drudgery later on. Of course we have Saint Jerome's Psalter *secundum hebraicam veritatem*, according to the truth of the Hebrew, but I think that a word for word study of the original can make one understand still more.... How sweet it is to read the Psalms! Far from boring me, it gives me pleasure. What could I do that would please me more? In the Psalms I praise and glorify my Creator; I appeal, I honor, and I beseech Him; I thank Him and bless Him; I confess my sins and implore mercy. In the Psalms I consider the vanity of the world and the deceptiveness of all things; I see myself mirrored and I understand the frailty of life, the paltry value of this mortal body, and how the senses distance us from God if the soul lets itself be governed by them; I understand how noble the soul is if it seeks true self-knowledge, without which it resembles the animals. And finally, in the Psalms I contemplate, in so far as the countless spots on my eyes permit, the infinite power, wisdom, and goodness of God.... If men studied the Psalter as eagerly as they study the sonnets of Petrarch or the Odes of Horace, they would find more poetic charm in them — to say nothing of higher qualities than in Horace. Only those who have never given any close attention to the Psalms could think otherwise, just as there are people who understand nothing of Petrarch and therefore find his poetry a laughingstock (which it really is). But for me the Psalms are my sonnets, my odes!

I learn them by heart so that I can say them without having to hold the Psalter in my hands. The literal sense by itself so ravishes me, I find in them thoughts so high and so divine, that I have not yet wanted to look up the commentators who give spiritual and allegorical interpretations. I intend some day to study them thoroughly, but for the time being I am satisfied with the literal sense. There I get an idea of what zeal for God filled good David's heart and of how far advanced he was in self-knowledge and real self-contempt, that is, contempt of the mortal part of his being, as well as in knowledge and contempt of the world. Often I say to myself: how mistaken are those who are fonder of Homer among the Greeks, Virgil among the Romans, or Petrarch amongst us than of that good Jew David, with his exquisite loveliness in poetry, nobility and subtlety of true philosophy, and tenderness of a man enamored of true, eternal, heavenly beauty. We can, moreover, find in the Psalms Jesus Christ prophesied so expressly that we might well believe that some of them were composed after, rather than before, His death, so explicitly does the literal sense speak of Him. I love to learn the Psalms by heart so that I can say them conveniently, unhindered by illness or any other obstacle.[16]

David deserves our admiration because he experienced in advance all the sentiments of a Christian, and especially those of a hermit: detachment from the world and desire for God.[17] Psalm 118 (119) in particular should fill us with enthusiasm, for it contains the sublime mysteries of Christ together with all that is necessary for our perfection.[18] A love of the Psalms is the mark of a true monk. Woe to those who scorn them! *Vae illis qui psalmos spernunt!*[19] On the other hand, those who esteem them and recite them willingly find consolation in them.

The main concern of monks should be to weep for their offenses, to praise God for His countless mercies towards us, and to embrace Jesus, who hangs naked and bleeding on the Cross, with all the affection of their souls. So no physical or spiritual occupation can offer them greater satisfaction than the recitation of the Psalter. Therein they can confess their misdeeds and ask God's pardon, often in words so

---

[16] F I: 40.
[17] Q I: 51.
[18] Q III: 151.
[19] F II:105V.

touching that the soul is roused to deep emotion. In the Psalms more perhaps than in any other part of Scripture, they praise and glorify our eternal Creator and Redeemer.[20]

We may well doubt whether any spiritual exercise can please the man who is bored by the Psalter. So suited is Psalm-reading to monks that in former times, when they made their profession, they used to be urged to keep the Psalter always in their hands or on their lips. This meant that whenever a monk was free of other duties, nothing was more suitable for him than to read the Psalms.... Nothing is more useful to the monk, who in solitude and silence wants always to meditate, often to pray, and at times to contemplate.[21]

---

[20] F I: 155.
[21] Q IV: 257.

X

PRAYER WITHOUT A METHOD

Study and psalmody are already genuine forms of prayer to the extent that they include attentive and meditative reading of Holy Scripture. For monastic prayer comprises these three inseparable elements which the whole tradition affirms to be indispensable: *lectio, meditatio, oratio* — reading, meditation, prayer. This concept of the life of prayer is recalled in the Rule of 1520:

All who know how to read will read Holy Scripture at least once a day.... But it is useless to read unless one meditates on what is read with all possible application. Therefore, during the times of silence each one shall reflect upon what he has read while he is in cell or at work. During the time when silence is broken to allow the brothers the recreation of fraternal conversation, they will speak of their reading. So they will avoid idle words and will make progress in the understanding of Scripture. But without God's help, reading and meditation would be of no avail, just as all other observances would be likewise impossible. We must, therefore, give first place to prayer: for the main characteristic of a hermit is that he spends his time in prayer. If our fathers have not assigned any definite time of the day or night for mental prayer — as is done in other religious institutes — they meant thereby to indicate that continual prayer is as necessary to the interior life as breathing is to exterior life. And so the hermits, whenever they have no other task, should always pray. Each one will choose the time best suited to him when he will remain motionless in prayer for at least half an hour, either all at once or divided into shorter periods. Even if at times his distracted mind can hardly pray, he must not fail to devote to meditation the time that has been appointed, kneeling before a picture of Christ or taking up whatever other position helps devotion. He may be assured that the time he spends thus will be counted as prayer, and if he perseveres he will soon, with God's help, arrive at sweetness in prayer.

Those who come to the hermitage from secular life or from a monastery must be formed in prayer before all else, for if a man who has been sufficiently instructed does not then devote at least half an hour daily to prayer, he cannot persevere in our life. It is as impossible to grow spiritually without prayer as it is to grow physically without food. Prayer makes the mind return with renewed vigor to reading and meditation, while the latter in turn foster prayer. These three activities imply one another and are mutually helpful. A man is a hermit in name only if he does not devote himself daily to reading, to meditation, and to prayer.[1] Each of these three acts of prayer must have its own characteristic feature: *studiosa lectio, ordinata meditatio, devota oratio* — careful reading, well-ordered meditation, devout prayer. Reading must be attentive, not superficial. Meditation is an effort at reflection, requiring that the mind should not wander but should fix its attention on very definite dogmatic and moral considerations. Prayer proceeds from it and takes the form of a direct conversation with God inspired by Him. For here again the only master is the Lord. No book can teach us to speak to Him: only the Holy Spirit can suggest how we should adore God and lament our sins. We must remain supple to His action. We must choose the time when the spirit is most tranquil and free[2] and let grace act. Then occasionally we will be granted contemplation. The rhythm of this process, however, varies according to the character of each soul and according to God's gifts to it. Happy are those for whom but a brief reading and a short meditation are sufficient to raise them up to a prolonged state of prayer! Happy are those who then become

---

[1] RVE f. 83-83V.

[2] Q III:52.

rapt in contemplation, that state proper to the angels and the blessed in heaven, but sometimes granted by Almighty God to those who, though in the body, practice a perfection verging on that of the angels! Their nature is then raised beyond its proper powers. Their spirit enjoys the sweetness of God. Blessed are those whose nature often suffers such violence and who experience such rapture for a longer time, if indeed it can last long.[3]

The most important exercise of prayer is prayer in the strict sense. Giustiniani has left us the beginning of a treatise on this subject. It is impossible to summarize it without distortion, for it contains what is better than mere theory: a demonstration.[4] Its fundamental principle is that "prayer is multiple and diverse." We can never find two men who pray in exactly the same way, and each man's way of prayer varies almost every time he prays. It is, therefore, vain and superfluous to seek a method of prayer. Rather the best method is to pray without a method. The Holy Spirit is an incomparable artist in this area, and we need only let Him bear us without looking backwards to find out by what path He is leading us. Just as a ship cuts its way through the waters of the ocean but leaves no trace of its wake, so the soul borne along by the Holy Spirit across the ocean of divine contemplation cannot, even by turning around, see either the route it has followed or the point it has reached.

If then we wish to present the method which follows no method but permits every way of prayer, we must first note that prayer, contrary to what the word itself suggests, is not limited to asking for something from God. More often prayer is truer and more efficacious when we ask nothing of Him. Thus we can say that each Psalm and each verse of the Psalms by itself alone is a prayer, even though many of them ask nothing of God. Saint Paul suggests to Timothy four kinds of prayer, of which only one means to ask: *postulatio*.[5] We gain more by thanking

---

3 F VIII: 2; cf. also Q IV bis: 173.
4 Fortunately the text has been published in *Vita cristiana, Rivista ascetico-mistica,* XIV (1942), p. 117-144.
5 1 Tim 2:1.

God for a benefit than by asking Him for one; we please Him more by acknowledging our wretchedness or His mercy than by imploring the help of His mercy to relieve our wretchedness. Let each one, then, freely cling to the way of prayer that attracts him. Let him not wish to observe some way of prayer or other, but let him follow the Holy Spirit, who will bring him from one way to another.

It is true that there are ready-made prayers that we can say and recite, but that kind of prayer resembles reading more than mental prayer. In mental prayer the soul is "suspended in God" without the aid of any printed text. The prayer that it exhales under the breath of the Holy Spirit, the cries and moans that it utters, perhaps even with the voice, constitute genuine mental prayer. That is why to try to set a method and an order to follow would be to debase prayer to an act of reading, whereas normally the opposite would occur — reading should give birth to prayer.

We must repeat, then, that prayer is not subject to any method, except the method of prior asceticism. Instead of seeking how to behave in prayer, it would be better to learn how much ardor, purity, and contrition should mark our prayer. Instead of trying to pin down a method of prayer, it would be better to strive to reach that proper degree of fervor and purity. This does not mean that prayer does not assume any definite form: man's finite spirit cannot grasp an indeterminate object. But the fact remains that the true way of prayer is to follow no particular way or, if you will, to follow them all. Blessed Giustiniani declares that he states this principle because it corresponds with his own experience: "truth forces him" to speak as he does.

Since he is asked how he prays, he gives these seven words that summarize all his attitudes:

> *I adore, I confess, I thank, I invoke, I await, and I desire*: but what must precede all this is the *avowal* of my misery and unworthiness. In these seven words I sometimes strive to confine the infinite multitude of the ways of prayer. I find each of these so vast and deep that they are like seven abysses into which the spirit can plunge without limit. Each of them suggests so many considerations

and so many ways and qualities of prayer that no spirit, however lofty, could exhaust them even throughout a whole long lifetime of prayer. We begin by recognizing our own misery; then we address God to adore, confess, thank, invoke, entreat and desire Him. But we can also produce other acts, such as praising God, blessing, glorifying, magnifying and exalting Him.

"One example can prove the inexhaustible resources of each of these words. Let us begin with the act that should precede and prepare for all the others: confession [about oneself]. Should we wish to classify the many considerations suggested by this word, we could think first of man's natural unworthiness, then of that due to his own transgressions, and finally of that caused by his negligence, his ignorance, his coldness, and his voluntary weakness." Here Blessed Giustiniani takes up more than ten pages to acknowledge his wretchedness. This interminable act of true humility proves, better than any theory, how easy it is for a contemplative soul to speak constantly to the Lord. Nor can we convey the "bittersweet quality" of the "gentle tears" that form the accompaniment of this interior dialogue. The confession of its misery suffices to keep the soul in God's presence: *sibi soli et Deo vacat* [it is empty for itself alone and God]. Then there ensues the whole intimate dialogue between man and God: all mankind confesses its poverty and receives the answer that God addresses to all men: the grace of salvation.

Prayer without any method and almost without any requests is possible; it exists. The only proof is the experience of those who practice it. We have the testimony of certain very long elevations written by Giustiniani on various mysteries and various Biblical texts.[6] "Particular intentions" have no place in these pages overflowing with a fervor that never abates. The soul expresses its faith and its desire for God. It interrupts its acts of adoration only to beg for one gift which is the Lord Himself. But could we say that such prayer, where there occurs no thought of other men, is a

---

[6] For example: Q III: 11: *Pii ad Sanctum Spiritum affectus*; F II: 100: *Soliloqui sulla santissima Eucaristia*; Q II: 51 : *Sulle parole: Signor mio e Dio mio*; Q II: 63: *Sulle parole: Perchè mi hai veduto Tommaso, hai creduto.*

form of egotism? No, for it is accompanied by a very strong feeling for the Church, an intense conviction of the reality of the Communion of Saints[7] and "that we cannot save ourselves without doing everything possible for the salvation of others."[8] Blessed Giustiniani has in mind all the great causes which involve the whole Church, such as the conversion of Islam and the union of separated Christians. These major intentions are his very life. From time to time he formulates them, just as he sometimes prays for his relatives, his friends, and his enemies.[9] But when he is deeply in prayer, he is engrossed with the presence of God alone.

* * *

While Blessed Giustiniani left no method of prayer, yet he clearly perceived the difficulty that all methods attempt to offset. Instead of trying to remedy the problem by some deceptively easy procedure, he strove to grasp the root of the matter. This he did in a treatise whose very title is a clear expression of the problem: "How is it that the soul, though experiencing great pleasure in prayer, finds it so difficult to devote itself to it, while the contrary is true of other actions?" The answer is as profound as it is original:

> I have often wondered whence it is that the pleasure we remember experiencing in certain agreeable activities draws us to return to them with ease and joy, while in spite of the incomparably greater pleasure tasted in prayer, the soul returns to it with difficulty and trouble, almost with reluctance. Those who at least once have derived great pleasure from sensual passion, from the delights of the table, from harmonious music, or from enthralling spectacles, are attracted to these activities by the memory of the pleasure they felt. But though our soul feels such

---

7 Cf. F I: 40; F I: 175; Q IV: 235. Cf. also above, p. 227, and below, p. 316. Consult also: HE, p. 52.
8 A collection of patristic texts illustrating this truth is found in Q IV bis, :214.
9 E.g.: Q IV: 365.

great pleasure in prayer, once it has advanced in God to the point where it begins to taste something of the divine reality, yet we continue to feel a repugnance that is both physical and spiritual on returning to prayer, even after we have felt these pleasures many times.

I, for one, can testify that my soul derives such pleasure from eating especially certain foods that, even without the stimulus of hunger or the serving of foods, I begin to eat so naturally and easily that I do not notice or pay attention to what I am doing. But I have to do violence to myself, so hard do I find it to return to prayer, even though, thanks to my sweet Lord Jesus Christ, the pleasures I have tasted therein more than once infinitely surpass all others that I have known.

Now I do not ask this question through mere curiosity, but in order to know and eliminate the reason that makes me postpone my prayer. I would like to be able to return to it as easily as I do the sensory acts that give me pleasure. Upon reflection, several reasons have occurred to my mind. The first is that the soul is a noble substance, or in other words, tenuous and subtle, while the body is a common substance, of coarse and hard matter. It is not surprising, therefore, that the soul receives the impressions of the body more easily than the body those of the soul. Sensual pleasures arise in the body and proceed to the soul, which easily consents to them because it is instantly affected by them: hence its feeling of satisfaction when it is carried by the body towards some pleasure. On the contrary, the pleasure of prayer first affects the spirit, the part of the soul farthest removed from the body. Thus when the soul is inflamed by the pleasure it has felt in prayer and wishes to return to it, the body, which did not taste that pleasure, or at least did not retain the memory of it, refuses its consent to the soul. For we assent easily to all actions in which the body and the soul act with common accord. That doubtless explains why it is so easy to return to physical pleasures, where the soul offers no resistance to the body, whilst it is hard to return to the spiritual pleasure of prayer, where the body resists the soul. This very resistance is the cause of the difficulty.

Similarly, for instance, when we go walking: we find it easy to descend a mountain, because in this action the heavy nature of the body is in agreement with the will of our spirit. But if, on the contrary, we wish to climb up the mountain, the body's heavy nature feels such repugnance that the soul must do violence not only to the body but to itself because of its own repugnance at forcing the body. The same is true of prayer: the violence the soul must do to the body is so unpleasant to both body and soul that both agree to flee from the pleasure of prayer.

In like manner, a man who well knows that a bitter medicine will restore his health consents to take it, but only with great repugnance, for the bitterness of the medicine grieves not only the body but also the soul that is affected by the bitterness our senses experience. So with prayer: while the soul, attracted by the memory of its pleasure, is inclined to return to it, nevertheless because this return is something violent for the body, a separation of body and soul, a kind of death, the soul keenly feels this violence suffered by the body. The soul is more sensitive to the sad feeling that precedes prayer than to the memory of the pleasure that accompanies it. It resists itself, fleeing the sadness that precedes prayer, no longer striving to attain the sweetness it experienced in the very act of prayer.

The contrary is also true: at times we refrain from present pleasure because of the sorrow that will result from it. Thus a man who rubs a wound that is almost healed feels great pleasure, but as he knows that an increase of pain will result if he reopens the wound permanently, he refrains from rubbing it. How many would like to eat honey because it is sweet, but finding that it causes stomach pains, deprive themselves of present pleasure because of future pain. So before prayer the prospect of a kind of separation of soul and body distresses the body, and through it also the soul, so much that prayer is forsaken because present sorrow, even though slight, makes a stronger impression than the mere portrayal of future pleasure, even though much greater.

I may add also that the attraction we experience towards corporal pleasures is a purely natural attraction, and whatever is according to nature is done easily because neither body nor soul feel it repugnant. On the other hand, our special attraction to the spiritual joy of prayer is not natural. I do not mean that it is contrary to nature, but that it is above nature. For the soul cannot attain to prayer by its own powers, but it must be drawn to it by a special gift of God, an actual movement on His part. As both body and soul are incapable of producing this by themselves, it has a hint of violence. That is one of the reasons why it is difficult to achieve prayer, even though one experiences great pleasure once it is achieved.

But I think that the main reason for this difficulty is lack of practice. Even easy actions seem toilsome through lack of practice, while difficult actions become easy and agreeable for those who make them a habit. Thus all day long I am busy reading or writing, and I do this with joy, without any sadness, because I am accustomed to it. To a person without this habit it would seem hard and almost intolerable. Similarly through force of habit we find it easy to keep returning to corporal pleasures, which are always at hand; but we find it hard to return to the spiritual activity of prayer just because we are little accustomed to it. A maxim of pagan philosophers states that men should choose the more perfect way, even if it be more painful, because practice will make it easy. I hold for certain that, whatever the difficulty or its source may be, there is no better, more potent, or more salutary remedy to counteract it than assiduous practice, constant exercise. Habit makes the soul prompt and capable of drawing the body after it. The divine movement which first seemed violent becomes, as it were, connatural. The pleasure that we frequently experience no longer as future but as already present exerts a stronger and stronger attraction as it lessens the distress we feel in achieving the habit.

In conclusion I shall say that the greatest obstacle to spiritual activity and the greatest difficulty in prayer is not practicing them. Nothing makes us so well-disposed and prompt as habitual practice. If you wish to pray easily, pray assiduously. If you want to taste the sweetness of prayer, make a habit of it and you will be filled with joy. Of course we should not make the pleasure it gives us the goal of our prayer. But the pleasure is a means of ascending further in God, referring everything to His glory, and uniting ourselves more closely to His love.[10]

---

[10] Q IV bis: 173. Published in *Vita cristiana, Rivista ascetico-mistica* XXI (1952), pp. 149-156.

PART FOUR

THE HERMIT'S ASCETICISM

XI

THE INNER WARFARE

The hermit's asceticism is wholly determined by eremitism itself. Since he is trying to live with God alone, he must achieve radical detachment from all that is not God. He must attain the only true solitude, that of the spirit. This interior stripping is hard and must be safeguarded by constant effort. "Only one thing is hard: to tame the spirit, to force it to abandon the world effectively and affectively, so to speak. We must not be anxious to see our relatives or friends or to hear news of the world. We must be really separated from the world like a new Melchisedech, without father, mother, brother, friends, or country — without attachment to anything of this world. We must leave the world and live for the Creator alone."[1]

Such interior detachment is necessary to some extent for every monk. But it is all the harder for the hermit who, because of his very solitude, is threatened by a more subtle enemy: self-love. Giustiniani denounces the danger with ruthless lucidity.

---

[1] F + :145, cf. Heb 7:3.

Man's whole life is an arduous, constantly renewed struggle, and we should be keenly aware of this inner drama. Each component of man, the flesh and the spirit, fights against the other and against itself. The flesh fights against itself: discomfort is involved if we sleep, eat, and drink little — but also if we sleep, eat, and drink much. If we cater to the flesh, we risk injuring it; if we treat it hard, we run the same risk. No matter what is done for it, it voices a protest, so hard is it to find the golden mean of its true needs. Even supposing this balance to be achieved, the flesh will not stop fighting against the spirit because their tendencies are opposed to each other. The flesh likes splendid buildings and vast estates; the spirit seeks a narrow cell with a tiny garden, knowing that poverty is the safer path to tranquillity on earth and happiness in heaven. The flesh is fond of pleasures and sensual gratification, which the spirit avoids. And so for the rest: every aspiration of the spirit is opposed by the flesh. Constantly and in every sphere of activity, the struggle must be maintained. Yet it becomes relatively easy, in proportion as the spirit succeeds in dominating the flesh and keeping it in submission.

There is, however, a still harder conflict, which only gets worse: the hidden struggle of the spirit against itself. The spirit becomes its own enemy and insidiously attacks itself. It often proposes sham goods under the appearance of genuine good, and it is difficult to make out the danger. If it does good, it spoils it by self-satisfaction. If it practices mortification, it remembers that discretion has its rights, as a pretext to relax its ascetic efforts. How often the spirit tells lies to deceive itself! For instance, if we yield to anger or impatience, it persuades us that this happens because of our concern for God's interests or our charity towards the neighbor whom we wish to correct. In short, the spirit disguises vices as virtues until it no longer distinguishes one from the other: it falls a prey to itself.

Whenever it wants to do good, such as by living the contemplative life, it manages to convince itself that there is a higher good, such as working actively for the good of others. It finds arguments against itself in Holy Scripture. Thus we should always distrust ourselves, for we are always at odds with ourselves. At this point we should seek advice, for we should fear more ensnaring ourselves than being ensnared by others. The spirit is exposed to illusions that it creates for itself. The greater our progress in good, the fiercer this interior war becomes.[2]

Only severe asceticism, controlled by strict obedience, can remedy this situation. The hermit's principal guarantee against the illusion that the contemplative life can be easier than active life is its austerity. A more perfect life must be more demanding. "You who with God's help have embraced the perfect and sublime life of hermits must practice very severe austerity. Nothing less than the great and the positively exalted is required of you."[3] Hermits are distinguished from cenobites chiefly by their greater severity of life. As eremitic life is a stage beyond (*supergressa*) cenobitic life, the hermit is held to more than the cenobite is. For him the practices of cenobitic life represent a bare minimum, to which he must always add and do better: *arctiora et perfectiora,* things more severe and more perfect.[4] All eremitic asceticism is putting into practice in detail this fundamental requirement.

The best training for bearing great austerities consists in first depriving ourselves of all pleasure. If life is hard, then things that others find austere may become pleasing to us, and what would be unbearable in a life of ease will cause but little suffering.[5] The first way to restrain the natural appetite for pleasure is privation, and we must begin with the appetite for food, that is, we must fast.

> The food must be cheap, plain, and scarce; the drink must be weak and meager. Your one meal a day must be preceded by a blessing of the food, accompanied in eremitic fashion by reading, followed by thanksgiving. You must not advance the time of meals, or care about the quality of the

---

2   Q IV bis: 129.
3   Q III: 245.
4   RVE f. 44V 54V,108,109, etc.
5   Q I:62.

food, or increase the quantity. Strive mainly to moderate your desire to eat, taking very modestly what is necessary and getting rid as quickly as possible of the necessity of eating.[6]

Similar directions are given on other points: "Sleep briefly, but for as long as nature demands...."[7] Your bedding should not include the fine linen that cenobites sometimes use.[8] Your clothing must be cheap, coarse, shabby, short, neglected, scarce — just what is strictly necessary."[9] The hair shirt and the discipline will be used, but always with modesty.[10] "If you cannot take the discipline without being heard by your neighbors, then have no scruple to dispense with it. Each of you may, if he wish, wear the hair shirt either always or only at certain times. But those who do not wish it will not be obliged to wear it."[11] Thus bodily mortification must always be controlled by prudence, which is "the seasoning of all the virtues," *omnium virtutum condimentum.*[12] Discretion does not excuse us from austerity, as a certain subtle egoism may often try to maintain. On the contrary, it safeguards austerity against the excesses of self-love and vain complacency. It keeps austerity in its proper place in the hierarchy of means of sanctification, preventing it from casting off the rule of the spirit.

Manual work is part of asceticism because it keeps the soul humble, even when it is not required to earn a living. As hermits are striving to lead a more perfect life, it is all the more necessary for them: nothing can dispense them from it. "The cenobites often try to excuse themselves from it, either because of the exertion of singing the Divine Office, or because of the inconvenience of their location if

---

[6] Q III:52.
[7] Q III: 52.
[8] RVE f. 108V.
[9] Q III:52.
[10] RVE f. 109Vff.
[11] Rule of 1524, Lugano edition, p. 159.
[12] RVE f. 110; cf. f. 95V, 97V, etc.

the monastery is situated in a city. But hermits can invoke neither the chant nor the location as excuses."[13]

Finally, the best occasions for mortification are those we do not choose or inflict upon ourselves artificially. Cold weather, rain, and snow are inevitable in hermitages which had to be built on mountains in order to assure isolation. We should accept willingly the bad weather: we have frequent opportunities to bear it, as our cells are not connected with the oratory by a roofed-in cloister as in the Charterhouse. During the long winters, before each liturgical service by day or by night, we should face the bad weather "for the love of Christ."[14] Giustiniani often refers to the cold. In his personal notes he has even sketched the outline of a meditation on the Christian acceptance of cold weather.

> To support the cold, remember that Christ was born in the Winter; He was covered with scanty cloths; He was warmed only by the breath of animals in a stable because there was no room for Him in the inn. He was crucified naked, still in the cold season, on a hilltop exposed to the wind. Do you want the proof that it was cold even in the city, even in a house, even for those who were clothed? Read the Gospel: "They were warming themselves by the fire, because it was cold."[15] Just think, then, of how cold the naked members of Jesus must have felt on Calvary. Remember how it is told that Saint Maur used to go out almost naked in winter in order that he could suffer from the cold. Think of the martyrs who were killed by the torture of freezing cold: in the readings assigned for All Saints, it says that many saints were tortured by the cold.[16]

Thus we see that the hermit's asceticism does not impose extraordinary mortifications but requires above all and in the first place

---

[13] RVE f. 99V-100.

[14] RVE f. 64V.

[15] Jn 18:18.

[16] F II: 125.

acceptance of the mortifications of everyday life, a joyful acceptance. The word most frequently used to indicate how the hermit is to fulfill his duties is this adverb that is hard to translate by a single word: *alacriter*.[17] The hermit should accept the observances of his austere life with zest, vigor, enthusiasm. He should be good-humored. The joyful tranquillity that his soul enjoys should be evident from his relaxed features and cheerful face.[18] He should possess and radiate the gift of joy, *iucunditas*.[19] His whole life has but one purpose: "to serve God voluntarily in a more perfect way, for the love of Christ, with spiritual joy."[20]

---

[17] F A :22C, 22A. RVE f. 42, 43, 43V, 100V, etc.

[18] RVE f. 7.

[19] RVE f. 71V.

[20] Prologue to the Rule of 1524, Lugano edition, p. 136.

XII

DESTITUTION

"The observances and rules do not contain perfection in themselves but are means whereby we may attain the perfection of the evangelical and apostolic doctrine."[1] This comprises two essential elements: to love one another and to renounce everything in order to follow in poverty the poor Christ. The fact that hermits live communally gives them at one and the same time the opportunity to practice fraternal charity and poverty. But the eremitic life makes them obliged to conform themselves with the utmost rigor to all the demands of this poverty, which should be one of their characteristic features.

The spirit of poverty and interior detachment is the natural consequence of their vocation. Since hermits leave the world in order to live with God alone, they should abandon everything that is of the world and every desire to possess anything in this world.

> In the use of those things necessary to support human weakness, the hermits, for love of poverty, should be satisfied with whatever is cheapest and meanest, and they should be on guard against any desire to possess anything or any attachment to the things they use. So they will truly live the eremitic life according to the apostolic standard. Then they will be in the world as if they were not in it, and they will use the things

---

[1] RVE f. 43V.

of this world as if they were not using them. Even if many things are lacking, no one should worry about it very much, perhaps wondering secretly: "What shall we eat? What shall we drink? What shall we wear? " But they will put all their trust in God, strengthened by these words uttered by the mouth of Truth: "Seek first the kingdom of God and His justice and all these things shall be given to you as well."[2]

Extreme poverty also meets another demand of the hermit life: simplicity. The hermit suppresses all artificial needs; he eliminates those superfluities which for so many others become necessities. From the fact that he breaks off all relations with the world in order to live with God alone, he reduces his needs to the basic essentials only; he is satisfied, we might say, with the indispensable minimum. So it is that his poverty merges with his simplicity, his characteristic purity of life: *eremitica puritas*.[3] It goes hand in hand with the humility of his state of life, for while the hermit life in the Church is conducive to the highest perfection, yet in the hierarchical order it is the lowest state of all. Since the hermit is separated from men, he has no right to any role in the government of the state and of the Church: he belongs to the lowliest class of society, among the poor. He should live like them and consider himself one of them. For him to accept a prelacy would be a betrayal.[4] He must ever avoid comparing his life with that of other religious, and only in case of necessity will he talk about the observances of the hermitage.[5] When he is traveling and stays in a cenobitic community, he should do the most menial tasks, which are best suited to the humility of his state.[6] If he is the major of the hermitage, he should behave like the last of the hermits. He will take

---

[2]   F A:7.
[3]   F A:6V.
[4]   RVE f. 42.
[5]   RVE f. 60.
[6]   RVE f. 107V.

his share of the necessities of life only after he has served the others, beginning with the last: the leftovers will be for himself.[7]

Detachment, simplicity, humility are but different names for the same poverty of spirit. The hermit who lives by these dispositions will find no difficulty in practicing concrete poverty. This involves two correlative obligations: first, to possess nothing of our own, but to receive and to use according to our needs a part of what the community possesses; second, to accept the fact that the community itself should have few possessions, for there would be no point in renouncing all personal property if a rich community then provided us with resources which we would probably never have enjoyed otherwise. The first requirements of religious poverty are: to possess nothing of our own, not to appropriate to ourselves any of the goods of the community, not to use things as if we owned them, to maintain things in the condition in which they were entrusted to us, to be always disposed to accept that things be taken away from us. The *Rule of Eremitic Life* not only contains practical rules in this regard, but it also points out their meaning. If, for example, the hermit is forbidden to have any key except that of the Church, it is to make it clear that nothing belongs to anyone. It will only be entirely evident that the hermits possess nothing of their own, but that everything is for common use, when they no longer need keys: "Nothing that is for the use of all should be locked up."[8] One should leave at the library a list of the books taken out: this is not only for the sake of organization, since it is important for good order to be able to find the volumes, but also because they belong to everyone and should be at everyone's disposal.[9]

The second condition of true poverty is that the community itself be really poor. It should avoid acquiring anything beyond the indispensable minimum of possessions. It should not seek to attract legacies or donations. When a rich young man announced his

---

[7] RVE f. 127V.
[8] RVE f. 53V.
[9] RVE f. 54.

intention of entering the hermitage and bequeathing his possessions to it, Giustiniani answered him thus in the name of all the brethren:

> We have learned of your desire and are ready to further it.... You can take it from me that you will find many weaknesses among us, for we are men and sinners. Our way of life is that best suited to sinners and penitents: we would not want to hide from you the fact that it includes many austerities. But nothing is so difficult and so arduous that it does not become easy to one who trusts in God's help rather than his own strength. As to your desire to give us part of your possessions, we congratulate you on it, but you must understand that we do not consider these riches as true riches. We do not love earthly riches, which we have rejected once and for all for the love of Christ. We do not seek that kind of gain: we desire above all God's glory and the salvation of souls. In you, then, my brother, it is you yourself and not your possessions that we welcome. If we receive you, it is not in order that we may become richer through your riches, for we wish to remain poor. It is in order that you, by becoming poor with us and by bearing the yoke of obedience, may walk in the footsteps of Christ, who was poor and naked, and may thus more easily reach eternal riches.... We wish to see you arrive in our midst full of virtues, not laden with gold and silver.... Whether you bequeath your goods to us or to other servants of Christ who are still poorer than we are, know that you will gain much by leaving all to follow Christ.[10]

Giustiniani often spoke of poverty, and one of his most constant concerns was to maintain real and effective poverty in the hermit life. He did not write any treatise on the subject, as he did on other points. But in this domain more than in any other it is the testimony of the facts that matters. Instead of devising a theory of poverty Giustiniani has described the poor life of his hermitages at the time when they

---

[10] F VII: 103.

were close to the ideal he had set up. Here are some extracts from this impressive text:

As to the life of the hermits, my fathers and my brothers, I shall tell you only the most ordinary and most evident facts.... As to food, they unfailingly observe the fasts of the Hermitage of Camaldoli and keep other even more severe fasts.... I do not think that in these four hermitages, during the course of a year, we have eaten more than about a hundred eggs: most of our hermits abstain from eggs as strictly as the more observant monks abstain from meat. During the last two years, some of the hermits were ill from time to time, but none ate meat: they had only a few eggs. In one hermitage where five fathers were living, they ate no more than seven eggs during the year. Most of them abstain from fish also. Some have tasted eggs and fish only two or three times in two years, and that because of guests.... Usually their food consists of hard bread or moldy bread. One of the fathers asserts that in one of the hermitages of which he had charge there was some of this moldy bread, and it was offered to the donkey, who refused it—but the hermits ate it! I myself have seen that in two hermitages, when the bread was put on the table (for sometimes before the cells were built the hermits ate together), each one tried to get the bread that was the moldiest. Besides bread, they eat herbal or vegetable soups. But do not imagine that they cook a meal every day: at times I have eaten for four successive days beans that had been cooked all at one time. Garlic, or scallions, or fruit are a real treat. They find boiled acorns as tasty as chestnuts: I have even learned to eat and enjoy them. The fact of the matter is that on some days they do no cooking because nature provides food that requires no preparation....

Their clothing is the poorest and shabbiest available. The tunic is a bit more than calf-length, with a scapular reaching a little below the knee and undergarments like sacks (pieces of cloth in front and back, but not sewed at the sides). I do not think that more than two or three of them wear stockings; the others wear none. Moreover some wear clogs, like those of Saint Francis, only during the winter. In the summer they go barefoot. During the last two years I have learned to walk without stockings and this year I shall try to wear the clogs with nothing else. So far I have felt the cold less than when I wore stockings.... I once had to buy all the clothing for one of the hermits. For everything — undergarment, tunic, scapular, and cloak — I spent at the most fourteen coppers. The cincture is merely a rope.... The hermits have only one tunic and few of them have two undergarments.... [11]

Unfortunately, this description of the life of Giustiniani's first companions was left incomplete. What was written is nonetheless valuable. Doubtless this heroic period could not last forever. But it remains as a symbol of a vocation that included destitution, because God alone suffices.

---

[11] On the circumstances in which this text was written cf. HE, pp. 118-120.

XIII

PERFECT OBEDIENCE

Unlike the topic of poverty, Giustiniani wrote a long and explicit treatise about obedience.[1] Real destitution, when voluntary, is the proof of interior detachment — if the former is present, we know that the latter has been attained. But the virtue of obedience is an interior attitude which is not so clearly evident in practice. Like poverty of spirit, it too resides in the soul; unlike poverty, it has fewer opportunities for exterior expression. In a well-regulated community, it is even possible that a life of apparent submission might be devoid of obedience. Giustiniani, therefore, felt obliged to emphasize the qualities required to make obedience perfect.

Many times he asserted the primacy of obedience in the life of monks, and more particularly, of hermits. The great originality of Camaldolese eremitic life is, in his eyes, that it *reintegrates into the eremitic life the obedience proper to the cenobitic life*. Obedience is the virtue that makes a monk. Without it, the cenobite can live in his monastery as in a prison. Without it, the solitary resembles a savage beast more than a Christian hermit. What makes us monks and hermits is neither the cloister nor the solitude, nor even all the other virtues together: it is

---

[1] There are several redactions of it. Here we quote from the edition published by Dom N. A. Giustiniani, O.S.B.; *Trattato dell' Ubbidienza del B. Paolo Giustiniani*, (Padua, 1753). Henceforth, it is referred to as *Trattato*. The treatise is also summarized in RVE, chaps. XI-XII, f. 55ᵛ-60.

perfect obedience.[2] This is common to cenobites and hermits, and the treatise dealing with it is only a commentary on the references to it in the *Rule of Saint Benedict*, which hold true for all monks. Here again, however, the hermit life is more rigorous than any other way of life, and it permits no mediocrity. And so, in order to point out the heights of renunciation to be scaled by any religious seeking to be perfect, he undertakes a refined analysis of what we might call the psychology of obedience. He maps out in detail its whole path of progress, or as he says, its degrees. Here is his own summary of the subject:

> The first degree is to banish all slowness in our obedience: we learn to obey immediately, without any delay. In the second, we learn to drop what we were doing, even if it was something necessary to us. The third degree teaches us to leave unfinished what we were doing. The fourth degree is that we no longer think about what we were doing, and we renounce continuing it, either now or later, if obedience prevents us. The fifth degree is to always desire that we may receive some obedience that will give us the opportunity to drop what we are doing. The sixth degree eliminates all hesitation and all feelings of fear in harsh, difficult, and dangerous things that we are commanded. The seventh degree precludes all delay or discouragement during the execution of what is commanded us, for one can begin eagerly and then slow down through negligence, when the order given is time-consuming, tiring, or seemingly unreasonable. The eighth degree frees us of all lukewarmness or coldness that can steal over us in the beginning, in the middle, or at the end of obedience. The ninth and tenth degrees curb all exterior and interior murmuring. In all these degrees we rise above the imperfections that menace obedience; we purify it of all that could besmirch it. But we have not yet attained perfect obedience, which begins only when we obey with spiritual joy — that is the eleventh degree. Finally, obedience reaches its twelfth and last degree of perfection when it is practiced with

---

[2] *Trattato*, pp. 6-7.

an upright intention, absolutely pure of all vainglory, hypocrisy, or false emulation — when we seek neither to appear good nor to be praised, but only to please Jesus Christ. Pure love of Christ enables us to obey no longer like servants, but like sons of God.[3]

This scale of twelve degrees is necessarily somewhat artificial. But it provides the occasion for many accurate and penetrating passages. Examples of the practice of obedience are based on the actual life of the hermits.

Suppose that a monk has settled in a corner of the church to say some Our Fathers. If the superior summons him, he will be ready to interrupt his prayers without completing the intended number of Our Fathers, even if there are just a few left. But he must even be ready to interrupt the Our Father that he had begun. If only the Amen remained to be said, and he consciously persisted in adding it before heeding his superior's order, that monk would not have obeyed perfectly....[4] Every year at the haying season we hermits are sent out for two or three consecutive days to pitch the hay that has been mown by the peasants. If a certain monk is sent there and goes without delay, he has achieved the first degree of obedience. But scarcely has he begun the haying when he is overcome by the heat or by fatigue. If he goes to sit down or stroll about in the shade of the forest, instead of persevering in the work he has been ordered to do, then he has not obeyed perfectly.[5]

In the realm of interior dispositions, the demands of perfect obedience are boundless.

Saint Benedict says that the monk should abandon his own will: that means that we should abandon all wish, thought, or desire for the work we were

---

3 *Trattato*, pp. 129-135.
4 *Trattato*, p. 46.
5 *Trattato*, pp. 95-96.

doing, when the superior's order has withdrawn us from it. Now it is easier to interrupt materially a work begun than to detach oneself from it. The will imposes its rule upon the body as upon a servant. But the mind, the imagination, and the affections submit less easily to the sway of the will. Nevertheless they too, along with the body, must leave off the work begun, when it is interrupted by a command....[6] It is not even sufficient to obey when the order is given; if it is not given, we should desire it and await it with pleasure. Of course the monk's spirit cannot continually keep on actually exercising this desire, but he must at least have it habitually, so that by virtue of a decision taken once and for all he may be always desirous of finding himself commanded something that forces him to leave off what he was doing with pleasure. It is not hard to obey without delay if we are doing nothing in particular, nothing that we find interesting or think urgent: then it is even agreeable to be prompt. But it is otherwise when we must interrupt work that we do gladly and find interesting.[7]

Therefore the spirit of obedience means not merely a passive availability, a certain readiness to receive orders. It takes the positive step of anticipating occasions for renouncement and accepting them even before they occur.

When an order is given, the obedient monk carries it out without discussion. "He submits like a beast of burden that does not try to find out what sort of load has been put on its back; it does not know whether the burden imposed be useful or not. Be it gold or manure — both are accepted in the same way. Moreover, it does not ask whether it is being led by the direct path or by a detour: it follows the route its guide sets."[8] Nor is it enough to obey without protest, for there is no point in exterior silence without interior peace. Placidity could be nothing but an abdication, if the spirit refrains from resisting but refuses its active consent. We must submit without strain, complaint,

---

[6]   *Trattato*, pp. 56, 59.

[7]   *Trattato*, pp. 64-65.

[8]   *Trattato*, p. 110.

or regret; in fact our obedience should even be easy, supple, and with satisfaction. Only then, as Saint Benedict says, will it become pleasant, agreeable to men and to God.[9]

> Obedience should be carried out with real spiritual joy: with elation, jubilation, merriment, and holy contentment. Of course we do not mean a purely natural pleasure, which could spring simply from the fact that what is commanded suits our own tastes, desires, and intentions. In that case we cannot speak of a spiritual joy, even if what is commanded seems to foster our spiritual good. But for our joy to be spiritual rather than natural, we must rejoice all the more in proportion as that which is commanded is the more contrary to our own personal tastes.[10]

The treatise on obedience concludes with a long contemplation of Jesus Christ, the model of perfect obedience.

> We should always keep before our eyes like a light the example of the Lord, who said that His food was only to do the will of the Father. Similarly the food of the religious spirit should be only to do the will of his superiors. He who is not nourished by this food can neither make progress nor even persevere in the religious life, even if he has all the other virtues. The body cannot be preserved or grow unless it is nourished: otherwise, to apply all sorts of ointments or to cover it with precious clothing is of no avail. So also a monk's soul, even if adorned with all the gifts of the Holy Spirit, cannot grow in perfection if it lacks the bread of obedience. And souls that do not wish or seek this bread, who do not relish it when it is offered to them and who eat it without joy and appetite, are cripples. They are like sick men, who can no longer savor the bread which is so pleasing to the healthy. Obedience is the bread that, as the Bible says, strengthens the heart of man.

---

[9] *Trattato*, p. 115.
[10] *Trattato*, pp. 124-125.

Each of us, therefore, should often say to himself: I want to have no other food than to do the will of my superior, so that I may follow the Lord who, becoming obedient to the eternal Father in all things, has left me a living example of perfect obedience. He was God, the eternal Word, equal to the Father, and He took on the form of a slave: Through obedience, He deigned to become the Son of Man and to be born of the Virgin.... Through obedience, He accepted hunger, sleep, vigils, weariness, all the miseries that are common to all men. Besides that, He accepted extreme poverty, exile, and subjection to the crowds that so pursued Him that it is recorded in Saint John's Gospel that He had not enough time to eat His bread. He did not refuse to bear the hatred of the chief priests, the scribes, and the Pharisees, as well as temptations from the devil and from men. He was not worried by the persecutions inflicted on Him by the very men to whom He had come, in obedience to His Father, to announce the Gospel. In spite of the detractions and insults heaped upon Him, He did not delay in the task He had to accomplish for the salvation of men. He never answered except with words wholly mild and meek. He endured the ingratitude of His own people, the ingratitude of His country, the ingratitude of the throngs to whom He served the bread of eternal life and the bread of mortal life. He even bore the unfaithfulness of the very men whom He had chosen in preference to all others — the betrayal of Judas, the denial of Peter, the desertion of all of them during the Passion. Finally, He bore the suffering of being taken prisoner, being bound, insulted, hit, tortured, whipped, crowned with thorns, judged, condemned, and crucified. From the Cross He heard reproach and blasphemy; He was given gall to drink. He wished to die like a lamb offered in sacrifice. His face remained serene; He did not complain; He simply said these words: "Father, not my will, but Thine, be done." Why, most sweet Jesus, did it please You to bear such pain, except because You wished to obey Your Father who sent You? You had come to do His will; Your only food was to do the will of the Father.[11]

---

[11] *Trattato*, pp. 140-151.

PART FIVE

UNIVERSAL LOVE

XIV

ANNIHILATION

Paul Giustiniani's teaching attains its completion and its crown in his mystical doctrine: to it all else is ordered. The hermit life, the spiritual exercises, and the ascetical practices lack all sense and purpose if they do not lead to mystical union with God, a certain experience of God. In this realm more than in any other, Giustiniani's teaching is linked to his own experience, and he expresses himself in long elevations which defy analysis. Even if we can summarize them exactly, we cannot translate their tonality. Because of the intense fervor animating these texts, it is desirable that they should be the first to see publication. Since we cannot yet read them in print, let us at least try to describe the states of soul that they imply and the doctrine that emerges from them. Needless to say, the reality we are dealing with here is one and simple, wholly united with each of its aspects and fully present in each of its phases. For the sake of explanation we can distinguish various degrees or elements in this reality, even though this will impoverish it. In our minds we must constantly rebuild the synthesis and restore its profound unity.

The fundamental attitude of the soul united to God is detachment from self. When a soul lives habitually in this state of radical renouncement, then at times it is given an experience of its nothingness. Keenly aware of its impotence, it plunges into God and receives all from His love. Giustiniani had the grace of experiencing, in an ineffable way that surpasses all explanation, that he was nothing without God. But he had merited this favor by his constant humility. We must, therefore, recall in the first place the basic principles that make such an experience possible and prepare for it.

In speaking of the degrees of perfection suggested by the beginning of Psalm 118 (119), Giustiniani characterizes the first as self-knowledge. By sin the soul cleaves to the earth: *adhaesit pavimento anima mea.* In a certain sense, it is dead and it asks for life: *vivifica me secundum verbum tuum* — "quicken Thou me according to Thy word." Then it regrets its transgressions and chooses to do good to the point of practicing virtue "eagerly and easily, or rather, gently and for love of God. Once this last degree is reached, a man can say to God: I have run the way of Thy commandments because Thou hast enlarged my heart."[1] Thus the first condition of every conversion is aversion from self and from sin: humility is acquired through self-knowledge. Giustiniani composed several prayers for self-knowledge.

> Lord Jesus, who are the light without which nothing is enlightened, who alone see the darkness that surrounds me, I dare not say: give me the light to see Your light. It is enough for me that You make me see my darkness. I am so blind that I cannot see it. I even take it for light. I am so deeply in error that I do not perceive my error: I mistake falsehood for truth. Death has advanced upon me so far that, wounded and all covered with sores, I no longer feel my pain and my wounds. Bring me back to myself: for in my misery I have strayed not only from You but

---

[1]   Q IV bis: 199V.

also from myself; I have become a stranger to myself. Bring me back to myself in order that I may then go towards You. Make me know my darkness, so that I may then look at the Light: if I do not know my own misery, I will not have recourse to Your mercy. Because of my sins I am reduced to nothing in the sight of Your Majesty: grant that I may be reduced to nothing in my own eyes also; grant that I may despise myself completely, that I may gauge the extent of my impurity. I am nothing in Your sight until I am brought to nothing in my own eyes. I cannot arise from my wretchedness as long as I do not see it. And so I do not say to You with Moses: "Show Thyself to me"; I only say to You: "Show me to myself."[2]

Ostende meipsum mihi. [Show myself to me.] How could I see You, I, who cannot see myself? Nothing is nearer or more intimate to me than my own conscience. And yet so thick is the cloud that hides me from myself that I cannot see my sins. Every day, at every moment, I sin and err; I offend God and neighbor. And, at the very moment that I sin, I am so blind that I forget what I am doing. All too often I neglect to do what You command, or I do what You forbid: in every way I transgress Your commandments. Yet I am not conscious of having broken Your commandments, or if I am aware of my sin, I forthwith forget it. How can I confess my faults, as I am obliged to do, if I do not know them? And so I say, Lord, and I keep repeating: "Show me to myself," that I may know my sins.[3]

This mysterious humility is not the egoistic and morbid complacence of those who cultivate feelings of guilt which they should discard. Humility, on the contrary, gives rise to trust in God. The deeper a man's misery and the more deeply felt, the more intense his calling upon God and his hope.

---

2 F+ : 201.
3 Q III:160.

The Lord, as one of the Psalms says, lifts up those who fall. I have fallen, Lord, and I continue to fall. I have separated myself from You and from myself in order to wallow in the vilest pleasures. See into what an abyss of iniquity I have sunk. If I hoped in myself alone, I could never get clear of it. And if I considered my offenses, I would hesitate to hope in God; but when I consider Your mercy, my hope knows no bounds. "The Lord lifts up those who fall": behold, I have fallen; I am falling lower and lower. Lift me up, Lord. Stretch out to me the hand of Your mercy. My fall has broken, shattered, soiled me. Who is going to pick me up, put me back together, purify me? Who is going to bring back my innocence and tranquillity? My soul, hope in the Lord; put your trust in Him, for He lifts up those who fall. Lift me up, Lord; I cling to my iniquities; my whole gaze is fixed on evil. But I am Your servant and Your handiwork: Your Son has redeemed me with His blood. Behold Your creature, stuck in the mire of his impurities, weeps as he asks You to fulfil the words of Your prophet, or rather of Your own Spirit: "The Lord lifts up those who fall." I never tire of repeating this word, which is the foundation of all my hope. I have fallen, Lord, but You are my God and my king: According to Your infinite Majesty and boundless Goodness, lift me up and I shall live again.[4]

Self-knowledge is the very condition of love of God: we must know our own wretchedness in order that we may begin to cease loving ourselves and to turn toward God. For the wise men of pagan times, the peak of wisdom was: "Know thyself." For the Christian, this is only a starting point and this self-knowledge is more perfect for him than it was for the ancient philosophers. The Christian knows himself as a creature dependent upon God and superior to all of material creation: such is his dignity. But he also knows himself as a sinner and separated from God: that is his wretchedness. From this point on, his wretchedness makes the creature realize his need of God; in

---

[4] F+ :233, cf. Ps 144 (145):14.

his wretchedness he gauges the measure of his powerlessness to attain God by his own efforts. Ought he despair? Is there no solution? Christ is the solution; He is the way of our return to God.

> Jesus Christ, true God and true man, removed all impediments. As man He has accepted the punishment due to men's sins; as God He has offered Himself to His Father on the wood of the cross. Now the debt is paid. We, who doubted that we could ever know the inaccessible Creator, are now allowed to contemplate God made man, the Word made flesh. Christ descended to our humility so that by knowing Him and loving Him, we might ascend to His sublimity. He lived among men in order that we might learn to live, in the midst of men, with God. He endured death — the most painful of deaths — to teach us to love Him. He, who was able to rise again when He pleased, could have come down from the cross. But He offered Himself for us willingly, freely. Now that our debt is paid, now that our souls have been purified in the font of baptism, there remains no obstacle to our ascent to God. Through the Mediator between God and men, let us ascend to the Father. Christ's humanity gives us access to His divinity.
>
> It is true that, even since the Incarnation, even since our baptism, our sins are countless and defile us utterly. But do they impede our approach to Christ? Are we condemned to die in despair? No, for God wills the conversion of sinners and that they should live eternally once they have done penance. There are two remedies for sin, two means of being released from it: the virtue of penance and the sacrament of penance.[5]

So humility and self-knowledge are the foundation of all ascetical and sacramental life.

A long meditation "on the perfect and true path of salvation" deserves full quotation. After ruthlessly denouncing the subtle self-

---

[5]   F II :61.

love that separates us from God, the pride that eats away at our hearts and vitiates our best actions, Giustiniani again shows that the only true path of return to God is humility, the humility that was perfectly exemplified in Christ.

> Our hidden self-love brings forth all manner of illusions: ecstasies, visions, revelations, prophecies, abstinences impossible to human strength; the experience of Christ's sufferings, the wound in the side, the stigmata, knowledge acquired without study, speaking in strange languages, the desire to be damned for the love of Christ; extraordinary humiliations, sublime confessions, fasting from all food except the blessed Eucharist, vigils beyond human strength, unduly prolonged prayer, knowledge of the secrets of hearts, miracles, and cures. All these marvels are, in some instances, nothing but the work of him who said, and would like to induce us to say: "I shall be like the Most High. I shall do what He does...." I think that these saints under the influence of Lucifer are much more numerous, or rather much better known and more admired by the world, than the true saints, who do nothing in order to be known by the world, but stay hidden. Christ's true servants love God totally and not themselves. So sheltered are they by humility that they are known to God and not to men.

We must not condemn all visions and marvels: some are authentic. But the touchstone for discerning them is always humility, a participation in the humility of Jesus.

Christ is the model of absolute humility. It can be said that Christ, in His human nature, practiced the most perfect possible spiritual humility. In the first place, because He did not consider as His own either His divine being or His heavenly doctrine or His miraculous power, nor did He wish that men should attribute these to Him. He knew and acknowledged that all came from the Father, and He sought not His own glory but the glory of the Father. Secondly, He who was equal to the Father voluntarily took on the form of a slave. In all things except sin, He became united to that human nature which was subject to the devil. Being God, He became man in a true human nature. Finally, He did even more than merely put on man's nature and flesh: in His deep humility He also voluntarily accepted the weakness of that nature, although it was not His due. He willed not only to appear in the flesh, but in flesh that is weak and subject to pain. Thus did He give us the true norm of perfect humility.

So it is that the last word on humility is the selfsame secret of the hermit life: God alone.

> Jesus Christ as man was perfectly humble because He did not love Himself, but purely and simply adored and loved God. He was not glorified in Himself, but only in God. He humbled Himself in order that He might contemplate only His Father's glory, and in that glory alone did He take satisfaction. By the light of Christ, therefore, we can define spiritual humility thus: Just as pride of spirit, the pride of Lucifer and of those who accept his dominion, consists in self-love and self-admiration, and self-satisfaction therein, so also humility means loving God, contemplating God, adoring God, and taking satisfaction in Him and in Him alone. Genuine, solid humility is nothing but this simple and pure love of God. Where such pure love dwells, no place remains for self-love.[6]

Blessed Paul Giustiniani habitually maintained these dispositions of self-knowledge and self-contempt, with a love of God that excluded all self-love. On one occasion he received the grace of an even keener realization of the demands of humility and of love for God. Towards the end of his life, on August 7, 1524, during the celebration of the Holy Eucharist, divine light revealed to him how one ought to die to self in order to live for God alone. That very day he took up his pen and

---

[6] Q IV bis:134V.

began to write while still under the influence of this experience. He had understood the absolute character of divine love, which permits no attachment whatsoever to anything created and which requires of man an absolute self-renouncement. And so he described at length this "annihilation of the soul" by commenting on a verse of the Psalms: *ad nihilum redactus sum et nescivi.*[7] Later he himself schematized that ardent contemplation.

There are four kinds of annihilation: the first two are evil, the other two are good. By the first, the soul is "reduced to nought" but "does not know it" when it is in a state of sin but does not recognize its own wretchedness and has no desire to escape from it. By the second, the soul is "reduced to nought" but is aware of its state. It is still in sin, but by grace it recognizes this and is beginning to wish to arise from sin. By the third annihilation, the soul is "reduced to nothingness" and knows it. Burning with love of God, it no longer lives in itself, but in God alone, or rather God lives in it and it knows itself only in God. Finally, the soul is "reduced to nothing" and "it does not know it," when its very intense love of God so transforms it in God that it no longer loves itself in itself, nor itself in God, nor God in itself, but only God in God. No longer does it know self in self nor self in God. It no longer knows God in self, but only God in God.[8]

It would be vain and even dangerous to try to summarize the further developments of these themes which a saint can give himself over to when he has been overpowered by God. It is better to have recourse to the original text, recently published. The expressions that a mystic makes use of to tell of his experience of God can seem forced when taken out of their context, but we should respect them, for the experience surpasses our concepts. Suffice it to know that

---

[7] "I was reduced to nought, and I did not know it." Ps 72 (73):22, Vulg. This text is the first of six "Arguments" which altogether constitute the book entitled *Secretum meum mihi o dell' amor di Dio* (ed. Frascati, 1941), pp. 45-53. Hereafter referred to as *Secretum.*

[8] *Secretum,* p. 19.

those expressions are being used by a theologian who is at home in our language when he is explaining the things with which we are familiar but who gives free rein to his fervor when he speaks to God to thank Him for His gifts. Nor does he stray off into obscure realms of speculation: on the contrary, he keeps ever in close contact with the sacraments. He keeps returning, as to the starting point and source of his experience, to the reality of the Eucharistic Body.

> And how will it come about, O my soul, that you become nothing, that you no longer are anything in yourself, that God alone is in you, or rather, you are in God? Not otherwise than by virtue of this sacrament, of which I was just now the unworthy minister. Oh, how blessed that torrent of doctrine that teaches us this truth: when we partake of food for the body, we are not transformed into it, but it is transformed into us; on the contrary, when we are admitted to the heavenly table of the Body and Blood of Jesus Christ, we partake of a food that is not transformed into us, but which transforms us into itself. Then self fails, and we begin to exist in God.[9]

---

[9] *Secretum*, p. 50.

XV

Transformation

"Blessed the soul annihilated to itself and totally converted to God, that lives not in itself but in Christ, wholly absorbed by His love. And happier still the soul that is liquified in the furnace of love, annihilated both to itself and to Christ, so that it no longer even lives in Christ, but lives only because Christ lives in it. *Vivo ego, jam non ego, vivit vero in me Christus.*"[1] Giustiniani now tries to make us realize what a pinnacle the soul thus transformed reaches. He does so by means of three "arguments," lofty discourses overflowing with fervor and sometimes disconcertingly subtle.[2] The state of such a soul is inexpressible and needs to be experienced to be grasped. Yet one can, at least, give some idea of it by dint of repetitions, reflections, and symbols.[3]

A series of comparisons helps to depict how the soul can live by God's love. The flesh does not live of itself, but by the soul from which it receives life, for by itself the flesh is dead. So the soul, when it does not love itself, does not live in itself, but in God. Let us go further: The flesh lives neither for itself nor for the soul, because it does not have in itself any life by which it lives in itself or in the soul. On the contrary, the soul lives in the flesh and communicates itself to the flesh, which receives from it the life by which it lives. So the soul, through a higher

---

[1] *Secretum*, p. 54. Cf. Gal. 2: 20, "I live, yet not I, but Christ liveth in me."
[2] These are Arguments II-IV of *Secretum meum mihi*.
[3] Cf. *Secretum*, p. 66.

love, lives neither in itself nor in God, because it does not love itself
either in itself or in God. Rather God alone lives in it, because it does
not love itself in itself or in God, but only loves God in Himself. Let
us rise still higher. The human soul lives because life lives in it. But
it does not live in itself, for the soul has no life in itself, as God has.
Moreover it does not live in life, because it has no other life by which
it lives than life itself: only life lives in it. Thus, the soul lives by love:
but it does not live in itself, nor does it live in God, nor does God live
in it. Rather God alone lives in God, and the soul lives by the very fact
that it is transformed in God, when it loves neither itself in itself, nor
itself in God, nor God in itself, but only God in God.[4] These words are
a constantly recurring refrain, the key to the whole eremitic mystery:
"God alone in God. *Solo Dio in Dio.*"

"God is love, and if someone is in love, God is in him and he is
in love, and God will be all in everything." How can we understand
that the soul can thus lose itself in God and be transformed into Him,
without, however, becoming identified with Him? By a new series of
distinctions. The human soul has two lives: essential life, received from
God, Who is life and the source of all life; and the life of love, received
from God, Who is love and the source of all love. And as essential life
itself comprises three degrees, so there are in the soul three lives of love.
By virtue of its essence, the soul is not in itself but in God, from Whom
it receives being. In like manner, the soul that loves does not live in itself,
but in God, for it does not love itself in itself. The soul lives neither in
itself nor in God, for it is not and has not in itself the life by which it
lives in God. But God alone lives in it, for it lives only insofar as God,
Who is life, communicates Himself to it. Thus God lives in it and not
it in God. In the same way, on a yet higher plane of love, the soul raised
up to God no longer lives either in itself or in God, it no longer loves
itself in itself or in God, but it loves God in itself. Finally when God,
Who is life and the source of all life, communicates Himself to the

---

[4] Schema, *Secretum*, pp. 19-20. This summarizes Argument II; *Secretum*, pp. 54-60.

soul and to living creatures, He does not live in the creatures but in Himself. And although He has one sole being, yet according to our way of understanding, the being of God in Himself is more perfect than that which He has in His creatures. And so the soul that reaches the highest love no longer lives in itself, nor in God, nor God in it, because it does not love itself in itself or in God; and it does not love God in itself, but it loves God alone, and no longer God in itself, but God in God, loving God not for the sake of itself, but only for His sake, and in His most perfect being. The soul does not live in itself nor in God, nor does God live in it, but God alone lives in God. The soul loves itself neither in itself nor in God, nor does it even love God in itself, but it loves only God in God, and this is the most perfect love: *solo Dio in Dio.*[5]

To get a still better grasp of this absolutely pure love of God alone for God alone, we can eliminate all other objects of love. The human soul can love things inferior to itself and outside itself: wealth, pleasure, honors; it can love beings inferior to itself but united to it: the flesh and the life of the flesh; it can also love things equal to itself: oneself (loved in oneself or in God) and its neighbor's soul; it can love, finally, a being superior to itself: God in self or God in God. Only at this final point does love become pure and perfect.

It is inevitable that such a chart of the degrees of love should be arid. To animate it, we need all the riches of the mystical vocabulary. Only a series of imprecise but suggestive evocations, abstractions, or images, can bespeak an ineffable state. These aim to express what it is like to lose oneself, to plunge oneself, to be converted, to be submerged in God.[6] This transformation is wrought by a blazing fire of charity from the hearth of love, which descends into the soul and utterly absorbs, consumes and liquefies it.[7] Given over to these flames of love, the soul loses sight of itself, dies to all self-love, is nothing but love of God alone for God

---

[5] Schema, *Secretum*, p. 20, Argument III, pp. 61-66.
[6] *Secretum*, p. 51.
[7] *Secretum*, pp. 54, 59, etc.

alone.[8] In this indescribable wedding, God gives Himself through love and the soul consents to receive this communication of God, to become His spouse. Just as two become but one flesh by a physical marriage, so the soul becomes no more than one thing with God in this spiritual wedding. No longer are there two spirits, two lives of love, but, as it is written, "He who adheres to God is but one spirit with God." Nothing is left but the life of God in God. The soul transformed in God no longer knows anything but God, no longer loves anything but God, no longer is anything but God.[9]

The soul that loves God in God is like an eye staring at the sun. It cannot see itself reflected. On the contrary, the more it looks and concentrates, the less it sees itself and the less is it capable of seeing itself. So the soul set ablaze by God in God has no concern for itself. All its love is fixed on God alone. No corporeal transformation can represent this fusion of the soul in God. For contrary to what takes place when a material substance burns and melts or when a drop of liquid mingles with the ocean, the soul lost in God does not lose its being in God. Rather it acquires in God a more perfect being. God's power and goodness can receive and assimilate, without destroying, the least particle of being.[10]

Divine love is a flame preserving what It consumes. It is also boundless: The more It absorbs a soul and transforms it into Itself, the more It makes it lose itself in Itself, to acquire in Itself a more perfect being. As Saint Bernard said, the measure of the love of God is to love Him without measure.[11]

Although some persons may find this style too poetic or speculative, yet the theology of love poured forth in all these discourses is eminently practical. The touchstone of all true love is always detachment. No experience, no sublime contemplation, can dispense with renouncement.

---

[8] *Secretum*, pp. 64-65, etc.

[9] *Secretum*, pp. 61-62. 1 Cor 6:17

[10] *Secretum*, Argument IV, pp. 104-106.

[11] *Secretum*, p. 109. [Cf. CS 127.]

To love God alone in God means to be attached to nothing other than God Himself, to seek nothing but God's glory.

How many there are who believe they are spiritual and wish to enjoy bodily and spiritual rest in God, not for love of God but for love of themselves. They prefer their illusory consolations to works of obedience and fraternal charity. They dislike whatever deprives them of the rest they think they find in God, but which they really seek in themselves. Their whole concern is to find peace: not, it is true, in things inferior to themselves nor in themselves, but in God. Yet that peace is desired for love of themselves, not for God's glory.[12] On the contrary, souls that have attained perfect love no longer desire for themselves either virtues, or sensible devotion, or tears, or spiritual consolations, or ecstasies, or prophecies. If they have such gifts, they value them lightly; if they have them not, they do not seek them, for it suffices them to love God alone in God.[13]

There are spiritual men who pass for saints and who rejoice in the progress of their order or their monastery. But so far as their neighbor goes, they are not exactly sad at his progress — for that would be a crime — but they rejoice less at it than at that which concerns themselves. If they will examine their attitude they will discover that they desire their progress or that of their monastery more than God's glory: they do not love God in Himself.

The soul which rejoices in God and in Him alone is willing to do without any consolation. If it could love God a bit more on condition that it never feel any actual devotion, spiritual tranquillity, or sweetness, and be deprived of all hope of these gifts in this life or the next, it would accept this exchange. For it loves God no less when it feels no consolation, no actual devotion. These are gifts of God, and we love Him equally whether we feel them or are deprived of them.[14] If, by hypothesis, we even had to lose God

---

[12] *Secretum*, p. 91.

[13] *Secretum*, pp. 97, 107.

[14] *Secretum*, pp. 110-111.

311

for His glory rather than lessening His glory by possessing Him, then the soul consumed with love would desire that by its damnation God receive a bit more glory.[15]

In expressing itself, pure and perfect love does not flinch from such expressions, excessive though they may seem. Blessed Giustiniani is sufficiently aware of the illusions of false mysticism to appreciate the danger of such formulations: indeed he himself condemned the temptation of those who wish to be damned for the sake of God's love. But when he wishes to make us grasp the demands of love, he is not afraid to permit such a comparison as a mere hypothesis. Moreover, at the end of his "Arguments" on the love of God for Himself, he submitted his whole teaching "to the judgment, the definitions, and the sentiments of the Holy Catholic and Roman Church" — a gesture not without merit in Renaissance times.[16]

Rather than defend his orthodoxy, which is above suspicion, we prefer to recall that he himself knew the limits of his language. He spoke mainly as a way of whetting his own desire to experience what he could not express.

Lord, I know that what I have tried to say, that what You have made me to some extent see and feel, is truly inexpressible, inexplicable.... But, Lord, what I cannot understand with my intelligence nor put into writing, make me taste and enjoy by experience.... Grant that I may be united to You in a way that the mind cannot grasp nor the pen express, that I may be so transformed into You that I may love You and enjoy You. I do not ask that Your joy may enter into me, but rather that I, like the faithful servant, may enter into it, and that reduced to nothing and annihilated to myself, I may taste Your love in a manner beyond all telling or understanding.[17]

---

[15] *Secretum*, p. 113.
[16] *Secretum*, p. 116.
[17] *Secretum*, pp. 52-53.

XVI

THE GIFT OF SELF

There are two commandments of love, not just one. It is true that we must love God, but the Lord has also said that "Thou shalt love thy neighbor as thyself." Therefore, he who loves only God in God seems not to have a full and upright charity, since he concentrates all his love on God alone, without directing any to himself or to his neighbor. But the Apostle John has said that there is no love of God without love of neighbor. "If you do not love your neighbor whom you see, how will you love God whom you do not see?" [1] To build up a love aimed at God alone without paying any attention to oneself or one's neighbor: is not this to destroy true charity? [2]

A whole discourse formulates the answer to this question. The solution of the problem is vigorously expressed at the very beginning in an invocation to eternal Wisdom.

O God who love Yourself and Yourself alone by one sole love, and who love all creatures in Yourself as in the adequate object of Your love: Grant that I may understand and express how one who concentrates all his love on You loves himself and his neighbor more than if he divided his love

---

[1]   1 Jn 4: 20.
[2]   *Secretum*, Argument V, p. 117.

amongst You, himself, and his neighbor. Show me how true it is that the human soul, inflamed with love for You, loves itself and its neighbor all the more, the less it turns toward itself and its neighbor. In this sense we may say, paradoxically, that the less it loves itself and its neighbor, the more it loves them. Grant that I may see and teach that, to love ourselves and our neighbor, we must not divert one bit of our love from You but desire to love only You. So the soul will love itself and its neighbor perfectly when, so as to love You only, it will have forgotten itself and its neighbor as if they did not exist and will direct toward self and neighbor neither thought nor love.[3]

"Since God is supreme Wisdom, Goodness, and Omnipotence, the best way to care for self and neighbor is to cast oneself and all others into God, to commit them to God with all confidence, and then to think of Him alone, to love Him alone. Then we will love self and neighbor more truly and more effectively than if we loved God less because we diverted part of our love to self and neighbor."[4]

This basic answer requires explanation. Two comparisons can help shed light on it: the first concerns God's very being, the second, His love. Doubtless God's love is not other than His being, yet we may be permitted to distinguish them for the needs of our argumentation. If, therefore, we speak of God's essential being, we can say that God, by one sole and self-same being, is in Himself and in all creatures, the latter receiving only a finite participation in His infinite being. But there is only one being in God: the being that He possesses in Himself is not distinct from the being that renders Him present to all creatures.[5] If God (supposing the impossible) wanted to deprive Himself of part of His being in order that He might be in His creatures by this part removed from Himself, then He would not be either in Himself or in

---

[3] *Secretum*, pp. 117-118.

[4] *Secretum*, p. 120.

[5] *Secretum*, p. 122. This formulation, while differing from those we are accustomed to find in classical theology, is by no means without value, as Dom Stolz has observed. *Prefazione*, p. 17.

creatures in a perfect manner: For He is in creatures only by reason of being perfectly in Himself the source of all being. He is in creatures only because He is perfectly in Himself. In like manner, the soul united to God by love, loving only God in God and not imparting any love to creatures, is more truly in God completely through love. Because it is completely in God, it is, by this same being, in all God's creatures that are worthy of love. It is there more truly than if it willed to be less in God in order to be more in His creatures.[6]

Let us now consider God's love and its object. God, in loving Himself and Himself alone, absolutely alone, as the only adequate object of His love, loves perfectly all creatures in Himself. So too, the soul that loves God and God alone as the adequate and principal object of love, by that same love also loves itself, its neighbor, and all lovable creatures. It loves the creature. not in itself, but in God. There is but one love in God by which He loves Himself and creatures. Were there two loves in Him, He would love neither Himself nor creatures perfectly. He can love only His being, and this love extends to all beings that receive of what is His. Similarly, in order that the soul may love God, itself, and its neighbor as perfectly as its limited capacity allows, it does not need two kinds of love. If its love were divided in two, it would be less perfect: whatever was given to one object would be taken away from the other. Therefore it should love only God in God, and its love will extend to all that God loves. This love of God alone not only makes it possible for the soul to love creatures; it also sets the measure of its love of creatures. The rule is to love them insofar as they are lovable in God. If we love God alone, we shall love them neither more nor less than God loves them and wants us to love them.[7]

This abstract explanation leads to some practical conclusions. The act of love of God alone in God spreads out to all lovable creatures and pours into them. All that remains is to evince this love by interior and

---

[6] *Secretum*, p. 122.
[7] *Secretum*, pp. 123-125.

exterior acts of charity. But this love, based upon the same love of God, will be sure of reaching the neighbor not in view of him, but of God. It will effectively help others to turn to God. The gift of self to God in our neighbor will take on many different forms: rejoicing on the conversion of sinners, cooperating with penitents in their repentance by prayer and mortification, desiring that sinners be pardoned, suffering for their sins, praying and weeping for evildoers, giving all men an example of the love of God, relieving the material needs of all whom we can reach, and using every effort and desire and resource to get others to supply such needs when we cannot do so ourselves.[8]

The result of the loving gift of self to all that God loves is the union of all creatures with God. The soul that loves God in God participates in the love by which God unites all the creatures that He loves, without at the same time depriving them of their diversity. Here again, the mystery is clarified by a comparison: A single soul vivifies a whole animal being, vivifying all its members by a single act of life. And yet it vivifies the members diversely, respecting, sustaining, and animating their different functions. Thus the love of God in God extends to all the creatures loved by God but flows into each of them according to its proper capacity. It reaches each of them by whatever deeds of charity each needs to be united with God.[9]

The perfect model of this universal love is Christ, who gave His life for the good and for sinners, for His disciples and for His persecutors, for His friends and for His enemies. Even those who were putting Him to death He saw in God and loved with the love that God had for them: the malice of their deed did not change the fact they were creatures of God, participating in His being and in His love.[10]

God alone knows the measure of His love for each of His creatures. Christ knew that measure in God. But man does not know this mystery: He can only throw himself on God. If he loves God, he will love all that

[8] *Secretum*, pp. 129-130.
[9] *Secretum*, pp. 132-134.
[10] *Secretum*, pp. 140-141.

God loves and as it should be loved. So it is in heaven with the blessed angelic and human creatures who already see God. They love creatures only for Him and gauge the measure according to which the creatures of God ought to be loved. When we ask in the Lord's Prayer that God's will be done on earth as it is in heaven, we desire to love God in God, and all creatures in Him, as do the blessed in heaven.[11]

The love of God is a mystery which man cannot perfectly understand or explain. But it is sometimes granted him to feel it. Then he sings the joy that inundates his entire being. Giustiniani has left us a sonnet composed as a thanksgiving in the grip of such an experience. Annihilated, forgetting himself but united to the Lord, he pours forth and radiates the joy that this experience brings.

> Why would my heart not be happy within
> And my face joyous and serene without,
> Since the Beloved before whom all woe takes flight
> I often see, hear, and feel close to me?
>
> That Lord whom I never repent of loving
> Calls me to Himself and then Himself conducts me;
> And such sweetness fills my every vein
> That I no longer remember who I am.
>
> When the Exalted Beloved enters my heart,
> I would want to keep Him hidden and do not know how,
> So brightly does He gleam forth from my brow.
>
> The Exalted Lord is not wont to come in secret
> To make so lowly a handmaid His spouse.
> O chaste, glad, lucky, O beautiful times of love.[12]

---

[11] *Secretum*, p.148.
[12] F II:115b.

XVII

Epilogue

The Cross of Christ and Martyrdom

Throughout his life Giustiniani desired martyrdom. Often he asked himself whether he should go off to distant lands to bear witness to Christ among the infidels. He wished to do so by mute preaching, by the very example of an existence wholly consecrated to God.[1] When he understood that his vocation was the hermit life, he never ceased to view it as a "clear and powerful confession of Christ." "The more a man is esteemed by the world, the more his conversion to the solitary life confesses Christ and gives glory to God."[2] He loved to read and to quote the texts where tradition has spoken of the martyrdom of the monk,[3] and he liked the liturgical hymns that sing of the martyrdom of confessors who, without dying, endured voluntarily a slow mortification.[4]

In the time of the primitive Church, in the age of the tyrants, the martyrs by dying confessed that Jesus Christ was the Son of God and that the Christian religion was the only way of salvation. Something similar

---

[1] Cf. HE, pp. 107, 112-113.
[2] Q I:211.
[3] F II: 102V; Q IV:492.
[4] Q IV:492; cf. F I:100; Q IV:257; F I:155, etc.

happens in our days when, in the midst of the tyranny of vices, amid the crowd of men great and small who hardly believe, a Christian who could live in comfort renounces the world, and not through weakness or discouragement. Such a Christian truly testifies, as by a voluntary martyrdom, that Jesus Christ is the true God, that our faith is right and true, and that the sinner cannot be saved without doing penance.[5]

Eremitical life, more than any other, is a martyrdom, because it implies more perfect forgetfulness of self: *sibi soli et Deo vacare.* But is there not a contradiction between this affirmation of oneself in God's presence and the desire to die to oneself in order to live for God and to love only God alone: *Solo Dio in Dio?* The antinomy is only apparent, for to live with oneself is not to live for oneself. The soul lost in God receives from Him, not from itself, all that gives it life: "*in seipsa, non tamen de seipsa, sed de eo qui est verum gaudium, vera quies, vera consolatio, Jesus dulcissimus.*"[6]

It receives from Jesus His peace and His suffering, or more precisely, His peace in His suffering. One of Giustiniani's last writings is an ardent proclamation of that true peace.[7]

Nothing can separate me from the charity of God that is in Jesus Christ. Will You take away from me, Lord, the very sweet sentiment I feel in loving You like this? I do not think so, for it is You who will that I should so love You. You may perhaps test me in order to know — or better, to enable me to know — if I love You truly. Very well! Lord, test and try my heart, and see if it contains any other love than You, if it loves You otherwise than in You and for You alone. Lord, make me dead and then give me life; lead me to hell and bring me back again;

---

[5] F I: 54.

[6] Q II:14. "In itself, not however from itself, but from Him who is true joy, true peace, true consolation, Jesus most sweet."

[7] This has become Argument VI in the *Secretum*, pp. 149-163. Only the outline was written for the seventh Argument which was to follow, p. 23.

make me poor or rich, just as You please; humble me and then exalt me; kill me and then raise me up; strike me and then cure me; should You make me die a thousand times a day, my love would be no less for You alone and in You alone. If You withdraw from me, Lord, leaving me like a barren and waterless land, stripped of all sensible and actual devotion or compunction or spiritual consolation, deprived of all these delights on which You so graciously feed me, despoiled of all the adornments of the spiritual life, poor, naked, wretched, abandoned — I shall still love You in the same way, and I shall know that You permit all that for the sake of my greater progress.

What could You do, Lord — permit me to speak thus — what could You do to make me stop loving You? If you give me peace, interior and exterior, I shall love you. If you give me war and battling, interior and exterior, I shall love you. If you console me, interiorly and exteriorly, I shall love You. If you leave me in tribulations, without consolation and in distress, I think I shall love You still.... Plunge me into the flames of purgatory and I shall love You, for they shall not consume me but will be a sweet comfort, since they will lead me to You, my only love.... If I love You alone, Lord, my good and my sole love, and not myself, I care not what may happen to me, so long as I may do Your will and that all Your good pleasure may be fulfilled in me, on me, and by me.

The soul thus at peace with God is at the same time, and inseparably, at peace with itself and with all creatures. Where love is, there is peace. As a shadow follows a body, so peace accompanies love — and that love, as we have seen, extends to all that God loves.

The soul wholly recollected in God is as imperturbable as God. It is always peaceful. Men of the world love things that change: therefore, as they are well aware, their peace cannot be stable. But the soul enamored of God cannot lose its peace, even in the midst of tribulation. In fact, true and perfect peace demands frequent facing of adversity, until the soul becomes so accustomed to it that it no longer feels it. Then it finds suffering a source of joy. It accepts without complaint or impatience, but with great consolation, being deprived of the Lord's visitations. It understands that being deprived of all sensible consolation is helpful to its progress and necessary for its salvation. Overwhelmed by troubles, it seeks refuge in none but God. Then only does it possess the peace of Christ, that peace about which the Lord said: "My peace I give you, my peace I leave you." He says: "My peace," for not every kind of peace is the peace of Christ: the world's peace cannot be His peace.

Where is the peace of Christ found? Nowhere else but in the cross of Christ, accepted voluntarily and joyfully. Our cross is nothing other than the cross of Christ: a cross formed by tribulations from above, from below, from the right, and from the left. Tribulations come from above, when we think we have been forgotten by God; from below, when the devil attacks us; from the right, when the holy angels and the just disdain us; from the left, when the wicked persecute us. That is the shape of the cross of our suffering. The soul enamored of God in this life not only does not flee the cross, it goes out to meet it, to carry it in peace and with great joy. Many who think they have heavenly peace really rest in themselves and in the world. They lack it because there is no peace elsewhere than in the voluntarily accepted and sweet cross of Christ. He who seeks peace elsewhere is mistaken.

Peace in this life lies in desiring and enduring with joy all tribulations, even if they be spiritual; in being unconcerned about temporal affairs, but rather in stretching forward in all one's desires toward the joys of eternity and aspiring for them in hope. Peace does not mean a life of pleasure and consolation now. We should be all the more consoled if our time of life brings greater tribulations, to make us more like Christ, more intimate participants in His tribulations. For a servant of Christ, no other peace is worthy of the name.

Blessed the soul which attains that peace which never, never can be achieved except by loving God, Him alone and in Him alone! Most amiable Lord Jesus, I beg You to give me peace, and let it be ever peace with You. If I have that, then I surely shall have at the same time, as far as it is in my power, "peace with all men," as the Apostle says. If I have peace with You, my Lord, I can sincerely say with the Prophet: "I was at peace even with those who hated peace." The soul that truly rests in the love of God alone, possesses a peace which not even the whole world can take away from him. No attack of the depraved, no insult of the demons can in the least disturb that peace, for the true love of God in God is a rampart for the soul that no force can break through. The peace of Christ is a rock and an impregnable fortress. I may be attacked from every side, but if my refuge is Christ, I am sure that I will not give way: I hope in God and so I shall be saved.[8]

---

[8] *Secretum*, pp. 149-163; Jn 14:27, Heb 12:14, Ps 119 (120):7, and cf. Ps 26 (27):3.

Appendix I

The Sources

The doctrine of Paul Giustiniani is original in more than one respect. He seems to have been the first since Peter Damian, at least in the Benedictine tradition, to assemble the elements of a coherent and complete account of eremitism, expressed in a notably personal style. But little of his work is wholly new. He had no need to discover everything by himself, for the spirituality of the monk and the hermit had already been fully treated before his time. His strength derives from his vast documentation, drawn from the best sources of general culture and Christian tradition.

A thorough study of the sources of his doctrine remains impossible, seeing as the greater part of the texts are unpublished. At least one can already indicate the authors and the currents of thought to which the Blessed is more indebted.

Giustiniani knows the ancient Greek philosophers. He often speaks of Aristotle, but seems particularly familiar with Plato (whose *Timaeus* he liked to quote) and Plotinus. His favorite Latin authors were Seneca and, more particularly, Cicero, whose *Questiones tusculanes* played a major role in his conversion.

The most important source of his religious thought is undoubtedly Holy Scripture, which he studied in the Greek text and in the Vulgate. He did not fail to consult also with those who knew Hebrew.

He was well-read in the Greek Fathers, particularly Origen, Saint Basil, Saint Gregory Nazianzen, and Saint Gregory of Nyssa. In the

Index of manuscripts at Urbino at the end of the fifteenth century (ms. *Urbin. lat.* 1761, f. 19) there is a note regarding ms. n. 110 *"est penes fratrem paulum iustinianum venetum.¹ Restituit."* That manuscript, now *Urbin. lat. 46*, consists mainly of writings by Saint Basil and Saint Athanasius (cf. C. Stornajolo, *Codices Urbinates latini*, I, Rome, 1902, pp. 51-54.). It is known that Giustiniani was acquainted with the Duchess Gonzaga of Urbino.

The Latin Fathers that Giustiniani quotes most readily are Saint Augustine (whose biblical commentaries he particularly admires), Saint Jerome (whose Epistles he often read), and Saint Gregory the Great, besides Saint Ambrose, Saint Leo, and the Venerable Bede.

He absorbed the Lives of the Desert Fathers. Though he did not give the collection his approval in every detail, yet he considered it as a bedside book for all hermits. When he noted what every hermit should keep in his cell, he gave this list of indispensable books: "a Bible, the Lives of the Desert Fathers, a *Rule of Saint Benedict*, and a Psalter". (FA 118V.)

He studied Cassian very thoroughly, reserving judgment on some theological points in his *Observations on Cassian*, but often relying on him with regard to the requirements of monastic and eremitical life.

He studied the *Rule of Saint Benedict*, seeking the help of whatever commentaries were available.

He studied the Camaldolese sources. His desire for martyrdom was doubtless derived from the biographies of Saint Romuald and his companions. He wrote out a whole volume of extracts from Saint Peter Damian (Q V bis). In drawing up his *Regula vitae eremiticae*, he was directly inspired by the *Constitutions* of Blessed Rudolph.

In the whole monastic tradition of the Middle Ages, the author with the strongest influence on Giustiniani is certainly Saint Bernard. Several times Giustiniani affirmed that he read him with joy and

---

[1] Read here *venetum* and not *veronensem*, as did C. Stornajolo, *Codices Urbinates graeci*, Rome, 1895, p. lxxvii.

profit. He often quotes Bernard or is reminiscent of him. Many of his fundamental ideas on the love of God, sometimes even the formulas in which they are expressed, are inspired by Saint Bernard, particularly the phrase about loving God without measure and the notion of loving God "in Himself and for Himself" (cf. *Brevis commentatio in Cantica ex verbis sancti Bernardi*, PL 184, 429 D), and also the ideas about the life of God in the soul (cf. Saint Bernard: *In Cant.* 81, 1-4, PL 183, 1171-1173). Saint Bernard's *De diligendo Deo* furnished some of the principal ideas of Giustiniani in his *Cogitationes quotidianae de amore Dei* [*Daily Thoughts on the Love of God*]. Giustiniani also composed a parable in the style of Saint Bernard's: *Rex omnium potentissimus...* (F VII, 92). He states that he wrote it after reading a series of parables, this being most probably the collection of Saint Bernard's parables (PL 183, 757-772).

Giustiniani made notes on Saint Albert the Great. He praised Saint Thomas, whose opinions he knew but did not always adopt. He often consulted him as a reliable master, far superior to the professors of what he calls "the new theology", that is, the abstract theology without contact with traditional sources, as taught in Paris in the fifteenth century.

Giustiniani knew the *Decree* of Gratian as well as the *Decretals*. He transcribed passages from these works. More than once he expressed his admiration for Dante and Petrarch.

Finally, one of the spiritual currents closest to him was the Franciscan. He had great devotion to Saint Francis and felt deep emotion whenever he passed near Mount Alverna. The original Franciscan spirit harmonized with his own tendencies in two respects: the quest for solitude and the quest for poverty. Naturally, therefore, he welcomed the first Capuchins with open arms. It has been written very accurately:

For the Franciscans as for the Benedictines, the primary and essential purpose was to *be* rather than to *do*. In this respect, the Benedictines and the Franciscans differ from other orders such as the Dominicans, which were founded primarily for the sake of an external apostolate. It is true that the Franciscan vocation implies activity for the benefit of neighbor. This is derived from the evangelical ideal of life to which the friars were bound to conform. But the principal purpose of the order was to revive in its members the perfect Christian life as portrayed in the Gospels.[2]

It is difficult to determine, from the manuscripts preserved for us, to what extent Giustiniani influenced the first Capuchins and was influenced by them.[3] In any case, certain similarities of detail in their dress and observances are an expression of the same desire to contribute to the reform of the Church and of religious life by a return to the spirit of poverty and solitude.

---

[2]   P. Cuthbert, O.F.M. Cap. *I cappuccini, Un contributo alla storia della contra-riforma.* (Faenza, 1930, p. 12.)

[3]   On this subject we have the studies published by Fr. Edouard d'Alençon, O.F.M. Cap., in the *Annales Capucinorum*, vols. XXV-XXXV, passim, and especially by Fr. Burchard De Wolffenschiessen, O.F.M. Cap., *De influxu Legislationis Camaldulensium in Ordinem Minorum Capucinorum*, in *Collectanea Franciscana Capucinorum*, I (1931) pp. 59-78.

Appendix II

Eremiticae Vitae Descriptio

The ideal of life proposed by Giustiniani is perfectly illustrated by a very beautiful painting of El Greco, now kept in the Instituto de Valencia de Don Juan in Madrid.[1]

On the left Saint Benedict, wearing a black cowl, holds a crozier and a book that probably represents his *Rule*. On the right Saint Romuald, in a white cowl and with a long beard, holds in his left hand a short staff, without scroll, and in his right hand a miniature image of the Hermitage of Camaldoli.[2]

Above these two figures is shown a hermitage, surrounded by a thick circle of trees and dominated by high peaks. In the center is a domed chapel; on the left of the entrance gate, a big building intended for common utilities; in the forest, separated by thick rows of trees, are twenty-four cells with their gardens in front. This picture of a Camaldolese hermitage corresponds exactly to the description given by Yepes in the *Cronica general de la Orden de San Benito*, V (1615), pp. 301 ff.

In a frame placed between the two figures the following poem, entitled *Eremiticae vitae descriptio* [A description of the eremitic life],[3] is written:

---

[1] On the history and the interpretation of the picture, cf. F. J. Sanchez Canton: *Catalogo de las pinturas del Instituto de Valencia de Don Juan* (Madrid, 1923, pp. 177-179).

[2] These same details are found in the engraving that serves as frontispiece to the original edition of the RVE.

[3] The phrases at the beginning of the first and second stanzas are taken from the liturgical hymns of the feast of Saint John the Baptist, as still found in the monastic Breviary. The second last line recalls the motto that Saint Gregory the Great applied to Saint Benedict: *soli Deo placere desiderans* (Dial., II, 1).

O nimis felix sacra solitudo,
Quis tuas laudes valeat referre,
Vita, dulcedo, requies, asylum,
    Semita portus.

Antra deserti coluere sancti,
Montibus sylvisque Camaldulenses
Nunc Eremitae satagunt beatam
    Ducere vitam.

Singuli plane rigide seorsum,
In suis cellis bene separatis
Iugiter degunt, comedunt, et orant
    Crimina plangunt.

Septies templum repetunt silenter,
Rite devote celebrant synaxim,
Ac Deum laudant, pariter canentes,
    Nocte dieque.

Si diu solus cupit esse quisquam,
Et frui vita penitus remota,
Is domi clausus remanet quietus,
    Celica cernens.

Regulam servant pietate multa,
Quam tulit Divus Benedictus olim,
Postmodum sanctus quoque Romualdus
    Ordinis auctor.

Hic Ravenatum procerum propago
Tesqua, vel saltus coluit rigentes,
Gratia, signis meritisque claris
    Regnat olympo.

Appetant omnes nemorum recessus,
Labilis temnant bona cuncta mundi,
Eligant soli Domino placere
    His in Eremis.

O holy solitude, happy beyond measure,
Who could be worthy to relate thy praises?
Thou who art life, sweetness, rest, and asylum,
    Path to safe haven.

Once the saints cultivated caves in the desert,
Now the Camaldolese, on mountains and in forests
Are occupied, diligent, busy with leading,
    The blest life of hermits.

Each on equal footing, strictly and in private,
Keeps to his own cell, widely separated.
Yet joined to the others–all eating, or praying,
    Or mourning offenses.

Seven times in silence they go forth to their temple,
Duly and devoutly to celebrate, assembled.
They praise God, as but with one voice chanting
    At night and in daytime.

If one of them longs for more time in seclusion,
Wanting to enjoy a life of full removal,
Shut up as a recluse, he with quiet discernment
    Thinks only of heaven.

They keep the *Rule* with a very pious observance,
That *Rule* that so long ago, Benedict gave divinely,
And that Saint Romuald also passed on later,
    In founding the order.

Here once the offspring of Ravenna's nobles,
Cultivated strictly this wasteland of the forest.
Now by the grace of their clear signs and merits,
    They reign from heaven.

All should be craving this wooded retirement,
Disdaining all the goods of this world so fleeting.
Would that many might choose to please God, and Him only,
    Here in the desert.

RULE OF THE EREMITIC LIFE

Seventeen Chapters Selected from the
Fifty-three of the Version of 1516

Blessed Paul Giustiniani

First published, in Italian translation, by Eremo di Monte Rua in 1984.
Second and revised edition, Abbey of Saint Benedict, Seregno, 1996.

Giustiniani composed this original version of his Rule during a forty-day period of reclusion.

"It constituted [for his new foundation] a precious codex not only in the book sense but also in the juridical and constitutional sense of the word." (E. Massa)

RULE OF THE EREMITIC LIFE

Preface: In Praise of the Eremitic Life

Just as outside the realm of faithful Christian piety, there is no scheme for living that can lead to eternal beatitude, so within the immense variety of the faithful in Christ, there are very many established ways of life by means of which we can direct our course toward the celestial fatherland and reach the glory of true happiness. Now of all the rules for Christian living, there is none that can more easily and more perfectly offer its followers the very sweet tranquillity of this present life and the highly desired happiness of the future one than the correct institution of the eremitic and solitary life.

This way in fact, in comparison with all others, more easily and securely directs the steps of those who travel in it to the perpetual beatitude of the heavenly kingdom. At the same time, it provides so much tranquillity in this mortal life to those who walk it uprightly, that it affords them, still passing time on earth, no small share of celestial delights. For it distances men to the utmost from all occasions of sin and from all things that are wont to disturb or confuse human minds during this pilgrimage. It almost compels them to upright endeavors and good works, to the point of making them, earthbound mortals, not very different from the angels, and of leading them on by a shortcut to angelic heights.

In bygone ages this singular kind of living had wonderful founders, famous eulogizers, and outstanding followers. Their teachings and their exemplary lives irradiated on the world an almost divine light, that in good portion still shines brightly in this miserable time of ours. But what formerly was considered the fairest and most honorable part of the Christian religion and religious profession is now the most diminished. And indeed the eremitic way, so upright and sublime, seems to have wholly disappeared.

Even so, there are twenty-odd Camaldolese, cultivators of solitude, who are leading the religious eremitic life legitimately according to the *Rule of Saint Benedict* and the currently approved Constitutions of the eremitic life. All others who, wearing any habit whatsoever, inhabit solitary places, or who in any way delight to be called hermits, are really neither hermits nor true religious. For they pronounce no religious vows, profess no approved rule, and are not subject to the teaching or obedience of anyone. Now these things are, in any form of religious life, necessary first principles. Their wretched fashion of living is deplorable. For without vows or rule, yet under the banner of the eremitic name, they serve their own inclinations rather than God.

Not that we claim to be worthy followers of so sublime a life, or somehow qualified to be founders of so distinguished a manner of life. But long ago we legitimately undertook the institution of this holy style of living, out of desire for the heavenly country and wishing, with His help, to please God as much as we can. We were zealously careful for many years, despite the feebleness of our powers, to keep this institution. Although it has been almost forsaken by others, it can still, if properly handed down, lead many of those who accept it to salvation.

Not trusting in our own powers, but relying on the divine assistance, we are about to write a rule of the solitary and eremitic life. We intend it for ourselves, for the brother hermits who are with us, and for all those who after us will want to adopt the plan of this kind of living. We exhort in the Lord all those who desire the very serene tranquillity of the present life and the superabundant beatitude of the heavenly homeland to undertake the institution of the eremitic life out of devotion toward God and, with firm purpose of soul, to strive to persevere in it to the end.

For even though there are in Holy Church many ways and diverse paths by which we may direct our course to the Lord, yet among all of them there is not one which like the regular eremitic way of life can guide its followers by so straight and clear a path, as on a journey free from all danger, to the ineffable joy of the Jerusalem which is above [cf. Gal 4:26].

1. Three Types of Hermits[1]

There are many and various types of eremitic life. But in practice they can be reduced to three.

To the first type of hermits belong those who take no vow of poverty, chastity or obedience, do not have an approved rule, and are not subject to any teaching or discipline. But because they have put off secular dress and wear a penitential habit in imitation of religious, they falsely claim they have renounced the world, just because they have changed clothes, wear the tonsure, and dwell in solitary places. They have not submitted themselves to the vows of poverty, chastity, and obedience, a thing that all those who renounce the world should do. They do not follow any regular discipline, but only their own feelings, and they are not directed by the teaching office of any superior, but by their own opinion. And so by these very things, they make it clearly understood that they still keep faith with the world.

These individually, or by twos or threes or even more, live in the same or different cells. They take what they need for food and clothing either from their own goods or from those that are common to all. Whatever the color or shape of their habit, whatever place of retreat or solitude they have chosen, whatever name they have given themselves, since they lack the three principal vows of the religious life, profession of

---

[1] Cf. RB 1 with this selection, RB 4 with the next selection, etc.

an approved rule, and the teaching of proven fathers, they evidently have not chosen a sufficiently sanctioned kind of living. For Saint Benedict, who calls these men sarabaites if they reside in a definite place, or gyrovagues if instead they move often from one place to another, plainly defines them as having the most disgraceful and miserable style of life. These are surely inferior to the cenobites and, what is much worse, are called acephalous, that is, headless. The sacred canons of the Church do not approve of this kind of life. Rather, they censure it.

To the second type of hermits belong those who have pronounced with solemn commitment the three principal vows of holy religion and have made profession before a regular superior according to an approved rule. After a long probationary period of observation in the cenoby or monastery they pass, individually and entirely alone, from the monastery to the hermitage. They proceed from the brotherly battle line of the cenoby, to single combat in solitude, to fight all alone, that is without any human encouragement, against every kind of vice and temptation.

Saint Benedict calls these anchorites or hermits. If they have truly chosen the solitary life, without any human companionship, they are to be considered, in the broad judgment of the Holy Fathers, more perfect and more honorable than the cenobites. But they do not entirely and publicly observe poverty and obedience, great and precious riches of the religious spirit, and are obliged to take care of their own bodily needs and to be concerned with arranging and directing their own lives. Since they expose themselves to these and to many other preoccupations and dangers that inevitably threaten those who live alone, as moreover is stated in the holy instructions and in the affirmations of the holy writers with regard to these hermits, one can suppose that this type of life is very dangerous. The learned and saintly Jerome says about them: "The life of certain solitaries, which I know very well, is difficult and dangerous. If it is very well conducted, it brings one close to God. But it is not as safe as that of those who dwell together."

Indeed, this solitary way of life was considered more perfect (even if less safe) than that of the cenobites at the time when no law of Holy Church forbade living a life in complete solitude. But at the present time ecclesiastical laws oblige all the Christian faithful, but especially professed religious, to confess their sins often, to receive Holy Communion, and to celebrate or attend Mass frequently, for the sake of their eternal salvation. Now since all these things are hardly possible in this kind of life, it would seem to be wholly prohibited. So it is held to be less safe (or rather completely illicit) for a Christian to attempt it or, more exactly, to persist in it.

The third form of eremitic life, which is not contemptible as is the first, nor somewhat dangerous as the second, deserves to be considered the most praiseworthy and the safest. There belong to it those who, withdrawing from the world or from the cenoby, live far from cities and, as much as possible, from frequent human contacts and other partnership in living. They reside in very remote and solitary places, that is, on mountains where the access is difficult and the passage fatiguing, in the barely accessible bends of trackless valleys, in unknown caves, and in the dark and secret solitary recesses of hidden caverns. They dwell individually in separate cells, professing vows of poverty, chastity, and obedience according to some approved rule, under prelates and the discipline of the same rule. Numbers of them live together for the same common purpose, in institutes of the religious life, and lead a more austere and stricter life than the cenobites.

These, because they pronounce the three principal vows and profess to live according to an approved rule, never moving away from the judgment and authority of the superior, certainly avoid that blame and bad reputation which, on the contrary, the hermits of the first type have. Although they live in solitude, yet they are never completely alone or deprived of the help and comfort of fraternity. Nay rather several of them, unanimous in the same purpose of life, live in holy solitude as in the house of the Lord so that each one may gain his own advantage from their fellowship. For if one falls, another immediately lifts him up, and if a difficulty prevails against one, it is overcome by many. They incite each other to every good work. They encourage each other and, as they mutually serve one another, they can safeguard all that is necessary for salvation.

They avoid with the utmost circumspection and discretion those many dangers that threaten the one who lives alone, and above all the risk of their own salvation that the hermits of the second type must face. Thus tempering their form of life, they have the advantages and the security of community life and obedience without the various occupations and the multiple distractions of the cenoby. They enjoy the glad and fortunate tranquillity of solitude, without any of the dangers of the completely solitary life.

If one of their number is eager for more freedom for contemplation and desirous of greater retirement and more perfect solitude,[2] he employs a quite admirable scheme devised with the help of divine rather than human ingenuity. Whoever retains this desire not only pledges himself not to frequent the people of the outside world, but he refrains completely from even the very living together customary with the other brother hermits, casting off absolutely every engagement of human life. He will not incur any solicitude about setting up and regulating his life. But he will never be released from the rule and the constitutions of the hermits or from the authority and obedience of the superior. So, too, he will never lack fraternal assistance on those occasions when, for the observance of ecclesiastical norms, the ministry of another is required. When it is granted to someone to live apart from all the others, according to his heart's desire, he is assigned a cell with a little garden. He may remain in it either for some preestablished time or else, if he prefers, even forever, without ever leaving it. The permanent recluse will be administered, through the diligent solicitude of the other brother hermits, everything that is necessary for both body and soul, timely aids and comforts. And

---

[2] I.e., reclusion.

so he will be loosed from every other concern and free, so that he can feel fully at ease to wait for God alone [*soli Deo vacare*].

This third type of eremitic life was pioneered by the most holy hermit Romuald, father and founder of all Western hermits. He, enlightened by the divine inspiration of the Holy Spirit, started the eremitic institution in the tenth century, when Saint Bruno had not yet founded the Charterhouse, nor Saint John Gualbert Vallombrosa, nor Saint Robert Cîteaux, nor Saint Bernard Clairvaux, and they had not yet made these monasteries famous by their life and doctrine. This was a long time indeed before Saint Francis had originated the Friars Minor and Saint Dominic the Friars Preachers, orders in which today an almost countless multitude of men and women do battle for God. It was a time in which a few abbots, not very observant of the *Rule of Saint Benedict*, alone or with very few monks completely alien to regular observance, were occupying the monasteries rather than governing them; when, that is, monastic observance was in decline. Then Saint Romuald shone upon the world through the divine mercy like the sun breaking through the clouds, and he also restored the cenobitic life that seemed then to be utterly ruined.

He established this admirable kind of hermits at the Holy Hermitage of Camaldoli. It is situated in Tuscany, on the summit of the Apennines, in the middle of forests abounding in very tall and evergreen firs. Here, with a tenor of life that has remained always constant for more than five hundred years until today, one can perceive, by the gift of God Most High and the prayers of the founder, a strict observance of the eremitic life.

This type of eremitic life seems more perfect than any type of cenobitic life and far superior to all the other types of hermits. For in it, one is not occupied in the many activities of the cenobies, nor is there that continual and harmful distraction of the things of the world, whether of persons or of business matters. There is no reproach of blame or disgrace as in the first type of hermits, nor danger or risk to salvation as in the second category.

Indeed, since both the pure cenobitic life and every other form of eremitic life have in themselves both advantageous and disadvantageous features, it appears that by taking away from both of them all or most of the latter, and by keeping everything that remains, that is, the things that are suitable, upright, secure and praiseworthy, by a sort of divine blending, the third type of hermits was formed.

Leaving out, therefore, the other two types of hermits, whose life is either unapproved, or insecure, or not even completely licit, let us begin with the help of God, to compile and to put in order the rule and the institutions of this third type, that is, of the hermits of Camaldoli. Since the holy founder they have been, as far as we know, his only indefatigable followers.[3] We are doing this not only so that the Camaldolese hermits may have the rules of their religious life collected and put in order, but also so that all those zealous for the eremitic life, to whatever rule or order they may belong, changing little or nothing, may have a common rule and a body of instructions for the eremitic life.[4]

2. Instruments of the Eremitic Life

The instruments of the holy eremitic life are principally these:

1. To take to heart, with a pure and free intention, the holy vows of poverty, chastity, and obedience; to profess them with one's own mouth and to perfectly observe them without ceasing, according to the *Rule of Saint Benedict* and these eremitic constitutions.

2. To keep inviolably with all one's might these rules of the eremitic life and the *Rule of Saint Benedict*, inasmuch as it is not contrary to eremitic profession, which requires many more austere and perfect observances.

3. To love the deep tranquillity of holy solitude.

---

[3] With the exception of Camaldoli, the hermitages founded by Saint Romuald were short-lived.

[4] On the possible option today of hermits making profession to the diocesan bishop and living by their own rule under his guidance, see CCL 603, number 2.

4. To enjoy the pleasant seclusion of the cell, removed and separated from the others.

5. To make every effort to avoid, insofar as charity permits, the concourse and company of men, whether of secular or other mode of life.

6. To love with all one's heart holy, voluntary poverty.

7. With perfect chastity of body, to keep the mind as well free from all stain.

8. Never to shake from one's neck the yoke of holy obedience, truly easy and light for the one who bears it willingly, but to carry it cheerfully until death.

9. With a constant longing to reach an ever higher peak of this virtue, to always obey one's seniors, also in those things in which obedience does not seem to be absolutely required.

10. To run with continuous strides of good works toward the high summits of all the virtues.

11. To guard the treasure of most perfect humility all the more carefully in everything as one makes more progress.

12. To avoid all elation of mind and haughtiness and arrogance in outward behavior.

13. Not to desire holy orders and the dignity of the priesthood and not to accept them except for love of perfect obedience.

14. To refuse with all earnestness prelacies and all preeminence of rank as if they were a treacherous and shipwrecking sea, not through fear of work, but through love of humility.

15. To wish for work that does not afford honor.

16. Not to refuse a service because it is not dignified.

17. To always be of profit to others and never to wish to preside over others.

18. To assemble together in church for the Work of God[5] not only compelled by a kind of customary obligation, but above all with the spontaneous desire to praise the Creator.

---

[5] Liturgy of the Hours.

19. To celebrate the just-mentioned Divine Office after the monastic fashion, with all gravity and reverence, great devotion of heart, proper and orderly ceremonies, without any singing, and with suitable moderation of voice.
20. To celebrate Mass with spiritual joy, or to hear it with devotion.
21. To take delight in the daily practice of private psalmody.
22. To love reading the Holy Scriptures.
23. To take time [*vacare*] often for devout meditation.
24. To bend the mind to holy prayer with tears and compunction of heart, if not continually, at least once a day.
25. To attend willingly to the study of letters, especially of the Divine Word.
26. To teach and exhort one another insofar as competent to do so.
27. To frequently confess one's sins with true contrition of heart.
28. To receive with great reverence the venerable sacrament of Holy Communion.
29. To maintain everywhere exterior good order of the body and of comportment.
30. To preserve honor and seriousness everywhere, knowing that one is always in the presence of God and His angels.
31. To be delighted with the rigorous abstinence, frequent fasting, and meager and commonplace food and drink.
32. To abstain from wine at least frequently, if not always.
33. Not to relax the observance of the common life, except through real necessity or by order of the superior, but instead to restore it, with fitting discretion at the right time and in a proper manner, in imitation of the ancient hermits.
34. To relax somewhat the rigor when reason appears to demand it, applying the poultice of kind discretion for the delicate, the weak, the old, those weary from work, and the sick.
35. To love much holy silence, in which is found just worship [Is 32:17, Vulg.] and progress in every virtue.
36. To preserve an inviolable silence at established times and places.

37. To accustom oneself to speak in a subdued, but not too weak, voice.
38. To strive to speak with few and well-considered words and only those that are required by necessity or for edification.
39. To diligently be on guard against long conversations, idle words, and any trace of the vice of murmuring.
40. Never to be inquisitive about wars or other secular affairs going on all over the earth, not to relate these things to anyone and not to listen to them willingly.
41. To flee idleness with manual work, preserving the good of humility and subduing the insolence of the body.
42. To always be occupied in some corporal or spiritual exercise.
43. To be happy to dwell continually at the hermitage and to stay constantly in the cell, and in this way to maintain stability of mind and body.
44. Never to enter the cell assigned to another, or even the common workshops, except with the permission of the prior and for an urgent need.
45. Not to roam outside the hermitage.
46. When through necessity or obedience you must go out of the hermitage, never to slacken the style and the rigor of the eremitic life where they can be observed.
47. To always sleep individually in individual cells.
48. Not to disdain a rough blanket and hard straw.
49. To sleep dressed and girt.
50. To take the discipline frequently and of your own free will.
51. To gladly wear rough haircloth and cheap clothing.
52. To consider the superior, whoever he may be, provided that he is legitimately elected, as chosen by God.
53. Not to pass judgment on the superior, but instead to be ready to be judged by him.
54. To revere the superior and willingly heed his orders and admonitions.

55. If the superior is virtuous, to imitate his good deeds; and to put his sound doctrine into practice even if, God forbid, he may do otherwise.
56. To obey the superior in everything, with all spiritual cheerfulness, as if you were obeying God.
57. The superior should love all his subjects without favoritism.
58. He should watch over the peace and the health of each one as though his own.
59. He should provide for the bodily necessities of his subjects even more than for his own.
60. He should always feel responsible when he finds some detriment or lack of progress in his subjects.
61. To gladly receive and eagerly carry out, when they are enjoined, necessary tasks of administration.
62. To assemble in chapter as often as necessary, to give counsel after a brief prefatory prayer.
63. To set forth your advice in the midst of the assembly with the fear of God and humility.
64. To gladly follow the judgment and decision of the majority, even if some think differently.
65. To keep secret what is said in chapter.
66. To give ear calmly to fraternal correction and the harshest reproofs of the superiors.
67. To do promptly, and with interior sweetness, the tasks imposed by obedience and penances for your faults.
68. Not to accept indiscriminately and indifferently everyone for the eremitic life.
69. To determine always with common counsel, diligent examination, and legitimate approval who is to be rejected and who accepted.
70. To give the one who is received an apt and authorized position in the community according to the established norms.
71. For each one to maintain everywhere his position in the community.

72. Not to disturb the order of the assembled community.

73. To readily accept an office enjoined.

74. Not to rashly beg off from such compliance.

75. Not to send anyone outside the hermitage for any business whatever, unless pious utility suggests or just necessity urges.

76. To see to it that, with solicitous care and fervent charity, the hermits are administered all necessary food and clothing at opportune times and according to the need of each.

77. To always have for the weak and the sick prudent discretion, conscientious care, and vigilant solicitude.

78. To welcome whoever comes to the hermitage with pleasant words, charitable services, and the fragrance of good example.

79. For the open hermits to be glad to minister to the recluse hermits.[6]

80. For the recluse hermits to pray with special consideration for the open hermits.

81. For whoever does not have the perfection of reclusion to venerate it and, insofar as an open hermit can, to imitate it.

82. For whoever has at some time attained reclusion to preserve it diligently and observe it in every respect.

83. For hermits, both open and recluse, to keep all the eremitic rules, aflame with zeal for God.

84. To be diligently careful that the eremitic rules are being kept.

85. To impose on transgressors the appointed penances for offenses, according to their nature.

86. Not to be of the opinion that the perfection of the religious life consists in these rules, but by means of them to pant after evangelical and apostolic doctrine and perfection and, in the first place, to always keep intact and unharmed the bond of fraternal charity.

---

[6] There were about twenty hermits at Camaldoli in this period, and of these five lived at times in reclusion.

87. To love one another perfectly.

88. As the ultimate end of all the virtues, to glow more and more fervently with all the powers of the intellect and the affections of the will in the knowledge and love of God the Creator, the Best and the Greatest.

Behold, these are the instruments of the holy eremitic art. If the hermits take them up eagerly and hold on to them persistently, they will receive the daily wage, the denarius of eternal beatitude [Mt 20:1-16]. In the last judgment their lot will be equal to that of the holy founders of this way of life, if not for their own efforts, then certainly by the goodness of the Lord. Now the workshop where we can wield these instruments without interruption and unhampered is the holy hermitage, with its most amiable environment of blessed solitude, and the firm perseverance until death in the purpose of the eremitic life.

3. *The Three Religious Vows and the Profession of the Rule*

Let whoever wishes to enter the eremitic life, before receiving the habit he has resolved to take, stay at the hermitage in a solitary cell observing all the rules of this way of life for forty days. In the meantime let him read the Rule, not in a perfunctory manner but with diligence. Or else let him hear attentively from other professed hermits the most important things contained in it, so that he may not be wholly ignorant of the form of life that he is about to undertake.

Having received his habit and changed his name, while living with humble devotion in everything, let him spend one full year of regular probation before making his profession. Only then, after finishing the year, may he pronounce his vows. If he himself and those whose duty it is to pass judgment on him agree, then publicly, during Mass on a solemn day and with his own voice and his hand on the Rule, let him make profession in these words:

In the name of the holy and undivided Trinity. I brother..., from...,
promise and vow to God Most High and Almighty to observe inviolably
poverty, chastity, and obedience all my life long, for love of our Lord
Jesus Christ. And before God and all His saints and in the presence of
the brother hermits residing in this place, I promise, according to this
Rule of eremitic life, the conversion of my manners and stability from
now until death in the purpose of this eremitic life.

Let the act of profession be written in his own hand in the parch-
ment book prepared for this purpose for all the professed. If someone
cannot write, let another do it for him. Then let him put what has
been written back on the holy Altar and to this let him affix, still with
his own hand, the sign of the holy Cross as a confirmation of the vows
and of his profession. Having done this, let him receive with suitable
ceremony and a solemn blessing the cincture of profession. And so, he
is held to be professed.

From now on, let him strive to observe the *Rule of Saint Benedict*
and the cenobitic norms much more diligently and strictly than is
done in the monasteries of the cenobites, provided they are not different from or contrary to the eremitic life and the norms in force that
concern only the hermitage. In fact, in the latter are proposed many
stricter and more perfect things than in the *Rule.*

Let those who take up the eremitic life know that, as the same
blessed author attests, the *Rule* does not contain the whole observance
of the religious life, but it delineates it so that by observing it we might
be somewhat fitted at the very start of our conversion for upright
conduct. So he calls it a "little rule for beginners."[7] It truly befits those
who undertake the greater and more perfect things of the eremitic life
never to neglect the lesser things that are proposed in the cenobitic
rule. This is in fact the teaching of the Lord, who says in the Gospel:
"These things indeed (that is to say, the greater and more perfect) you

---

[7] RB 73:8

ought to do, and those also (namely, the lesser) not to leave undone"
[Mt 23:23].

For indeed, the complete observance of all the *Holy Rule* and
the perfect custody of the norms of the cenobites, when they are not
contrary to the eremitic rules, is nothing other than the foundation
of the most perfect eremitic life, without which one would endeavor
in vain and to one's own ruin to reach the apex of eremitic perfection.
For how will anyone who does not fulfill those lighter things that are
proposed by the *Rule* and by cenobitic customs be able to keep the
weightier and stricter precepts of the eremitic life?

4. Poverty

One who has made profession of the eremitic life should be
diligent to observe poverty always and in everything. Let him not
only appear truly poor because he possesses nothing at all of his own,
but especially let him love holy and voluntary poverty. It behooves
him to very carefully beware all that which, even in part, may violate
or harm the vow of poverty.

First of all let him possess nothing, absolutely nothing. He ought
not consider anything as his own or in his exclusive use always or
for some time, no matter how slight and very little, even if it is very
fitting for him or absolutely necessary. He should clearly understand
that whatever is conceded to his use by choice of the superior is
common to all. And this is so, not merely in name or in a manner
of speaking, but in reality and by force of the inviolable authority
of the rule.

Let him always remember that those things that he uses, such as
clothes or work tools, he ought not to employ in such a way as so to
change on his own initiative into another form or another use. Rather
let him be assiduously careful to keep intact, as far as it is possible,
anything conceded to him for personal use, as is rightly demanded of
an object held in common.

He must always be ready, without proffering an excuse or becoming troubled of heart, to return everything at the beck of his superior. Furthermore, he should thank him for letting him use a common article for such a long time. With humility, let him be prepared to excuse himself for alone having used, for a long time and for his own convenience, an article that belongs to all and is perhaps more useful and necessary to someone other than himself. Let him excuse himself, finally, in the event that he has indiscreetly or inadvertently damaged or soiled an article.

He should never presume to call or designate anything "his"[cf. Acts 4:32]. Furthermore, he ought never give anything to anybody, nor receive anything from anybody, without first having informed his superior about the article, the person, and the reason, and having gotten his express permission to give or to receive. Even if someone receives something as a gift or as a loan from his own parents or brothers, let him immediately present it or hand it over to the superior. And let the latter decide freely what should be done with it or to whom it is to be given, as he does for all other things.

If somebody has received a gift that later was not given to him but to some other brother, or placed at the disposal of everyone for common benefit, he ought not feel sad or regretful. Moreover, unless there is a very urgent need, no one is permitted to have in his own use those things that he has brought or acquired or received as a gift from his loved ones. Thus he will not think that, because they have been conceded to him, he is almost their owner or at least has more right than the others to use them. If he really needs these things, let him get them from those in common use, if the prior of the hermitage judges it advantageous, in order that all private ownership be completely eliminated. Nothing can be promised to anyone or by anyone with any word or gesture, not even the smallest, most insignificant article, without the superior's knowing and having given permission.

Let the brother hermits avoid exchanging, promising, asking for or receiving anything, without having asked and obtained the permission of the superior. Neither the professed nor the novices who have received the probationary habit, as long as they live in the hermitage, can have with them or use money. This is deposited with and kept by the superior and the assigned cellarer. Whoever goes out of the hermitage should receive what he needs for the trip or the business at that very time. Staying outside the hermitage, he is not forbidden to use and have money with him. But when in a group, this is granted only to one, who acts in behalf of the others. After returning to the hermitage, if they have money, let them hand it at once to the superior or to the cellarer even before entering their assigned cells.

Let the hermit not have anything superfluous in his cell. Rather he should give back those things conceded to him that truly he does not use. He ought not venture to keep for himself for a long time garments, books, and tools of any art, or any other thing that is not necessary to him at that time. It should not be permitted that there be in the hermit's cell anything in any way remarkable, anything precious, anything that serves more for the pleasure of the senses than for some necessary use, but let there be only those things that are very necessary. And let everyone see to it that these are very cheap and fit for voluntary poverty and for eremitic purity. Therefore the father of the hermitage, with the cellarer or some other brother hermit as examiner, should inspect the cells frequently in the absence of those concerned, not superficially but with great care. If he finds something superfluous or not in conformity with holy poverty, let him not hesitate to remove it. Let he himself, however, try to be poorer than the others in everything.

Nobody ought to have a special key except the cellarer. For nothing must be locked up of that which is held in common and available for the use of individuals with the permission of the superior.

One who changes cells is by no means permitted to transfer vessels, iron tools, icons, or anything else, except for the clothes that have been given to him for his use, books that he really uses, and tools of a special art, if he has them. Thus the things one uses in cell are considered as assigned to the cell rather than to the person.

Finally let everyone strive, through love of holy poverty, not only to rejoice in the extreme commonplaceness of the things whose use human weakness must have, but also to remove likewise from his heart every desire of possessing and every attachment to things he uses, so as to be in truth a follower of the eremitic life according to apostolic discipline. That is, he will be in this world as if he were not in it and make use of the things of this world as if he were not using them [cf. 1 Cor 7:31].

In short, even if many things appear to be lacking, let nobody, and not even the local prior himself, who has more reason to take an interest in the matter, be concerned overmuch about those things that are necessary for human life. And let no one think within his heart: "What shall we eat, or what shall we drink, or with what shall we be clothed?" But let him cast all his care upon God [cf. 1 Pt 5:7], faithfully heeding what was spoken through the mouth of the Truth: "Seek ye first the kingdom of God and His justice, and all these things shall be added unto you" [Mt 6:31, 33].

5. *Chastity*

By many testimonies of the Holy Fathers, we know that all the other vices sometimes may be defeated by fighting, but that the concupiscence of the flesh cannot be overcome other than by flight [cf. Gn 39:12 and 1 Cor 6:18a]. For it is perhaps not very difficult to keep the body clean from every blemish of sin, yet this is not enough, but it is necessary that the mind also be free of every base desire. Indeed, "whoever looks at a woman to lust after her," says the Lord in the Gospel, "has already committed adultery with her in his heart"[Mt 5:27].

Therefore, let each one strive with great care and diligence to guard the chastity that he has professed. Let not only the body be free from all pollution of lust but the mind also be pure and undefiled by any stain of concupiscence, setting before one's eyes in all one's actions and thoughts the Lord, "searcher of loins and hearts" [Ps 7:9]. In order to accomplish this more easily, one must be quick to dismiss all stirrings of base thoughts when they have not yet occupied the mind and all occasions of sin from their beginning. Let everyone be especially prompt to turn away from, as soon and as long as possible, those thoughts that are wont to be the starting point of a transgression.

In order that the hermit never deal with women, let him in the first place remain willingly in the hermitage. This ought to be characteristic of the hermitage, that women are by no means permitted to enter it. A place easily accessible to women cannot be called a hermitage, in the true sense of the word. Those hermits who do not reside together within the enclosure of the cloister, but as private individuals in solitary cells, are not in a safe dwelling place. The more solitary and removed from human habitations it seems to be, so much the less secure must it be appraised.

With the exception of his own mother and sisters, let the hermit carefully avoid sending to or receiving from women, letters, greetings, or little gifts, even if the women happen to be blood relatives, whom he has never seen or whom he thinks he will never see. Such things, in fact, tend to arouse in the depths of the soul no slight heat of concupiscence, even though the one to whom it happens may not be fully aware of this. Therefore permission of this type is never to be given to anyone unless an urgent need or a great spiritual utility persuades and the father of the hermitage so decides. The hermits should avoid absolutely all conversations on this subject.

Those pages of the Holy Scriptures that may arouse base thoughts are to be read rarely and with due precaution. Other books of this kind are never read. Unless they are depicted in quite decent attire, images of the holy virgins must also be removed from the hermits' cells and oratories.

Let no one touch those little animals, whether male or female, that are customarily kept to catch mice. Let no one carry them in his arms, play with them, pet them, or stroke them.

Take diligent care not to look at your own nakedness. And do not touch very softly any part of your body.

When going out of the hermitage, on the street or wherever they are, let the hermits get accustomed to keeping their eyes fixed on the ground. Thus they will either not see women at all or at least not gaze intently upon their countenances. Hermits are forbidden to speak with women, as propriety and right reason suggest. Yet, out of consideration for human frailty or in the event of some need, it is permitted to talk with one's own mother or sisters. But let them not talk with other women, unless there occurs a necessity or an urgent need. And when speaking is called for, let the conversation not be prolonged, and let there be present some confrere as listener and witness of all that is said.

The hermits who exercise the priesthood absolutely must not, by inviolable institution, hear the confession of any woman. An exception occurs when there is imminent danger of death and no other priest is available. They are never to take on the direction of monasteries of nuns.

Furthermore, the following usually avail much for keeping chastity of body and mind whole and inviolate, namely: constant and earnest consideration of the eternal punishments reserved justly for sinners and of the heavenly joys mercifully promised to those who persevere in penance; the heartfelt and continual remembrance of the certainty of death and of the uncertainty of the hour of death; the frequent recollection of one's vows and profession, together with the devout renewal of them within the heart. Also quite helpful is the disdain of one's own body and the unwearied correction of the insolent flesh with fasting and vigils, with taking the discipline[8] and continual mental and corporal exercises. And needed above all, to be sure, are continual devotion of mind, assiduous holy prayer, true humility of heart, and last of all, the indefatigable and attentive observance of the regular life.

6. Obedience

Whoever has made the vow of obedience has completely renounced

---

[8] NCE 4:895.

his own will. Anyone who has made the vow of poverty and chastity and then in practice seeks and loves in some way the riches of the world and the pleasures of the flesh is considered a manifest offender against his profession. Likewise, if one who has made the profession of obedience afterwards wants to do his own will, or if he takes pleasure in accomplishing it, he becomes an open transgressor of his vow. Let everyone, therefore, since he has made a vow to the Lord, be very careful not to do his own will, but in all things let him strive to do the will of the superior and, for the love of Christ, to submit himself to him in all obedience. Therefore, by no means let him think of refusing or directly trying to avoid with excuses, in a harsh and impolite manner, any charge enjoined, whether a task of administration or a business matter, even if he considers it very unfit for him.

Perhaps he truly and sincerely considers himself unfit for a given task. Then he should patiently and at the right time and with all humility bring to his superior's attention once only the reason for his inability and inadequacy, without pride, or resistance, or contradiction. But if after this he sees that the superior stands firm in his view, he ought to accept the task entrusted to him with much holy spiritual cheerfulness, with gentleness and calmness, and putting aside all evasion and excuses.

Here are some of the most frequent examples of obedience: to accept an assignment, to give up an assignment received, to change assignments; to change place, to move from one cell to another; to return articles that seem most useful and much needed; to give up doing what one is accustomed to do, to accomplish what one has never done; not to practice the art that one knows, to learn an art that one does not know; to speak during the time of silence, or else to observe silence when others are permitted to speak.

One should obey promptly, with all humility and cheerfulness, mindful that this is advantageous, also in the following situations: when one wishes to remain quietly in the seclusion of the cell and instead is obliged to go out of the cell and the hermitage to accomplish something; or else when one wants to go out and instead is asked to remain quietly in the cell and is even constrained to stay enclosed in the cell for a long time; when one wishes to lead a more austere life and is obliged to live more easily, or else when one wishes to eat more amply and instead is compelled to fast more strictly; when one freeborn or brought up in the nobility is more suited for the study of letters and frequent prayer and is assigned to cultivate the vegetable garden or to do some other humbler and heavier work; or later he is ordered to take care of the cattle or to frequent cities and markets to sell or buy something; or else when, as it were for opposite reasons, someone of humble origin and used to hard work is more fit for outside and manual tasks and instead is told to stay in the cell to write, to read and to pray; when one wishes to have some free time and is ordered to take care of others, or else when one who has been given the assignment of taking care of others has it taken from him.

And finally, let each one strive to keep, fulfill, and obey with patience, humility, and cheerfulness whatever things are ordered by the superior, even if they seem unreasonable, provided they are not clearly against God's commandments. Let him do all these things no differently than if they were divinely commanded, for one who does otherwise does not keep the vow of obedience. In fact, if we are ready to do something willingly but not something else, we do not seem properly to have entirely given up our will, even if we are unwilling to carry out one single order.

For the integrity of obedience it is not only necessary to follow orders, but also to do nothing at all without the permission and blessing of the superior. Furthermore, anyone who has made the vow of obedience should do nothing that does not come within the customs of the eremitic life, unless he has informed the superior and has obtained permission to do it. Even for little things or those for which permission usually is not required, the hermit ought ask permission and blessing just the same before starting them. Asking permission even when it is not required, he gets used to doing it often. And it is better thus, instead of acting without permission even a single time in one's life when it is required.

Let the brethren, then, serve one another with deference in those things that are not against the rule or the order of the superior. Let the juniors help the seniors with all humility, the seniors the juniors with all charity. This, indeed, is deemed part of perfect obedience.

And it is also necessary for one who wishes to attain perfect obedience to obey at once in all things without delay, as soon as something has been ordered. On that account, it behooves him to put aside any other work, even if it has to do with an urgent personal need, and even leave unfinished a task that is being carried out. In short, the hermit should be prepared to give up wholeheartedly his own will and attachment to any work for himself or for others. Thus, with free hands and mind, let him begin the work assigned. Let obedience be practiced to the degree of wanting to be frequently compelled to give up a material or spiritual task undertaken on one's own initiative, even a personal necessity. Finally, it is needful to accept any order with a superior strength of soul and without any anxiety or fear; to persist at the task resolutely and carefully and without any slowness or negligence; to bring it to completion with a devout and fervent soul and without any tepidity.

The hermit must not only keep his mouth from all unseemly murmuring, rude excuses, and any word that could indicate that the obedience was not gladly accepted by him. He should beware in addition lest, by sadness of face or some gesture or external sign, it is seen that the point of obedience was accepted unwillingly. He must also cast out of his heart, where nothing can be hidden from God, every vice of this kind, of murmuring, excuses, or silent and hidden impatience. And let him never judge openly or secretly an order given as unsuitable, burdensome, or useless. But in all things let the hermit embrace obedience with a holy readiness and spiritual gladness of both soul and countenance. Let him do this even in things irksome and unbecoming, harsh and difficult, base and laborious, and even with the added contrariety of scorn, rebukes, and wrongs.

And finally, the hermit ought to do all this neither from servile fear of punishment in this life or in eternity, as is characteristic of beginners, nor from a mercenary desire for present or future rewards, as are wont those who are making some progress. But let him act out of pure and simple filial love of Jesus Christ our Lord, as he promised by vow and professed to observe forever. He should imitate Him who did not come to do His own will but the will of Him who sent Him [cf. Jn 6:38]. He declared that His food was to accomplish the will of His Father in everything [cf. Jn 4:34]. And according to the dictum of the Apostles, He became obedient unto death, even death on the cross [Phil 2:8], leaving us an example so that, by following in His footsteps through the labor of obedience and having become partakers in His passion, we might be worthy to reign with Him forever [1 Pt 2:21, 4:13].

7. Humility

Hermits must be very zealous to practice humility. On that account let them note that, just as all the vices sprout from the root of pride, so from the seed of humility all the virtues grow up. Truly, where the type of life seems more praiseworthy, it is there that pride more often lies in wait. For when the adversary does not succeed in staining some with manifest enormities or other vices, he strives to lift them up with pride in their good works, in order to hurl them down all the more wretchedly into the precipice of arrogance and vain elation.

Therefore, above all, hermits must keep themselves from every kind of proud arrogance. They must not, in pharisaical fashion, put on airs, either personally or as a group, and so reckon others as publicans. It will be good for them always to think well of other religious and religious communities. They should strive to speak in their honor and avoid making comparisons, which hardly ever can be made without a hint of pride. Except out of necessity or for edification, let them never speak of their eremitic observances. To practice humility, they ought to willingly busy themselves with the commonest and lowliest activities. Let them be glad to wear cheap rather than expensive clothing.

Let them decline with a humble apology, to preserve true humility, the position of superior or other offices, instead of rejecting them with the proud assertion of liberty.

It is better to obtain by modest entreaties that certain things are not commanded than to dare to refuse them obstinately if they have already been commanded. As a matter of fact, as holy authors affirm, it often happens that some may be even more proudly arrogant because of their disdain of honors and their contempt of vainglory than many accustomed to vain boasting.

In fact, hermits will be truly humble when, through love of humility, they will never refuse to submit in obedience to the superiors even in things in which they have a free hand. For humility proves itself true when it does not forsake obedience. Certainly pure humility is never alien to full obedience. For these two virtues are sisters, and they always follow one another.

8. Solitude and the Site of the Hermitage

After the perpetual observance of poverty, chastity, and obedience, required by common profession of hermits as of all religious, nothing more properly befits those who are zealous for the eremitic life than to strive for solitude in preference to everything. For indeed, the names "solitary" and "hermit" are derived from "solitude" and "desert." Hence those are falsely called hermits who do not love and assiduously pursue solitude.

For this reason, those who take up this kind of life may on no account and under no circumstance, however reasonable it may appear, establish their dwelling place in or near cities, towns, villages, or even cenobitical monasteries, which we read was done at times by all monastic institutes. Nor may they inhabit a spot near frequented public roads or bordering on cultivated fields. But let them have separate cells, at least two or three miles away from cities and as far as possible from all the other crowded dwellings of men. When wishing to construct eremitic cells, they should always choose sites that are wild, rough, solitary, deserted, hard to reach, on steep mountain tops, in hidden recesses of the woods, in unknown caves and caverns of the earth, or in solitudes with vast horizons.

Let them take care not to draw a multitude of men to those places for any reason, whether under pretext of devotion or of spiritual utility. For where access is permitted to women or where a throng of men is tolerated, it is not possible to keep uprightly the institution of the eremitic life.

To preserve solitude let them try, insofar as the needs of human life and necessary charity toward neighbor permit, to direct all their attention and diligence toward avoiding both familiarity with anyone and keeping company with those of a different style of life. Therefore it is never permitted, or very rarely that is, when it is necessary to offer service out of charity and the scandal of the little ones [Lk 17:2] cannot otherwise be avoided, to give food or drink to the inhabitants of nearby places or to let them spend the night. Because of their nearness they usually frequent the hermits' places more and can easily bring along food for their meal and then go back home. Indeed regarding these things, when such service is to be either denied or extended, always let the prudent discretion of the superior, with the counsel of some of the senior brethren, make the decision. In this great care ought to be taken lest either through an excessive desire to conserve solitude, necessary services of charity are neglected, or on the contrary, because of putting forth greater exertion than necessary in service to charity, seclusion and tranquillity, so very necessary for cultivators of solitude, are disturbed. Let no guest, however noble and distinguished, secular or religious, if familiar with the hermits or even a benefactor or blood relative, be permitted to eat, drink, sleep, or stay for a long time in any hermit's cell, even if it is empty. In this matter, exception is made if and when there is a pressing and unavoidable need, which according to the common opinion does not come under the law but rather is itself a law.

The cell or cells where religious and suitable guests are received, who can never be lacking however solitary the place may be, are never to be built amongst those of the hermits, but apart. Let them be built most preferably in that area of the hermitage that is near the entrance, at a distance of at least a bowshot, yet not much more than 500 feet, from the church or from the cells of the hermits. All of this has been arranged so that it will not happen that, because of extreme proximity, the noise of those guests who are coming and going will break the tranquillity of the hermits and disturb their quiet, whether they are in church or remain in their cells. Likewise, the distance will not be burdensome to the superior and the other brother hermits when the needs of the guests require them to go there and from there to return to their cells. Instead it will be easy to go and come, even many times a day. And so they will neither neglect their cells nor fail to meet the obligations that hospitality requires.

Near the guests' cells let there be a stable for their beasts of burden and for those of the hermitage. Thus someone sitting on his beast, or the beasts themselves, are prevented from going into the hermitage, that is into that area where the hermits' cells and the church are, unless an extreme need arise.

The cells of the hermits must not be built like those of the cenobites, inside a cloister or joined under one single roof, but separately and a bit distant from one another and from the common oratory, scattered here and there within the bounds of the hermitage. In this way each one, abiding in cell, may freely read, psalmodize, pray aloud or with sighs, or do other things of this kind if he pleases, without being heard by anybody.

The other common workplaces necessary or useful for the hermits include the sacristy, the chapter room, the library, the common kitchen, the refectory, the cellars in which wheat, bread, wine, oil, vegetables, fruit, and other things necessary for human life are laid aside, and also those rooms in which the hermits have their hair cut or can wash their clothes and those that can be assigned to the sick.

These may be built near each other and joined together under the same roof. They may be built next to the church or in some other part of the hermitage, according as the location of the place and the prudent consideration of the majority of the hermits may dictate. Let great care always be taken so that psalmodizing, praying or celebrating the divine mysteries in church, or lying in bed in the cells of the sick, the brethren are not disturbed by some untimely noise from nearby places of work.

In constructing either the cells of the hermits or the common places of work, take care not to build them over refectories or the *tristega*.[9] If it is indicated that a room should be constructed underground, as happens especially in mountainous places, nothing prohibits this.

And if it happens that you receive a place to live where there are cloisters, and cells joined together, and also refectories constructed in the cenobitic fashion, let the hermits by no means live in them, but try to adapt buildings of this kind as places for necessary common work. As for refectories on the upper floors, unless serious damage is caused to the building, they are to be demolished. For high-situated refectories do not become hermits, but living in lowly huts.

The area of the hermitage where the church is, the cells of the hermits, and the common work rooms for the hermits must not be open and accessible to all who wish to enter. But according to what the situation of the place seems to require and what resources are available, let it be closed with a ditch or a trench, or else with hedges or even a wall, so that entrance and egress are through only one door. As for the locality itself, if there are woods, let them strive to preserve and increase them. But if there are none, they shall see to it that they are planted and maintained with great diligence, both to foster the splendid appearance of the solitude and for the sake of firewood, so very necessary for hermits.

---

[9] A room in a Camaldolese Hermitage, at times above ground level (cf. "third story" at Gn 6:16 Vulg. and Acts 20:9 Greek), used on a few occasions each year for common refectory with dispensation of silence.

Let the same hermits, then, gladly reside at the hermitage for the love of solitude, so amiable and pleasant to holy souls. They ought to go out of the hermitage rarely, only when an urgent need or pious usefulness requires it. Nevertheless, they must never go out without the superior's consent and blessing. When going out, let them try to take care of several business matters that have occurred or seem immanent at the same time, so as not to be compelled to go out more frequently, that is for each piece of business separately. When outside the hermitage, if they expect to return the same day, let them not eat any food without the special blessing of the father superior and except in case of extreme necessity. But, as the cenobites also used to do, let them return to the hermitage fasting. Yet, if they think that they will have to eat and drink outside, having informed the superior and gotten his permission, they may take along food they judge sufficient for the trip. Thus let them prefer to refresh the body with suitable food outside, along the road, in a remote spot, instead of entering for this necessity into the public or private places of seculars, or even into monasteries.

While they are abiding at the hermitage, on those days and in those hours devoted to silence, nobody should presume to approach the cell of any brother or any common work room without the special permission of the prior. Absolutely never without permission of the superior, who is to concede it quite rarely, may anyone go into a cell that is not assigned to him, or into any common work room except that one entrusted to his special care. Nor may anyone at all enter his cell. And so, let each one occupy his own cell, and in no event let it be permitted for two or more to eat or sleep in the same cell.

If the brothers do not observe these rules completely, although they abide in the hermitage and in solitary cells, they can never be solitaries. And indeed they ought to guard very attentively against solitude being stolen from them by others. Yet it is they who will deprive themselves of it, gaining practically nothing from having renounced the crowded cities and the company of outsiders, if they do not most diligently beware of too frequent fraternal socializing. This takes away, as easily as disastrously, all solitude.

9. Rules for the Acceptance of Brethren into the Hermitage

There may be received into the hermitage for the eremitic manner of life men coming from the world, whether laymen or priests. The same holds for religious of any order, including the mendicant friars and the Carthusians.

Concerning seculars there are the ancient documents [constitutions] of the hermitage produced by Blessed Rudolph, in which he describes the customs of the hermitage: "In our times," it is stated, "many laymen, having turned their backs on the world, have taken refuge in this hermitage as in a safe port." Whence it is satisfactorily established that in those olden times laymen were received into the hermitage. But even the important authority Peter Damian, in his wisely written rule for hermits,[10] advised giving the preference to laymen rather than to cenobitic monks for reception into the hermitage. He gives some very convincing reasons in favor of this opinion.

What was said in the most recent Constitutions of prior Gerard, namely that "only those who have lived in Camaldolese monasteries for three years are to be accepted into the hermitage", referred only to monks of the Camaldolese order. It stands written like this: "Monks" (and here must be understood those of the Camaldolese order, as may be gathered from the words that follow), "wishing to go up to the hermitage, cannot be accepted there if they have not spent at least three years in a monastery of our order." These things were stated to remove all ambiguity, if there ever were any, and reasonably there ought not to have been. And so the very ancient custom which has endured to these times, providing that men from the outside world (whether

---

[10] Letter 50, Blum 2:289-334 (329 referred to here).

priests or ordinary laymen) may be accepted into the hermitage, may be observed in the future.

With regard to religious there are ample indults of many Roman Pontiffs, recently, in fact, confirmed by Leo X (1512) and strengthened by the latest apostolic letters. In these, among other things, we read:

> With the present letters I permit you hermits to accept and retain, without anyone being able to oppose it, all and each who have decided to serve the Most High perpetually in your hermitage and order and with your habit. They may present themselves from any order and may come from any congregation, house, or monastery, whether they are mendicants, non-mendicants, or even Carthusians. They must have asked the permission of their superiors, even if they have not obtained it. All this holds notwithstanding any kind of constitutions or ordinances, privileges or indults to the contrary, whether existing or yet to exist, including any which, with their tenor, have had special mention in the present context.

Besides the fact that for five hundred years the custom has obtained without any contradiction, it is permitted to all even by common law to pass over to a stricter way of life.

There is not, therefore, any human condition making it impossible to enter the eremitic style of life, provided the one who asks is adjudged suitable by the hermits. Yet both the tenor of the ancient constitutions and a custom observed until these times provide for this: that nobody should be accepted into the hermitage who has not reached the age of twenty-five.

10. Reading, Meditation, and Prayer

Let it be the common practice of monks and of lay brothers to read every day at least one chapter of the Sacred Scripture, or else of some other devout book that may more easily suit their capacity. Each one is, then, to be assigned a Bible or another book, according to his capacity, and he is to be advised how he ought to read.

Reading alone is too little. What one reads he must afterwards meditate on with a clever and silent mind, according to his own ability. For this reason, let everyone preserve in silence what he has read, whether he is ordered to do something outside the cell or to remain in it. He should strive to meditate on these things and turn them over in his mind. What he catches a glimpse of in his reading, let him continually press on to put into practice. Forgetting the things that are behind and always stretching himself forward by desire to the things beyond [cf. Phil 3:13], let him busy himself with advancing from one virtue to another [cf. Ps 83 (84):7].

But when at the proper hours when silence is dispensed, they want to refresh their minds in brotherly conversation, they should confer with one another about what they have read. If their discussion is gladly occupied with these things, they will be able to avoid useless and idle discussions more easily and thus attain knowledge of the Sacred Scriptures more quickly.

Since unless divine assistance is present, neither reading nor meditation is worth anything and no practice of the religious life can be accomplished, let the hermits devote themselves, first of all and above all, to prayer. This is the characteristic of hermits: to apply themselves to prayer. No particular time of day or night, as other religious institutes have, is appointed for prayer by the ancient fathers. We should believe that the founders of the eremitic life did so because, by not setting a fixed time for prayer, they wanted to make this understood quite clearly: Just as breathing for the exterior man, so praying for the interior mind is always opportune and well-nigh necessary. So hermits, when they have free time [*vacant*], ought always to pray. The rule of this hermitage is that each one establishes for himself the hours he reckons most suitable for prayer, so that during a whole day he persists immobile in prayer for at least half an hour, either all at once or on several occasions.

Even if the hermit sometimes cannot pray because his mind is occupied and distracted, he must not omit drawing near to the place of prayer. There on bended knee before an image of Christ (or in another way according to his own devotion), let him remain for the usual interval, fully convinced that such a space of time will also be credited to him as prayer. If he perseveres in this, he will soon be able to reach, by the Lord's bestowal, the sweetness of prayer.

Coming to the hermitage either from the world or from the cenoby, first of all and above all let everyone be instructed about the time and the manner of praying and about insistence and constancy in prayer. In fact, no one can easily persevere in the hermitage unless, having been sufficiently taught, he applies himself to prayer for at least half an hour daily. For it is just as impossible to grow in perfection or even to last for long in the spiritual life without frequent prayer as it would be to grow to adult stature or even to survive very long without bodily foods.

If the prior enjoins some common prayer, all are held, even setting other prayers aside, to persist at it with insistence. Whenever a brother sets out on a journey for some business, or if he falls sick, let everyone daily remember in prayer the wayfaring or ill brother. Prayer itself, thus attended to, makes one pass on briskly to reading and meditation, and these in their turn serve prayer. They embrace one another and, in turn, they defer to and assist one another. Therefore let it always be of greatest concern to the hermits to daily apply themselves to reading, meditation, and prayer. Otherwise, they should know that they are hermits in name only and that they will not be able to carry on for very long this way. Because without these things it is not possible to persevere in the hermitage, as is proved by manifest declaration of the ancient hermits and by the evident experience of many.

11. Study and Spiritual Conferences

In the first place, let the prior of the hermitage be careful to explain the *Rule of Saint Benedict* as is prescribed by the holy canons. He ought to do this for all, according to their diverse capacities, either himself or through another he judges to be qualified. No one is to be admitted to profession unless first, as the *Rule* itself ordains, he has read the whole *Rule* three different times or heard it read by others. In the chapter meeting on the days it is customarily held, let there always be read a section of the *Rule* or of the constitutions. Let the prior himself make a commentary on what was read or do so through some other person, so that the *Rule* or the constitutions may be more expressly understood. And he should add some words of exhortation.

Furthermore, these constitutions are to be read and explained often. They are to be proposed for reading to all those who wish to be part of the eremitic community, so that they may know what they must observe. They should strive to observe the dispositions of the *Rule* and the regulations of the constitutions which declare at what hours and for how long they ought to have time for [*vacare*] corporal exercises and when for study and reading. So they should understand that all the time they are not occupied with [*vacare*] corporal exercises ought to be devoted to study, psalmody, and prayer.

It is permissible for hermits to devote themselves to that study of letters not prohibited by the Church. Let them take care not to have with them or to read banned or superstitious books. Everybody may read all other books, according to the native capacity of each. Yet those who give preference to the study of the Holy Scriptures over other literary genres have chosen the better part [Lk 10:42]. For all the other disciplines are not comparable to the Holy Scriptures. Therefore those who are so perfect in understanding as not to need the help of profane books, in order to delight in the continual reading of the Holy Scriptures, should by all means leave other reading aside. But whoever needs other studies should have time for them, provided that all this is directed to the end of coming to understand the Holy Scriptures more thoroughly.

Furthermore, on the days and at the hours in which silence is not observed, the professed hermits may confer together by twos or more on some subject. In order to instruct one another, they may read some selections from Christian books, especially, and interpret. Novices cannot participate in these lessons without the permission of the prior or of the novice master. On the days and at the hours reserved for silence, let no one do this without the permission of the prior.

If there is in the hermitage someone to whom God has granted a word of exhortation, he can, with the permission of the prior, preach a sermon or else expound some passage of the Holy Scriptures. He should do this not in the church, but rather in the chapter room. Only the members of the hermitage family may participate, in order to avoid a concourse of secular or any other persons. Whenever religious who are wont to preach come to the hermitage, let the prior be sure to ask and urge them to deliver a devout exhortation for the consolation of the brother hermits.

The hermits should do their best to have the common library of the hermitage adapted so that all the professed hermits may enter it without special permission. Let all the books in it be arranged in order and an index of all of them be made. And so everyone, with the permission of the prior, may take with him to cell as many books as he may need, provided that he leaves in writing in the library the titles of the books he has taken out. In the library always observe a strict silence. Every year those books should be bought that are considered better and more useful.

All this has been established accordingly because it has been sufficiently ascertained by the witness of experience that the study of letters stimulates every virtue in religious souls. Likewise, no one doubts that idleness and ignorance are the mother and incitement of all evils.

12. Discretion and Care for the Weak, the Weary from Work, the Old, and the Ill

Because of a more delicate bodily constitution or some indisposition, some hermit may not have sufficient soundness and health of body to bear the rigor of fasting and abstinence without evident bodily harm. If he confides his manifest or hidden infirmity to the prior, it is right that he be fully believed, even if that kind of infirmity does not appear on his face or if it is entirely hidden. The religious brother would not claim this unless it were completely true.

So it is proper that the prior, out of consideration for the kind of weakness or infirmity, come to his aid discreetly and prudently with some dispensation. In all this, neither should the eremitic institution be wholly undone through excessive relaxation nor the weak or delicate brother incur some more serious infirmity due to harsh austerity. It should be done so wisely and cautiously that the kind discretion granted to those who need it may not give rise to harmful laxity among the stronger. Let special concessions never become common usage, nor a necessary concession made to one give rise to the blameworthy irregularity of many.

Deal discreetly with newcomers, since they are little accustomed to fasts and abstinences, and do not hold them at once to the full rigor of the eremitic institution. Rather the observance should be somewhat relaxed for them for some time in certain things of no great moment. Thus they will grow accustomed little by little and not be scared off by the first experience of stricter abstinence. Novices, then, whoever they may be, are never to be permitted before making profession to practice more abstinence and fasting than common discipline requires.

Furthermore, for those who work at manual labor, or have returned to the Hermitage after a wearisome journey, or are tired for other reasons, let there be reserved not downright laxity but a discreetly moderate treatment. Also lend a hand to the elderly who are weak and infirm, with prudence and kind discretion, when and where it is needed. For to the elderly, old age itself is a continual infirmity.

As the Rule and all the ancient constitutions ordain, the prior and those assigned to serve the infirm and the sick should always do their utmost to care and provide for them. As soon as someone in the hermitage starts to bear up under some infirmity, the prior should visit him and see to it that he gets special care, both for the sustenance of his body and the consolation of his spirit. If the kind of illness appears to require it, let the prior assign two of the brethren to care for the sick brother who will know how to do so in a more agreeable fashion. One of the two should be a priest or cleric, who will say the Divine Office day and night, with the patient either joining in if he can or else at least listening. But let the other be a lay brother, who will prepare and serve the special foods necessary for the body. Both ought to do their best to serve the sick brother in every way. All the hermits may visit him at any time of day after Prime and before Compline. Everyone is permitted to go into the cell of the sick brother who is not a recluse at the above-mentioned hours, even without the blessing of the prior. However nobody is permitted to enter the cell of a recluse, even when he is ill, without special permission of the prior, except those who have been assigned to take care of him.

As long as he is ill, the brothers must not neglect to pray for him both at Mass and at private prayer. Thus let them always and in everything employ tender care and prudent discretion for the sick, those of delicate constitution, those worn out from some work or journey, the elderly, the infirm, and the convalescent. And so while human frailty is taken into consideration with all charity, still care of the body will never turn out to be indulgence.

13. Silence and Moderation of Speech

Silence and moderation of speech are the chief and special adornment of solitude.

Hermits should do their utmost in this, if they wish to preserve that solitude which they have professed. For where silence is not properly observed by the brother hermits, they become completely alienated from solitude. As much the more frequent as conversations among the brother hermits can be than conversations with outsiders, so much the more do they disturb all solitude.

Therefore let them most diligently take care not to dare to speak at all with the guests without permission of the prior, even if they are familiar friends, or their own relatives, or the relatives of some brother. Only the porter and those who are assigned to the reception of guests may do so. If somebody is greeted or asked for something by one of the guests, let him return the greeting with all humility and promptness and reply only that he is not allowed to speak with a guest without permission. He ought not presume to listen further or to add anything.

The hermits should beware, with no less diligence, of brotherly conversations at unsuitable times and places. In the church, the sacristy, the chapter room, the library, and the refectory always observe so great and inviolable a silence that not even a slight whisper may be heard in those places. If anything must be said to or enjoined on someone, let this be signified and declared by some gesture or audible sign rather than by words. Also make an effort to observe silence in the bakery, the laundry, and other places of work, except in a case when speaking is required for a real need. Reckon all the area of the hermitage which contains the church and the hermits' cells as a cloister or dormitory. Therefore do not enter into conversation with the guests or one another in that open space, unless it be really necessary to ask briefly or answer about something urgent. In this case speak with a few words, cutting the matter short, and in a low voice.

Let the times both of keeping silence and of speaking be so arranged that, by prolonged silence, we may learn to speak at the opportune time. Indeed, nothing can teach one more than a long-held silence when, what, and how it is fitting to speak. Therefore Holy Scripture puts keeping silence before speaking, for "there is a time," it says, "to keep silence and a time to speak" [Qo 3:7]. Thus it shows that silence comes before speech. Elsewhere the Scripture points out how very necessary silence is for hermits when it says: "He will sit alone and keep silent"[Lam 3:28]. For there is truly nothing more proper and necessary for those who cultivate the solitary and eremitic life than to sit in the cell and keep silent. Therefore, even if not always, at least for some periods of the year, on certain days and at certain hours, let the followers of this eremitic way of life try to observe silence with special diligence.

During the two Lents, one of which comes before Christmas[11] and the other before Easter, preserve a continual and wholly inviolable silence. At other times, to be sure, conversation is allowed at certain hours: two days a week from mid-September to holy Easter and three days a week from Easter to mid-September. But on all other occasions, observe silence utterly, and let no one presume to talk without permission, which is not to be granted so easily. On Sundays and on days of fasting on bread and water, and also especially on holy days when work is prohibited and on Fridays, let permission to talk never be given unless an unavoidable need urges it or a praiseworthy and very timely spiritual benefit suggests it.

Accordingly, they are permitted to speak with one another on Tuesdays and Thursdays in winter and, in summer, on Saturdays as well. On the above-mentioned days they may converse among themselves, not at all hours, but only from the end of the hour of None until the signal for Compline. In fact, after Compline and until the end of None of the following day, the right to speak even with the superior himself should be understood to be taken away with the strictest observance. During these hours, let there be no one who dares ask permission to break the sanctity of the silence. If anyone imprudently requests such permission, it may only be granted with much more difficulty than at other times and only if there is a really valid reason. Let the father of the place himself order and arrange everything beforehand at suitable hours with such foresight, that there will be no need to break silence at those hours.

But if guests surprise them at those hours, or something unforeseen of no light moment occurs that cannot be postponed, only the prior himself

---

[11] It begins November 12.

and the brothers assigned to receive guests or those needed to execute the matter that has occurred may speak. They must do so, however, with the utmost gravity and moderation, and only about what is necessary. As for the others, let them keep inviolate the rule of holy silence.

Also during those same hours devoted to perpetual silence, or at least from Compline to the end of Prime, let them even refrain from confessing. For it is not proper to violate the silence of those hours even for confession. When they go to confession, let them very carefully guard against all conversation that has nothing to do with confession, lest while they seek to amend by confession, they sully themselves the more with vain and harmful words.

When a feast day or a fast day that requires silence coincides with one of the days on which silence is usually dispensed, change the dispensation of silence to some other day of the week, so that there will always be two days in winter and three in summer on which silence is dispensed. But never break silence on holy days on which you abstain from work because of a precept either of the Church or of religion, nor on days of fasting on bread and water.

On the days that by rule silence is dispensed, at the first stroke of the bell that announces any hour of the Divine Office, interrupt every discussion and discourse immediately. One who having heard the signal presumes to carry on his discourse further becomes guilty of having broken the silence, just as if he had violated it in the places and on the days dedicated to silence.

It is particularly important that silence be kept inviolably when going to church for the celebration of the Divine Office or when returning to the cell after the celebration. When leaving the church after the completion of any part of the Divine Office, let everyone return straight to his cell in supreme and inviolable silence even if silence is dispensed at that time. Let nobody take it for granted before entering the cell to direct his course to another or to engage in conversation with another. But as soon as he has entered the cell, if he wants to speak with some brother or to go see somebody, let him go forth from the cell and do what is permitted. It is understood that this rule was made in order to take away certain slight opportunities for speaking or for roving about. In these cases the less circumspect are accustomed to frequently get entangled, apart from all necessity and beyond any purpose of their own mind, in many useless chats and rambles, with great loss of time and distraction of heart.

Perhaps someone even more zealous for silence will choose to observe it on those days and at those hours when speaking is allowed according to the rule. With the knowledge and permission of the prior, he may affix to the entrance of his cell a tablet on which is written in capital letters: SILENCE. Then all authorization to converse is taken away, not only from him regarding others but also from others regarding him, no differently than if the superior had given a special order. Therefore when this tablet is at the entrance, let no one approach the cell of that brother. And let him so much the less presume to go to the cell of another, unless by chance the prior has not only allowed it for some reason and conceded it but has rather expressly ordered and mandated it. When he is outside the cell, let no one speak to him, and he should neither give ear to nor reply to someone wishing to talk with him. Rather let him at once bring his finger to his mouth, indicating with this sign that at that time it is not permitted for him to talk with others or for others to talk to him.

At no time may the professed speak with the novices or the novices with the professed without the consent of the superior. The novices may not venture to converse among themselves without the permission of the prior or the novice master. But the novice master himself can grant this only on the days and at the hours when silence is dispensed for the professed. At other times, if an occasion to speak arises, permission must be asked of the superior, who will hardly grant it unless a really clear reason urges him.

The rule of silence should be observed with more care by the younger and by the newly professed of any age, so that by persisting in silence from the very beginning of the eremitic life, they may learn to stand firmly upon their own two feet. Ceasing from human conversations, they grow accustomed to speaking with God and begin to taste the very sweet tranquillity of the solitary life. Once imbued with this, they will be able to persevere cheerfully until death in the purpose of the solitary life that they have undertaken. In fact it is very important that, from the beginning of any change to a different kind of life, one be imbued with its customs. Therefore, never relax anything beyond the disposition of the rule for the younger and the newly professed. But rather sometimes when the rule permits going out of the cell or speaking, let the superior order them to remain in the cell and be silent. When they speak, they should use few and well-considered words, and let them learn to keep silence until they are questioned. In fact, it behooves such as they to listen and to learn rather than to speak and to teach. It is quite unseemly for someone junior in age or profession to appear to speak more than necessity requires.

Let all, then, be most diligently on guard everywhere against long and useless confabulations, particularly on worldly subjects, idle words or such as move to laughter, and every kind of scurrility. But above all they should be wary of murmuring, detraction, contempt, and noisy arguments.

14. Manual Labor

To work with one's hands in silence according to the admonition of the Apostle [cf. 1 Thes 4:11; 2 Thes 3:12], even if not for the sake of obtaining food, is not only useful but necessary in order to avoid idleness, which is the enemy of the salvation of souls, and in order to preserve humility, which is the root of all virtues. If it is necessary for all monks, it is all the more so for hermits, who have taken upon themselves a stricter manner of life. The *Rule* of our blessed father Benedict teaches this.[12] So does the authority of the most holy doctor

---

[12] RB 48.

Augustine, who wrote a precious opuscule *On the Work of Monks*,[13] against the wrong-headed opinion of some monks, who were asserting that manual labor does not befit religious.

Now it is particularly suitable to speak here of hermits, both because those who strive after loftier things ought not bypass any of the regular ordinances that pertain to perfection, and especially because they seem to have no excuse whatever. In fact cenobites, either because of the great exertion exacted by singing or the unsuitability of the place, that is because they have monasteries that are cramped and located in town, often maintain they are excused from manual labor. But hermits, who can be excused neither by exertion at singing nor by the restriction and indisposition of the place, should devote themselves to working with their hands, according to all the more ancient constitutions of the hermitage. Thus, it is written in the *Rule*: "Let the brothers be engaged at certain times in manual labor, but at other times in divine reading [*lectio divina*] and other spiritual exercises, and let them have time for prayer and meditation."[14]

Then indeed is a plan for living at its best, when all things are allotted their proper times. Thus everything proceeds in order and nothing confused and disorderly can vex the spirit in troublesome situations.

First of all, on all Sundays and holy days of obligation, let the hermits do no manual labor, even if minimal, nor in any way order or permit seculars to work. On all other Solemnities, even if not observed by precept of the Church, and on every Friday, and finally, on all days of abstinence, no work must be done either outside or inside the cell that might especially make a noise or raise a din. These customs, then, exactly observed from when the hermitage was first built down to the present day, should be kept inviolably in the future. Let the hermits be zealous to observe what has been established from of old. Accordingly,

---

[13] Cf. NPNF I:3 and FC 16.
[14] RB 48.

whenever they must go to gather hay, let them go and return with psalmody: that is, let them at least manage to say some Psalms. For nothing prevents a servant of God, while working with his hands, from meditating on the law of the Lord [Ps 1:2], and psalmodizing to the name of the Lord Most High [Ps 7:17]. And surely this should be done not only in the present instance, but in all manual labor whatsoever. Whether it is done inside or outside the cell, it should always be accompanied either by meditation on the law of the Lord or else by the chanting of the divine canticles, as a kind of relief from the work. Nothing hinders one from praying during work, and this is not at all useless. Rather a single prayer said with the fear of God, a free spirit, and a cheerful countenance, by one who is working, is sooner heard favorably than ten thousand prayers of one who scorns manual labor because of idleness and negligence.

No craft is allowed to take place in the hermitage that might disquiet the solitude, with its disengagement for God [*Deo vacans solitudo*]. Let hermits chiefly pursue the more commonplace and abject tasks and those that tend toward the common advantage and the comeliness of the hermitage. They should try to keep clean all the paths, the open areas, and the other common places, either by the common effort of all, or by everyone whose cell and garden extends nearby, or else according as the prior allots to everyone. In this way, none of these locations will be allowed to get dirty or untidy. They ought not fail to cultivate the gardens. Whatever they produce should belong to all in common. Let them get used to putting together little boxes and to weaving both little baskets and little hair shirts, to making those tokens of the Lord's Prayer and Angelic Salutation that they call rosaries, or to producing other things of this kind. Let all even learn to sew, so that everybody knows how to repair his old clothes. If someone knows a craft, he should practice it after getting the prior's blessing. If some craftsman is ingenious and able enough to cut stones to build cells, to raise walls, to do woodwork and make windows, let him work especially at that job for which he shows expertise. But let those who know less about how to practice a craft of this kind assist those who are practicing it and be employed when there is need of bearing burdens.

Perhaps those who will have come to the eremitic life after having left and distributed their riches, and who are physically fit, will do some manual labor to set an example of working for those who have come from a humbler state of life and will make no excuses. They should know (as Saint Augustine says) that they then act more mercifully than when they apportioned all they had to the poor. But those who come to the hermitage from a humbler state of life and are used to toil should blush if, where the rich humble themselves, the poor are insolent with pride. For "it is certainly not proper" (as the same doctor asserts) "that in a life in which senators and nobles are put to work, there workers and stewards grow idle, and that where the landed gentry come after forsaking their enjoyments, there rustics get to be dainty."[15]

It will be praiseworthy, if conveniently doable and circumstances do not demand otherwise, for both those who have come to the hermitage from a nobler and from a humbler estate to work with their own hands in everything needful. Thus workers need not be brought in from outside, but they themselves will work at the hours and days prescribed. By so doing, they will both flee idleness and pursue humility. They will also tame down the insolence of the body, or flesh, by their constancy at work, and they will keep the hermitage free of a retinue of laymen.

15. Avoiding Idleness and the Loss of Time and Gaining the Good of Quiet and Stability

There is nothing hermits ought to shun more than idleness, which (as Saint Benedict says) is the enemy of the soul.[16] Indeed idleness more

---

[15] *On the Work of Monks*, 33.
[16] RB 48:1.

usually lies in wait in the life of hermits than in that of cenobites and, once it has been let into the hermit's cell, can hardly ever be driven out except with much zeal and effort. Idleness is perverse in and of itself and deceitfully snatches from our hands all the instruments of good works. Yet it seems even more mischievous in this, that it always opens the door to all temptations. Whence not undeservedly does Scripture say: "Idleness teaches many wicked things" [Si 33:29]. Hermits, therefore, must be very earnest, according to the authoritative teaching of the Holy Fathers, to be always doing some work, so that the devil will always find them occupied and never have the leeway to tempt them.[17]

Let everybody strive to devote his time [*vacare*] to manual labor at the opportune and set hours, and to reading and to prayer, as well as to other disciplines of the soul, at other hours. In this way, concerned and intent now upon corporal and now upon spiritual endeavors, the whole expanse of day and of night will seem brief and insufficient to him. May he always be convinced that what superabounds for him is work to be done, not time in which to do it. Otherwise, if either the days or the nights begin to seem overlong to somebody, he will soon on his own initiative waste his time, which must be considered most precious, on superfluous sleep. Or else through gadding about and profitlessly chatting, he will make himself and the others lose many opportunities for doing good.

Let the hermits also strive to maintain a perpetual and uninterrupted stability in the hermitage and in the cell so that, by the grace of God and their own unremitting constancy, dwelling in the hermitage and in the cell may get to be pleasant for them. They should neither ask nor desire to go out of the hermitage, and let such permission not be granted easily to those who ask and desire it. For indeed, by this kind of wandering the whole correct scheme of one's living is thrown into disorder, and every virtue starts to languish and, little by little, to die out. So on no account may

---

[17] Cf. Saint Jerome, Letter 125:11, in NPNF II:6.

hermits (monks or lay brothers) be permitted to go out of the hermitage, unless compelled by necessity or urged by some evident advantage. On the days and at the hours in which silence must be observed, nobody may go out of the hermitage or stroll about the hermitage. And on these same days and during these same hours, especially before the hour of Prime or after Compline or during the noonday repose, nobody should go to the cell of any brother or to any workshop, or roam through the hermitage, unless perchance, for some necessity, he will have first asked the prior's permission. Nor should anybody, on these same days and during these same hours, go even to the prior's cell without a legitimate reason. But if somebody is seen to be restless, he is to be reported to the prior, who can first speak to him to urge him to amend and finally, if need be, make him do so with due severity.

Although it may be permitted to walk through the hermitage on those days and during those hours that silence is dispensed, let the hermits nevertheless try at those times also to persist steadfastly at some task, preferably inside or else outside the cell. In fact, not everything that is permitted is advantageous [cf. 1 Cor 6:12]. For if they begin to take pleasure in wandering about, the cell will start to seem like a prison to them. For the cell is sought again with more eagerness and delight when it is left rarely and for a short time, out of necessity or by the order of the superior. But when it is frequently neglected and forsaken on one's own initiative, then it is consigned to oblivion and becomes irksome.

They should strive to flee, cut off, and tear out of themselves by the roots the vice of wandering and instability. To accomplish this, they must not only not be quick to course to and fro outside the hermitage or outside the cell, lest the dignity of the outward man and purity of soul be marred, as was Dinah, daughter of Jacob [cf. Gn 34: 1-2]. But even in the cell itself, they must willingly remain in one place and steadfastly and immovably at one work. For those who are less eager for stability can sometimes, while staying in the cell, be driven about all day long as if by a certain demonic impulse and spirit of wandering.

They go around the different workplaces of the cell and in the same hour begin and leave off doing various tasks. This is truly the most wretched form of the vice of wandering and is very detestable. They should try, therefore, to remain firmly grounded in the same place even in the cell, stably keeping at the same task insofar as the matter calls for this. They must not easily give way to boredom, passing from place to place and from task to task.

Indeed, all should recognize the following point, that was commonly held by our holy fathers in accordance with what is set down in their constitutions: Just as for the hermit who is quiet and zealous for stability, the cell and silence hold out the most pleasant refuge and refreshment from all the fires of the world and flames of temptation and offer a certain share in the delights of paradise, so for the restless and unstable hermit, the cell turns out to be like a jail and a torture chamber, and it occasions the utmost affliction.

And just as the sea quickly casts a corpse upon the shore, so does the hermitage speedily thrust forth like a dead man the hermit who is restless and a stranger to stability. It casts him out like an untimely birth, or rather it quickly vomits him out like food useless and harmful to the stomach. The workshop of piety cannot long suffer deep within it the restless and unstable worker. But if such a one endures for some time at the hermitage, that will not happen because of constancy of virtue, but rather because of wretched stubbornness. Nevertheless, he will come to an end soon and without honor. From the time that the cell becomes, for one so very unfortunate, practically a prison or the grave of a man buried alive, truly he cannot last until the very end, as has been seen of many by experience. For a corpse, that is, a man dead at heart, cannot remain long in a holy place and on holy ground.

16. What Kind of Hermit the Prior Should Be

The one who is elected prior of the hermitage is summoned to toil rather than to honor. He ought not utterly and obstinately refuse the office enjoined on him, even though he might seem to have some excuse. And although he is not strictly held to accept such a burden, nevertheless he should know that he will receive a greater reward from the Lord if he gives his consent with humble zeal to the will of his electors and the persuasion of the hermits. Even if he feels he lacks the strength, yet confident of divine assistance through the interceding prayers of the hermits, let him gladly accept the office enjoined on him by the definitors and imposed by virtue of obedience.

In his gait, posture, dress, speech, and work, in short, in all the actions of his life, let him do nothing that could offend the mind or gaze of anyone, but in everything let him do his best to conduct himself as befits eremitic holiness. In his very self, he must needs put before his subjects an example of all the virtues and particularly of the observance of eremitic standards. For the example of those who are in leadership is more effective than their words, and it is far more perfect to teach by deeds than by speech. In everything he should follow, not his personal preferences, but the eremitic constitutions and the praiseworthy customs of the hermitage. Let him neither establish anything new nor venture to change anything in the hermitage, except after mature consideration and after having heard the counsel of the hermits, especially the seniors. And in anything that is needful, he should act with the consent either of the majority or of everyone. Everything that he tells the others to do, he ought first to do himself. Let him employ discretion, to be sure, with others, and severity toward himself.

As for manual labor, let him show the way to others if his age and obligations permit, undertaking first the most commonplace tasks. He must beware being one of those who impose hard and harsh burdens on their charges and subordinates, while they themselves do not want to lift a finger to move them [cf. Mt 23:4]. For in sight of the Lord, a diversity of weights and measures is an abomination [cf. Prov 20:10 and Dt 25:13-16]. This parable certainly reproaches those who reserve the lighter tasks for themselves, while they lay the heavier ones upon their subordinates.

He should take very careful heed to always hasten to arrive first at the Divine Office insofar as possible, whether by day or by night. Let him not try to plead the many occupations of his ministry and, under their pretext, hold himself excused. He can rest assured that it is precisely then that all business is conducted with the utmost diligence when, at the approach of the time of the Divine Office, matters of even the greatest moment are left suspended and unfinished, so that we can draw near to render to God due homage of service. Then, in fact, are we truly committing our interests and affairs to God. And He, "whose Providence in His designs does not fail,"[18] directs them far better than any human prudence could.

Since he has received a double assignment, that is to say, of directing souls and of administering temporal things necessary for human bodies, let him always pay more attention to the care of souls than to the disposition of temporal things. He ought never neglect the salvation of souls for any want of temporal things whatever, but rather bend his efforts toward the salvation of souls even to the greatest detriment to the property of the hermitage.

As our blessed father Benedict says,[19] let him not dissemble the sins of offenders. But so that he can prevail against those sins, he should endeavor to root them out immediately, mindful of the condemnation of Eli, priest of Shiloh [1 Sm 2:11-4:18]. Now superiors usually dissemble the faults of offenders in one of two ways: either they do not care to take cognizance of them or, even though they are perceived, they do not make an effort to correct them. Let him not neglect through carelessness the little and least faults. If they are not eradicated right away, when they start to arise and are very small, they get to be very big because they are committed with impunity. Whoever neglects little things gradually declines to the point of failing at greater ones and despising them. He ought not to abstain from correction through fear

---

18 RM, Collect of the Ninth Sunday of Ordinary Time, Latin text.
19 RB 2:26.

of occasioning scandal or of inconvenience. For necessary correction is not to be omitted for fear of scandal, especially by those who are in charge, lest greater scandals gradually arise because of impunity, even if this is not at once apparent.

Even if he sees that someone is scandalized by good, he ought not to be troubled, because often, by the Lord's will, in this way the plant that the Heavenly Father has not planted is uprooted [cf. Mt 15:13]. And so it does not occupy the land uselessly, but another takes its place that may bear fruit [cf. Lk 13:6-9].

He must not refrain from correcting faults through indiscriminate humility or false kindness. In fact, all humility of this sort and all such kindness are reckoned quite damnable in the one who presides over the community. Nay rather, there can be no greater pride in a man than to neglect, under the pretext of humility, such necessary, divine commandments. And so as he seeks indiscreetly to preserve the one virtue of humility, he allows the souls entrusted to him to fall into the various transgressions of the vices. For there is no greater impiety than to leave the sins of one's subjects unpunished and uncorrected through false kindness. And truly, one can show no greater kindness and mercy to anyone than not to leave even his least sins uncorrected and unpunished. If he discovers some long-standing vices that he doubts he can correct, let him not regard the capability of his own powers, but let him look to the power of the One in whose place he stands.[20] And so what he would not presume to attempt by his own powers, let him set about doing, trusting in the help of the Lord. Nevertheless, he ought always be careful lest he himself appear to deserve rebuke for that which he proposes to correct and reprove in others, or even for some other kind of fault. For when somebody's manner of life is disdained, it is inevitable that his admonitions are also easily slighted.

What was just said about the necessity of correction has perhaps been presented less extensively than would have been called for,

---

[20] Cf. Second Vatican Council, *Perfectae caritatis* 14, and CCL 601.

inasmuch as in our time almost all religious institutes seem more wanting in nothing else than in the necessary virtue of correction. And on account of nothing else more than want of correction, it appears, have they declined and gone astray. Yet while wishing to avoid one vice, one ought not to play the fool by going to the opposite extreme, that is, by overdoing correction. In fact, our blessed father Benedict teaches in his *Rule* that the bruised reed must not be broken. Rather, one should be careful lest, while the vessel is being scraped too hard, it break with worse damage.[21] And so, let him do everything with discretion. He will achieve this easily if, according to the admonition of the *Rule*,[22] he will hate the vice, but so love the brother as not to hate him in any way for his vice or apply himself with any less concern in seeking his salvation.

If he is loath to read the work that Gregory has divinely written about pastoral care,[23] or the treatises of other doctors, let him at least frequently read, reread and memorize chapters 2 and 64 of the *Holy Rule*. Thus he will know how to adapt his approach to circumstances, warning of terrors now and proffering blandishments later, showing at one time the kind love of a father and at another the sterner love of a master.[24] Furthermore, he will know how to be of service to many dispositions. He will teach those capable of instruction with words, the simpler with deeds and examples, holding in check the more honorable and intelligent by admonitions, the stubborn and troublesome with threats and stiff discipline. Let him keep some within the regular and eremitic discipline by means of coaxing, others through advice, and still others through reprimands, according to the persons or the kinds of faults in question. According to the mind of the Apostle, he must become all things to all men in order to gain all [cf. 1 Cor 9:22]. He should know that the care of souls pertains entirely to him alone, nor can he delegate it to others without always being held accountable for it himself.

---

[21] Cf. RB 64:12 and Mt 12:20.

[22] RB 64:11.

[23] Gregory the Great, *Pastoral Rule*, NPNF II:12 and ACW 11.

[24] RB 2:24.

All the administration of temporal goods devolves upon him, and anything that is done improperly by any assistant is deemed wholly imputable to him, unless he applied all diligence and showed all concern. It is his duty alone to correct all offenders. And he is responsible for convening the chapter, as often as it is necessary or is humbly requested by the majority of the hermits, and for proposing the things to be done in it. Whenever he leaves the hermitage, he may appoint whomsoever he wishes as his vicar, even if he wishes to choose different individuals each time to whom to entrust this charge. Nor is he obliged in this matter to observe the order of profession.

It pertains to the prior, in addition, to pay careful attention that the things to be provided to the sick, to guests, to the poor, and to pilgrims are supplied diligently, with charity, and in a suitable manner. He must also be attentive that all temporal goods are well managed, and that at fitting times everything necessary is furnished to the hermits. In fact, just as one soul in man rules and vivifies all the members, whether lowest or highest, the nobler as well as the more ignoble, and to it alone are assigned the praise or the blame for all actions, so it is with the one set over all the brethren and assistants. He ought to care for and direct these as if they were his members, and whatever any of them accomplishes, either well or ill, he should believe devolves to his credit or his blame, except where all his care and diligence were to no avail.

Finally, it is necessary that he be learned in the divine Scriptures, if not through assiduous study, at least through a good manner of life. That is, he must be chaste, sober, merciful, not anxious, not going to extremes, not obstinate, not jealous or suspicious,[25] and especially a keeper of the *Rule* and of the eremitic constitutions in everything. And thus may he not incur guilt on account of neglect and carelessness, but rather acquire merit before God for the hard work of administration and for earnest diligence in all things.

---

[25] RB 64:9,16.

17. That the Entire Observance of the Religious Life is not Contained in These Constitutions[26]

The Camaldolese hermits, and all others who would like to observe these constitutions of the eremitic life, should not regard them as having been set down so that in them they could have a complete instruction on religious and eremitic living. Rather they were written so that, by observing them, they might be able to have a certain outward pattern of eremitic conduct.

As for the other things that pertain to the perfection of the inner man and to the conduct of the eremitic life, let those who long to understand them and desire to attain them read, in the first place, the Holy Gospel. And they should also read the commentaries on the Gospel that make some points in it clearer, namely the epistles of the holy Apostles, which are nothing else but expositions of the evangelic doctrine. For indeed, all the principles of Christian perfection are fully contained in this evangelic and apostolic doctrine, and the perfect pattern of religious life is described, not only regarding outward conduct, but also as regards inward cultivation. For first of all, we are not taught therein by human wisdom, which can be deceived and mistaken, but by the infallible divine Wisdom, which fully understands what we need to know and what we do not need to know.

Moreover, a doctrine that is not corroborated by the example of the one who propounds it does not seem complete. For this reason, to the Gospel doctrine is added the fully complete example of all the virtues that divine Wisdom has proposed to us through His assumed humanity. And so we who are human have no excuse if we fail to imitate those things which, in His true humanity, the Lord Jesus did and endured. It is written, in fact, that Jesus began to do and

---

[26] Many of the less precise Biblical references, as well as those to the Sermons on the Mount and on the Plain (Mt 5-7 and Lk 6:17-49; CCC 1965-1970, 1983), are omitted.

teach [Acts 1:1], so that the doctrine set forth might be confirmed by example and that we might thus be attracted to imitate Him. If, then, we wish to have a perfect model of religious life, let us search the Gospel and the teaching of our Lord Jesus Christ. Let us put into practice and imitate His example, and in this way we will attain the summit of the perfection of all virtues.

In the Gospel, we are fully instructed especially how God is to be loved with all our heart, with all our mind, and with all our strength [cf. Mk 12: 30, 33]. Thus everything is referred to Him and nothing is preferred to the divine will, but rather we desire and also pray that not our will but His will be always done [Lk 22:42].

We are also taught how love must be proved by works. For indeed, that love which is not followed by the doing of works is vain. "For I love the Father," says the Lord, "and as He has commanded me, so I do" [Jn 14:31]. And to us He proposes the same thing: "Whoever loves me," he says, "keeps my commandments" [cf. Jn 14:15, 21]. This is the first and the greatest of the commandments, that we should love God more than ourselves and refer every other love to Him, so that we might be able to love Him as much as we ought. Accordingly, we are taught to hate father and mother and brothers and sisters, and finally our own life [cf. Lk 14:26]. For whoever does not hate father and mother, yes also even his very life, does not appear capable of divine love.

Following closely upon that commandment, and like it [Mt 22: 39], is this one: to love our neighbor, not in himself, not with carnal affection (a thing that the imperfect do also in the world), but in God, with spiritual affection, as we love ourselves. Accordingly, the holy doctrine and example of Christ teaches His disciples and servants who are eager for religious life nothing more than to love, after God, our neighbor as ourself, to consider all men as neighbors [cf. Lk 10:29-37], and to extend love not only to parents and relatives, but also to those we do not know, to strangers and foreigners, yes even to broaden it as far as enemies. To wit: not to curse those who curse us; not to seek or desire revenge for insults, but rather to bless those who curse us; to do good to those who hate us, to pray for those who persecute and calumniate us, to give food and drink to an enemy who is hungry and thirsty [Prv 25:21; Rom 12:20]; not to render evil for evil but to eagerly render good [cf. 1Thes 5:15]; to forgive those who sin against us not only seven times, but seventy times seven, if we want our greater sins against God to be forgiven [Mt 18:22]. Not only not to have anything against our brother, but if he has anything whatever against us, to take care with all humility and by all means that we are reconciled before we present a gift to God. Not to address a brother with mocking or slanderous words, such as "you fool" or "*raca*". Not to get angry, or if angry sometimes through human weakness, not to cherish anger, or by any means to let the sun set on our anger [Eph 4:26]. To patiently bear from our neighbor the loss of material goods, words of slander and open curses, as well as the pain of words and of every insult, nor on this account to forsake love. To the one who takes away our coat, we give our cloak as well; we do not ask back what has been taken away; compelled to go one mile with someone, we accompany him for two; struck on the right cheek, we also offer the left. In order to preserve love of neighbor whole and inviolate in the midst of even these adversities, He would admonish us not to be sad when suffering something unjustly, but then to rejoice exceedingly. We should indeed deem it all joy [Jas 1:2] to bear various even undeserved afflictions and injuries due to both slander and gossip. And finally, we should lay down our life not only for friends [Jn 15:13; 1Jn 3:16], but willingly for the salvation of enemies, so that, if possible, through our bodily death they may be recalled to the life which is in God.

And so it is that He teaches us with words and instructs us by example, He who was mocked [Lk 22:63] and kept silent, was accused and did not reply [Mt 26:60-63], was beaten [Lk 22:63] and endured it like a sheep that is sheared [Is 53:7; Acts 8:32], was crucified and prayed for His crucifiers [Lk 23:34], who indeed laid down His life for all those who lay in wait for His life, who did not refuse to die for us even though we were His enemies [Rom 5:10], the just for the unjust [1Pt 3:18]. Yet He suffered these things undeservedly, He who committed no sin [1Pt 2:22]. Certainly, no injury can be inflicted undeservedly on us, who are sinners [1Kgs 8:46; Rom 3:23] and receive what our deeds deserve [Ps 61 (62):12]. Any insult or injury inflicted on us by our neighbor is not an offense but a punishment. For we first sinned against God, and on that account we ought to believe that whatever we suffer happens, not by human counsel, but by the will of God [cf. Ps 38 (39):9; Heb 12:5-7]. Furthermore, from this fount of twofold love, all the rivulets of the holy and religious life are derived. Thus the soul, watered by them, brings forth not only flowers but also perfect fruit of every virtue.

For in the life and teaching of Christ Jesus we learn, after charity toward God and neighbor, to pursue humility in everything: to shun haughtiness, to avoid also all dignity of rank offered to us; to become little children regarding malice, but not in our way of thinking [1Cor 14:20]; for the greater to become as the lesser, and one who ranks ahead as one who serves [Lk 22:26]. And in all things to strive after the humility of the one who, although He was in the form of God, emptied Himself, taking the form of a servant [Phil 2:6-7]. He who, when He knew that they were coming to take Him by force and make Him king, fled to the mountain alone [Jn 6:15] and refused all the sovereignty offered Him, even though it was His by right.

[This humility will imply, in practice, the following:] To be in harmony with everybody [cf. Heb 12:14], never to argue with anybody [cf. Phil 2:14], to avoid useless questions [cf. 1Tm 6:20]; not to have the practice of arguing, but of maintaining peace with all, even with those who are averse to it, insofar as this lies within our power. Not to insult or slander anybody, but rather to bear with equanimity the insults inflicted and the slanders spread against us. Not to pass judgment on anyone, but to judge ourselves lest we be judged by the Lord [cf. 1Cor 11:31]; not to imitate the haughtiness of the Pharisee and his rashness in judging his neighbor, but the humility of the publican, who accuses himself [Lk 18:9-14]. Neither to long for prosperity nor to be in dread of adversity; not to worry about tomorrow, but to seek first the Kingdom of God and His justice, and to cast all one's care upon the Lord [cf. 1Pt 5:7]. If the Lord has given us some talent, not to wrap it up in a napkin and hide it underground, but to double it by doing business with it or investing it [Mt 25:14-30; Lk 19:20]; yet not to pour the oil we need into the lamps of the foolish, lest perhaps it fail us and not suffice for them [Mt 25:8-9]. To do good works openly as effective examples, and to carry them in our hands like burning lamps, but to keep them hidden regarding the intention by which we wish to please God alone. Not to seek our own praise in employing God's gifts, but only the glory of God; not to glory in ourselves or in our virtue, but to glory only in the Lord [cf. 2Cor 10:17]; not to take pride in what we have received, as though we received it not [1Cor 4:7]. To keep the eye of our intention always simple and clear, so that our whole body may be lightsome. Not to fear the tongues that perversely interpret our deeds; to beware of scandalizing the weak and the little ones, but not to care about the scandal taken by the Pharisees at our good deeds; not to heed the judgment of the blind about our deeds. If our right eye, hand, or foot scandalizes us, to cut it off and cast it away. To willingly listen to those who rightly admonish us, even if they themselves do otherwise [cf. Mt 23:3]. To guard against not only evil, but any hint of evil [cf. 1Thes 5:22]. To avoid occasions of sin. Not only to keep the body free from any wicked deed, but the soul also free from any concupiscence for worldly things [cf. 1Jn 2:15-16]; not to give in to temptations, but to pray without ceasing not only for oneself, but also for all human beings; to weep continually before God for one's own guilt and that of one's neighbor, that is, of all human beings, and to make entreaty for them, imploring pardon; also to persevere in prayer with longanimity, even when not receiving what we ask for [cf. Lk 18:10]. To work so cautiously in secret that one's left hand cannot find out what one's right hand is doing; when fasting, to wash one's face and anoint one's head with oil. Not to fear poverty, exile, persecutions, curses, imprisonment, torture, and finally death itself, considering them beneficial after the example of the one who innocently bore them all; to bear the mockery of men and the temptations of the demons with equanimity, not giving in or giving up, but undergoing them manfully; to endure patiently the loss of anything whatsoever, the death of friends and any infirmities of one's own body. To tame the insolence of the body with fasting, taking the discipline, exterior good works and continual meditation on death. To guard diligently against vain and idle words and much speaking [cf. Prv 10:19 and Mt 12:36]; with great care, to keep one's mouth from the vice of murmuring and detraction; to shut one's ears from these with the bolt of divine love. To always be truthful, not only in word but also in deed; to shun lies and pretenses like deadly poison; to tell the truth by simple affirmation or negation, without any kind of oath. To laugh seldom or never [cf. Si 21:20]; to weep bitterly and frequently over one's own and others' sins; to often moisten one's countenance with sweet tears at the thought of heavenly delights. Never to leave off doing good works [cf. Gal 6:9]; to watchfully expect the Lord, who will come at an hour we do not know [Mt 24:44]; to believe and to understand that God is always present to us [cf. Prv 10:19]; not only to begin good works, but to persevere in them to the end; and in addition, never looking back, but forgetting the things that are behind, to always stretch oneself forward toward the things that lie ahead [Phil 3:13]. And finally, when we have done all that the Lord has commanded, to regard ourselves as unprofitable servants [Lk 17:10]. And even if we are not aware of anything against us [1Cor 4:4] (which is, however, unlikely), not to suppose ourselves justified by this, but with sighs and tears coming more from the heart than from the eyes to implore unceasingly the mercy of the Lord, of which we all stand in need.

As we ceaselessly do these things, we ought ever to have before the eyes of our mind that those who really desire to serve God the Most High Creator must do them all (and many other things of this kind that would be tedious to enumerate), neither from love of human fame or glory (as hypocrites do), nor merely out of pleasure in virtue (as we believe philosophers alien to the true worship of God have done), nor either from dread of eternal punishment or from desire of heavenly happiness (seeing that the former is servile and the latter is mercenary). No, they must do them only for the pure, simple, and most burning love of God, the Best and the Greatest, reposing in His will alone and seeking His glory in preference to everything.

These things, and very many others of this kind, are the lessons of the holy Gospel and the holy Apostles and the precepts of Christian perfection. Since they truly contain the perfect institution of the religious life, they are to be attentively reflected upon day and night and effectively carried out by the hermits, who have embraced the institution of the perfect solitary life. Because it is indeed difficult to attain to these principles of a perfect life without some standard to regulate outward conduct, these constitutions of the eremitic life have been set forth: not that we might suppose that in them the perfect pattern of religious living is described, but so that through them we might be able to ascend to those more perfect evangelic and apostolic precepts.

For those who diligently observe these constitutions will most certainly arrive at those more perfect precepts. And putting them into practice, they will without doubt obtain eternal life and reach heavenly joys, in Christ Jesus our Lord, to Whom be glory, praise, and thanksgiving unto the ages of the ages. Amen.

SANCTUS ROMUALDUS ABBAS, CAMALDULENSIUM FUNDATOR.

Saint Romuald's Brief Rule

Raphael Brown

Here is the hundred-word Latin text of this bright gem of eremitical spirituality, recorded about 1006 — twenty years before Romuald's death — by Saint Bruno of Querfurt in his *Life of the Five Brothers* (VFr), as reported to him by one of those martyrs named John, who, like Bruno, knew Romuald well (VFr 19). First the simple Latin text; then a translation with commentary. (Numbers added by R.B., and other additions made by the editors.)

Et hanc brevem regulam a magistro Romualdo accepit, quam custodire in vita ipse multum sollicitus fuit:

1. Sede in cella quasi in paradiso;
2. proice post tergum de memoria totum mundum,
3. cautus ad cogitationes, quasi bonus piscator ad pisces.
4. Una via est in psalmis; hanc ne dimittas. Si non potes omnia, qui venisti fervore novicio, nunc in hoc, nunc in illo loco psallere in spiritu et intelligere mente stude, et cum ceperis vagare legendo, ne desistas, sed festina intelligendo emendare;
5. pone te ante omnia in presentia Dei cum timore et tremore, quasi qui stat in conspectu imperatoris;
6. destrue te totum,
7. et sede quasi pullus, contentus ad gratiam Dei, qui, nisi mater donet, nec sapit nec habet quod comedat.

And he received this brief rule from Master Romuald, which he was very careful to practice throughout his life:

1. Sit in the cell as in paradise;
2. cast all memory of the world behind you;
3. cautiously watching your thoughts, as a good fisher watches the fish.
4. In the Psalms there is one way. Do not abandon it. If you who have come with the fervor of a novice cannot understand everything, strive to recite with understanding of spirit and mind, now here, now there, and when you begin to wander while reading, do not stop, but hasten to correct yourself by concentrating.
5. Above all, place yourself in the presence of God with fear and trembling, like someone who stands in the sight of the emperor;
6. destroy yourself completely,
7. and sit like a chick, content with the grace of God, for unless its mother gives it something, it tastes nothing and has nothing to eat.

How beautifully simple and profound and powerful! Saint Romuald evidently spoke like Saint Francis, with the same brief, pungent, realistic, practical tone and vocabulary and the same deep insight and soaring inspiration. To find such common sense and wisdom together in the history of spirituality one must turn to the pithy Sayings of the Desert Fathers and to the strikingly similar Golden Sayings of Blessed Brother Giles of Assisi — or to some of the Zen and Sufi masters.

It is indeed difficult to understand why this minor masterpiece of contemplative spirituality in the authentic words of a great mystic and saint has not yet received the thorough study which it merits. A comprehensive critical analysis, tracing its roots in the Desert Fathers, illustrating applications by the first generations of Camaldolese hermits, and indicating echoes in later spiritual writings, is definitely needed. Here I will only submit a few reflections which its seven steps have suggested.

1. Sit in the Cell as in Paradise

Dom Jean Leclercq has shown how meaningful was the use of the word *sedere* in medieval monastic literature.[1] Stemming from the contemplative Mary sitting at Christ's feet (Lk 10.39), it also appears in a scriptural passage often quoted: "He shall sit in solitude and silence" (Lam 3.28). Cassian had: "Sit in your cells..."[2] And Jerome wrote: "Have a cell as paradise."[3] Romuald was probably familiar with these texts, but the whole point is that for him, as for all true hermits, the formula became a living, existential truth, confirmed by years of daily experience. It was the essence of the oral rule of life which he gave to the first five

---

[1] Jean Leclercq. "Le devoir de s'asseoir." *Chances de la spiritualité occidentale.* (Paris: 1966) pp. 313-28; and *Le Millénaire du Mont-Athos* (Chevetogne: 1963) I, 253-64. For the connection with the hesychasm (stillness) of the Eastern Church, see *The Privilege of Love* (Wong), pp. 86-92.

[2] Conf. 7.23.

[3] Epistle 125.7.

hermits at Camaldoli, as reported by the short constitutions: "the rule of fasting, keeping silence, and remaining in the cell."[4]

In practical application, despite its use in the first and seventh step, the word *sedere* meant not just to sit, but also to remain, to stay in one place. While urged not to keep getting up and down or to stray restlessly in his cell, the hermit did not literally remain seated all day. When praying he stood or knelt and prostrated himself on the ground. And he took his fast-day meals of bread and water sitting on the floor of his cell.

The cell itself is such an important phenomenon in the history of Christian spirituality that its evolution must be briefly sketched. It was of course the basic housing unit of the hermits and anchorites of the Near Eastern deserts. The *laura* was a group of separate cells, sometimes two- or three-room cottages, and even the large cenobia of Pachomius comprised villages of cells. But, in the West, the spread of the *Rule of Saint Benedict* introduced and made standard the common monastic dormitory. The two fundamental motivations of this drastic change were the fostering of poverty and chastity — at the cost of privacy and solitude.

Consequently, in the eleventh century, a monk who felt called to a life of greater solitude could not transfer to a community or order whose members lived in cells for the simple reason that none existed. He had only two options: go off, with or without his abbot's consent, and live as an independent hermit; or settle in a hermitage on the grounds of the monastery. The latter arrangement became the traditional solution for such rare vocations. Many abbeys came to have one or two hermitages, but they were not much used.

It is in the light of this situation that we should appraise the enormous significance and originality of the contribution to Western monasticism of Saint Romuald. He was the first to provide foundations in which hermits could live in community. It was this revolutionary

---

[4] *Camaldolese Spirituality*, p. 214.

new creation which effectively reformed and repaired eremitism, i.e., the solitary contemplative life, in Europe. He did so by making the solitary life communal, semi-cenobitical — or, in a word, Christian. And he did it just at a time when the need for such a reform was widely felt, in what has become known as *the crisis of monasticism* in the eleventh century, which resulted in the founding of the similar eremitical institutes of Fonte Avellana, La Grande Chartreuse, and Grandmont. It was also reflected in a new stress on contemplation and solitude among congregations of regular canons, and later even in the Silvestrine and Olivetan Benedictine reforms.

Saint Romuald not only revived the *laura* or community of cells. He also revived and reformed the radical eremitical institution of reclusion, the more or less permanent residence by a hermit in a cell, without joining his brethren in church for major Offices, chapter, meals, or weekly walks. Saint Anthony of Egypt, the father and model of Christian hermits, spent twenty years as a recluse. Many of the Desert Fathers retired to a cave for entire Lents. Many medieval towns had a recluse, usually a woman called an anchoress, living in a cell adjoining the wall of a church. Half a dozen rules or treatises written for them are extant; they are invaluable documents for the study of medieval eremitical spirituality, notably that by Saint Aelred of Rievaulx.[5] Saint Francis of Assisi knew an anchoress named Prassede in Rome and urged her to persevere in her vocation.[6] And he made his own free adaptation of reclusion by occupying a remote cell in his hermitages. Incidentally, when he spent several weeks on retreat at the Sacro Eremo at Camaldoli, it is probable that the saintly Blessed Leonardo was then in reclusion.

---

[5]   Aelred of Rievaulx. *De Vita Eremitica. A Rule of Life for a Recluse.* Latin and French in *Sources chrétiennes*, 76. (Paris: 1961). English: *The works of Aelred of Rievaulx*, I (Kalamazoo: Cistercian, 1971), pp. 41-102. See also NCE 1:487-488; F. Darwin. *The English Medieval Recluse* (London: 1944); and A. Savage and N. Watson. *Anchoritic Spirituality* (New York: Paulist, 1991).

[6]   3 C 17.

The theme of the cell as anticipated paradise or heaven on earth is frequently found in the writings of the Desert Fathers and medieval contemplatives. Likewise the allied theme of the cell as teacher of infused wisdom. The Egyptian Abba Moses used to say: "Go sit in your cell, and your cell will teach you everything."[7] Saint Peter Damian wrote: "The cell will fully teach its dweller our entire way of life."[8] An early Syriac compilation of the lives and sayings of the Desert Fathers bears the apt title *The Paradise of the Holy Fathers*.[9] Medieval Benedictine and Cistercian writers referred to the cloister as a paradise and the soul of the monk as a cell. Only in the thirteenth century was the private cell reinstituted by the Benedictines, just as the Cistercians are doing today.[10]

Obviously the material cell or private room is simply a helpful but not essential means to ensure silence and solitude for prayer and recollection, which has traditionally been safeguarded by the monastic stress on silence, even reinforced by sign language among the Cistercians. The evolution of the spirituality of the cell is an illuminating illustration of that basic process in religion: internalizing or interiorization. Saint Gregory the Great enunciated the fundamental principle: "Of what good is solitude of body if solitude of heart is lacking?"[11] Saint Francis rephrased that psychological rule in the following statement, which is a perfect summary of his contemplative spirituality: "Wherever we are and we travel, we always have the cell with us: for brother body is our cell, and the soul is the hermit who stays inside the cell, to pray to

---

7 PG 65, 284; CS 59:118.

8 Op. 15:18, Letter 50:51, Blum 2:314.

9 *The Paradise of the Holy Fathers*. Tr. by E. A. W. Budge (London: 1907).

10 On the history and spirituality of the cell, see: J.B. Hasbrouck. "The History of the Private Cell vs. the Common Dormitory," *Monastic Exchange* 5:1. Spring 1973, 33-6; J. Leclercq. "Pour une spiritualité de la cellule," *Collectanea Cisterciensia* 3. 1969, 74-82, and *Le défi de la vie contemplative*. (Paris: 1970), pp. 208-20; Thomas Merton. "The Cell," *Contemplation in a World of Action*, Pt. 2, Ch. 2. (New York: 1973) pp. 265-272; G. Penco. "La dimora interiore," *Vita Monastica* 20. 1966, 195-205, abs. in *Cistercian Studies* 3:4, 1968, 125.

11 *Moralia* 30.16.

the Lord and meditate on Him. So if the soul does not remain in quiet and solitude within its cell, a cell made by hand is of little good to a religious."[12]

We should take care to note that, when he uttered those golden words, he was not speaking to brethren living in a hermitage, but to friars setting out on a preaching mission.

This same principle of internalizing the cell was later applied by extension to such concepts of the soul or heart as "the cell of self-knowledge and knowledge of God" by Saint Catherine of Siena and the many-mansioned "interior castle" of Saint Teresa of Avila, culminating in the profound psychospirituality of the heart in the writings of the modern Russian bishop Theophane the Recluse.[13]

2. Cast All Memory of the World Behind You

Here we find the traditional monastic attitude of separation from "the world", with all the semantic confusion enveloping that ambiguous term. This stance has ranged from scorn and flight through detachment and disengagement to liberation, depending on the particular sense of "world". Those senses are three: (a) the creation or cosmos or planet; (b) mankind or human souls; and (c) sin-permeated society. The best treatment of this complex topic of which I know is that of Louis Bouyer in his very valuable *Introduction to Spirituality*, the only work in its field broad enough in spectrum to cover eremitical as well as lay and priestly spiritualities, while correctly stressing that basically there is only one Christian spirituality. In his Chapter 8, Father Bouyer masterfully explains why "those who are free of the world, and they alone, can contribute to its salvation." No doubt there has been in monastic spirituality a tendency toward an unchristian absence of compassionate concern for worldlings, but only to the extent that it has occasionally

---

[12] SP 65. LP 80.

[13] Thomas Špidlík. *La doctrine spirituelle de Théophane le Reclus. Le coeur et l'esprit.* (Rome: 1965. Or. Chr. Anal., 172).

deviated from a full ecclesial sense of community with Christ's Mystical Body the Church. No such deviation can be seen in the work and words of great Catholic contemplatives like Saints Romuald and Peter Damian, who labored to "repair" the House of God in souls by strengthening their inner life of prayer and union with Christ.

In this second item in his Brief Rule, the founder of Camaldoli instructed a novice hermit to set aside all memories of the past and the potential pleasures of life in the world, which very naturally tempt young religious to return to family and friends. This ever-valid rule of all ascetics and mystics is strikingly similar to the practice of astronomers of locating their observatories on mountains, remote from the bright lights and the murky smog of great cities, in order to be able to "contemplate" more effectively the mysteries of the universe — so as to help mankind with the fruit of their efforts (*contemplata aliis tradere*: "to hand on to others the things contemplated").[14]

3. Cautiously Watch Your Thoughts, as a Good Fisher Watches the Fish[15]

How vividly Saint Romuald introduces to his novice the

---

[14] Saint Thomas Aquinas, *Summa Theologiae* II-II, q. 188, a.6.

[15] "The sight of a tranquil sea is delightful, but it is certainly not more lovely than a state of peace. Indeed the dolphins swim in the sea in a calm, and thoughts directed to God are immersed in a state of serenity" (Evagrius, *The Eight Evil Spirits*).
"One who finds himself in the struggle ought always keep his mind serene. Thus the spirit, discerning the thoughts passing through the mind, will know how to put away in the treasury of the memory those good thoughts that God sends it and to drive away from the receptive natural inclinations those evil ones that the demon suggests. In a similar fashion, when the sea is calm, the fishers cast a glance so as to grasp the movements in its depths, so that nothing escapes them of the living beings that traverse the paths down there..." (Diadochus of Photice, *A Hundred Considerations*).
"The monk who keeps watch is a fisher of thoughts who easily knows how to catch sight of them in the tranquillity of the night and is able to catch them" (Saint John Climacus, *Ladder*).

primary contemplative exercise of self-observation and self-analysis! "Watch yourself, Anthony," said an inner voice to the father of hermits. Ever since, monks, hermits, and mystics have taken that basic rule to heart. Hence the introspective Danish philosopher Kierkegaard could characterize monks as "those deeply serious souls" who "tirelessly scrutinize each secret thought to discover the obscure impulse hidden in all human life." The Desert Fathers became masters of the fine art of remaining on guard against the intrusion of negative, evil, or impure thoughts (*logismoi*). No doubt Romuald learned that skill from their *Lives* and Cassian's *Conferences*, those amazing masterpieces of psychological insight.[16] Saint Peter Damian's two works on eremitical spirituality and life, his Opuscula 14 and 15,[17] should also be studied as essential background for all seven sections of this Brief Rule of Saint Romuald. The entire chapter 19[18] of the second work deals with "idle and harmful thoughts that must not be received but expelled," and chapter 22[19] with "the discerning of thoughts" by using the soul as a net in which to retain only wholesome fishes, i.e., thoughts. Strange to say, neither saint quotes the most relevant scriptural passage, often used by the Fathers: "With closest custody, guard your heart, for in it are the sources of life" (Prv 4:23). Here modern psychiatry confirms the enduring wisdom of the contemplative tradition: constant self-observation is the price of self-knowledge. Incidentally, Saint Romuald also taught an independent hermit "how to resist his thoughts and how to repulse attacks of evil spirits."[20]

---

[16] John Cassian. *Institutes and Conferences*. Tr. by E. Gibson. NPNF II: 11. More recent and complete translations: *The Monastic Institutes*. Tr. by J. Bertram (London: 1999); *The Institutes*. Tr. by B. Ramsey. ACW 58; *The Conferences*. Tr. by B. Ramsey. ACW 57.

[17] Letters 18 and 50, Blum 1:159-170 and 2:289-334.

[18] Sections 52-53 in Blum.

[19] Sections 57-62 in Blum.

[20] VR 24.

4. In the Psalms There Is One Way[21]

Here we reach the principal occupation of the hermit, in some cases apparently his only occupation, as some recluses recited at least one Psalter and a half every day. Again, Saint Peter Damian's two eremitical treatises supply rich material regarding the theory and practice of psalmody at Fonte Avellana (and Camaldoli). Saint Romuald's advice in this section contains an explicit echo of 1 Cor 14:15, *"spiritu...et mente"* ("with my spirit...and with my mind"). His stress on striving to recite the Psalms with understanding of mind and heart was noted by his biographer: "He used to say that it is better, if possible, to chant one Psalm with heartfelt compunction than to run through a hundred with a wandering mind."[22] After he received the gift of tears, he was often overcome with weeping while reciting his Office, whether in a chapel or even riding on horseback.[23] The early Camaldolese included in their first constitutions these lines which no doubt reflect their founder's liturgical spirit: "All the brethren except the recluses come to the church for Matins and the other hours and chant the Psalms very distinctly and slowly and with great care: without haste, but very deliberately, meditating."

---

[21] Pope John Paul II, in his General Audience of March 28, 2001, stated:

...the Psalms came to be adopted from the earliest centuries as the prayer of the People of God. If in some historical periods there was a tendency to prefer other prayers, it is to the monks' great credit that they held the Psalter's torch aloft in the Church. One of them, Saint Romuald, founder of Camaldoli, at the dawn of the second Christian millennium, even maintained, as his biographer Bruno of Querfurt says, that the Psalms are the only way to experience truly deep prayer: *"Una via in psalmis"* (cf. CCC 2597, 2762).

Has this *una via* a reference-point? We are told Pascal prayed Ps 118 (119) daily (General Audience of November 14, 2001), and for the Holy Fathers (cf. Delatte on RB 18:2-3), this longest of Psalms was also the richest and particularly normative for Christian life.

[22] VR 9; cf RB 20.

[23] VR 34-35.

And that is exactly the spirit and tempo in which the Camaldolese and Carthusian hermits recite their Office even today.

You may notice that this Brief Rule does not once mention Jesus Christ. Nevertheless we know that Saint Romuald's spirituality was intensely Christocentric. Often, when overflowing with consolations, he would exclaim: "Dearest Jesus, beloved, my sweet honey, ineffable desire, sweetness of saints, suavity of angels!"[24] We must not forget that for him, as for all Catholic contemplatives from the fifth to the thirteenth century and beyond, each Psalm was considered to have been either uttered by Christ or written to foretell His redemptive work or to be recited with reference to His mysteries (Dom Jean Leclercq).

5. *Above All, Place Yourself in the Presence of God with Fear and Trembling*

Here we have three basic themes of patristic contemplative spirituality: the presence of God, humility, and compunction. This inner awareness and humbling was perfectly formulated by the Epistle of Saint James (4:7-10): "Submit to God...Draw close to God, and He will draw close to you. Cleanse your hands, you sinners. Purify your hearts...Begin to lament, to mourn, and to weep...Be humbled in the sight of the Lord." As the Desert Father Poemen put it: "When a soul blames itself before the Lord, the Lord loves it." A rich treasury of early monastic writings on compunction motivated by "placing oneself before God with fear and trembling" has been compiled (in French) by the modern master of early Christian spirituality, Father Irenaeus Hausherr, S.J., in his *Penthos*.[25] Saint Peter Damian's Opusculum 15 has two chapters (24 and 26)[26] on

---

[24] VR 7, 16, 31.
[25] Rome, 1944 and 1966; CS 53.
[26] Sections 65, 68-70 in Blum.

this subject, which no doubt faithfully reproduce the attitude of Saint Romuald.

6. Destroy Yourself Completely

Such is the lapidary recipe of the great hermit for that crucial inner process which is the real Christian revolution, also known as overcoming, self-mastery, self-annihilation, and naughting. It is a vivid echo of the Desert Fathers' equally pithy shock treatment: "I kill the one who kills me!" Or: "If someone does not kill his soul's passions with the fire of tears, he can never acquire charity." True to his radical nature, Saint Peter Damian wrote in his epitaph: "Better that the spirit kill the flesh than that the flesh kill you!" The later constitutions of Camaldoli discreetly rephrased the founder's words thus: "The concupiscence of the flesh is to be killed and not its nature...You are to slay the carnal desires which war against the soul (1 Pt 2:11), and not the sensible members which serve her." Logically, this advanced stage of asceticism leads to the process of passive purifications in the dark night of the spirit (cf. the doctrine of Saint John of the Cross).

7. And Sit like a Chick, Content with the Grace of God

Probably because this Brief Rule was designed for a novice, only the last section deals with the higher levels of mystical union, and only in a simple yet vivid formula using the barnyard image of a baby chick (*pullus*) being fed by its mother hen. *Pullus* is found in Christ's lament over Jerusalem in Mt 23:37; also in Saint Francis' dream of himself as a hen and his friars as her brood.[27] This was Saint Romuald's way of evoking what we call today openness to the Spirit's guidance, inspirations, graces, and charisms. We should note that he does not mention desiring such favors, but just being content

---

[27] 2C24.

with whatever God chooses to give. This stand is in accord with the traditional principles of Catholic mystical theology — and in contrast to a potentially dangerous stress on seeking such manifestations of grace which is evident in some elements of the current charismatic movement. Like all great saints, Romuald, Peter Damian, and Francis certainly were bearers and channels of the healing power of the Holy Spirit, but they were not examples or exponents of spiritual gluttony or sectarian "enthusiasm."

It goes without saying that Saint Romuald's chick-novice received needed guidance not only from the Spirit but from an experienced spiritual director or novice master, as the early Camaldolese custom was for master and novice to reside together in a double cell. Hence there is implicit in this last section of the Brief Rule the theme of trust, confidence, self-abandonment to God through monastic obedience, i.e., the essence of spiritual childhood.

In summary, Saint Romuald's seven-step Brief Rule for novice-hermits comprises a surprisingly rich set of exercises for training in contemplation which succinctly cover the following topics:

(1) posture, place, solitude, inner peace, and joy;
(2) detachment and liberation for concentration;
(3) self-observation and analysis for purity of mind and heart;
(4) attentively praying the Psalms as seeds of meditation;
(5) reverent, compunctious practice of the presence of God;
(6) intensive ascetical inner overcoming of faults;
(7) childlike humility and receptivity to grace.

If this summary strikes the reader as rather modern and up-to-date, there is a simple explanation: the basic process of the inner Christian reform as lived and transmitted by Anthony, Romuald, Francis, and Charles de Foucauld is a permanent fixture, like the death and resurrection of Christ, which does not change with passing trends in spirituality.

By radiantly living and teaching the powerful principles of his Brief Rule, Saint Romuald made a major contribution to the spiritual health of the Church in the West, because he renewed in it that essential element of its inner life: the contemplative, semi-eremitical small community. Today his sons are continuing to make that healing gift to the House and People of God.

Abbreviations (unique to the Supplement)

C (i.e. 1C, 2C, 3C) Thomas of Celano. *First and Second Life of Saint Francis*, and *Treatise on Miracles*. Latin: *Analecta Franciscana* X (Quaracchi: 1926-41). English: *Saint Francis of Assisi, Writings and Early Biographies, English Omnibus*. Ed. by Marion A. Habig (Chicago: 1973). Cited below as *Omnibus*.

LP Legend of Perugia. Latin and English: *Scripta Leonis, Rufini et Angeli, Sociorum S. Francisci*. R. Booke, ed. and tr. (Oxford: 1970). English tr. by P. Oligny in *Omnibus*.

SP *Speculum Perfectionis*. Latin: *Analecta Franciscana* X; and ed. by P. Sabatier (Paris: 1898; Manchester: 1928-31).

*   *   *

O God, Who chose Saint Romuald to renew the eremitic life in Your Church, give us the strength to deny ourselves in order to follow Christ in the way of the Cross, and to go up with Him into the glory of your kingdom. For He is God, and He lives and reigns with You in the unity of the Holy Spirit, for all the ages of the ages. Amen.

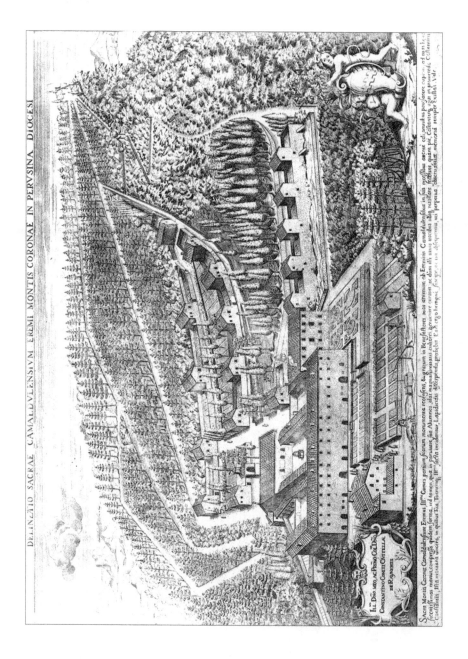

DELINEATIO SACRAE CAMALDVLENSIVM EREMI MONTIS CORONAE IN PERVSINA DIOCESI

ILL. DÑO. AC PIÐO. CO. DÑo.
CONSTANTINO COMITI CASTELLA.
DE RAINERIIS.

Sacem Montis Coronæ Camaldulensivm Eremi. Illmi Comes pertium suorum monumenta recessus, & gratiarum in Benefactores mea animum ab Eremitis Camaldulensibus in suis specissimus sacræ celsitudinis prospicere cupiens, ad manisecretissimos motus, compressa quidem forma, sed tamen quod in parviant, sui Alumnes dixit magnanimitatis cultori, & gratiarum curam ac dum illi unus urcibus illius, redditur seddent quam pie Constantino, non in præsentibus Costantiniis Costantiniis. Illa micinam uiscere, in quibus Ita. Ticinum, Illmi actas incidantur. Lapidicidis prospiciendis prospicit ille, forsque; et sui adsequenies, ut perpetua obæcusibilis memoriæ semper existat Vsu.

Monte Corona

New Camaldoli is the name of the American Hermitage of the Camaldolese Benedictines. It is located at Big Sur, California, and commands a magnificent view of the blue Pacific from the elevated coastline. In days of yore their sister congregation of Giustinianian provenance had its own new Camaldoli: the Holy Hermitage of Monte Corona. Monte Corona was originally called Monte Acuto. It is at the center of a majestic mountain range, of which it is the crown (*corona montium*), and overlooks Umbertide (formerly Fratta Perugina) in the province of Perugia.

The Hermitage of Monte Corona was intended to be a kind of "new Camaldoli" for those who, although regarding themselves as being among the heirs of Saint Romuald, did not have possession of the "old Camaldoli" he founded in Arezzo. The parallels between the Perugian house and its archetype (of Arezzo) are many. The chapels of both were dedicated to the Most Holy Saviour. The abbey of Monte Acuto, which lay below the mountain, was transformed into a hospice and administration center in imitation of Camaldoli's Fontebuono. Both hospices operated a pharmacy of considerable importance. The new Camaldoli, like its precursor, was ample in size and was built to serve as the temporal and spiritual focal point of an expanding congregation. Little wonder, then, that artists sometimes have depicted Saint Romuald holding, not Camaldoli, but Monte Corona.

The previous monastic history of the spot is worth outlining.

The abbey of Monte Acuto's eleventh century origin was attributed to Saint Romuald. In 1234 Pope Gregory IX gave it to the Cistercians. Two hundred years later, it was returned to the Camaldolese monks by Pope Eugene IV, but, since they never actually took possession, it passed into commendam. Thus it was received in 1506 by Cardinal Gabrielli, who in turn gave it to his nephew, Monsignor Galeazzo Gabrielli. In 1524, Galeazzo Gabrielli joined Blessed Paul's Company of the Hermits of Saint Romuald, taking the name Peter (of Fano). The Company eventually secured his great wealth and his benefices, which included the Abbey of Monte Acuto.

In 1523, Camaldoli recognized the Company of the Hermits of Saint Romuald. It celebrated its first general chapter in January 1524; its second at Monte Cucco (Pascelupo) in August 1524; and its third (a month after the separation of the Company from Camaldoli had been approved by the general chapter of the entire Camaldolese order) in June 1525. It was this initial assembly of the Company as an independent entity that called for the erection of a hermitage above the Abbey of Monte Acuto. The task was undertaken straightaway at San Savino, a spot between the Abbey and the summit of the mountain. In 1530, two years after Blessed Paul's death, the building of the Hermitage at its present location began, and it is likely that the community started dwelling there around 1532. The construction was completed very much later according to the Montecoronese historian Luke of Spain: "We should be aware that they continued to work on it for about forty years or more."

Since the new Hermitage was under construction at the beginning of 1532, the general chapter that met early that year was convened at the Grottoes of Massaccio. Peter of Fano (Galeazzo Gabrielli) was elected major, and since then the congregation has been called "of Montecorona." The monumental construction had been costly, and so Peter of Fano went to Rome in 1534 to seek papal financial assistance. There, in the heat of August, he died and was buried.

For 330 years, the Hermitage of Monte Corona was to be the generalate of the order: seat of the general chapter and residence of the father major and father visitators. Over the two centuries to come, the Hermitage's homonymous congregation would grow to a total of 550 members in 30 hermitages located in Italy, Poland, Austria, Hungary, Slovakia, and Lithuania.

Then there came, however, two major setbacks: the suppression by "the sacristan emperor," Joseph II, and later that by Napoleon. The secularist advisors of Joseph, and Bonaparte himself, saw the contemplative monastic life as useless and to be done away with. They were like Pharaoh, who could see only idleness in the Israelites' desire to worship the Lord in the desert (Ex 5:1-9), and like those who grew indignant over Mary of Bethany's anointing of Jesus (Jn 12:1-8) and said, "Why this waste?" (Mt 26:8) The congregation suffered some heavy losses that it would never recoup. The hermits were expelled from Monte Corona in 1812. Nevertheless, it was restored to them by Pope Pius VII in 1814, after his release from Napoleonic imprisonment and his return from exile.

Toward the middle of the nineteenth century, the Holy Hermitage itself was enjoying prosperity. The influx of vocations was so great that in 1858 construction commenced for the expansion of the novitiate. But Josephinism and Bonapartism were succeeded by the Risorgimento. Although it is customarily defined as simply a nineteenth-century political movement for the unification of Italy, all too often its result was the plundering and attempted subjugation of the Church. Its foremost leaders were the swaggering apostate soldier, Joseph Garibaldi, and the more diplomatic and less bitterly anticlerical politician, Count Camillus Cavour. It was the latter who was to oversee Monte Corona's demise — as he met his own.

On December 13, 1860, the government of Piedmont declared the suppression of religious corporations. Monte Corona might have been exempted from this decree; that it was not, the contemporary Camaldolese chronicler charges to the influence of the members of "a certain Masonic club."

In the spring of 1861, the congregation dispatched the visitator

Father Emilian and the procurator general Father Maurice to go to Cavour, in an attempt to dissuade him from letting the law be applied to Monte Corona. The Count made some flattering promises at first. But at their final meeting on June 1, he was sneering and inflexible. He said that there were too many religious in Umbria and that they would not keep pace with the times. But Father Emilian had a response ready. He read Cavour the eulogy that the historian Botta had written in honor of Napoleon for having spared Monte Corona. The message was too clear for the doughty, self-styled patriot to miss: If an impious foreign invader had hesitated to touch Monte Corona, were the sons of Italy themselves, then, to lay profane hands upon her?

The Count, whose motto was "a free Church in a free State," was taken aback. "All right," he said, "if that is the way it is, you have nothing to worry about." And he bade them farewell. In spite of his statement, the decree was applied with all severity to Monte Corona. So the two hermits returned to try to get Cavour to make good his word. They were not, however, admitted to see him, for he had fallen ill. So they headed for home, and as they were awaiting a train at the Turin station, on the night of June 5-6, Count Camillus Cavour died.

Still, there remained a court of last resort. The King of Italy, Victor Emmanuel, had the power to set right the injustice. And so to him the valiant cardinal archbishop of Perugia, Joachim Pecci, registered his protest. The adjective "valiant" has not been lightly chosen, because, not long before, similar gestures by Piedmontese bishops had been rewarded with long prison terms or perpetual exile. A passage from the cardinal's intervention follows:

> These virtuous recluses to whom an illustrious ancestor of your Majesty, Charles Emmanuel, Duke of Savoy, at the solicitation of the venerable Father Alexander di Ceve, gave an honorable abode in his states about the close of 1601, are now made the object of ignoble and rancorous calumnies.... Dispersed within the space of eight days, they were compelled to tear themselves away from the famous sanctuary which

414

they had themselves founded. Men of stainless life, of unbounded popularity among our country folk, whom solitude, silence, and prayer separated from all worldly pursuits, were accused of mixing up with politics. Men whom the world never saw coming down from the lonely peak of their inaccessible mountain, except when the offices of brotherly charity compelled them, and whose convent was the refuge of the pilgrim, the infirm, and the needy — these were held up as persons who imperiled the interests of the nation!...

The King, unwilling to disquiet the anticlericals, replied nothing and did nothing. As has been the case with so many political figures of our own day, what he was personally opposed to was one thing, and what he was publicly willing to allow quite another. "For they loved the glory of men more than the glory of God" (Jn 12:43).

After the suppression, the function of generalate devolved upon the Sacro Eremo Tuscolano, Monte Porzio Catone (commune: Frascati), not too far from Rome, in the Alban Hills. Meanwhile, Monte Corona had become an agricultural estate that from 1863 passed through the hands of various owners and occupants. The congregation would make numerous attempts to recover it, all of them in vain. The longest proprietorship was that of the Roman family Marignoli, from 1870-1935. The renowned operatic tenor Beniamino Gigli had it from 1938-1941. He sold it to a firm associated with the FIAT motor corporation, whence it passed to an insurance company. The hermitage proper, so long abandoned, was dilapidated.

There were two tenants, the Cassinese Benedictines of Saint Peter's of Perugia (1975) and the guru Yogi Sri Satyananda (1977), who attempted to restore the Hermitage, the second for use as a self-realization ashram. But their efforts were short-lived and accomplished little.

And so we reach a turning point. The appointed time had now been completed "...until the land had made good her sabbaths; all the days she lay desolate she kept sabbath, to fulfill seventy [or here, seventy plus fifty] years" (2 Chr 36:21). It was counseled from the beginning that her exile should end in honor. The Lord's holy mountain could not remain "a widow and bereaved of many" (Bar 4:12) forever.

On July 9, 1981, the Charterhouse of Farneta (near Lucca) bought Montecorona for the Monastic Family of Bethlehem and of the Assumption of the Virgin. This new institute, of Carthusian inspiration, originated in 1950 as a female community under the auspices of the Most Reverend Gabriel Matagrin, Bishop of Grenoble, which is the diocese where the Grande Chartreuse is located. Since 1976, there has been a male affiliate. At last the Holy Hermitage was host to a religious community that would abide there.

That Christmas, midnight Mass was celebrated, and on January 1, 1982, the Bethlehemite Sisters moved into the Hermitage. On August 30 they had electricity. The church was thoroughly cleaned up but not yet restored.

Eventually some of the Brothers of Bethlehem who were studying at Rome began to come to Monte Corona. In 1989, the Brothers replaced the Sisters, renaming the Hermitage in honor of the coronation of Mary, assumed into heaven. It is said at this writing that the Bethlehemites are happy to occupy the site, the bishop is likewise content to have them there, and that no turn of affairs is discernable on the horizon.

The Camaldolese Hermits of Montecorona cannot but be pleased that their ancient motherhouse once again accommodates a monastic community, and even one with a way of life similar to that of its first inhabitants. "What of it, then? So long as in every manner...Christ is being proclaimed. And in this I rejoice. And indeed, I shall continue to rejoice...." (Phil 1:18-19).

Index of Names

Index of Places

INDEX OF SUBJECTS